Into Helmand with the Walking Dead

In the Name of God

*Dedicated to every fallen warrior in Iraq and Afghanistan
who has reported to their final overwatch position.
We ask that you save us a seat at the bar.*

*And for Zau Seng
Captain, Kachin Independence Army
Free Burma Rangers
Killed November 3, 2019, outside Tel Tamir, Syria.*

Into Helmand with the Walking Dead

A Story of Marine Corps Combat in Afghanistan

Miles Vining and Kevin Schranz

Pen & Sword
MILITARY

First published in Great Britain in 2020 by
Pen & Sword Military
An imprint of
Pen & Sword Books Ltd
Yorkshire – Philadelphia

ISBN 978 1 52676 786 8

Printed and bound in the UK by TJ International Ltd,
Padstow, Cornwall.

Pen & Sword Books Limited incorporates the imprints of Atlas,
Archaeology, Aviation, Discovery, Family History, Fiction, History,
Maritime, Military, Military Classics, Politics, Select, Transport,
True Crime, Air World, Frontline Publishing, Leo Cooper, Remember
When, Seaforth Publishing, The Praetorian Press, Wharncliffe
Local History, Wharncliffe Transport, Wharncliffe True Crime
and White Owl.

For a complete list of Pen & Sword titles please contact

PEN & SWORD BOOKS LIMITED
47 Church Street, Barnsley, South Yorkshire, S70 2AS, England
E-mail: enquiries@pen-and-sword.co.uk
Website: www.pen-and-sword.co.uk

Or

PEN AND SWORD BOOKS
1950 Lawrence Rd, Havertown, PA 19083, USA
E-mail: Uspen-and-sword@casematepublishers.com
Website: www.penandswordbooks.com

Contents

Glossary of Terms

In an effort to reel in the reader to the human terrain and language used in the infantry, I want the reader to pronounce the occasional acronym and slang words we used, in the same way we would have said them.

0311	Military Occupational Specialty of Infantry Rifleman
0331	MOS of Infantry Machine Gunner
0341	MOS of Infantry Mortarman
155mm/one-five-five	155mm heavy artillery shell
8th & I	Marine Barracks Washington DC, infantry battalion used mostly for ceremonial purposes
2590s	rechargble tan batteries that power communication and THOR devices; about the size of a brick
5590s	same as 2590s, but single use and OD green in color
A-driver	Assistant driver or vehicle commander, sits in the front passenger seat of a tactical vehicle, directing and aiding the driver
AAFES	Army & Air Force Exchange Service
AAV	Amphibious Assault Vehicle, capable of assaulting an enemy objective on land or over a beach
ACOG	Advanced Combat Optic, four-power rifle scope issued to every Marine, mounted atop an M16A4 or M4
Advon	advance party of troops that goes ahead of the main force to prepare the way, whether in training or on deployment
AIR-O	Air Officer coordinating all interaction with the air support
ANA	Afghan National Army

AO	Area of Operations, denoting the geographical area that a certain unit is responsible for and holds
API	Armor-Piercing Incendiary (ammunition)
Armadillo	an upgraded version of the Seven-Ton truck; it is used to counter roadside IEDs and has thick side armor, an armored cab, and a rotating turret. Thus, the nickname
AUP	Afghan Uniformed Police
BAMF	bad-ass motherfucker
BC	Battalion Commander
BLS	Camps Bastion-Leatherneck-Shrobak, the British-American-Afghan base that made up the largest logistical hub in Helmand Province
boots 'n' utes	boots and utilities, meaning a uniform of boots, trousers, and an undershirt; no blouse or cover; used to PT in, or conduct working parties where a blouse and cover would get in the way
CAAT	Combined Anti-Armor Team (usually a platoon in a Weapons Company), pronounced "cat"
camelback	bladder-like device that holds three liters of water and attaches to the back of a plate carrier
Camp Cup Cake	derogatory term for Camp Geronimo
CAR	Combat Action Ribbon, pronounced "car"
CENTCOM	U.S. Central Command. With ISAF NATO forces, Helmand fell under CENTCOM Regional Command South West
chai	tea (Pashtu and Dari)
CH-46 "Phrog"	twin-top engine troop transport helicopter similar in appearance to the Army's CH-47 Chinook, referred to as a Forty-Six
CH-53 "Sea Stallion"	heavy lift helicopter, in use extensively for troop transport, referred to as a Fifty-Three
CHB	Clear Hold Build exercises, designed to simulate asymmetrical warfare, fighting an insurgent enemy hiding among the population, referred to as "Chub"
Chucks	slang for Dress Charlies, the short sleeve, no tie khaki dress uniform Marines are authorized to wear in garrison or off-base

CIF gear	Consolidated Issue Facility gear (now known as IIF, or Individual Issue Facility), referred to as "siph"
CLIC	Company Level Intelligence Cell, Marines trained in intelligence collection, referred to as "Click"
CLO	Community Liaison Officer, a civilian liaison between a unit and the families, prounounced "Klo"
CLS	Combat Life Saver, a program to train infantry Marines to be better trained medically
COC	Combat Operations Center, the operational control nexus of a platoon, company, etc.
(Weapons Conditions) Condition One– M16A4/M27/M4	round in chamber, magazine inserted, bolt forward, weapon on safe
conex box	large metal shipping container, used to create houses for training cities or storage/living spaces on deployment
Core frame	shiny uniform dress shoes, only worn with dress uniform
Coyote	slang for Range Safety Officer who ensures a live-fire exercise is going safely
COG, SOG	Corporal of the Guard, Sergeant of the Guard overseeing a watch
CONUS	Continental United States
CP	Command Post, where a company or larger unit will have their headquarters
CTEP	(Supporting) Contingency Training Equipment Pool: special gear issued before a unit deploys, FROG uniforms, deployment bags, plate carriers, etc., referred to as C-tep
DD214	Military separation papers, issued to a Marine on his EAS date
Deuce Gear/ 782 Gear	nickname for an issued chest harness of any sort, holding magazines and other gear on a Marine's body while in the field
DF	Directional Fragmentation (as a type of explosive device)

DFAC	dining facility, pronounced "D-fak"
DFL	Depart Friendly Lines, denoting the exact time a patrol has left the wire
DMO	Distribution Management Office, the household goods/ transportation agency at Camp Lejeune agency that holds your personal vehicle and belongings while you are deployed; notorious for stealing your stuff while overseas
DMOC	Deployment Medicine Operators Course, pronounced "D-mock"
DMR	Designated Marksman Rifle
EAS	End of Active Service, the end of an active duty Marine's active service obligation
ECM	Electronic Counter Measure, used on deployment to deter remote-controlled IEDs
EDL	Equipment Density List, an accountability measure that tracks all weapons and issued equipment
EFP	Explosively Formed Projectile, essentially an explosive force channeled in a linear direction
EFL	Enter Friendly Lines, to denote the exact time a patrol re-enters friendly lines
EOD	Explosive Ordnance Disposal
FAS	First Aid Station
flak	short for flak jacket, referencing to the protective armor/plate carrier that infantrymen wear; initially, we had Intercepter carriers in OIF, later changing to heavier MTVs, and then to lighter plate carriers mostly associated with OEF fighting
FMF	Fleet Marine Force: active duty operating component of the Marine Corps, shortened to "the Fleet"
Fobbit	derogatory term for a Marine who rarely leaves a Forward Operating Base (FOB) *see also* POG/ REMF
FROG	Flame Resistant Organizational Gear, essentially lightweight uniforms with the torso areas turned into a silky, smooth material

G-BOSS	Ground-Based Operational Surveillance System: thermal/ infrared tower mounted at bases and on trucks
Green Weenie	common slang to refer to the Marine Corps
GRG	Gridded Reference Graphic used on military maps
GSW	gunshot wound
Hajji	a Muslim who has gone on a pilgrimage to Mecca, used as a derogatory name by grunts to describe local Afghan men
Hesco	a contraption of canvas and steel wire filled with dirt to make instant fortifications (named after the production company)
HIIDE	Handheld Interagency Identity Detection Equipment, a biometric machine that scans a human facial, finger, and iris features against a database of known IED emplacers and Taliban members, pronounced "Hiide"
HME	Homemade Explosive, cheaply purchased and mixed-together chemicals designed to inflict maximum damage upon ISAF forces
HOG	Hunters of Gunmen, an informal name for a school-trained Scout Sniper
Holley stick/ sickle	named after EOD Master Sergeant Floyd Holley who invented it and was later killed by an IED blast (used to probe for IED components when on patrol)
IAR	M27 Infantry Automatic Rifle
ICOM	commercial Chinese radios, favored by Taliban but used throughout the world
IED	improvised explosive device *see also* VBIED and SBVIED
IFAK	Individual First Aid Kit, pouch worn by every Marine on their plate carrier, pronounced "I-fack"
Index	the official end to a training event, usually called out by RSOs or officers conducting the training
ILBE	Improved Load Bearing Equipment and a nickname for the issued main pack, between the old Alice pack and the new modular main pack

IPBC	Infantry Platoon Battle Course, a specific live-fire range in Fort Pickett, Virginia
IRR	Individual Ready Reserve, non-obligated time a serviceman is in after his EAS
ISAF/ANSF	International Security Assistance Force/ Afghan National Security Force, pronounced "I-saaf" / "An-Saaf"
ISR	intelligence, surveillance, and reconnaissance
Ivan Target	green plastic target that imitates the outline of a Soviet soldier, used extensively on U.S. live-fire ranges
JDAM	Joint Direct Attack Munition, a guided airdropped bomb, pronounced "J-dam"
jingle truck	large cargo truck covered with various shiny bits and symbols, sometimes making lots of noise as it drives
JSOC	Joint Special Operations Command, pronounced "J-sock"
J-ville/ J-Vegas	Jacksonville, the town (of crime and vice) outside Camp Lejeune
Kevlar	a Kevlar helmet
LEP	Law Enforcement Program, policemen turned contractors in Afghanistan and embedded with the Marines, pronounced "LB", pronounced "lep"
Liberty/ Libo	authorized free time ashore or off station, not counted as leave, known in the Army as a "pass"
LSA	Logistics Support Area
LVSR	Logistic Vehicle System Replacement
M4 two-oh-three/ M203	a rifle-mounted 40mm grenade launcher
MarineNet courses	similar to MCIs, but completed online
Maruit	sarcastic combination of Marine and Recruit used by Drill Instructors to poke fun at recently graduated recruits who do not yet have the maturity and experience of being Fleet Marines
Mat-V	*see* M-ATV
M-ATV	MRAP All-Terrain Vehicle, pronounced "Mat-V"
MCI	Marine Corps Institute, professional military educational classes, presented and tested remotely

MCMAP	Marine Corps Martial Arts Program, pronounced, "Mick-Map"
MDO	Machine-gun Day Optic, a magnified optic for the M240 General Purpose Machine Gun
Mdub	*see* MWR
M-E	Marine-Enlisted
MEPS	Military Entry Processing Station, where the military adventure begins, pronounced "Meps"
MEU	Marine Expeditionary Unit, pronounced as Mew; *see also* UDP
MICH	Modular Integrated Communications Helmet, an advanced helmet that some units and the Marines had access to
MOLLE	Modular Lightweight Load-carrying Equipment, a system of canvas that allows the custom attachment of various pouches to the fighting load on a flak or pack. Also used as a verb: e.g. to "molle" a pouch to a flak
MOS	Military Occupational Speciality, denoting a service member's numerical job designation
Motor T	Motor Transportation, vehicle drivers; each battalion has a Motor T platoon
MOUT	Military Operations on Urbanized Terrain, pronounced "Mount"
MRAP	Mine Resistant Ambush Protected, essentially an armored monster truck with either four or six wheels, pronounced, "M-Rap"
MRAP All Terrain	*see also* M-ATV, a vehicle with same armored capabilities as the MRAP, but smaller and more maneuverable over rough terrain
MRE	Meals Ready to Eat, military rations
MWR	Morale, Welfare, and Recreation, also referred to as "M-dub"
MWTC	Marine Corps Mountain Warfare Training Center, located outside of Bridgeport, California
NBC	Nuclear/Biological/Chemical
ND	Negligent Discharge (of a weapon)

NIPRNet	Non-classified Internet Protocol (IP) Router Network
NJP	Non-Judicial Punishment, a lower form of military punishment, often resulting in a reduction of rank/ loss of pay/ confined to barracks; also known as getting ninja-punched
ninja punch	*see* NJP
NCO	Non-Commissioned Officer, E-4 and E-5 ranks of corporal and sergeant
NVG	Night Vision Goggles, typically referring to an individually issued PVS-14 monocular device that clips to a Marine's Kevlar.
OCS	Officer Candidates School
op-check/ ing	operational check/ ing (of equipment)
OpFor	Opposing Forces, friendly troops in training who play the part of an adversary
Oscar Mike	abbreviated slang for "On the Move"
OIF	Operation Iraqi Freedom
OEF	Operation Enduring Freedom
Page 11,6105	administrative punishments
PB	Patrol Base, usually occupied by a squad- to a company-sized element.
POG	Person Other than Grunt, all non-03XX MOSs; *see also* REMF, Fobbit, pronounced "Poog"
PID	Positive Identification of an enemy combatant: that he is firing a weapon/ laying an IED/ or carrying a weapon and displays hostile intent/hostile act
piss/ ing hot	testing positive in a drug urinalysis
PMO	Provost Marshal's Office, Marine Corps policemen
PRC 152 (-3)	tactical encrypted radio, also known as "green gear" to differentiate it from "black gear" (PRC 153), which can be less encrypted; pronounced "Prick-one-fifty-two (-three)"
PSO	Position Safety Officer on a live-fire range
pump	slang for a deployment
QRF	Quick Reaction Force, typically, a squad/platoon/ company designated to rush to the scene of a battle when needed

quad	quadrangle: flat, open area in front of a barracks, where formations are usually held
RAT boot	Rugged All-Terrain boot; during OEF these were only issued to units deploying and not generally worn in garrison
RBE	Remain Behind Element, the portion of a battalion that cannot go on a deployment, and thus stays in the States
RC	remote-controlled
RCO	Rifle Combat Optic, scope on an M16 rifle
REMF	Rear Echelon Motherfucker, another term for POG; *see also* Fobbit, REMF
RIP	Relief in Place, the process in which one unit actively relieves another unit while forward deployed, pronounced "rip"
River City	slang for temporary communications shutdown on a base where a casualty has occurred
RO/ RTO	Radio Operator/ Radio Transmission Officer
ROC	Regional Operations Company
Roll Tide	is the motto of the University of Alabama football team that we used as an arbitrary brevity code when we suspected an IED. So instead of saying "IED!" you could calmly mention "Roll Tide" without the whole patrol freaking out.
RP	Religious Personnel, chaplain's assistant, enlisted sailor, entitled to carry a firearm
RPG	rocket-propelled grenade
RSO	Range Safety Officer, usually an officer, Staff NCO, or NCO monitoring a live-fire exercise, making sure things go safely
RTB	Return to Base, used by patrols over the radio to denote returning to a base of operations
SAF	small arms fire, pronounced "saaf"
SAPI	Small Arms Protective Insert: curved ceramic plates an inch thick, designed to stop rounds up to 7.62x39mm; four are issued, two front and back, two for the left and right side, pronounced "Sappy"
sat-phone	satellite phone used to call home

SAW/ M249	Squad Automatic Weapon, previous to the M27's adoption, pronounced "saw"
SDO	Squad Day Optic, light machine-gun scope mounted on the M27 or M249 SAW
SEEK	Secure Electronic Enrollment Kit, an updated version of the HIIDE, pronounced "seek"
Seven-Ton	Troop-carrying transport truck, capable of carrying a maximum load of seven tons offroad, and fifteen tons on a highway.
SMAW	Mk 153 Shoulder-launched Multipurpose Assault Weapon, used in Weapons Platoons in a Rifle Company by 0351 Assaultman-designated infantry, pronounced "Smaww"
SNCO	Staff Non-Commissioned Officer, E-6 to E-9; said as "Staff NCO"
SOI	School of Infantry, MOS training school that every infantryman attends after boot camp
SOP	Standard Operating Procedure
SVBIED	suicide vehicle-borne improvised explosive device
taskera	Afghan national ID card
T and E	Traverse and Elevation, the mechanical device on the tripod of a machine gun that allows for minor adjustments
TBI	Traumatic Brain Injury
Terminal Leave	taking the balance of leave due and not returning to active duty
Terp	short for interpreter, Afghans who could speak Dari, Pashtu, and English who worked at the patrol-base level to enable communication with the local populace
TIC	Troops in Contact, radio transmission abbreviation to signify friendly troops taking fire, pronounced "tick"
TO/E	Table of Organization/and Equipment
TSE	Tactical Site Exploitation
UAV	unmanned aerial vehicles

UDP	Universal Deployment Program, rotational program the Marine Corps has in place wherein units are based/ deployed to Okinawa, *see also* MEU
UGR-E	Unitized Group Ration-Express modules serve hot meals for up to 18 soldiers without kitchen equipment, cooks, fuel or power source
UNCW	University of North Carolina Wilmington, located in Wilmington, NC, an hour from Camp Lejeune
USO	United Service Organizations
UTM	Universal Thermal Monocular, a thermal-imaging device that can be clipped to the picatinny rail of a weapon system
VBIED	vehicle-borne improvised explosive device, pronounced "V-bid"
VC	Vehicle Commander
VCP	Vehicle Control Point, where searches of civilian vehicles are conducted
V-22 "Osprey"	Tilt Rotor Helicopter used extensively in later portions of OEF
vic	vehicle
Victor unit	administrative name for an active duty infantry battalion, e.g. V19 is Victor One-Nine, or First Battalion, Ninth Marines
wadi	Arabic/ Pashtu word for a small canal/ ditch
Water Buffalo	A military mobile water tank with faucets to allow Marines to fill their camelbacks in the field
wook	derogatory term for female Marine, derived from the wookie race of Chewbacca, from *Star Wars*, because of the amount of hair that female Marines have compared to males.
XO	executive officer, the second-in-command of a unit, starting at the company level
Z-MIST	technical portion of 9 Line Medevac where a patient's vital signs are listed, pronounced "Z-mist"
ZAP card	laminated card with personal information and EDL printed on it, for use with the 9 Line on WIA or KIA grunts

Preface

"Sometimes the scariest gunfights, the longest patrols, the most lonesome posts, the hardest hikes, don't take place in Helmand, Lejeune, or Bridgeport, but instead in the confines of our conscious."

I want to tell you a story. This isn't a tale of high valor with medals and presidential speeches. Nor is it about America's elite Special Forces warriors. You won't find any scenes that are in an action film or the latest video game. This is a simple tale. This is about the grunts. This is about those who are readily used and abused in political discourse, elections, campaigns, and forgotten wars. My war could be dismissed. I won't let that happen.

Low-intensity conflict. What a succinct way to sum up these events which keep me up at night. What a great way to ignore the reason I feel like I constantly have to guard my back. Could there be a better way to explain why I always know where the best place to find cover is? I still wince throughout the day, waiting to hear that singular loud "SNAP" or that disturbing whirring ricochet announcing the nearby flight of an incoming piece of supersonic metal.

What really gets me is that my war truly was low intensity … on paper. My battalion "only" had three men die in action. My company had no men killed and only a handful of wounded. The actions we were engaged in were small affairs by standards of battle. The engagements we were in usually had us enjoying superior numbers and, as far as I saw, the Taliban didn't have tanks or helicopters in support. But what is battle apart from a large group of individual people trying to kill each other? Let that sink in. I was not at Kursk, Normandy, Okinawa, or Hue City. But the fields, hills, wadis, and compounds of Boldak, Habibabad, Showal, and Mattaque all had young men from different parts of the world trying their best to outsmart and kill each other. You tell me your war was worse than mine. All are the same.

Kevin Schranz
Ohio, 2015

This is the tale of a generation of young American men who became infantrymen and conducted America's foreign policy in its most brutal and straightforward manner. But war, in and of itself, only plays a small part. This is about our lives, our ambitions, our aspirations, our struggles, and how we came to understand the cataclysm of the odyssey that we embarked upon. We lived, we laughed, we loved, we suffered, we were maimed, physically and mentally, and some of us were killed.

Together, as Infantrymen, we formed a side of America that is not often brought to bear, and when it is, it is often categorized as some awesome war machine. Within that war machine, we had our own culture, our own way of being, our own semblance of identity that allowed us to become what we were, for better or worse, a band of brothers, and killers of men. That identity is in being a Marine infantryman in the wars of Iraq and Afghanistan. This is about and for the enlisted 03XX Military Occupational Speciality: the riflemen, the mortarmen, the assaultmen, the machine-gunners, the scout snipers, the LAV crewmen. This is about those fine individuals who sling lead and stack bodies. If you happened to have sweated with us on our patrols, bled with us in our fights, and mourned with us at our memorial services, then this is for you. If your father, brother, son, husband, or ex-boyfriend filled that role, then hopefully this will offer a glance into that tale, and might help you find the answers to questions you never asked.

Welcome, the grunt.

Miles Vining
Iraq, 2019

Kevin began writing simply to cope and make sense of his experiences. When he had the idea to write a book it was more about connecting with his fellow Marines than for any grander purpose. While he was passionate about sharing his story and the stories of those he served with, I have a suspicion he missed his buddies and wanted an excuse to talk with them about their shared deployments. There are experiences written here that Kevin would never have shared with me; not for a lack of love or trust, but for an intense need to protect me as was his nature to protect and serve all he loved. Including his country, family, and fellow Marines. Thank you, Miles, for keeping Kevin and his story alive through this book. Your willingness to incorporate Kevin's unfinished work into your own fills my heart in a way in which words fail me. Miles, I know Kevin is smiling that big, goofy grin as he looks on you and all you have accomplished and will continue accomplishing. And Kevin, you did it! As always, I am so proud of you. I love you. I loved you, and I will always love you.

Abby Schranz
Ohio 2019

This story is a true account and testimony of the author's experiences while serving with 1st Battalion, 9th Marines. Every event described in these pages actually happened. However, to present a fuller account of the culture and times, some characters have been merged, some names have been changed, some events have been reordered to make the flow of the story more in tune with the journey. Dialogue is approximated as close as possible to what we remember. Most of it was never recorded at the time it took place. To more fully peek into our particular slang and way of speaking, I've changed acronyms and abbreviations to how we would have said them. Instead of spelling CAX, I've spelled out Cax because we didn't pronounce it "C-A-X." However, with EMV, it is spelled EMV, because we did pronounce it "E-M-V." With numerical designations, pronounce it normally: M16A4 is "M sixteen A four." If necessary, I will spell it out. Such as PEQ16 should be pronounced "Peck-sixteen," and I'll write it as Peq 16.

With the exception of our battalion commander, not all commissioned officers are mentioned by name in this narrative. I refer to them in the way that infantrymen refer to their immediate commanding officers, as "The Sir." This is in no way to discredit them, protect their identity, or retain their anonymity. It is merely done to keep the focus on the enlisted infantrymen, our story and our narrative.

Unit Organization

The Marine Corps is organized into four divisions. It only has enough divisions to constitute a corps, and not an army. The divisions are the 1st Marine Division on the West Coast at Camp Pendleton and Twentynine Palms, the 2nd Marine Division on the East Coast at Camp Lejeune, the 3rd Marine Division in Hawaii at K-Bay and Okinawa (otherwise known as overseas), and the 4th Marine Division as the Corps' reserve division. The first three divisions, combined with the Marine Air Wing, form the active duty component of the Marine Corps, otherwise known as The Fleet, short for Fleet Marine Force. Within these divisions are regiments, usually three per division. Within a regiment, there are three battalions, otherwise known as a Victor unit in the OIF/OEF period. The battalion has been the primary deployment force when it comes to post-Vietnam Fleet deployments. In other words, the Marine Corps does not deploy units by regiments or divisions unless it is a big fight.

These battalions are numbered sequentially within a regiment. Thus within the 8th Marine Regiment, you'll have 1st Battalion, 2nd Battalion, and 3rd Battalion. These will be shortened to 1/8, 2/8, and 3/8. 1/9, or One Nine as I have written in this book, had a unique history during the OIF/OEF period. One Nine was originally the Fleet Anti-Terrorism Company (which formed the nucleus of One Nine) in the early 2000s. Due to the needs of the war, the 9th Marine Regiment was stood up after being deactivated in the early 1990s, but it only existed as individual battalions that fell under different regiments. While we were at Lejeune, we as well as Two-Nine and Three-Nine fell under 2nd, 6th, and 8th Marine Regiments all at different times as we were shuffled around. All of the 9th's battalions deactivated post-OEF.

A battalion has three line companies of riflemen, one weapons company of heavy machine guns, 81mm mortars, and an anti-tank platoon (CAAT) to support the rifle companies. These companies are alphabetically numbered depending on where they fall within the regiment. The 1st Battalion of any regiment will have Alpha, Bravo, and Charlie companies. Then the 2nd Battalion will have Echo, Foxtrot, and Golf while the 3rd Battalion will have India, Juliet, and Kilo. Delta and Hotel are skipped because these used to be a battalion's heavy weapons companies in Vietnam, but are now simply called Weapons Company irrespective of which of the battalions they fall in. The Headquarters and Support (H&S) Company consists of motor transport, Intel, Comm, and admin assets. Sniper platoons are typically organic to either a Weapons Company, or H&S, but overseas are usually tasked out to the various rifle companies for supporting operations. In the OIF/OEF era, many weapons companies fufilled line company duties as their heavy weapons weren't needed as much.

The rifle companies are then further divided into three platoons, a weapons platoon of Two-Forty machine guns, light mortars, SMAW rocket gunners, and finally a small headquarters platoon. The line platoons are further divided into three squads, which are then divided into three fireteams, which consist of three Marines and one fireteam leader.

The "Walking Dead"

The 1st Battalion, 9th Marines was activated in the First World War and later fought in the Pacific theater of operations during the Second World War. But it was during the horror of the Vietnam War that it was given

its moniker of the "Walking Dead." Through costly combat operations –
Operation Buffalo, Dewy Canyon, Khe Sanh – the battalion suffered one
of the highest casualty rates within the Marine Corps infantry during the
war while being involved in sustained combat operations. The narrative has
it that the Viet Cong referred to the Marines operating in One Nine's Area
of Operations as the "Walking Dead," or "Đi bộ chết" in Vietnamese. One
explanation of the name claims that a North Vietnamese leader's son was
killed in action while facing One Nine. Soon after, "Hanoi Hannah" came
on air warning the Marines that in retribution for the death of the NVA
officer, the "Marines and Sailors from the First Battalion, Ninth Marines
are Walking Dead." This is the legacy that we inherited as Marines and
Sailors serving in the First of the Ninth Marines.

Introduction

The enlisted Marine infantryman is a force to be reckoned with. Renowned the world over, he is forged in the furnace of Parris Island and San Diego, refined at the School of Infantry, and introduced to the Fleet Marine Force as a junior Marine, equal to his peers and eager to achieve success. He is led and emboldened by his NCOs. As he completes his MCIs, runs First Class PFTs and CFTs, does as many MarineNet courses as possible and scores Expert on the rifle range, he too will one day become an NCO, dedicated to training new Marines and influencing the old. In battle, he follows the Law of Armed Conflict and is flawless in executing the orders of those appointed over him.

Bullshit.

The average 03 goes to the Recruit Depot with the misconception that every Marine is a rifleman, no matter his MOS. He is taught how to speak, how to dress, and apparently how to kill. However, this propaganda is dished out to every recruit, making them believe that "I'm up, they see me, I'm down" and firing at the enemy from a proper prone position with a web-sling wins wars. The "Marauit" graduates from boot camp and reports to the School of Infantry where his combat instructors tell him to distance himself from his Pog recruit friends and focus on the actual business of killing human beings. Here he learns the fundamentals of fire and movement on a battlefield, and the mission of the Marine rifle squad – "To locate, close with and destroy the enemy through fire and maneuver" – becomes all too apparent as he pores over the textbooks of war. He takes his final exams and his trade: rifleman, machine gunner, mortarman, assaultman, or anti-tank missileman. However, his final exam, his instructors tell him, will be in combat.

Now he reports to the Fleet, where technically he is seen as equal to his peers who have deployed before him. But below all the politically correct Marine Corps terminology of junior Marines and being treated equally, he knows who he is. He is a boot, a scourge of society and condemned to being hazed and treated as lower than whale shit, that is, at the bottom of the ocean. His sentences begin and end with "Yes, Lance Corporal" and "Aye, Lance

Corporal." He is on every working party, every Sunday morning police call after his seniors have used him as a beer courier the night before. In fact he is fearful of even opening his door during the work day or getting out of line. Every mistake, every mishap, every wrong usage of rank is met firmly with a beat-down, PT, or an easy let off, writing his Medevac 9-Line eighty times.

But there is a method to this madness. His seniors remind the boot of this from time to time. This is not Tanks, or Admin, or Com Cam. This is a profession of arms, the infantry and he is a grunt. His job hazards include possible death, decapitation, PTSD, suicide, or loss of limb. Doing well in this profession isn't enough. In fact, it is a job where he can do everything perfectly right and still die a meaningless death on the battlefield. Surviving a deployment will depend on the actions or inactions of the grunts to his left and his right. Whatever notions of freedom, love of country, and adventure he had before he deployed, they evaporate when the first round zips by his head and is replaced with fighting and dying for some obscure compound or GRG location.

However, he doesn't know any of this yet, because all he knows is what he hears from his seniors. They talk of blood-lust and confirmed kills. He sees this and yearns for it, and even burns for it. If he wasn't fully committed to killing another human being, he certainly is now. The chevron reticle in his 3.5 power Trijicon RCO becomes imprinted on some Talib shooting at him in his fantasy. However, he also hears the downside of deployment: their stories, their fears, their friends dying, and their brothers screaming in pain. This is what they see in his mistakes and mishaps. So they punish him and run him into the ground because they know their lives and his will depend on one another. The next combat deployment is coming, Cax is only weeks away and after that, the Wild West.

So in the meantime, he trains, and he trains, and he trains some more. He memorizes his 9-Line and is repeating it in his sleep. He can spit you a polar mission while covered in mud in the push-up position. His shoulders burn from doing repeated reloading drills because he is told the difference between life and death might be one more gun in a fight. His feet are done for from all the hikes and forced marches his unit completes in a workup. His notepad and pen are always present, dip and cigarettes in his right shoulder pocket, and dog tag in his left boot in case he is so wholly blown to pieces that identification would be required to tell the difference between him and his boot friend because their dispersion was all fucked up on that dismounted foot patrol in Mout Town. However, that's all right. A few buddy-drags across a field and a notional letter to his mother explaining why he is now coming home in a pine wood box is in short order. This is okay. Because it is training, this is the time to make mistakes and ask stupid questions. Just remember this on deployment, when this is a no-go.

So the boot deploys, and he finally understands what deployment is all about. What standing an eight-hour post behind a Two-Forty is, what the difference between a *crack* and a *whizz* are when taking fire, and what an IED sounds like when it explodes during his foot patrol. He sees death all around him, both locals and Americans dying, men wounded and disfigured, and corpses. He will never forget the sight of his first corpse, the stench and the glazed-over look on the face if there are even eyes or a head still present for that matter. But the intense adrenaline rush is a high, better than heroin. He lives day in and day out in fear for his life, never knowing if each breath, each footstep, each sector scan on a patrol will be his last.

He is surrounded by a group of men he would lovingly die for on the field of battle. But he loves it, because this is what he joined up for, he knows he is making a difference. He is at the forefront of America's spearhead, he is the grimy face of the infantry. He is the proverbial "Chesty's raggedy-ass Marines." But this doesn't mean anything to him on a seven-hour, ten-klick foot patrol. His flak is cutting his shoulders and his boots are heavy and soaking from crossing the wadis instead of risking the footbridges and turning into pink mist. All that matters now is the grunt in front of him and his sector of fire for which he is responsible and owns.

Then he returns to the Land of the Big PX. He is a senior Marine now, with more combat experience in his boot bands than most career Marines will have in their lifetimes. But he is uneasy and uncomfortable. He does not feel safe without a gun on him like he had in-country at all times. He jumps at loud noises, he doesn't understand the peculiar mannerisms and customs of a civilized society that didn't exist on the PB. What is the meaning of formal speech to the man who kills to earn his keep?

The thing that bugs him most of all is the next deployment. He yearns for it, as he did when he was a boot. This is a different kind of yearning. When he was a boot he wanted the honor, the chance to prove himself, and especially that combat action ribbon that no one can shut up about. But now he is a senior, and he misses the simple life of kill or be killed. Back in-country everything is simple. Either you go on a patrol and come back alive or you get schwacked. Your priorities are keeping your rifle within one arm's distance, your next post schedule, and chow.

Now he is home and he has to deal with bills, civilians, and all the other nonsense that garrison life offers. He has a whole new perspective on being a Marine and a grunt. He cannot believe he was fooled into believing every Marine a rifleman, can't believe he has to look up to and respect staff NCOs and boot officers who are convinced they know how to kill, know how to make war as he does. He only looks up to those who have deployed and proved their worth under fire. Training almost becomes irrelevant because most of it has nothing to do with what he actually accomplished or how he went about fighting the Taliban. But he persists and takes care of his boots as his seniors did and keeps them in line. As his seniors were hard on him, he is hard on his guys because he knows what the next deployment has in store.

This is the Marine infantryman in his element, behind the staged parades and pompous award citations. Underneath the clean-cut chucks and starched cammies is the rough-and-tumble lovable bastard. Wasted on the weekends is an understatement, relationships with women hold little to no value unless she has stayed true throughout a pump or two. Supposedly immune to forced marches, he hates them with a passion and moans about every inconvenience.

But despite all these seemingly horrible, poorly disciplined shortcomings, these are the men America calls for in times of great distress. These are the men who greet the wolves at the door with smiling faces and say, "If you want some, come get some." We will go into harm's way whether we agree with the reasoning or not because our profession is that of controlled chaos and surgical violence.

The Marine Corps PR machine hates our true face of cuffed sleeves, cut-off glove tips and "Devil may care" attitudes because we have nothing to do with the cleanly pressed blues of 8th and I or the smooth flaks of E-7s and above. It's not our fault our Frog suits are almost black from all the grime and our Kevlar red from the blood of a slain brother. However, that is us, the true zeitgeist of the Marine Corps infantry. These are the men who have faced down the enemies of our nation in mortal combat, from Belleau Wood to Marjah. This story is an insight into the nature of the rough-and-ready men to whom the art of killing is more than a profession of arms. Our job description wasn't nine to five; it was every beating moment of our existence.

Chapter 1

Boot

"Dude, come downstairs! I just finished putting together my Nativity Scene!"
"Isn't it beautiful?"
"It's wonderful."
"Merry Christmas."
"Um ... how long do we have to be like this, lance corporal?"
"YOU SHUT THE FUCK UP, boot! ... You're Baby Jesus! You think Baby Jesus could talk? ... No! Babies don't fucking talk!"
Maximillian Uriarte, Terminal Lance #76 "LOL, boots III"

The Fleet enters the mind of the boot in SOI, through his instructors. It isn't talked about much in boot camp, partly because drill instructors are more interested in churning out identical little tinker-tailor soldiers. At that point, the boot is still a recruit, and to him, every Marine is a downright killer, and his drill instructors reinforce this by not acknowledging the differences between the Wing, grunts, and even reservists. Regardless, he comes back to square one at SOI. There, his instructors chuckle every time the "Maruits" can't do some absurd punishment and they say, "You kids got it easy this time, wait until you get to the Fleet." Because strict rules bind them, and when SOI kids aren't exploring their new jungle of Jacksonville or Oceanside, they make great tattletales.

So, the instructors go along with their day, realizing how clueless these kids are. The Maruits are still curious: How does this Fleet thing work anyhow? Which units are better to be with and which bases are better than others? One-Six is a bunch of Marjah body slayers, but Three Three hasn't done a thing but Mews and UDPs. It's all a silent, forbidding mystery that sits there, and doesn't grow any bigger until graduation day when it smacks them in the face on bus rides across New River to Marine Corps Base Camp Lejeune, North Carolina. Because there are more pressing matters than the Fleet, like studying for the 0331 test, mopping the squad bay, or banging that new girlfriend flying down from Michigan this weekend. Either way, the whole Fleet thing is a non-issue.

But then it becomes an issue, front and center. SOI kids learn what unit they'll be going to several days before they graduate, whether it's East Coast, West Coast, Hawaii, or Twentynine Palms. The poor reservists get to go back home, their Marine Corps adventure has just about ended, where they will possibly remain in perpetual boot camp until their EAS six years later. Then there's the 8th & I poster boys, twirling Garands for a living and claiming that one of the more progressive cities in the United States, Washington, D.C., is a waste of time, and not something worth leaving the Xbox controller for.

The Security Forces dudes aren't much better off, except they picked their fate by signing that Security Forces contract. The most elite of these high-speed individuals get to go on presidential support out at Camp David, where they learn the most extreme methods of room-clearing and urban operations, a skill that is hard to translate back to the Fleet when they eventually do return as corporals and take up spots that combat veterans were originally slotted for. All these guys get to go on a relaxing air-conditioned bus that takes them on a lovely journey to Norfolk, Virginia, for Security Forces School.

Then, of course, we have the recon babies; an extremely small amount of 03XX contracts are recon contracts, an opportunity to be assigned to a Basic Reconnaissance Course holding platoon. Most will never earn the fabled parachute/wing/bubble combination that makes up the Reconnaissance Battalion's crest.

Not the Fleet Maruits. They pack their SOI gear all up and wait outside in the parking lot for their respective Motor T sections to come to turn their world into something else. Seven-tons and buses show up and out come the Motor T drivers and A-drivers. There's something off about them, though. They have a look on their faces of disgust, as if they hate life and every form of it around them. Their plate carriers are different from what the boots have been used to, strange in a way, going against everything they were taught in SOI about magazine pouch and IFAK placement. These guys have little use for manners as well. "Are you bitches with 1/9? Yes? No? Get your shit on those seven-tons."

The boots instinctively follow all these new commands because this is where their new careers are starting. From this point on, every comment, every "Sir" and "Yes, Lance Corporal," every obeyed command is a hallmark of who this boot is, and just what kind of Marine he will turn out to be. This isn't the time to be acting goofy.

Motor T takes the boots over to the battalion CP, where they get checked into medical and admin. This, in typical Marine Corps fashion, should take all day, no less, much more if need be. Here, the excitement of finally getting to the "Fleet" dies down a little bit because of the waiting and the typical mind-numbing hurry up and wait that the boot has gotten accustomed to at SOI. But just as he slips into his comfort zone, thinking that this Fleet thing won't be so bad, the platoon sergeant gets some senior lances to come up to the office to bring the boots to their new home, the Barracks. Also, "help" them with their gear, but that won't ever happen. Lo, the Barracks.

An infantry barracks exhibits some of the most festive debaucheries to ever exist aboard a Marine Corps base. Barracks are usually organized by company, and then by platoon. Squad and fireteam members typically don't live with each other, but room with other Marines from the same platoon. For example on a typical Lejeune three-story rectangular barracks, first will be on first deck, second on second, third and Weapons mixed in on the third, and headquarters mixed in between all of them.

Each room will have three Marines, a bunkbed alongside the wall with a wall locker, computer desk and bedside table for each Marine. In addition, each rack has a "coffin locker" that opens up, where the boots gear is all stored. The back of the room will have a bathroom and outside sink for all three to share. It will also have a refrigerator and microwave but God forbid you have a rice cooker or burner. Sheets, pillows, and comforters are signed out by the barracks NCO. Doors are locked with keys that the boot is expected to keep on him at all times, even when PT'ing in the morning. These keys are essential, can't be copied, and the repercussions of losing a set can be a page eleven or sixty-one o'five. Get enough of those and the boot is looking at getting ninja-punched.

But then again, a Marine isn't a legitimate Marine until that ninja punch. It's bound to happen. By the way, that DoD CAC card – Department of Defense Common Access Card – is crucial as well. Losing one will most certainly lead to further non-judicial punishment. However, regardless of it being small and easy to lose in the first place, the chain of command fully expects the boot to keep it on him at all times. Similar to his weapons cards or Humvee license, which come in paper form, but that doesn't stop half of everything a Victor unit doing from happening in the pouring rain.

The common-sense approach to this predicament would be to laminate them, but that is against the rules as well. These same rules also apply to meal cards, which the boot will need at every meal from now on. Well, the meals he does manage to scarf down by the grace of God of his seniors. Most of these will be takeout as well, because who the hell ever got healthy off of main meals? Also, the company has formation in five minutes, so get that shit quick, boot!

Described from the outside, the Barracks doesn't sound too bad at all. Free-living, free food nearby, the amenities of a refrigerator, microwave, a sense of individualism away from mom's house. But this is merely the facade created to lure innocent youth into signing away their wretched existence. Grunt barracks generally suck. The only reason why they aren't completely miserable is because sleeping in a snow hole when it's negative 15 below is miserable, and the "Bricks" is certainly a calamity compared to that lovely field environment.

There is no privacy, the chow hall food sucks, the boots don't understand why they're getting hazed all the time, and the senior lances don't understand why they're getting inspected all the time, and all are wondering aloud why they can't just live their lives in peace without some higher-up in their personal space every second of the day. Or why there is black mold growing out of the vents, and what dim-witted Marine stuffed that dead hooker who had OD'd in the top wall locker before deploying?

We arrive at the barracks and suddenly all these seniors in civvies descend upon our motley group of boots. Like hyenas, they circle us, catcalling.

"Hey, Garner, look at this one, and his stupid moto SOI backpack!"

"Toledo, get a load out of this fucker, his name's Slaughter!"

"Move it, bitch! Upstairs right now! You fuckers are fresh meat!"

They herd us upstairs where the duty unlocks the doors, and then hands us the keys. Into the room, the seniors follow us. A fine young gentleman by the name of Spiegel jumps in along with Garner.

"Get at parade rest, bitches! You think you left boot camp two months ago? Well, you're back in it now! Say 'Aye, Lance Corporal'!"

"Aye, Lance Corporal!" we all yell in unison, just now realizing the debacle we just got ourselves into. From there, the seniors rifle through all our packs, our dress uniforms, throwing everything about. We make a mistake, and we're all in the push-up position on the floor. We get back up, and we are promptly ordered to field-day the entire room.

A little bit too slow, one of the seniors yells something at me, and I yell out, "Aye, Lance Corporal!" Immediately, he punches me in the chest, pushing me several feet back, telling me to shut up with that volume. Another senior notices I'm saying something somewhat sarcastically, regardless if unintentional, and orders me back into push-ups. He kicks me in the stomach when I'm not doing them fast enough, rolling me over on the floor, but soon I get back up into the push-up position. Sneering at me and leaving, I slowly stand up and get back to work.

Borrowing mops, buckets, brooms, and baby wipes, we get to work. Going after every dirty part of the room we can find, we try our best and get inspected on the hour by Garner. Every inspection we eventually fail, thus waiting a full hour until we can attempt to pass the next one. Finally, at zero three, we somehow pass, and we go sleep. Only to wake up in two hours for the morning formation. It's cold, we don't have any warming layers on, and the platoon sergeant takes a roll call. We may be tired, we may be ridiculed at every level, we have a lot of work ahead of us, but finally, we are in the Fleet.

Third platoon, Charlie Company gets word that the company is going out on a field op. We as boots are excited because this is our work station, where we will be able to prove ourselves to our seniors and to each other. The seniors know the amount of suck that is entailed in this, but they are giddy because the field is where they can screw with us, away from prying eyes in the barracks or officers in the rear.

The gear list gets passed down, and, just like the boots we are, we pack every single thing there is, making our packs much heavier than our seniors'. Sleeping gear, warming layers, MREs, this is what the experienced seniors know to pack: not your entire hygiene kit, a spare book, spare this, and spare that. Ounces equal pounds, and pounds equal pain, says the salt dog. However, I'd rather have it and not need it, than need it and not have it, says another salt dog. Caught in between, what do you do? Well, the novice packs everything, every single thing. Gasmask? Kabar Molle adaptor? Yeah, might need that.

When getting ready for deployment, the unit thought process works around the concept that each field op is to complete a certain task. A unit can only function once the smallest level within that unit can function. In order for that lowest level, that fireteam level, to function, it needs to be tested, to be put through the wringer. Thus, field ops start at that smallest level, and eventually work their way up the chain. So in a deployment training cycle, the company will go out on a fireteam range, where only the fireteam will attack a live-fire range, then the next field op will focus on the squad, working with those fireteams.

When the squads of a platoon are solid, the next one will be a platoon live-fire attack, making sure those individual squads can work with each other, firing, maneuvering, possibly bringing in machine guns from weapons platoon for fire support. Now that the three platoons of a company are competent, the entire company will go on a live-fire range. The platoons will support each other, working to fire and maneuver toward their objective. Mortars and assaultmen will now come into play, suppressing the company objective as the platoons move underneath their SMAW rockets and arching mortar bombs. Twentynine Palms is usually the culmination of this training matrix, where the entire battalion will work together, each company supporting each other on the defense, or even the offense, with Weapons Company bringing in the big guns, the 81s, the 50s, and Jav missiles, in addition to supporting arms like the overhead fast-movers and Cobras.

However, we don't understand any of this. All we know is that it is going to be a cold week in the North Carolina woods. Super-early wake-up at O'dark-stupid, draw weapons at the armory, get our counts, get on the trucks, and head out. We get to the assembly area where the company is bivouacked for the night and set up a terrain model, laying out our packs with sleeping gear. That night we go to sleep, and it is insanely cold. I get woken up for fire watch and have to pace around the packs to get some semblance of warmth and feeling in my feet. One of the boots even gets hypothermia from not packing the right sleeping bag. Sucks for him. The next morning we get up, and patrolling exercise, or "Pex," begins.

Our little platoon becomes weighed down with enough MREs for several days, radios, extra batteries, all sorts of oddball gear. I'm given the task of carrying the radio, and being the point man, directing the patrol. Fuck me, right? We start off, and our packs are heavy, cumbersome even. It doesn't get better because soon we enter the thickest of the thick that ever did thick. I'm talking straight-up Vietnam vegetation. To get through it, the first man has to push his body against the vegetation, pressing it down, while the next guy walks over him, only to push down on the next part, while the guy before him humps past him.

Eventually, we get to the point where the patrol leader, a stellar veteran of Iraq, Charles, says, "Fuck this, we're going round to the road before we have to go through more of this …" Charles has one more deployment to go before his eight years in will come to an end, and apparently, he left all his fucks behind in Fallujah. He got demoted to corporal after sleeping with an MCT wookie while an instructor there. In his own words, "So what? They demoted me for fucking a chick; that should be an accomplishment, not a demotion. I don't mind."

We take the road, and our packs are still almost as heavy as when we left because we haven't eaten any of our MREs yet. They are a tad bit lighter though because we shed off some of our blank cartridges back in the bush. In addition to having fewer blanks to carry, it makes cleaning weapons easier which isn't a fun task when all you want to do is get back to your room at the end of a field op. Eventually, we get to a security halt, and fan out into a 360-degree security circle, laying back on our packs, completely exhausted. One of the seniors in third, Kennington, looks up at the sky and says to no one in particular, "Man, I wish a fucking stray one-five-five round would just land directly on me right now, I'm so fucking done!" Not only is this funny, but it's hilarious because of the situation we find ourselves in. The whole patrol cracks up, life is good you know.

The patrol gets back up, and we eventually find our way to a patrol base location. A patrol base, by definition, shouldn't be occupied for more than twenty-four to seventy-two hours. It is meant as a temporary base, from which the unit will send out patrols, ideally in the middle of Indian country, alone and unafraid. Here we set up the same defensive posture, with the center being the command and control center. I'm at this location because I have the radio, and thus need to be next to the patrol leader, Sergeant Michael, and his assistant patrol leader, Wilbanks. Wilbanks is a portly fellow from Tennessee who hates life, and will punch your face out for looking at you funny. I'm managing my radio, monitoring all the comm traffic back and forth between the company headquarters back at the assembly area. Here I make my first mistake on the radio by ending a transmission with "Ten Four" instead of "Out." Wilbanks laughs at me, and says, "Vining, don't ever do that again; we don't say that stupid shit here." I feel embarrassed because I thought I was a proactive little boot, but instead was being a normal, stupid one. "Good to go, Lance Corporal, I won't do that again."

Night falls, and so does the mercury, getting very cold, very fast. We take turns watching the radio or watching the lines. Our platoon commander and platoon sergeant come walking in through Vietnam to see how our little base is set up and organized. They make some corrections and then leave. Finally, we have our small fort to ourselves. They tell us that we'll probably be probed during the night by one of the other platoons as the OpFor. The night gets colder, and we get more miserable. Suddenly there is some noise nearby, rattling the vegetation. Charlie is upon us, with his vengeful ways. Wilbanks tells me to be quiet, as I'm shifting around for the radio. I make another noise, and Wilbanks whispers, "Vining, make some more noise and I'll break your fucking nose." I don't want my nose broke, so I keep quiet. The rattling gets closer, and suddenly the night lights up with fire as the other platoon opens up on us with their blanks. We respond in kind, firing back. No one knows who has the upper hand, but we are in a good position, in good cover, and in the prone. The OpFor break contact and pull back, but they did catch us somewhat off guard. The next time they come through, I'm so tired, and I'm not on watch, that I fall asleep amid the gunfire and screaming. Not a good thing to do, but no one notices in the darkness.

Another day of this training, and we are back on the seven-tons going back to the Bricks. We clean weapons, turn them in and hump it back to our rooms, the cold still in our very bones. Strip off our disgusting uniforms, and jump in the shower, taking turns with Stinson and Smith. It feels great, phenomenal to get cleaned off after that stint in the cold. It would be the first of many showers of this kind. Almost as soon as we are done, 96-hour liberty papers are passed out, to be filled for the upcoming Veterans Day 96. Temporarily alleviating myself of this Fleet nonsense and filling it with Lynn is all I can think about.

* * *

I first met Lynn the night before I shipped off to Meps, and therefore into the great unknown. My close friend and I were walking along the boardwalk on the Jersey shore. With the full knowledge of leaving for three months without a single sighting of a vagina, my primary focus was on somehow convincing a promiscuous female to sleep with me before the haze-fest known as boot camp began.

As we walk up and down the shore without much success, we agree that we would make one more lap and then call it a night. I spot a group of girls and say to my companion, "Nick, how about them?" He takes one look at them, mutters "No," and keeps on walking. I, on the other hand, look back at them, and say, "No, Nick, we're talking to them, like NOW!" Nick, who is the Lord's gift to the feminine variety says, "Fine," and proceeds to walk right into the middle of the group, and asks the girl at the center of attention if she wants a drink. Which is stupid because both of us have just graduated high school and are underage. Thankfully, Nick's Italian features of being tall, a dumb blond, and stupidly built make him attractive to this girl and he goes off to buy her a Red Bull.

As she tails next to him, I'm left with this other group of girls. We are left walking about ten to fifteen feet behind Nick and their friend. I'm feeling awkward, Nick taking my thunder away from me. What happens next I will never forget as long as I live. I glance up to one of them, the one that seems to glow from out of the friend group, and she asks me my name. She tells me hers is Lynn and is graduating high school at the same time I am. She lives in New Jersey and is going be starting college in Canada. I tell her I was going to be going into the Marines. She asks me when. I tell her "tomorrow." Her cute face goes, "Wow! That's soon!" Although she has two other friends around her, we sort of zero in on the conversation, ignoring anyone and everyone else. The journey takes us out into the Atlantic sand, where we sit down and talk. And talk, and talk. Nick comes back, her friend with him now has a bloody nose due to the heat. They had been making out too, which made it somewhat awkward.

Somehow, through leaving the beach, swift texting on both of our ends, we return to the beach. This time alone. We walk down it again. I can't even remember what we talk about, but I can barely feel the soft sand beneath our feet over my heart twisting and turning as I start falling in love. We pick a spot on the beach to lie down on. The conversation continues, but we're facing the lights of Point Pleasant, turning Lynn's face into a flicker of amber. She looks out at the lights for a second, then looks at me. Nothing could have felt so right in my life. Heart throbbing through my throat, I lean in and we lock with a kiss. I close my eyes, concentrating on how my lips and tongue are interlocking with hers. Then I roll her onto the sand where it doesn't stop. I don't want it to ever stop.

The friends come looking for us, and we have to push away, acting as if we were just sitting there in the sand for some stupid reason. And the next day I went to MEPS in Philadelphia and on to boot camp.

I almost lost contact with her while at boot camp, but we would eventually write letters, long letters, with hers smelling of perfume, a welcome respite to the sweaty odor of the Parris Island squad bays. The only phone call I made at the end of boot camp was to her, and it went along these lines:

"Lynn, is it you?"

"Hi, Miles? Yes, yes it's me! Oh my God, how are you?"

"I'm fine, I just got done with boot camp and have so much to tell you … Can you be in New York next weekend?"

"Ummm, yes, I think I can! Email me as soon as you get out, and we'll put all the details together."

"Okay! That sounds good! I have to go now, but I've really missed you a lot."

"I've missed you too. I can't wait to see you."

I try to surprise her at Penn Station in the city; it doesn't work, but she giggles and we kiss. For the next week of boot leave, days roll into nights as we are interlocked most of the time, loving, living, and laughing. From New York to New Jersey, to the bus ride down to Washington. We are so locked in this sphere of pure bliss that we completely book the train tickets for her to go back home on the wrong date entirely, but it doesn't matter in the least.

Lynn then went off to college in Canada while I went to Lejeune to learn the art of killing. This 96 Liberty was the first time I was going to see her since coming into the Fleet. We agreed to get a random hotel in Vermont, sort of a midway point in between us, so I would take a plane there, and she would take a bus from across the border, and we could be together. It was a convoluted sort of lovers' rendezvous plan, with a million different things that could go wrong, but we actually pulled it off.

I get to Vermont and pick her up at the airport in Burlington, all happy and romantic, taking a cab back to the motel. I'm so anxious to make love to her again, especially after being in the field, but she tells me, "No, we're snuggling first, I want this feeling to last!" I agree, and we do that for several minutes, my hands still moving places they shouldn't have been. Finally, she gives in and says, "Okay! Let's do it."

The clothes come off.

For the next few days, we live in this fairyland, where her college and my Marine Corps are irrelevant for the time being. Where we're back to just being curious people in a strange world, exploring a small town in Vermont, eating at fancy restaurants, playing with reindeer, and telling each other stories. This is the first of many trips of the sort, where I leave one world for another if only for a few days, only to return to the world of Death and Destruction 101.

* * *

Coming back from Libo, we apparently have a hike the next day. The seniors groan while we're almost still in the mindset of the whole training thing, so a hike isn't something utterly horrible for us. Regardless, hikes in the Fleet are more at an adult level compared to the kiddie hikes in boot camp and SOI. Hikes in the Fleet have more weight, a faster pace, less cuddling, and heavier weapons. While a hike in boot camp would get you apples, in SOI the instructors and corpsmen would be pestering you to see if you were all right, in the Fleet you were on your own. Papa Doc, our platoon corpsman, might check up on guys, but that was about it.

As much as technology allows us to be even more mobile in the twenty-first century, through helicopter inserts, and AAV beach landings, the simple act of walking still remains a central element of being an infantryman, just as it has from the times of yore. We don't walk as much as Stonewall Jackson's "Foot Cavalry," but being able to hike, hump or "ruck" as the Army calls it, is a central pillar of being an infantryman. And in an entirely theoretical and unworldly way, the concept is a beautiful one. To take a fighting unit, and relocate it to another portion of the battlefield, with everything it needs to survive and fight, is a sound notion, one that no other job description in the military can really imitate. You can't relocate artillery or generators by foot but you can move an infantry unit.

That being said, others retain the concept that we are immune to hiking, to walking long distances, and we like to perpetuate this idea when not around our own kind. But the truth of the matter is that the hikes are an orgy of pain and suffering: the longer the distance the more intense the orgy. Officers love this misery, and staff NCOs smile at every corner, uttering silly clichés like, "If it ain't raining, we ain't training" or "Good training gents, good training." While the corpsmen just say, "Drink water, change your socks."

Depending on where you are in the admin column formation, the hike can be manageable or downright miserable. Usually, if you're toward the rear of the formation it's the worst because you have this slinky effect going on. The back is always trying to catch up with the front, and thus you're either going much too fast or much too slow. Either way, it's a painful process, and you're limited to the grunt in front of you, you step into where he is stepping. And if he has really long legs, then it sucks even more so, because now you have to compensate with his strides because he is stepping it out much faster than you are.

So you play little games in your head to keep yourself occupied. Akin to the scene in the Halo books where the commander keeps coming up with happy memories to hide the coordinates of Earth, with each one getting sucked away, never to appear, you go through similar thoughts. Sexual experiences serve well for this, remembering the way you had this girl, or that girl, or that position, or the one time on the beach outside of Wilmington, or even the quick Plenty of Fish hookup that happened last week. But you keep yourself occupied until the next halt, when you hear "Ten minutes!" and you rip off your main pack as quickly as humanly possible, sitting down on it. Surprisingly enough, this is actually where most of your blisters will occur, because the weight of your body that was on your feet now isn't there anymore, and the skin starts popping up, sometimes breaking and bleeding.

But the hike continues with "TWO MINUTES!" echoing up and down the line of march. At once the entire company gets up, bitching and moaning throughout. Flaks are thrown back on, main packs are hiked up, and weapons are slung, as guys help each other out down the line with this arduous process. Cummerbunds are tightened while the waist and sternum straps are clipped into place. Then all of a sudden, as if part of a sick joke, "STEPPING!" And with that, the company is Oscar Mike, Onward Christian Soldiers. Usually, for the first ten or twenty minutes of being back on track, the grumbling, joking, and complaining continues. Guys are trading stories of achievements with all levels of women, or the debauchery they got themselves into the weekend before, and the upcoming safety briefs they're going to violate the weekend coming up. Eventually, this dies down, as the pain mounts, and everyone resorts to their personal misery, suffering alone.

The funny thing about suffering is that as long as someone else is suffering more than you, it makes it all the more bearable. You have this sense of, "This sucks a lot, but it sucks exponentially for Lateef over there; thank God I'm not Lateef," and that helps alleviate the mind-numbing pain of each additional step. Usually, the body becomes numb after a while, especially midway through the hike, and all the joints kind of freeze up to allow you to push onwards. NCOs go up and down the line, seemingly with ease (if they are good NCOs that is), checking on guys, making fun of their dudes, encouraging them to drink water and suck it up. A man drops, face first to the ground, causing all those behind him to wiggle out of his path, and keep on pushing. While in front of them everyone is thinking, "Phew, poor old Lateef, the bastard always falls out anyways; it's not a good day to be Lateef." PFC No-Brains-Lateef has suffered a rolled ankle, dehydration, or is just being a weenie and wants to ride in the safety vic that trails the column at the rear. In the old Corps, the safety vehicle used to be at the front, so those who fell out would watch their buddies hump while they were sitting the ride out. But not anymore; apparently that was deemed mean and degrading. So how is mortal combat not degrading?

We often underestimate the endurance of the human body. Our mental capacity has the ability to quit, long before our physical capacity is ever near the edge of shutting down. Thus, during a hike, the closer we get to the end of it, the worse it seems to hurt. When in fact, if we just set off, without any sort of known ending, just walking onwards, we would most likely surprise ourselves with how far we could actually push before shutting down. But alas, usually the end of the hike can be spotted, or at least felt, like when the familiar environment of the barracks or Camp Wilson in Twentynine Palms come into view.

The column reaches the destination, the company disintegrates into the platoons, broke dicks come back in shame and the packs come off, dropping to the ground with a resounding thud. Best "thud" sound you've heard all week. Platoon sergeants get their EDLs in, making sure all the weapon ducks are in a row. Counts are up, First Sergeant or the CO makes some pathetic speech about how the company is God's gift to not only the battalion but the entire Marine Corps. Moto tirade over, the company hobbles over to the armory to turn in weapons. Hopefully, the custodian doesn't care what condition the weapons are in, as this usually separates the Marines from their much-beloved Libo.

At this point in the Fleet experience, I'm starting to get a better feel for the platoon, learning more about them individually. The boots are myself, Weitoish, Stinson, Schroyer, Dunbar, Mahoney, Smith, Todd, Mauler, and

Rich. Rich, Weitoish, Todd, Schroyer, and Dunbar are all Pennsylvania boys, from different parts of the state. Weitoish is a little stocky, and talks with very unique hand motions when emphasizing things. Todd is short, well built, and, coming from one of the really rough coal-mining parts of PA, he grew up around a lot of drugs. Rich is older, having been to college and thus usually gets treated better than the rest of us. Schroyer is a lanky kid with a big head who figured out that if you get international service, you can text back home on deployment. Dunbar is another short kid like Todd, but a former wrestler. My introduction to Mauler was him covered in sweat, with his flak, Kevlar, and pack on, doing laps around the Bricks because he forgot his rifle at the armory that day. Stinson and I were in the same boot camp platoon, that of Alpha Company 1066 at Parris Island; he was older as well, but suffered right alongside the rest of us. He is a former guitar player from Florida and can belt out some volume if you need someone to scream. Smith is from Detroit and loves being a Marine so much that he took his girlfriend out on a date in his Blues. His face is continuously covered in pimples, but this wouldn't stop him from kissing Katy Perry onstage during Fleet Week 2012. Spencer is a Tennessee boy who made the bitter mistake of getting married after getting in the Fleet. He has this very distinct Southern accent that he can almost whistle with when making jokes.

Our seniors are a mixed bag, to say the least. Two would get kicked out for pissing hot on drug tests later on in the workup. All of them have been on One Nine's previous deployment which was the 24th Mew to Africa and Haiti. So no combat deployment but they too, like us, are itching for it. Garner is a super-tall guy who sometimes likes to exaggerate a bit too much, but he is my team leader down the line. He can be a complete jester one second, laughing with everyone, but the next can switch to straight evil as he hazes you in your barracks room on a Saturday night. Range is a Georgia boy whose introduction to the Fleet was getting punched in the face after he cleaned his room. He is one of those people that you really want as your friend because if you aren't, he'd have no qualms about knocking you down if you got in his way. He takes his job of being a rifleman seriously and is proud of it. Martin is one of the team leaders who is a career guy through and through. He is from Florida, married and is the poster image of a Marine NCO despite being a lance corporal. He lives, sleeps, and breathes Marine Corps in everything he does, which can be frustrating if he is your team leader. I'm sure he has USMC-branded condoms somewhere at home. Caldwell is another older senior who has actually been with One Nine since the very beginning of its activation and the Iraq deployment afterward. He is one of those seniors whom you vehemently respect because of what he has done and his knowledge base. He doesn't have to haze boots or scream at them to get their attention. Dimauro is another senior who doesn't have to haze us for us to listen carefully. Tall and lanky, he is straight out of the Pennsylvania wilderness with his ideals and personality as a true-life mountain man. Very self-reliant, he stitched together a leather coat and carved a staff out of wood that he would bang on the ground, and scream, "You Shall Not Pass!"

Miller, the platoon's resident jacked dude, came from Security Forces and is continually getting "taped" for being "overweight" and technically a "Fat Piece of Shit" by admin standards. His arms are enormous, and his idea of fun is going to the Gold's Gym out in town because the base one isn't good enough. Hamaker is our platoon corpsman, tall and from Alabama. Another one of those quiet southern boys that you really would want as a friend in any situation. He lost his coveted FMF pin status because he got a DUI on base one day, but kept it pinned underneath one of his pocket flaps. He'd eventually test out and get it back though. Dejesus was the resident black guy in the platoon until we got Sergeant Michael. Very quiet kid from South Carolina who played video games in his room most of the time. Wilbanks is another team leader, a Tennessee fellow who has a little gut and always a big smile. Older as well, with a wife named Whitney. When he came out of the field, she put a small gift-wrapped package in the freezer for him to find and open. He thought it was a can of dip; instead, it was a message from her telling him that they were going to have their first child. Salisbury is a tall, stocky guy from PA, usually quiet and keeps to himself. But he has this secret reservoir of strength that he can summon when flipping tires or putting someone in a headlock. Kennington is another character from South Carolina, whose great accomplishment was banging his former English teacher. He is always trying to compete with Martin when in the field during training.

Haylock is one of our squad leaders who came to us from another platoon, quiet, tall and quite serious about his job. Although this didn't stop him from having a buddy take a picture of him splayed out on the floor with ketchup smeared by his mouth to fake his death to a nagging girl who wouldn't stop texting him. Sergeant Michael is my squad leader, our other resident black guy. He was in Fallujah and Ramadi with One-Eight back when things were nasty, before being transferred to the ceremonial post of 8th & I in Washington DC. We have this feeling of security around him as if he has that sixth sense that true warriors have. He always knows the right thing to do, whether how to clear a building, which side of a field to cross on patrol, or even just where to put the generator fuel at a patrol base.

Our platoon sergeant is a career staff sergeant whom I'll call Himmler. Very much by the book, he most likely has USMC condoms at home as well. In Afghanistan, he would make the Marines at his patrol base smooth out the rocks inside the perimeter. He runs an extremely tight ship with third platoon, at the cost of our sanity. Above him is "The Sir," our platoon commander. Tall, with blond hair, Second Lieutenant Buck is from Texas and graduated from the Naval Academy. You can tell the guy knows how to throw down and party with the boys in his spare time as he brings some of that cheery atmosphere to work. Some of us hate him, some of us don't mind him. We are his first command. But the most eccentric character in the platoon is Paul.

During one work week, I walked into Lance Corporal Paul's room. Paul, or Paulie, is one of those rare breeds of infantrymen. The guy was a functioning alcoholic who couldn't have completed a personal budget if it was gold on a balancing scale. Paulie could grunt, and grunt he did. He outdid every team leader and senior in the platoon when it came to tactical proficiency and pure grit. He knew his operations orders backward and forwards, he could out-PT everyone, and he made it known, regularly. But Marine, he didn't. The guy could have cared less how high his boot blouses were, what the Libo rules were, or how to stand in formation. He was the epitome of being a top-notch infantryman, but a garbage Marine. Which, in the Marine Corps' eyes, means he was still a garbage person overall. This is the guy who was graduating top of his class in Infantry Squad Leader's Course, but then accidentally took a Tornado soft drink from the Seven Day store on Lejeune and got dropped from the course. His arch-nemesis was Lance Corporal Martin, a career-centered guy, through and through. Whether it was criticizing his team, or out in the field, you were never safe from being lit up by Martin for some trivial matter.

Paul, unlike the other seniors, didn't take to hazing as much. He was older, in his late twenties, and probably didn't care for it much to begin with. He was the senior who allowed us to drink with him while we were scared to walk by the other seniors' rooms. And he was great for just talking stuff over with. That day I came in, pretty flustered.

"What's going on, Vining?" He looked up at me and said in his deep New England accent. I sat down in the nearest chair. "You're welcome to sit in there, make yourself comfortable!" The sarcasm flew right by me.

"I'm pretty pissed, Lance Corporal."

"Why's that, Vining? Lay it all out."

"Well, today at the CP, Staff Sergeant Whatley called me out for wearing fucking white socks with my boots. I didn't realize white socks weren't allowed at all, and so he was going to go tell Staff Sergeant. Then I went over to the admin section in S1 where I had to sign some stupid shit, and the fucking corporal in there yelled at me for using a blue pen."

"Well Vining, that sounds like a rough day ..."

"It really is! Like, why'd that retard have to fuck me over for the socks? He could have just told me to go back and change or something."

Paul looked at me and nodded. "What was that you said again?"

"What? Telling me to go back and change?"

"No, that other one."

"I'm not sure what you mean, Lance Corporal ..."

He just continued nodding. "Vining, you like chairs?"

This was getting odd. "Chairs? Chairs are cool."

"Great! Then get out of that one, and sit in this one," he said, pointing to an empty spot against the wall, where there was no chair.

"But there's no chair there?"

"So? Put your back up against the wall and make a ninety-degree angle with your knees; it'll be really comfortable."

Oh, I see. He was putting me on a wall-leaning punishment, but for what? I assumed the position. After that he just made small talk with me, talking about what I had planned for the next 96. All the while I was starting to break out a sweat against the wall. Weitoish walked by outside, and Paul called out to him, "Hey Weitoish! Get in here! Vining said he wanted you to sit next to him."

Weitoish walked in, saw what's happening, and immediately understood that I had screwed up somewhere. "Dammit, Vining! What the hell did you do now?" as he too assumed the position next to me, back against the wall as per Paulie's orders.

More time passed, and then Mauler walked by, "Hey Mauler! Weitoish and Vining were just talking about you! Come see how they're doing!"

Mauler realized what had happened, and didn't need Paul to tell him to "sit" next to us.

Paul then said, "Hey guys! Pretend like you're driving! Get your hands up!" We got them up. "I want to see some action! Some racing! Let's see some NASCAR stuff going on okay!" We imitated racing each other. Mauler put his hand into a gun, pointed it at us, his adversary drivers, and plugged us as he ran ahead. We kept driving, with bleeding head wounds.

"Do you guys know why you're doing this?"

"Because of Vining's dumbass?" yelled out Mauler. We were all covered in sweat now, slipping up and down the wall.

"It is true, but what did he do exactly?"

They all looked at me.

"I don't know! I don't know what I did! I was just talking about my day, Lance Corporal!"

"Yeah, well you said something, Vining."

Mauler got the hint. "Fucking A Vining! You said the R word, didn't you! In front of Lance Corporal Paul!"

Weitoish groaned, "Dammit Vining! You idiot!"

Finally, I realize what had happened. When we first got to Third, Paul had pulled us aside and said, "Look, guys. I'm pretty fucking chill, I'm not like these other seniors. But one thing I will not tolerate is the R word, for retarded. My sister is mentally handicapped and I'll fuck you up if I hear you guys saying that." I had completely forgotten when I was talking about having a rough day at the CP.

Paul let us drop down, as Mauler walked off and slammed me in the chest with his fist. I deserved it, for getting them screwed over as well.

Paul asked, "Now Vining, you gonna use the R word again?"

Sweating through my pullover and panting, "No, Lance Corporal, I won't." And to this day, I don't use it in a derogatory context, because of Paulie.

* * *

After Fox Two Five, we are told that Fort Pickett, Virginia, is next up on the schedule. Fort Pickett is crucial because it is the platoon live-fire field op in the deployment workup schedule. There is this monster range there, called the Inter Platoon Battle Circuit, or IPBC. One of our seniors, Toledo says, "Fuck, IPBC again? You boot fucks are going to get broke the fuck off, don't fucking worry." One Nine did Pickett for the 24th Mew workup back in 2009, in addition to training at an old mental asylum by the name of Muscatatuck in Indiana. Fort Pickett was a world of suck for them, not only because of IPBC but because they were hazed pretty bad in the woods by their seniors, essentially our granddaddy seniors, very few of whom are left with us in the battalion. Caldwell is one of these salt dogs – the bastard has been with One Nine since the very beginning, when the battalion was only a company and deployed to Iraq as a security force.

Fort Pickett is undoubtedly an adventure, and for us boots an exciting one. Doing a field op here and there in Lejeune is business as usual, but picking up and leaving for another state with the entire battalion is a new concept to us. The battalion splits into three groups: the advon, the main element riding by bus, and a helo element that will be assaulting an objective in one of the role-playing exercises. I'm in the advon, which for this particular time, is responsible for taking some of the battalion's vehicles up to Virginia, including seven-tons, Humvees, and Mat-Vs.

Usually, a civilian car trip from Lejeune to Pickett is around five hours or so, but with tactical vehicles driving below the speed limit, and following in convoy order all the way up Interstate 95, this turns into an eight-hour ordeal. I'm an A-driver to Koppers, a senior lance from first platoon. Koppers is that typical senior who enlisted in the infantry for one thing but was drastically disappointed. Regardless, he does his job, trains his boots, and doesn't screw around. But make no mistake, Koppers won't be your first volunteer for anything: he has had enough of the Green Weenie in his life.

The convoy draws weapons, trips out vics, and gets in convoy order outside the base theater at Lejeune. One of the Humvees won't start, so a Motor T gunny is pissed: "Get that fucking thing towed out of here and get a goddamned new Humvee asap; we're already behind schedule." The gun truck is towed, and a new one is brought in. When I say brand new, I mean this sucker drove off the assembly ramp, to our very parking lot. It still has plastic wrap on all the seats. The wrap gets ripped out, convoy brief goes out, and off we go. The trip itself is entirely uneventful. I busy myself with listening to my iPhone and texting Lynn the entire way up, apart from when Koppers tells me to look out the window for oncoming traffic. Because these tactical vehicles are so vast, there isn't any way for the driver to really see another car on the other side of the truck, so the A-Driver has to be his eyes.

On one of the stops, Koppers's door gets stuck while he is outside on a break. I can't get it to open from the inside because the latch technology is from the 1980s. In some bout of hilarity, Koppers has to throw his flak into the truck, through the tiny square where the armored window rolls into. After this, Koppers squeezes his entire body through the square and gets in the driver's seat with just enough time to start the truck and get moving with the convoy. Eventually, we arrive at Fort Pickett, park the trucks, and get all our gear inside the barracks we have been assigned to. These are wooden army things from World War II that are freezing cold. Two stories, with open squad bays for the platoons, closed-off rooms for the NCOs, and the head is downstairs on the first floor. I'm greeted by my platoon sergeant, Staff Sergeant Himmler, who hands me some frozen pizza leftovers that the platoon had ordered earlier. I lay out my sleeping system on an empty rack, and sleep. Some start to this adventure.

The next morning the field op begins. EDLs are completed, MREs are doled out among us, and we flak up, headed out on seven-tons to a fake village. Fort Pickett is undoubtedly one of the best training facilities that the military has to offer a conventional infantry unit. This is mostly because it is an army base, and they get tons of money for this stuff. It has mocked-up villages, kill houses, remarkably well-put-together live-fire ranges with tons of targets. But in this case, we head out to one of these fake villages where we patrol out of for several days on end. Afghan role players are there as well. These are Afghans who have immigrated to the U.S. and are hired to play the part of insurgents, police, and the local populace per our training. They are given scripts to follow to make it realistic, from cooperating with us on patrols, to shooting back at us with blank AK rifles. Great stuff overall. After a few days of role play, patrolling, and sleeping in miserably cold weather, we switch to our live-fire attack at IPBC.

Before we get into the attack planning, the company hikes to a nearby range where we zero all our small arms, so we don't look like total noobs in the live-fire. Heindl, one of the boots from 1st Platoon, is overheard saying to a buddy, "Man, I'm so happy we've got a combat deployment coming up, at least we don't have a damned Mew." Dammit, Heindl, word choice and context are everything. A couple of the seniors in second platoon don't take that too kindly, coming from a Mew themselves. Heindl gets taken into the treeline while the NCOs and officers aren't watching and takes a "flight down some stairs." It serves as a somber reminder to the rest of us about who calls the shots.

We go over the plan in this little briefing room that is set up outside the range, and then we actually go to the range and do a simple walkthrough. The range itself is enormous, from start to finish probably several miles in length. We're going to do a night run and a day run. But before this, the company gets a new boot drop. This will be the second boot drop since my own, and probably the fifth or sixth one overall for the line companies. Third hears that our very own platoon will be getting a new boot. This kid's name is Michael Hand, and along with the whole boot drop, they show up in an advon convoy straight from Lejeune.

This is probably the second worst way to enter the Fleet, the first being right before or during a deployment as a combat replacement. Things are already arduous enough for the boots going into the field, but at least we have some sort of semblance of what to do and what rules not to break. A brand-new boot in the field has no clue about what he just got himself into, and is guaranteed a ticket to pain city … So this kid Hand comes over to us, and the platoon sergeant takes him aside, laying the ground rules, telling him that the seniors will watch out for him, and for him to listen to him, also for him to band with us, the already established boots. So we take him off the packs and get him sorted, telling him to say "Aye, Lance Corporal" as if it was the latest style, cutting him dummy cords for his weapon and PVS14s, molle-ing his pack and flak together, trying to brace him for what is about to come down.

The first live-fire attack on IPBC is called up from the Sir. We go by platoons because it is a platoon attack, so first platoon goes, then second, and then we get the word to flak up. We already have our ammo loaded, pyro stuffed away, lead trace markers set up, comms checked. Pre-combat checks and pre-combat inspections take place, making sure zap cards and tourniquets are available. For some reason, Lance Corporal Martin, one of the team leaders, starts talking about the possibility of getting shot by accident, so we have this discussion about leaving one button undone so it is easier to get a zap card out, and other tidbits. It strikes me as funny, talking about friendly fire in such a casual manner as if we're making plans for a night out in Wilmington.

Word goes out to get in the gun trucks that'll take us to the release point for the attack, so we mount up. Once we hit a small valley, we get in our patrol formation and start moving forward through the forest, in order of squads. The first targets come into view, about 400 meters away on top of a small hill. These targets are plastic humanoid-shaped cones that are nicknamed "Ivan" for their deliberate resemblance to Soviet infantrymen. When shot, they have a sensor that triggers the base, and it folds back, only to pop back up after a predetermined period. We start engaging them with fire from our M16A4s and M4s. Wilbanks goes down as a notional casualty because he was standing while shooting. But he comes back into play a little bit later: no use keeping him away from his team for the whole attack. We push forward, our flaks heavy on us, especially with all the ammunition now loaded in my magazines. I'm thinking, "Holy fuck, this is heavy, fuck, fuck, fuck, damn all this ammo!"

Eventually, the platoon gets a quarter of the way down the range, and we push the squad online, firing at the now closer targets. One of the other squads has peeled off to the left, for their flanking maneuver. At this point, my squad begins the buddy rush, but I can't tell because my earplugs are stuffed in my ear and I'm banging away at targets with my M27 automatic rifle in the prone. I hear people screaming, but not really at me. Finally, I turn to my left, and I see Range, mouthing, "VINING, MOVE!" Forget the earplugs, this will be the last live-fire range I wear them on, especially when I can't even hear the commands.

I push up from the prone, and *crack!* The stupid grip pods on my M27 are broken, damn those things, never putting those on my rifle again. We move up in pairs, two guys rushing, two guys laying down fire as the others are exposed, only to reverse the process once the frontal two are set in position. We keep pushing, moving in this rhythmic beat of shooting, moving, and screaming, with the team leader Wilbanks yelling out our rates of fire and movement. Eventually, we get to our forward limit of advance, and all we have are targets out to 700 meters. I know this because the profiles of the targets fit in my stadia lines for 700 within the scope on my rifle. I take well-aimed shots, and each target goes down. This kind of shooting would be very difficult with an M16A4, never mind an M4 carbine. But with the new M27, dropping plastic Ivan targets at that range is child's play.

All of a sudden, this huge car-shaped target pops up at 200 meters, and Garner yells, "Vehicle in the open, two hundred meters! Get it, Vining!" I traverse my M27 to the right, flip it on auto, hold the gun as tight as I can, and proceed to dump an entire magazine in a single burst into the fake pop-up vehicle. I see it go down through the jittering of my scope as the recoil rocks the rifle back and forth. Goddamn, I love this job, I wish I could do this every day, minus the rest of the bullshit. Garner is now feeding me magazines, as soon as I'm dumping one, I eject it, and he jams another one in there, only to dump it, and load a new one in.

An index is called out, the attack is officially over. We all get up, immediately checking our EDL to make sure all our gear is still there. Apart from the whole hearing thing, I'm feeling really accomplished, I've proved my spot in the fireteam and the squad, by being able to competently manage my weapon system, and work within the team, minus hearing my name that one time. We debrief a little with the Coyotes, the Range Safety Officers, who have followed our movements throughout, then get in the gun trucks and push back to the packs, where we reload our magazines for the night live-fire range. Apparently, poor Hand did alright and didn't mess up too much. Good for him, as staying low profile in the Fleet is a good thing.

The night shoot starts closer to the limit of advance because it's at night and inherently more dangerous than a day run. We flip our PVS14 night vision goggles down over our eyes, the green glare reflecting on each other's faces in the dark. But this doesn't stop us from tripping over every hole, root, and elevated piece of turf there is. This isn't Seal Team Six with their six NVGs on their polymer hockey helmets and super-light gear. This is the infantry, and we deal with the lowest bidder. Night attacks are slow by nature because friendly fire can be a real party stopper, especially when you trip in the dark and blow your buddy's face off. The army range is well designed though, the Ivan targets have IR markers on them that flash at night, to simulate enemy muzzle flash, so you can see the target through your NVGs, lase it with your Peq, and drop that plastic Commie where he stands. When they get hit, the IR stops as the target goes back down, only to come back up when it resets. The attack goes well, but in the background, we can hear the Sir getting chewed out by the CO for using black gear, i.e., Motorola Prick-one-fifty-threes, instead of encrypted green gear, i.e. Prick-one-fifty-twos for the attack. This is because in-country, apparently only green gear is used and train like you fight, right Marine? The whole thing is ironic in retrospect because in-country we used both, and our black gear is exponentially better than the green gear. But alas, this is training ...

We get back to the bivouac site, and it is drizzling a bit. Wilbanks and a couple other seniors start talking about the idea of building a small tent city with our tarps. Because of the trees surrounding us, it isn't a bad idea. At first, it is only talk, but it turns into a half-decent plan of rigging up tarps between three specific trees around our sleeping area. Soon Wilbanks goes to Himmler and asks permission for us to put our tent city into action. The platoon sergeant gives us his blessing and all of a sudden a platoon of grunts turns into a mischievous Boy Scout troop. Everyone's tarp comes out, five fifty cord is affixed, and guys are gathering long sticks to prop up the tarps in the center. Third works together in clipping the different tarps together, which takes much longer than it sounds because the clips on these issued tarps seem to have been designed to be used by giants with massive thumbs, and not human beings. The drizzling increases, and so does our work, anxious as we are to be sleeping under cover. Eventually, we complete it, and it is a grunt mansion, shaped like an "L" with a tree at each end, and one at the base to hold it down. We pull our packs and weapons underneath it. That way the tarps have an anchor point to the ground, giving us space underneath. Inside, we're all a bunch of teenage girls, giggling and telling jokes, laughing about how the other platoons are too stupid to come up with our grand idea of keeping us dry and warm. And indeed, we are dry.

But soon the giggling dies down, and we fall asleep, a nice sleep indeed. Hand even looks happy at this point, despite his dummy-corded 17-Charlies, his lanyarded PVS17C night vision, Fire watch lists are passed around, and I see that I'm on from 04–05, an all right time, instead of the 01–02 or 02–04 times that really suck because you can't get back to sleep afterward. My phone almost dead, I send off a text to Lynn, and fall asleep to the soft patter of the rain against the tarp ceiling.

"Fire watch ..." The words spoken by the platoon sergeant wake me up. This is quite normal, as usually the leadership will want to get with fire watch in the morning, to wake everyone up and get the day moving. "Fire watch," he says again. No one responds. Fuck. Is it my watch? It can't be my watch: no one woke me up. Did someone fall asleep on another watch?

Somebody better respond because this is a tornado in the making. Again, this time with more agitation: "FIRE WATCH! Where the fuck are you!"

Everyone is awake now, rustling about, racing to get out of their bags. "Alright Third! I'm cutting your goddamned tent city down!" He means it, as he whips out his knife and starts slicing the five fifty cord away from the tarps, collapsing them on us. We're all out of our bags now. "EDL right goddamned now fuckers! I guess you don't want to maintain fire watch, Third, what the fuck is this!" The platoon all gets out and formed up; the other platoons are already awake and moving because their fire watch didn't fall asleep on them.

Garner comes over to me, "You got all your shit, Vining?"

PVS14s, check; PVS17s, check; weapon, check; optics and Peq, check. "Yes, Lance Corporal, I'm good".

Himmler, done with his EDL, declares, "Alright fuckers, you obviously can't maintain fire watch on your own, with the boots standing it, so from now on, every fire watch will have two Marines on it, one boot, and one senior, to show the boots how it's done properly."

Uh oh. This isn't going to go over well with the seniors, because now they're in trouble and are going to take it up on us. This can only mean one thing: treeline …

The EDL now complete and Himmler fuming at the mouth, some of the seniors start investigating. Wilbanks and Garner call out, in a low voice, "Hey fuckers, every boot who was on watch get over here, right now."

We run over, because we don't want to be seen as lethargic. Wilbanks starts off, "Okay, we're going to go through this one by one and see who fucked up. First on watch from twenty-two to twenty-three, Todd?"

Todd answers, "Yes I was on, Lance Corporal. I woke up Weitoish."

Weitoish says, "Todd woke me up and I woke up Mauler at zero hundred."

Mauler says, "Lance Corporal, he woke me up and I had it from zero hundred to zero one, then I woke up Stinson."

Stinson says, "Mauler got me up, and I woke up Smith at zero two."

Smith says, "I can't remember being woken up by Stinson very well."

Fuck. Busted. We're all fucked. Range chimes in, "So Stinson, you stood your watch, but didn't adequately wake up Smith; you should have fucking known to make sure that he's out of his bag, and fully dressed, before you yourself go back to sleep."

Stinson did wake up Smith, but he didn't ensure Smith was up; instead he went back to sleep thinking Smith was up. Smith was woken up, but he went back to sleep, a common thing when you're tired and woken up. However, it is the fire watch's job to make sure the next guy is completely woken up, thus taking the responsibility off the watch and transferring it to the next guy. Stinson and Smith are about to learn the meaning of "treeline."

The seniors gather round in a little circle, as do we boots. We're worried, because we're an extension of Smith and Stinson, and their actions just murdered us all. How do you learn in the grunts? Pain and repetition. We see the seniors give out looks to see if anyone is listening to them, then nodding at each other while talking in low whispers. All of a sudden, Range comes over and says, "Mauler, Rich, come here." This can't be good. The seniors tell Mauler and Rich to take Stinson and Smith into the treeline, one at a time, down a slight depression and beat them without leaving any marks. So, first Stinson, they escort him down into the depression, and sort of just look at each other, then suddenly hit him in the gut. He doubles over in pain, and they keep hitting him, then kicking him while he is down. Once this is done, they help him back up, and then get Smith down there and proceed to do the same thing. This all over, we're back at the packs, no other platoon the wiser. Mauler and Rich are seen as the senior boots, because Rich is older than most of the seniors, and Mauler is just built like a tank and performs as well. But in this way, the seniors get what they want, without actually touching us, while corrective actions are still performed. A crime has been committed, and the punishment has been delivered.

It's time to go back, and we get a final EDL at the packs. Himmler is still pissed at us, so we have to make up for it by being good little grunts at his every command. EDL complete, I stuff my 17-Charlies in my LB and load it up on the Seven-Ton. I come back, and Garner says, "Hey Vining, you didn't put your 17-Charlies in your LB, did you?"

Uh oh, boot move. Cardinal Sin. "Umm, yes I did, Lance Corporal, I thought we wouldn't need them until the hooches."

"Stupid fucking boot! Go and fucking get them!"

I run to the seven-ton, throwing packs aside until I find mine, retrieve my 17-Charlies and run back to the packs, showing him that I have them with me. Just in time for "Load up!" We all get on the trucks, flaks and weapons included.

On the ride back, Kennington is talking to Wilbanks, and they're talking about Hand. "You know that fucker forgot his shit in his pack again? Stupid fucking boot, YES HAND! I'm fucking talking to you, BITCH! Get the fuck up at parade rest! Now, on your fucking knees!"

I'm lying down on the deck of the truck right next to Kennington, who is sitting toward the rear, while Hand is at the far end by the tailgate. Hand doesn't get on his knees but he says "Aye, Lance Corporal!"

"No MOTHERFUCKER, on YOUR FUCKING KNEES!"

I think this has to do with domination of some sort. Hand gets on his knees, with his hands behind his back, taking in everything Kennington is saying. Kennington gets up on the moving truck and sticks his finger in Hand's face, then sits back down, then gets up again, only to sit back down during his tirade. "You stupid motherfucking boot, you think you fucking rate, you think you fucking know shit, don't you? Well guess what fucker, this is the fucking Fleet, and here you're nothing but a completely worthless piece of shit; in fact you're the most worthless piece of shit and most worthless boot I've ever …" His speech is cut off as Hand lunges at Kennington, flak, Kevlar and all. This is quite disadvantageous to me because as he crumples against Kennington, the two loaded-down Marines roll over onto me on the deck of the truck.

Immediately every senior in the truck jumps on Hand, punching his head, his face, his thighs, his arms, everywhere that isn't covered by his armor. Salisbury throws a punch that gets me in the face, and I try to lean away from it. Eventually, they get him off of Kennington and sit him back down, screaming bloody murder at him the whole way. Salisbury leans over to me and says in his slow accent, "Hey Vinning, I'm sooory man, I was only trying to puunch him and I thinnk I gooot youu."

I respond, "It's okay, Lance Corporal, you did get me, but I realized what was happening."

For the rest of the ride back, the seniors put Hand back in his place at the back of the truck, most of us in complete disbelief at what just happened. Hand was to become a solid boot and then became an even better grunt, leading a fireteam on the second pump, and stacking bodies as a good grunt does. He got out, married a smoke show and went to school on the GI Bill. Sometimes the Fleet just has a really nasty learning curve, and he took it pretty hard, but eventually came out on top.

Apart from forgetting the 17-Charlies, Hand getting beat by the platoon, Smith and Stinson missing that fire watch, Fort Pickett was an excellent training opportunity. It was a great chance to get out on a battalion training operation, move away from Lejeune, and do grunt shit. It was a stepping stone to Cax. This is the hallmark of predeployment training. A month out in the desert of California, working with large towns of Afghan role players and running conventional infantry ranges for score. If a battalion fails the ranges, it might not get a chance to deploy because of the importance these ranges have.

However, the CO comes out to one of our afternoons off work, and says, "Gents, what I am about to tell you is going to change a lot, and I ask you to please, please not to tell your wives this, for their own sake.

But due to a battalion imbalance in theater, there has been a shift in the deployment schedule. At this rate, I cannot for certain say that we'll even get predeployment leave, maybe a 96 if we can wing it. In fact, we're making plans right now to deploy directly from Cax."

Wow, Sir, deploy directly from the Stumps? Guys are making leave plans, buying plane tickets, family arrangements, moving cars into storage. However, this is the grunts, and Semper Gumby remains supreme. Our platoon sergeant passes some more word afterward, something about making sure to get a will and power of attorney completed before Cax. A living will and testament. A power of attorney. How many American kids have to fill out a will, in preparation for their death, before they reach their twenties?

Cax, Enhanced Mojave Viper, ITX, whatever each generation of Marines decides to call it, the concept remains the same. Put a grunt battalion in the desert, with all of its assets, see how it does when you amp up the pressure. Do the platoons and squads mesh well? Can the company commanders control their Marines over an extended period of patrolling? Do TSE and Clic Marines know how to use the Hiide systems, and do docs know how to triage simulated wounded? The whole ensemble is a final exam for deployment: essentially, can this unit complete every necessary task that will be asked of it when overseas. And if it can't, is it even worth sending?

Cax was the big test for sure, even more so because the majority of the battalion hadn't been to it, most of our seniors being Mew guys. Although a Mew work-up was certainly an extensive training regime, Cax is a different animal in some ways. In the desert you are pushed, through the heat, the sun, the dehydration, the long ranges, 400 being the most infamous of all the live-fire ranges.

Days prior to Cax are filled with readying the battalion. Gone are the worries about deploying from Cali, replaced with how we will perform in California. Blood draws, dental appointments, gear inspection after gear inspection, C-tep issue of Frog uniforms, plate carriers, deployment bags, prepping weapons, fixing armory issues. Mostly it is the admin process of readying for war. Something about all these pieces of equipment issued for the deployment make things feel that much more real. What we wear in training is not the same thing as what we see in the pictures and videos coming back from Afghanistan. Even down to the uniforms and boots which are designed to be more flame-retardant than the standard-issue stuff. Receiving it in person somehow makes things real, as if to say, "This is finally happening." At the same time, we are entering into that world of war that is Operation Enduring Freedom: in a physical sense with the equipment, but in a more emotional sense where "here" and "there" become a distinctive mentality. It is becoming apparent that what we do "here" in the States might not be the same as what we would do "there" in Afghanistan when it comes to tactics and procedures.

Unfortunately, though, this is sort of an illusion because when you get off the big bird and step foot in Helmand Province, you don't enter into some kind of video game where you act differently, your attitude changes, your spirit becomes braver, etc. You remain the same person, with the same amount of training and mental fortitude as you had in the United States under that controlled environment. Some aspects might change when combat becomes a reality, but for the most part, your reasoning and logic remain the same.

But being the concerned and loyal boyfriend I am throughout all this, I'm thinking of Lynn, and how she is going to take it all. My objectified and immature mind immediately considers the lack of sex a serious issue over the next seven months. So, obviously, what does she need in my absence? A battery-powered dildo of course. I go out the night before we bounce out to Cax, and I buy this awesome gel-covered dildo that vibrates and can be twisted into all sorts of shapes. The thing is epic, and will do well to compensate for my absence.

I come back to the Bricks, and throw the plastic bag with the dildo and assorted other stuff onto my bed. Of course, no one else is going to look at it, right? Realizing this, I go up to Weitoish's room to check on something. Having done that, I walk down the catwalk, back to my room. I open the door, and half of the platoon is clustered around my bed. Range turns and says, "Vining! What the fuck is this!" while waving the giant dildo around the room.

"Umm, I thought it would make a good gift for my girlfriend, Lance Corporal…"

"Gift? Holy shit, Vining, you don't have a girlfriend, you're a fucking faggot! I always knew it!"

"Umm, no, Lance Corporal…"

"Whatever, let's go fuck with the new boots!"

The rest of my buddies are finding this hysterical, and I want to suck-start a 12-gauge. The gang follow Range out the room and instantly come across Dunbar, someone from the latest boot drop. Range tells Dunbar to assume the position of attention, saying, "Listen up, Dunbar, do you have any composure? We're going to test your military bearing!" He then smacks him upside the face with the dildo until Dunbar balls up in laughter. Then he moves on to Smith, doing the same thing, but Smith keeps his composure throughout, dildo smacking him in the face and all. So embarrassed, I neglected to tell Lynn any of this when I handed it to her on leave, and thankfully we both decided to toss it before it was ever employed.

The next morning, Charlie Company wakes up at the usual time around 0630, but there is no PT, as we have a workup to get on with. We wear our sleeves down, because by God, we are going to Cax, and after that, Helmand Province. The married guys start coming in, some of their wives with them. One by one, we make our way over to the armory, rolling our deployment bags behind us on the brown Lejeune dirt that we keep getting yelled at to get off of, on the premise that it'll stop the grass from growing. Slowly, the company starts forming, team by team, squad by squad, always shifting down when some latecomer shows up. Our mood is that of curious enthusiasm, as most of us, including the seniors, haven't been out to Cax.

Staff Sergeant Himmler calls out to Sergeant Mike, "Michael, your squad up? Haylock? Peterson?"

All of them give the thumbs-up, showing we have full accountability. The EDL kicks off now, "M27s, get them up!" … "M16A4s, get 'em up!" … "PVS14s! Get 'em up!" … "Come on, Dejesus, waiting on you … Okay, LBS kit? Good, I'll get these numbers to First Sergeant, the rest of you wait here." The first of many EDLs was upon us, and God help you if you're late to this.

While waiting in formation, Hoopi, one of the seniors from first platoon, and a body-slaying, grizzled Marjah vet from 1/6, goes over to hug his mother, the battalion CLO. The whole company lets out an "Aaaahhh!" as the sight of a lead-slinger such as him with his M4/203, in cammies, gingerly hugging his mother is too funny not to embarrass him in front of us all.

Soon third platoon turns to each other in formation, bored with waiting for the school buses and seven-tons to show up. I send off a quick "Good Morning, I love you" text to Lynn. Toledo notices something about my gear. "Hey, Vining, what the fuck is an IFK?"

I turn, slightly red in the face. "It's an IFAK, Lance Corporal. I stenciled that on there."

Toledo picks up the pouch and shows it to the seniors, "Okay, Vining, but you spelled IFAK wrong, there's an A in there, you dumbass."

A couple of the seniors laugh, Garner shakes his head. Range says, "Damn, Vining, forget how to spell? I knew you weren't American."

I have proved that I, after being in the Fleet for six months, am still a boot.

The buses roll up, not the nice double-deckers that take you to combat but the white school ones driven by Marines. After some barking and screaming, we boots load up the deployment bags on the seven-tons. After another EDL and personnel count, we are off. The whole thing just feels like a field trip and we are middle-schoolers with guns.

Lejeune to Cherry Point via county highways, get off at Cherry Point and go through the flight manifests, get everyone weighed, take a picture with your ID, and now the waiting in the staging bay, with the lines of plastic chairs set out. Commercial planes come in, form up, one more EDL, walk across the tarmac with our packs on our chests, and board the planes, lowest rank to highest. This process takes at least five hours.

The planes take off, bound for March Air Force Base in California. We land at night, all groggy and sleepy, do another EDL, getting on buses to Twentynine Palms. As we drive onto the base, we all start waking up, seeing the entrance to the base in big bold yellow letters against the red welcome sign: MARINE CORPS AIR GROUND COMBAT CENTER TWENTYNINE PALMS. Cammies are sweaty from the ride, eventually, the buses wind their way into Camp Wilson, the smaller outpost that all the temporary Cax units stay at. We get out, odd shapes against the background of the darkness on one side, metal hangars on the other. Home for the next month.

There is much commotion with all the yelling going on, "First platoon! Over here!", "Third platoon! Move to that hangar!", "H and S! This hangar!" Eventually, the platoons get sorted. Third gets assigned a hooch, and we move in with all our gear, slamming into each other as we shove our way through the doorway, anxious to drop like rocks. Canvas cots are laid out in rows on either side of the hooch, and we order up by teams and squads, picking out spots next to each other.

"Peterson! Set up a fire watch!"

Peterson, coming from Security Forces, is seen as the junior NCO in our platoon and is thus charged with the mundane task of writing down all the boots for watch. I've got from three to four, so I lay out my sleeping bag on the cot, climb in and doze while the lights are still on.

Mauler wakes me up at 0245, "Hey, Vining, you've got watch."

Groggy-eyed, I say, "All right man, let me get my cammies on." Slowly I crawl out of my bag, slip into my trousers, tie my boots on, grab my weapon, and take the list from him. I'm on watch now with a red lens light, serious stuff to say the least. I pace round the hooch, going from one end to another, really out of boredom more than anything. I'm thinking to myself about how crazy this all is. Ten months ago, I was just another wild-eyed senior in high school. Now I'm a PFC in the Marines, in the middle of the Mojave Desert, preparing to go to Helmand, one of the most violent pieces of real estate in the modern era. I'm not able to buy a drink yet, but I'm about to be on the tip of America's spear, the ugly end of foreign policy, if you will. I'm doing something that none of my peers from high school are remotely coming close to being a part of. I pace some more, I turn on my phone, and text Lynn. And I think about her too: her smile when I'm with her, how she fits into me when I wrap my arms around her in bed, how I feel timeless when she visits me. And that body, Lord that body and those curves …

It's time to wake up Todd for watch. I nudge him, and say, "Hey, Todd, time for watch, man." He lets out a huge breath and rolls over. I nudge him again, and he gets up, puts on his cammies. I give him the list, and I'm released from watch.

* * *

Those dark shapes in the background of the night? They turn out to be gigantic mountains in the day. The morning air is fresh, as if it shouldn't be, because, well, this is the desert, right? We get off to a late start, on account of the company still unpacking itself. Days soon turn into madness, as we turn to drills, rehearsals, planning, shots, everything necessary for the training about to occur. You can feel the pressure just ramping up as if some invisible hand is slowly turning a dial to our deployment training.

Cax is separated into a number of CHBs, or Chubs for short: "Clear" is the fully kinetic phase of warfare, slinging lead and dropping bodies; "Hold" meaning we hold the positions/villages we just took, and "Build" meaning we work with the local populace – in this case, role players – to solidify our gains. The realistic implication is in applying all this to counterinsurgency in Helmand, so thus we train for it back home.

But before we get to the training ranges on the base we work out more of the kinks in the platoon's spare time. Out patrolling in front of the hooches one day, Himmler yells out, "Contact right!" Immediately the platoon as a whole switches to kill mode, getting online and returning fire by screaming, "Bang, bang, bang!" as we imitate a wall of lead from our weapons. We move up, bound by teams, picking up from the prone, advancing a few meters, slamming into the desert sand and returning fire, allowing other guys to do the same. As one organism, we push across the desert, screaming and yelling in a sort of controlled chaos. We are absolutely in our element at this point.

However, when the drill finishes, Himmler is over by Baby Doc, obviously pretty pissed. Baby Doc is on his knees next to a simulated casualty, all his medical gear turned inside out; something doesn't look right.

"What the fuck, Doc? You took like five minutes to even get to the casualty and another ten to even find the right equipment. All the while, Wilbanks is here bleeding out on the ground from a femoral artery bleed … he's dead by now."

Oh no, Baby Doc, new to the platoon, seems to be messing up already, especially when it comes to his job of taking care of one of us. Papa Doc, we have supreme confidence in, the guy is an Alabama medical genius who we know would be there if we need him. But Baby Doc is brand new to the Fleet, and his constant stuttering and seeming inability to treat us under fire is a liability none of us can afford.

"Look at all these guys around you, Doc, look into their faces," Himmler starts out. "These are the guys who are going to be dying if you can't do your job, these men right here. Don't worry about the enemy, these grunts will provide the covering fire, you just worry about tending to the wounded and saving their lives when they need you."

Awkward silence as we all sort of look at him, thinking, "Yeah, that's right, listen to him, he's actually right this time." Baby Doc sort of looks at all of us and says, "Aye, Staff Sergeant." Papa Doc lays into him, going over all his medical supplies while we walk back to the hooches, and he continues to school him back there as well. All I'm thinking is, "God, I hope I don't get stuck with him on my PB."

Moving into the "Clear" phase, we start on the 400 series of ranges: 410, 410 Alpha, and the big one, Range 400. The first two are relatively simple, your run-of-the-mill platoon fire and maneuver both day and night. Except in the desert, where the ground is rocky, the sand is hot, and your water source gets depleted quite quickly. But 400, that's the big one. Range 400 is the ultimate test of any rifle company in the Marine Corps: pass or fail, it will show if your company can actually integrate a combined arms solution successfully.

We run through 410 and 410 Alpha with relative ease, mostly it's assaulting into a cliff face that ends with an index. Then for 400, we wake up real early, with the company commander giving this pep talk beforehand, demonstrating just how vital this range is. Loaded down with extra mortar rounds for the gun crews, we start the range early in the morning by running. The entire platoon is running through these small rock canyons, while guns are going up machine-gun hill to get their suppression in. We don't even see the green Ivans they are so far down the range. Out of breath, we get to a staging area, doubling over, under cover, trying to suck air and water in at the same time. Garner yells out, "Let's move!" and off we go, getting to the mortar crews, and dropping off our rounds, one by one. We back off, at the same time hearing the mortar crews screaming at some poor boot. Looking over, I see a 60mm tube being tipped over, part of the misfire drill of a mortar team. Panting, Range says, "Oh God, it would suck to be that guy trying to catch it as it comes out!"

Moving on, we roll through some ditches, and I see Sergeant Mike being lowered as a simulated casualty. I can almost see the frustration on that killer's face: "C'mon? You gonna take me out now? I've got a squad to lead!" Soon enough we actually see some Ivans, and we open fire. I deploy the bipod legs on my M27 and fire quick bursts at the targets through my horseshoe reticle, silently murmuring, 'Die, motherfucker, die! Die, motherfucker, die!" to time my bursts to the verbiage in order to keep my rate of fire down. Dunbar runs right out in front of Range and Weitoish, both screaming out to him, "Dunbar! Get the fuck out of the way! You're in our line of fire!" A surprised Dunbar turns and sees half the squad right behind him, weapons pointing toward him. He flees back to his spot under the cursing and screaming of the entire squad. Real boot move there, "Jack."

The engineers run out to an obstacle and we pick up our rates of fire, covering them on the way; soon the word comes down the line, "Apob out!" Everyone echoes it and digs deep into the ground, keeping our mouths open to allow the blast wave to flow through. The Apob is fired – *whewwwwwww* – silence for several seconds, then a tremendous *boom!* echoes throughout the valley. America, and savagery at its finest. Sergeant Mike, now back from the simulated dead, screams, "The breach is clear! Move out!" Rushing in single file, we push through the breach, clearing it to the other side. Going into the Ivan positions, we move as a platoon up the huge hill at the end of 400, barely running, now just walking, with all our gear, ammunition and water.

Finally, we are at the objective and consolidate, facing outboard and prepping for any counterattack. In the prone, I turn to Weitoish and say, "Fuck man, that was rough, but thank God it's all over."

"Yeah man, I agree, that really sucked."

Index is called and we slowly get up and begin to make it back the mile where we started.

Schroyer calls out, "Hey! There's an unexploded mortar round here!"

Range goes, "Fuck you're right, Pass that shit back and let's go into a ranger file."

Mortar rounds are sticking out of the sand in every which place, so we watch our step as we trudge through the sand in single file. Martin finds out that Dunbar and Schroyer had warming layers on that whole time and is busy chewing them out, the rest of us puzzled as to how you keep warming layers on in 90° heat.

At night, we form a sort of rock formation around our bivouac site, trying to keep the high winds out. It may not actually get very cold in the desert, but it certainly feels like it, because of the difference in the day–night temperatures. The setting sun forms a sort of odd afterglow, as we can see it at the curvature of the horizon, the desert just being so vast. Joking around, eating our Mr. Es, we feel quite accomplished, considering that the company did well on the range, or at least that is what the CO tells us. But everyone knows this is what officers are for: tell the minions they performed like kings, and they'll eat that up like cotton candy.

The next week is spent in the defense, first clearing through a live-fire MOUT town by inserting with CH-46 "Phrog" helicopters close by and flowing through the little city like water. 81mm mortars from Weapons Company set up, the night draws on us, and planes come over, dropping bombs down-range, while targets are illuminated at night for us to hit with small-arms fire. We dig these sort of improvised fighting holes on a berm where we spend the rest of the night.

That morning, first squad goes out on a training patrol around the town. Range makes me point, and I take the helm of the foot patrol. I'm looking all around for IED indicators, on the ground, the walls even, swiveling my head this way and that. We get back to where we started and Range comes up to me, "Hey, Vining, what was the number painted on the last house we patrolled by? Don't turn around either."

Umm, umm, ummm, "I don't know, Lance Corporal, I didn't see it."

Range just looks at me with his bipolar blank stare as if to emphasize how much of a dumb boot I am. "Well, the number is fifty-three. You didn't notice that, or the other five houses before that, why? Because you were too busy walking too fast and looking at everything. When you're on patrol you need to focus on the details, you need to take it slow. What if those numbers were an EFP IED, placed at head level so it'll take your torso out? Or better yet, you'll walk through it, but it'll take us out, behind you? You better start bringing your A-game because a month from now, there won't be any indexes, or a barracks room to go home to. It'll be for real. You got that?"

Dammit, I screwed up again. "Yes, Lance Corporal, I understand."

Range looks at me closely for a second. "Show me your fucking NVGs." I pull them out of my dump pouch, and he walks away, obviously furious.

Charlie Company has just one more "clear" training operation to do, before we move into the "hold" stage of training. This consists of a coordinated attack on a town, with tanks and AAV tracked vehicles. There will be role players in the town shooting back at us with blank rounds, just as we will be shooting back at them with blanks.

To facilitate this, and the rest of Cax, the company, gets trucked out to this random Fob in the desert, to help us get used to living on a patrol base in Helmand. We ride in Armadillos, seven-ton trucks with huge slabs of armor plating along the sides, to protect troops sitting down the center on benches. They have these really intricate ladders out the back, that most of the time are held together by five fifty or some other improvised cord, making getting off or on a challenge, especially with flak and Kevlar because you have to fit through this tiny opening in the armor. Then you have these top bars that are for a canvas roof section that is of course never installed, because Motor T is always a bunch of tightwads and probably chucked the things to begin with. But essentially you are constantly smacking your head on these bars while trying to fill up the wooden seats that allow for a squad to fit on. Riding in one gives a good view of the surrounding area, unlike being in a normal seven-ton where all you see is the guy in front of you. But in these, the dust spewing through is intense, covering anything and everything. The weather isn't much better, and because of the open top, you get whatever is bearing down on you, be it sun or rain, but most of the time cold desert air.

Getting to the Fob, we raise this tent, large enough for the whole platoon to sleep in when laying down. The place starts to take on a life of its own, with chow every morning, and the boots standing post in this small wooden enclosure on a hill, where I find a huge spider on Dunbar one night that I admire for quite some time before I let him know. Himmler also announces earlier in the day that he is going to be rationing the platoon to one MRE a day, to get us ready for deployment.

Toledo makes the offhand comment when the platoon sergeant is out of earshot: "Wait, so because I'm going on deployment for seven months, I'll just not have sex for a month prior, because I won't be having sex for the next seven, right? That makes literally little to no sense, what-so-fucking-ever."

To us boots, we're just taking it as it comes but the seniors realize how stupid this idea is. Either way, we only draw one MRE apiece.

We wake up stupid early the next morning, quickly filling up on water, getting everything we need for the day, doing an EDL real quick before we start off on this death march across the sand to this combined arms attack. In trying to keep up with the platoon, I'm flat-tiring Lance Corporal Martin in front of me and he blurts out, "Dammit, Vining, stop fucking stepping on my heels!"

"Sorry about that, Lance Corporal, I'm just trying to keep up!"

Heck, it's still dark by the time we get to our little staging area. But doing another EDL there reveals that Baby Doc forgot his NVGs either in the tent or somewhere along the way. That isn't something to be forgetting right now, so Sergeant Mike runs him back over the tank trail to find it. This poor kid is just screwing up left and right, and he's supposed to be the guy we count on when we get shot.

The attack goes off without a hitch, we load up in AAVs and move in with Abrams tanks against an enemy-controlled conex city. I ride topside with the AAVs, careful not to put my fingers between the openings to prevent them being chopped off by the top hatches if they shut by accident. We storm the town, shooting role players with blanks, while the tanks empty their main-gun blank rounds at the city. Dismount from the AAVs, and bound into the town, clearing room by room, house by house, moving with the flow and the screaming, rolling like white rapids through the rooms. I screw up by entering a room alone, and Range gets furious at me for it. Another fuck-up. Stupid boot. But Dunbar takes the cake when he starts arguing back at Garner about a room-clearing technique, and all of us, boots included, are screaming at him, "Dunbar! Shut the fuck up! Just shut the fuck up and listen, you dumb bitch!" The kid has a lot to learn, and at least I'm not the only one screwing up.

Going back to the Fob, via the same AAVs that offloaded us, we begin a series of patrolling exercises, pushing out in squads from the Fob and entering another conex town. The point of this is to hold the gains we just made in a town, and eventually to move into a patrol base in the town center.

But before that, Himmler comes stomping into our little bivouac area, sticking his big bald head up into the ceiling, looking at all of us to be quiet. "Who the hell told on me about the one-MRE-a-day issue? Fess up now fuckers. Or else I'm going to actually make your lives a living hell." Super-awkward silence among all of us, as both seniors and boots sort of look at each other as if now on sort of equal terms, being in this together as it were. "No one? No one at all? Very well then, I'll deal with you fuckers later, Third!" And off he trumps into the distance. Slowly whispers are going round, "Was it Sergeant B? Did he tell someone?" We don't know. But thank God, whoever that was.

By this point in the game, Range practically hates me: to be hated by a senior team leader isn't a good thing for a boot. It is further complicated by Range's bipolar mood swings. You never know if you'll catch him in a good mood or a disastrous one, which can either lead to you getting hazed or sharing a cigarette with him. He is also taking a lot of his frustration out on me, the poor boot.

Thus, I don't find it too enjoyable when our team gets sent out on a VCP patrol outside of this town. We set off from the Fob with a Prick-one-fifty-two; my team consists of Range leading, Dejesus, and Weitoish. Topped off on water, and loaded up with blanks, our big ugly Rat boots pound the desert sand as we push out in a column. IEDs being one of the biggest problems in-country, our eyes are peeled for disturbed earth, ant trails, odd trash, or any anything else that could get us nailed in training. Despite it not being the real thing and only Cax, we're trying to get in the mindset of looking for this stuff.

Walk a few steps, slowly turn to the outboard side of the patrol, make a connecting file with the grunt behind you, slowly turn back the same way, following in the footsteps of the grunt in front of you, always keeping your weapon up, propped up on those magazine pouches mounted to the kangaroo pouch of the plate carrier, thus if not actually holding the weapon up, giving the appearance of doing so. A patrol can look far more menacing depending on how vicious it appears to the enemy through their weapons carry. Every security halt, we're fanning out to the nearest cover, trying to get eyes on the surroundings.

Moving like this, the patrol silently burns through the hot day in Twentynine Palms, Range motioning for us at the end of it to set up this ad hoc VCP on a road leading into town. He takes one look at me and tells me exactly where he wants me, then turns away. The hate must keep him warm at night. After setting up at this road for hours, what looks like a desert sandstorm starts coming in. Nothing too big but with enough wind to make you want to get behind something, so we are all huddled under this small watchtower sort of thing by the side of the road, trying not to choke on the sand being whipped up all around us. Range is getting on the green gear, trying to get a hold of the squad leader, Garner, and the Sir. But to no avail.

Range is extremely frustrated. "You know what? Those fuckers back there are sitting in their seats, listening to music, inside that stupid covered COC back there, and they've all but forgotten about us out here, in this fuckin' sandstorm. We're out here, on this pathetic VCP, getting torn up by sand, without any word on a relief either. It would be so easy too, if they just used a Humvee, load up the relief team minus the driver, then we'd switch places, also minus the driver. But no, something like that would be too complicated for them. You know what, Vining? I'm not even pissed at you anymore, compared to how mad those COC fucktards are making me."

"Good to go, Lance Corporal, I agree, it really sucks."

"You're damn right it sucks, Vining! Fuck them!"

Who cares about the sandstorm, the wrath of Range scares me more than anything our company COC – Combat Operations Center – can do.

After about another two hours of waiting, Toledo's team comes out and relieves us, appearing as angels through the dust. Thank God they are here because the sandstorm is really whipping up into something none of us want to be outside in. Range briefs Toledo on what has been going on, which is really nothing and with Smith, Stinson, and Floyd, they immediately head for a conex box. Those turds, we could have done that all along, but that's because first squad is much harder than third squad will ever be.

Back into a fireteam column, we head to the Fob, through the sandstorm. Getting back, we strip off our gear and lay down on our sleeping systems that are already there. It feels great, but Garner pokes his head back in and says "Hey don't get too comfortable, we might have to send you guys back out in a bit." A collective groan from my team, why, whyyyy, WHYYYYYY! It's getting dark now, the sandstorm is still raging, why can't they just let us rest before sending us back out?

Nonetheless, Range, being the exemplary team leader that he is, goes to find out more, and tells the rest of us to fill up on water and chow. The water bull is right outside. I grab Weitoish to come with me, we fill up our camelbacks, then we fish through our packs and get some MRE snacks, as it's probably going to be a long night.

Range comes back. "One of you grab an assault pack, fill it up with chow, and bring it for the rest of us, we don't know when we're coming back."

All set, and EDL taken, we move out into the night, pretty much in the same direction as earlier. Except this time, we are heading to a traffic circle, with conex boxes surrounding it, supposedly to hold another VCP. Using NVGs, the desert turns into this enormous green ocean, calming while we move through it, and then hurting us when we step on things we can't see. Our team gets to the traffic circle, and we relieve some guys from third squad. The poor bastards now have to walk back in a sandstorm, but at least they get to go back to the Fob and relax. We, on the other hand, have to maintain security at this random traffic circle, in the middle of nowhere. Range sets Dejesus and me up on either end of the circle, so we are facing outboard security. About twenty minutes later, this white car drives into our checkpoint, and we stop it, motioning for it to halt about thirty meters away. Still in training, we motion for the occupants to get out, and they do. They are role players, dressed in man dresses and wearing Afghan headgear, known as pakols, circular cloth things. It is blatantly obvious that they are Marines dressed up tonight as OpFor for the training scenario, because they are acting like a bunch of lance corporals, in other words, like idiots. But we search them and their car nonetheless, take pictures before sending them on their merry way.

Dejesus and I get back on security, and not ten minutes later Range comes out and pulls us back in, the sandstorm being much too thick at this point. He tells us to hang out in the conex box for a bit while he sees when we'll get relieved. "Man, I knew those fuckers, they're some Pogs from H&S Company. I remember seeing those idiots in Indiana when we were there for the Mew workup."

"Sounds like an odd coincidence, Lance Corporal."

"Yeah, damn right it is, they were acting stupid up in Indiana as well. Whatever ... I'm going to see what's going on with this post situation. They can't have us out here for more than long. It's a fucking sandstorm outside."

Dejesus and I nod as he is right: this sucks. Range gets on the radio and chats for a while, but whatever is coming out of the radio seems to be inaudible. "Roger, One One out ..."

"What's up, Range? No relief?" asks Dejesus.

"Fuck no, the Sir wants us to stay out here until like zero six."

"Damn son, they really stuck it to us, they said we could go fuck ourselves!" Dejesus is a pretty quiet dude, mostly keeping to himself playing World of Warcraft in his room, so to hear him swear like this is pretty funny.

Range thinks for a little while, figuring out what to do now. Suddenly he pipes up, "Listen up, Vining, Weitoish, Schroyer. At this point, they've fucked us pretty hard, and there is a freakin' storm going on outside. I'm not going to treat this as an OP or something, because this is completely stupid to begin with; we shouldn't even be out here. So each of you stand watch on the radio in this corner, while the others go to sleep over there, spread out, share poncho liners, whatever. Try to rest though; it'll probably be a long and cold night."

We couldn't agree more: "Aye, Lance Corporal," almost in unison if we weren't so tired. Weitoish and Schroyer take off to sleep, while I get on the radio for the first watch, Range right next to me, and taking out a fat dip from a can he had in the ankle pocket of his Frogs and putting it in the left side of his mouth, spitting out the doorway. I'm holding the Prick-one-fifty-two right now, always anxious about what to say on the net, not wanting to say anything out of radio protocol.

"One One, this is Three Papa, radio check over." Staff Sergeant Himmler is checking on us.

"Roger, Three Papa, I hear you. Lima Charlie, over."

"Roger, same. Out."

Whew, that was easy ... Range looks over to me. "So where the fuck you from again, Vining? China or some shit?"

"Well, I grew up in South East Asia, Lance Corporal. Burma, and Thailand."

"So, what you are saying is, you're practically a foreigner?"

"Eh ... I enlisted and am going to Afghanistan in a few weeks. Does that make me unAmerican?"

"I guess you have a good point there, can't really argue with that one."

The howling wind outside the small conex box doesn't get any better, or the conversation easier to hear. Crackling noises echo from the green gear radio leaning up against the wall.

"I hear you're from Georgia, Lance Corporal?"

"Yep, just outside of Atlanta. I love Georgia, always have. Our family used to live in a pretty rough part of town, but then moved out of it when I was a kid."

"And do you have any siblings? I don't have any."

"Yeah, I have a sister back home …" Range then looks at me closely. "Vining, do you know what my first day in the Fleet was like?"

That was a quick change of topic. "No, Lance Corporal, I don't."

He leans back against his plate carrier and starts tearing open a sealed MRE cookie. "After checking in, I get my room key, bring my gear up to the room, and don't see anyone there, so I start unpacking and field-daying, mopping the floor, wiping down the surfaces, and so on. After a little bit, I hear this knock on the door so I go to open it. When I do, it's one of the seniors from Weapons Platoon with some buddies. Before I have a second to even say anything, he punches me right in the face and I go down to the floor. The rest of them come piling in after me, and beat me down right there in my own room. This was my welcome to the Fleet and I think it happened just about every day for the first week in." He takes a bite out of his cookie, slowly chewing it as he stares into my soul, the Mojave desert wind still swirling viciously, into the connex box shelter.

I stay quiet for a little bit. "That really sucks to hear, Lance Corporal. I'm sorry to hear how that went."

Range looks back at me. I can feel his angry glare in the darkness. "Don't be sorry, Vining, just be glad that your generation of boots doesn't get treated near as bad as that. I never agreed with that sort of hazing and don't want it done today."

I nod in the darkness, stiffening up a little. "Well, thank you for your generosity. It looks like you turned out well despite it, being a team leader now, and all."

"Indeed …" His voice trails off, looking out into the night. The only light we have is the occasional headlamp or issued Sidewinder light. Those, or we just click our Peck-sixteens on the permanent setting, leaning our rifles up against the wall of the conex. The problem with the issue Sidewinder light is that it costs around 60 bucks, so it would really suck to replace if you ever lost it in the field.

"You like guns, Vining? Of course, you like guns."

"Indeed I do, Lance Corporal, I don't own very many because I haven't lived here for a while yet."

"Gotcha … what's your favorite pistol?"

"Well, I'll give Glocks a point for just being so reliable and economically priced, but if I'd have to pick something, I'd pick the Nineteen Eleven. Tons of history, the thing is what all other modern handgun designs are derived from, and when it came out, it was one of the most reliable and effective handguns of its kind."

"True, yeah, I like Nineteen Elevens as well: that's 'Merica right there. I've got an FN Five Seven, and a Three Fifty Seven Magnum back home, at my mom's house now."

"Ah, the Five Seven. The Pee-Ninety takes the same cartridge; pretty cool pistol, especially with a capacity of twenty rounds. I've shot one before at Knob Creek."

"Oh yeah, that thing is a great time, and I love it. When it isn't at my mom's, it's in my truck, at all times. I bought it when I got back from the MEU, all that deployment money I had, that and a truck."

"Wait, so do some guys keep their guns on base? I thought you weren't supposed to?"

"If you get caught, you'll get fucked. But you just have to be smart."

"Well, I'm glad you like it. Wouldn't mind shooting one myself."

I reach into my right pocket and pull out my iPhone. Click it on. No bars or data show up on the screen. As per usual in Twentynine Palms. Sometimes you can get lucky in the field if for some reason the cell towers are broadcasting nearby, or you have the right network. A text from Lynn about how boring her one economics class is would help distract me from the cold wooden floor I am sitting on.

"How much money do we usually make on deployments?"

"Eh, it depends, but you'll probably come home with a solid fifteen grand, combat deployments a little more, because of the combat pay."

"Damn, that's a good chunk of change. Why is it so much?"

"Well, you have to consider, all of your salary is now tax-free, so the government is giving you the full amount that you normally rate. Then you realize you're not spending any of it at all: it isn't like you are eating out every night." Range leans out the doorway to spit some dip out; like he's finished with the majority of it but leaving it in helps with the oral fixation.

"That makes sense, a lot more then. So what is this new truck you got?"

"You've probably seen it in the barracks parking lot. Big, black Ford F-One-Fifty. I really like it a lot. I'm still making payments on it, almost a year later, but I'll soon be done with these, hopefully during the next deployment. Either way, it's my first truck and I'm super-happy with it."

"Nice … I don't have a car yet, but hopefully, I'll get something when we get back, something used, maybe a truck. I don't know yet. I'll have to do some researching."

"Yeah … that you do. Make sure you get a good payment plan and not some stupid amount of interest, and don't buy from anywhere local in J-Vegas: all them dealers will scam your ass." Range fishhooks his finger into his mouth, wiping out the dip, flinging it outside the doorway.

"Will do, Lance Corporal, will do …"

Range sort of turns over and tries to go to sleep, in his flak and all, knees up, back against the wooden corner. Leaving me with the radio. And time. I look down at the time and see I have a few minutes until I get off watch and have to wake up Weitoish. I go to wake him up, him still in his flak as well. I hand him the radio, and he moves into the next room, me falling asleep before he settles down in the doorway.

Field sleep never seems to last as long as it should, seconds instead of the hours it takes. Even if you do get some solid rest, it's usually rudely awakened by someone yelling at you to move somewhere. "Vining, get up bro', we're being relieved." Weitoish pushes me awake as he walks through the conex. Holy smokes, I thought the day would never come. Groggy-eyed, I stretch out, feel for my M27, my NVGs in my dump pouch, and my PVS24s in my assault pack, recheck the SDO and the Peck-sixteen dummy-corded to the M27, making sure they are still there. I take a peek outside the doorway, and I see the fireteam coming to relieve us, walking through the twilight of the early morning, wind still whipping all around. Range does the handover with Martin's team, completes a touch EDL with us, and we head back to the Fob, walking in a tac column. The wind is still strong, ripping through my thin Frog top, despite my plate carrier. Finally, we see the main entrance of the training Fob, call out the challenge and pass to the guys on post.

Range keys the mike, "Chaos Main, Chaos Main, Chaos Three One requests permission to enter friendly lines, four packs M-E." A muffled reply comes back, someone in the COC writing numbers on a dry-erase board. Range replies with a weary "Roger, out" then leads us the rest of the way to our tent, Kevlars hanging off of our plate carriers, rifles drooped across our magazine pouches in front. Getting into the big tent, we drop our Kevlars on top of our LB packs still arranged at the edges, lay our rifles up against them, then rip off our flaks, slowly working them off of our heads from our shoulders. Our Frog tops have the outline of the plate carriers from the sweat. We let our weary bodies fall to the ground and enter a solid sleep, not knowing when we'll get a break again.

Several more training scenarios later, and Twentynine Palms is history. Probably the only hiccup being that a senior left his M4 two-oh-three in the head at the PX, making Charlie the laughing stock of the battalion. The entire company has to get formed up outside the hooches and do a complete weapon and radio number by number EDL, courtesy of the XO, whom not many guys are very fond of. The dweeb seems like a high-school nerd playing college football, and not fully competent in either arena.

Putting on fresh cammies, we load up the seven-tons with our deployment bags, and LBs, then get on the buses that seem to take all day to show up, while we wait in the now empty cots in the cans. During the ride back to March Air Force Base, Toledo, infamous for his ability to always have this exhaustive need to hit the head for a number two, manages to take a dump in a paper bag on the bus, before throwing it out the window at around 55 miles per hour. Improvise, Adapt, Overcome, right Marine?

Get off the buses, EDL, load up the plane, get on the plane, EDL, don't sleep on the plane because of the excitement of finally being done with all the workup. Land at Cherry Point, get off, do an EDL, unload the plane, packs onto the seven-tons. Get chewed out by Garner and Range at the same time for not replying fast enough, get on the buses, back to Lejeune main gate, slightly saltier than before, back to the armory. Do an EDL, unload the seven-tons, turn in weapons and NVGs, safety brief by the CO, safety brief by First Sergeant, safety brief by Sir, safety brief by Himmler, safety brief by squad leader. Team leader says screw this, get dismissed, back to the Bricks, into civvies (except Paulie, he gets drunk in boots 'n' utes), crack open a beer despite being underage, relax. Party.

Mattresses fly off the decks onto the quad below, and boots are low-crawling across the quad in cold-weather gear. One of the seniors comes running into my room buck-naked, wasted, and with a row of stitches down his scalp. He jumps on top of me and starts wrestling me. It takes Paulie coming in from the other room to get him off. CNN comes up with a special announcement from the president. Osama bin Laden has been smoke-checked by a DEVGRU SEAL team in Pakistan. All of Lejeune explodes with celebration. I take another swig of my beer and text Lynn how many times I want to bend her over before we leave. She thinks I'm cute. It's a good day to be a U.S. Marine.

Field training at Lejeune and Pickett are done, predeployment checklists are complete, all are up on medical and dental, all up on C–Tep issue, extra tourniquets are issued. Now we check out on predeployment leave. Next on the checklist? Helmand Province, Afghanistan. One of the most violent places, in one of the most violent countries, in one of the most violent regions of the world, and we are destined for the middle of this massive geopolitical conflict that has been going on for most of our teenage lives. Enjoy your leave, don't smoke dope, call your squad leader if you have any problems. Any questions? Now for five more safety briefs. Don't worry, your ill-timed plane ticket out of Raleigh-Durham Airport can wait, should have picked Wilmington.

I go home to my parents. Lynn has a section of the summer off, and she is able to squeeze part of it in spending the fifteen days of leave with me, in addition to the week or so afterward in J-ville, before we push off. We spend as much time as possible with each other, sightseeing, sleeping, cuddling, making love ... lots of making love. In fact, this is the longest, continuous time we have ever spent together since we began dating. It feels crazy that we could be so close, yet soon be so far and possibly one of us gone forever.

One night, while Lynn is asleep, I go to my Dad's smoking spot. He has a chair in the kitchen where he smokes Nat Shermans: the oven sucks the smoke out of the house so he can smoke inside during the cold nights.

"Hey, Dad, mind if I bum a cigarette from you?"

"I guess so, you're of age now, might as well." He's the strict type.

Of age. What does that even mean? I can smoke a cigarette, vote for office, go off to war, but God forbid I purchase an ounce of alcohol. He hands me a cigarette, and I light it up, semi-proud of smoking with my Dad.

"So how is Lynn taking all this?"

"Yeah, I think she sees it as part of the deal sort of thing, something she got herself into and feels it might be worth staying for. Or least I hope so." I really hope so. She doesn't know how hard I want this to work.

"I imagine it being very hard on both of you; you are in a very serious occupation, something that neither she nor you have ever seen the likes."

"Guess so ... I agree with you."

He takes another drag, I take another drag, we sit in silence. The oven clock changes its digital number pattern.

"Dad?"

"Yes?"

"What would you do ... or what do you think ... if I get killed?"

A long pause. I can't believe this is ever an easy question for any parent to answer. But I want to hear the answer. I need to hear it.

"Well ... I mean, we can't joke around with this. It is an extremely real possibility. I think you know that Mommy would be devastated by it. I would be too. But I know that this is what you want, and it is something you believe in very deeply, and means very much to you." He takes another drag on the long, brown Nat Sherman. They always smelt so particular while I was growing up. "Of course we hope that you will be okay, and have nothing happen, but we have to be realistic."

Silence. I don't know if this is what I want to hear, or if there ever is a right answer, but he is truthful, and that is important to me.

"Thanks … thanks, Dad."

We don't say much after that. We finish our cigarettes, and him his coffee, then head off to our separate bedrooms. I close the door, feel my way over to the bed, climb in, under the sheets. Lynn makes a low rumbling sound, as she turns over in her sleep, and I wrap my one leg over her knee, my arm underneath the pillow, my other arm around her back, to her shoulder, slowing caressing it from shoulder blade to hip. It doesn't wake her up. I kiss her on the cheek, and whisper, "I love you." She doesn't hear it, but she already knows it in her subconscious. I think of my conversation earlier.

* * *

Leave couldn't have been any shorter, and soon enough it is over. Lynn and I are in J-ville, spending the week at Spencer's house with his wife, before our flight date. All the crazy preparation has pretty much already taken place, and we really don't have much to do when it comes to admin tasks. Range tells me that he half-expected me to not come back from leave, that I was probably going to desert like Lateef did during our Christmas 96 Libo. That coward. But Range is pretty much doing his bipolar thing. I've gotten quite used to that. The mood around the company is an ominous one. Getting back from Cax, we felt like we were hot shit, the cool guys on the block, for spending a month in the desert and becoming BAMFs out there. It showed too, because our sleeves were always down, showing that we were within sixty days of deploying. But as each day slips by, we start feeling anxious, and realizing, you know, this is the white elephant, the Moby Dick, this is the real thing, and some of us might not actually come back home with air in our lungs.

You can see it in the guys holding onto their wives or girlfriends, the awkward jokes about what we are going to do to each other at our patrol bases, the funny comments made to their significant others, "Don't go hitting up all our friends from high school, looking for Jodie, ya' hear?" Behind every laughing face is a nervous soul, one that is sort of expecting the unknown, but also welcoming it at the same time. Even our seniors are antsy, this being their first combat deployment as well.

We go to work in the morning, spend a couple hours on this or that, mostly last-minute gear inspections, of which there are multiple permutations. We don't know what to pack, so instead just pack everything listed on every list. Reading it though, Stinson abruptly says, "Why are there four trashbags on here? Like just four? Not five, not three, not a whole box of trashbags, but four." Smith and I look at the list, and sure enough, it says, "TRASH BAGS 2 GALLON (4)." Kinda odd. Papa Doc is walking by, so we spit out to him, "Hey Doc, you know why there are four trashbags on this list?" Without missing a beat, he turns and says, "Oh, the trashbags are for your body parts, so if you get blown to bits, we have something to put your pieces in when the routine medevac bird lands." And just like that, he walks off. All of us kind of look at each other, as if to say, "Damn, that was unexpected." We turn back to packing everything for the gear inspection, trying not to think of ourselves as a bloody mess. I tell Lynn it was a good day at work and neglect to mention the bodybag trashbags.

Each day I come home with Spencer, working through the gridlock Lejeune traffic, wishing that we could scream to all the cars how we just want to be with our women, and not deal with anything else, that we might be heading home dead in as little as a couple weeks. We get home, squeeze our rolled sleeved blouses off, walk into the apartment, and sort of just go to our separate rooms and stay there, Spencer with his wife, me with Lynn, the one couple texting the other if either needs food or something. Lynn and I try to forget about the impending deployment, watching movies, telling stories, or having sex. I get the bright idea to play Lonely Island with Akon's "I Just Had Sex" comedy song immediately after one of our acts of coitus, Lynn finds it hilarious as we finish. We're trying to hold on to each second, each minute, trying to make it last just that much longer. As if somehow, by some miracle of time travel, we could pause the moment forever and make the world not exist.

The day before Charlie Company, 1st Battalion, 9th Marines deploys, we have a massive company PT run, with our company shirts on. The pace isn't bad, the cadence even enjoyable, as each platoon competes with the other for volume and ferocity. Weitoish gets out on the left of third platoon's formation, belting out, "LEFT, RIGHT, LEFT, RIGHT, LEFT, RIGHT, KILL! LEFT, RIGHT, LEFT, RIGHT, LEFT, RIGHT, 'CAUSE YOU KNOW I WILL!" Running back to the quad, the company slows down, transitioning to marching instead of running. Having been a former drill instructor, First Sergeant Hambaugh gets up on the PT table, leading us in the cool-down stretches. He gives a little pep talk and practically releases us for the day, reminding us that, "Sixteen hundred tomorrow, gents, form up in the CP parking lot, ready to fucking rock and roll, with all your gear. Platoon sergeants, you got them."

Spencer and I go back home and do our separate thing again. That night we shave our heads, as is the custom in the Fleet when a boot goes on deployment, Lynn and Spencer's wife helping us out. Afterward, Lynn and I stay in bed, kissing and caressing each other until we fall asleep, my arm becoming numb under the pillow as she rests on it. The next morning we sleep in; we don't have to be anywhere until fifteen forty-five, but we'll show up to the Bricks at around fourteen hundred just to be on the safe side, with all our gear. After all, it isn't every day that you go on your first combat deployment. In bed, we are trying to really soak everything in, every feature of our faces, our bodies, our moans, our silly tendencies, and funny quirks. We make love twice that morning, slumbering in between. After a bit of just facial memorization and gazing, I kind of choke out, "Lynn ... I ... I ... don't want to die." I've got a tear rolling down my face.

Lynn kind of smiles and wipes it away, saying, "Ahh, me neither Miles. Me neither ... I don't want you to die either." She's trying to be upbeat, trying to act as if this is all just a bad dream. That kind of makes me feel better, but it doesn't make the realization any less. Despite three months of the hardest entry-level service training, another three months learning my infantry trade, learning how to better kill another human being, then many more weeks and field ops in the Fleet, being toughened up by the seniors, getting beaten down, hazed, living on my own and managing my life as an adult, even writing a last will and testament. I am still just a teenager, about to take part in one of the most chaotic and defining challenges that a human might ever experience. So although I am going to war, I am still a boy, playing a man's game.

There is this picture of the third platoon guys on the second-deck catwalk. Some of us are mid-laugh, others look bored, Spencer has his hands on his hips, with a beer in his left hand. Lynn and I are off to the right of the center, against the wall. She has one arm around my waist, and I've got my arm around hers. My desert cammies are looking smart, with some pretty sharply rolled sleeves if I don't say so myself. I'm looking down, sort of anxious, like someone has just motioned me off to the right. But Lynn, she is staring into the distance, and the look is plain as day: she doesn't want me to leave. If she could squeeze the very blood out of me to stay, she would: you can tell she is halfway trying already.

But this look, this image, is timeless. A couple, before a Vietnam tour, before a Korean deployment, before being sent off to Europe. We can take this back to the Revolutionary War, and before that, to ancient battles with the Greeks and the Romans. Maybe even the Mongols, however vicious they were, maybe their women wanted to squeeze the blood out of their men, to get them to stay, not to leave, to not die. Some years later I'm at a museum in London, in front of a painting called *Eastward Ho!* depicting British soldiers shipping off to India in 1857, hugging their wives. Whether the artist served or not is irrelevant because he gets the same expressions down as in the photograph from 2011. I sit down, in front of the painting, and I just study it, for something like half an hour. I see myself in the soldiers' faces, I see Lynn in the wives. It's so real I could almost fall into the painting and find myself on their wooden boat, in a red coat and with a musket, ready to fight for the Queen during the Sepoy Rebellion.

The time has come, and what does that mean? EDL of course. Lay the packs down in neat rows, platoon by platoon so we can load the trucks up when Motor T comes along. Now we sit round the packs, Range hanging out with Rich and White, Dejesus doing his thing, Garner with his whole family, Martin and his wife, Lynn and me … the list goes on, each grunt in his own way, clutching this little diamond of time. The guys without families are almost bored, as we usually are during this hurry-up-and-wait ordeal. We've already drawn our weapons from the armory. The only thing left is the movement to Cherry Point.

"Yooooo, Seven-Tons are here."

I don't need that: the rumbling tells us that enough. Sergeant Mike spits out, "Hey, get all the boots up there, get those packs on." Leaving our weapons behind, we strip our blouses and start chain-ganging packs onto the trucks. Time goes by. Eventually the buses show up, lining up next to each other against the company CP. Third gets in formation, in the U.S. for the last time, EDL yet again. EDL complete, Himmler tells us to get in line, to get on the buses. I'm toward the front because I'm in first squad, but I'm looking for Lynn; where is she? Time is winding down, War isn't going to slow down for me. I spot her, behind the platoon, next to Spencer's wife who is squeezing Spencer tight at that moment. Lynn looks a bit lost, confused, not understanding what is happening, looking round for me.

I look at Range, "Lance Corporal? Can I go say goodbye to Lynn?" Range sort of looks over at Spencer, sees that we need to keep the line on the buses going, but also sees that Spencer is getting his time, and I'm not, and the humanity part of his bipolarity just nods and whispers, "Go, but be quick." So I go, and I run to Lynn, assault pack on my back, M27 slung down my chest, preventing me from pressing my body completely up against hers. I hug her really tight, she's sobbing, almost uncontrollably, but just keeping it together; she can't seem to get a word out either. I cup her cheeks in my hands and bring her head in to kiss her. I kiss her, through our tears that form droplets together.

"Lynn, I love you, okay? I'll always love you. I'll think of you always."

She sort of nods, her face glistening, and I wipe away her tears. Then I split off, ever so softly, turn my back, and rush back to the line on the buses. Range is waiting for me to get on, and I do, sitting down, next to the platoon clown, Toledo. We do a personnel count-off, and I'm in tears. Toledo puts his arm round me and pats me on the back, saying, "It's okay man, it's gonna be okay. This is what we signed up for man; she knows that just as well as you." It doesn't help much, but it also doesn't do any harm. My sobbing slowly fades as the air-conditioned tour bus rumbles into the dark Carolina night to Marine Corps Air Station Cherry Point.

I was 19 years old, and that is how I went to war.

9-LINE MEDEVAC REQUEST

You, this is Me, Stand by for Medevac 9-Line

Line 1. Location of the pick-up site:

Line 2. Radio frequency, call sign:

Line 3. Number of patients by precedence:
A – Urgent
B – Priority
C – Routine

Line 4. Special equipment required:
A – None
B – Hoist
C – Extraction equipment
D – Ventilator

Line 5. Number of patients:
A – Litter
B – Ambulatory

Line 6. Security at pick-up site:
N – No enemy troops in area
P – Possible enemy troops in area
E – Enemy troops in area
X – Enemy troops in area

Line 7. Method of marking pick-up site:
A – Panels
B – Pyrotechnic signal
C – Smoke signal
D – None
E – Other

Line 8. Patient nationality and status:
A – US Military
B – US Civilian
C – Non-US Military
D – Non-US Civilian
E – EPW

Line 9. Obstacles and Terrain report:
<u>Z-MIST</u>
Z – Zap Number
M – Mechanism of Injuries Sustained
I – Injury Sustained
S – Signs and Symptoms
T – Treatment Rendered

Chapter 2

Them Grunts

"Now, brotherhood is different from friendship. Friendship happens in society, obviously. The more you like someone, the more you'd be willing to do for them. Brotherhood has nothing to do with how you feel about the other person. It's a mutual agreement in a group that you will put the welfare of the group, you will put the safety of everyone in the group above your own. In effect, you're saying, "I love these other people more than I love myself."

Sebastian Junger

As our 6x6 Mrap pulled out of company patrol base Jaker, Stinson, Todd, White, and I peered out of the thick armored windows at this new country. Peculiar sights, sounds, people in turbans and burkhas, oddly shaped, mud-brick village compounds. Apart from the occasional motorcycle, this country hadn't changed since Shakespeare was knocking boots. Since we left Cherry Point, our plane had gone to Maine, then Ireland, several days in Kyrgyzstan, a week at Camp Dwyer in the Garmsir district of Helmand Province, then Jaker in Nawa District, and finally being pushed out to our platoon PBs. We were in southwestern Afghanistan, falling under ISAF's Regional Command South West. Nights were cool, mornings were sticky, and days were so hot that it would melt the glue off of envelopes in direct sunlight.

The lumbering truck pulled to a stop along a dusty road at the edge of a village called Loy Kolay, literally meaning "large village" in Pashtu. The eight of us in the back peered out of the four-inch-thick blast windows at the Afghans. Some stared back at the steel monster that had become a common sight in Nawa District. Others went about farm work, walking to their fields or sipping on *chai* outside their houses.

"Alright, this is the PB, get out!" shouted the vehicle commander from up front.

We looked at each other for a brief second, as if to say, "This is it, there's no turning back now." But there was little time for a philosophical discussion: a halted tactical vehicle is a perfect target for anyone with an RPG within

300 meters. Granted, the V-shaped hull sat several feet above ground and could take small-arms fire like a BB gun shooting at a vault but that didn't negate a lucky rocket coming in through the turret and turning the insides to a bloody mess, which would not be a good day at all: precisely what those trashbags were for on the gear list. Being the closest Marine to the door, I turned the creaking latches down on one side and then the next and pushed both open. The Afghan heat and sun flooded through the opening, quickly wiping the breeze from the air-conditioning off our faces. The rear part of the truck was facing an engineering bridge that leads to the patrol base that will be home for the next seven months.

I looked down at the dirt under the ladder steps leading up to the Mrap, trying to compress every counter-IED class we had ever gone over into actionable movement. Check the ground you're stepping on first before you even step off the truck, then the surrounding five meters, and then twenty-five meters beyond that. Even if you have done them already, do them again. Looking is cheap, prosthetics are not. What you are looking for are ground signs, disturbed dirt, ant trails, and anything out of the ordinary: something to give away a victim-operated pressure plate because the IED planter was either lazy that day or the weather has brushed away the sand he used to cover it up. Most of these anti-personnel IEDs are made with ten to forty pounds of homemade explosives, a deadly concoction of fertilizer and various nitrate acids that, when ignited, turn into a blast that takes off limbs and can kill someone in an instant. IEDs designed for vehicles are packed with even more HME, up to several hundred pounds and these usually blow the engine block of an Mrap or Mat-V clean off. If placed correctly in a directional charge they can penetrate the armor of these vehicles and kill the entire crew, despite all the expensive metal.

That first step I took, I was absolutely certain I was going to be blown to shreds, without even stepping into the PB. What a story that would be. "Hey remember that Vining kid? Yeah, well, he barely got out of the truck and bought it right there." But it wasn't to be so, not today at least. So I continued walking, gingerly of course, and took a knee beside the vehicle, pulling up a sector of security watching the village while my buddies piled out behind me, also taking up sectors. What we didn't know was that this was Route Shiner, a busy commercial road for Afghans traveling along the Helmand river valley, in addition to being a main supply route for ISAF forces. The likelihood of a pressure-plate IED at that intersection was very low as it would have had more of a chance of killing civilian Afghans than Marines: not a rapport-gaining move on the part of the Taliban. It was also in full view of the Marine standing post in the concrete guard tower at Loy Kolay, so unless a particular

Taliban member had a dying wish to be one with his creator, no one would spend several hours digging a hole and placing the components inside it and covering it up. Although later in the deployment, there was an IED meant for us, emplaced down a side road from where we stepped off.

But we didn't know this, and even if we had, we still would have been fearful even opening up the Mrap double doors. We gathered our gear, mostly LB packs filled with all the essentials we would need to sustain ourselves for several months, plus our tan boxlike deployment duffels, and began walking across the bridge to the PB. The closer we got the less fear we felt; more of a "Holy shit, is it hot, and I stuffed way too much gear inside this thing." Across the bridge was a sort of winding Hesco serpentine barrier, to slow vehicles down approaching the main gate. The irony was that nobody used it, and it was easily apparent that vehicles simply drove around it. We walked up to this wrought-iron gate with a small door, a pedestrian entrance, where Sergeant Mike stood waiting for us. He had his M4 two-oh-three in one hand and a radio in the other, not even a flak on.

"Welcome to Loy Kolay. Drop your shit off inside the storage room." Classic word choice, Sergeant Mike, flawlessly delivered.

Pushing through the gate, I had a good view of the PB. It was mainly three buildings, two guard towers at either end of the square, and a perimeter wall topped off with razor wire. All the structures were concrete and painted white, with the three buildings of equal size, and arrayed with two facing each other, the third one by itself. The guard towers were on either end of the base, one next to the front gate and the second next to the back entrance. Home sweet home indeed …

Patrol Base Loy Kolay was a partnered patrol base located in the northern portion of Nawa District in central Helmand Province, right along the Helmand River. The lifeline of Helmand is this river: everything revolves around it. The fertile land on either side of the river is sometimes called the Green Zone by the coalition. Beyond the river is the desert, where nothing too much happens apart from migratory camel-riding Kuchies, a nomadic tribe. The river is controlled by a critical dam known as Kajaki Dam, located farther north in Helmand. This was a crucial part in the fight for Helmand because whoever controls the dam also controls the flow of water into the valley on which the livelihood of the Afghans there depend. Using a system of culverts and canals, some put in place by the US Army Corps of Engineers in the 1950s, the Afghans use the water to bring the desert to life and grow crops such as corn, wheat, and, of course, hashish and opium.

PB Loy Kolay was typical of the small squad-sized patrol bases that were scattered over the area of operations. Beginning in 2008/09, when a surge of

Marines took over from the British forces at Camp Bastion, patrol bases like these were established all throughout Helmand, from Now Zad in the north to Garmsir in the south. Victor units such as Two Eight and One Six pushed through and cleared the valley, setting up these bases that usually comprised between twenty and sixty Marines, or a reinforced squad or platoon most times. These, in turn, reported back to the larger PBs which consisted of the company headquarters such as the one that controlled Chaos Company's AO at PB Jaker. More significant than that were Fobs, such as Geronimo for us or Hanson in Sangin which was where the battalion operations and logistics were located. The mothership for all these bases was Bastion-Leatherneck-Shorabak (BLS) which was ISAF's logistics hub for all of Helmand Province.

Our PB consisted of around fifteen to twenty Marines, partnered with a similar number of Afghan Uniformed Police (AUP). In other AOs Marines were partnered with the Afghan National Army (ANA) as well. Working with ANA and AUP were two entirely different experiences. The ANA was usually okay to work with, more professional, and more determined in taking the fight to the enemy. Of course, some ANA units were complete garbage, but for the most part, the ANA were soldiers that could be expected to do soldier things. The lack of a coordinated and robust logistics system was probably one of their most substantial weaknesses. We had IED-jamming technology, air support, medevac flights, some pretty advanced minesweepers, and all our personal armor. Our trucks could take some extremely severe beatings, and still come back all right; Mraps more so than Mat-Vs because of the armor, and their V-shaped hulls. But the ANA, all those poor folks had were weapons and uniforms, and that was it. We often talk about the adversity we faced in dealing with the Taliban, our casualties, our tactics, and so on, but something that is rarely discussed is the ANA's fight with the Taliban, where they almost always got the short end of the stick.

The AUP, on the other hand, was much less desirable to work with than the ANA. A lot of the AUP were merely in it because it was a job and some didn't seem too interested in fighting the war. Never mind body armor, these guys had AKs and Ford "Danger" Rangers, supercab, four-wheel-drive pick-up trucks with PKM medium machine gun mounts in the bed. None of these was a match for some of the Taliban's weapons and IEDs. Occasionally you would have some great patrolmen though. At our PB, we had an AUP named Darman Khan, whom we just called "Rambo" (there seems to be a Rambo within every partnered unit in ISAF for that matter). The guy would go out on patrol loaded with belts of ammunition, and a PKM, leading the way. He was almost the AUP ringleader, certainly the most motivated of the bunch, always corralling them up to head out, or even checking them like a good NCO should be doing. Then we had other AUP guys who were less than stellar, an all-out safety risk on their own accord. One of them threatened to kill one of our interpreters and was absolutely nuts. We learned to keep our distance from him and others we found out to be off the wall.

The aim was to have us live together, run operations together, and for us to support the police in training or anything else they needed. Ultimately we would hand over control to the AUP, and our physical presence would slowly melt away, giving the security role to the Afghans themselves. The problem with this is that the AUP knew what was going on, and for the most part, realized that they couldn't do the job on their own. They had to deal with local tribes, horrible management from the top, bad logistics chains, corruption within their own organization, in addition to fighting the Taliban as well. They needed us, for our water, our supplies, our medevac support. Thus, everything was a push-pull sort of dilemma: we were pushing them to be self-sufficient, while they were pulling us in for their own support. This relationship created much strain between our two forces, sometimes erupting in "green on blue" violence when one of them would shoot the Marines they were working with.

A simple example of this situation was water. They wanted us to provide them water to patrol; we wanted them to source their own water, so they wouldn't have to be dependent on us for their supplies. So, in the beginning, we gave them water. Usually, it was in the form of water bottles from our COC. Then we started cutting down on how much water we gave them. It almost felt like we were a mini water-welfare state. Then we started only giving them water for patrols. Then we eventually stopped that, and they started refusing to patrol unless they had water to go out with. A similar problem happened with generators. They were relying on our generator for electricity, and we tried to get them off of it, eventually buying a civilian generator from Lashkar Gah for them. It was like this with almost everything.

None of this was evident within those first few weeks at Loy Kolay. Working, patrolling, even just surviving in Helmand was a tedious process where we learned every lesson, every trick, through hard experience. Whether it was cooperating with the AUP, figuring out how to run the post watch, or just burning our own poop. However, one thing that always remained pretty constant was the patrolling. That, we did a lot of.

The first combat patrol a boot goes on changes things. Whether the patrol gets in contact or not is irrelevant. But it is where everything that boot has ever learned, ever studied, ever got hazed for, has undergone, becomes real. This is the point of no return because, beyond this, it's for real: it's not training anymore. When he returns he's no longer a boot, regardless if he acts like it afterward, if he hasn't learned, if he does boot things and gets boot consequences. After weeks or months of training, he is finally doing his job description and earning his paycheck, because he has finally gone on his first combat foot patrol.

The patrol brief goes out, and everyone starts slipping on their plate carriers, clipping war belts on hips, and strapping on Kevlars, not to mention throwing that fat lip of Grizzly in. Double, triple, quadruple check water, magazines, Thor IED-jamming packs, NVGs, batteries, kill cards. The weight is heavy, more cumbersome than it should be because the boot doesn't know that half the junk he has on is just bearing him down.

This first patrol starts, in a single-file column out of the gate of the patrol base. With fifteen to twenty meters of dispersion between each Marine and Afghan, this is the most conducive formation in Helmand. It minimizes the chance of a single IED detonation taking out as many Marines with it as possible. This formation has been drilled into the boot's head since the second phase of boot camp, during Basic Warrior Training, but actually doing it for real brings a whole new meaning to why it works. This is also the line of departure, or Departing Friendly Lines (DFL) as the patrol leader will call out on the radio back to the COC. From here out, there is no safety net of the patrol base, no overwatching post stander, no almighty G-boss to look over the boot's head as he moves. It's weapons condition one and outside the wire, into the previously unknown. Nervous? His nerves are entirely shot. He's done this hundreds of times in training, but this is the big one. This time there won't be an index after a notional firefight, there won't be friendly officers and NCOs to critique what he did wrong or right. Those aren't blanks in his magazine, and these tourniquets are ready to be ripped out if necessary. There'll be critiques all right, about what happened when his buddy gets shot through the chest or passes out in the 100° heat.

Every mound of dirt, every odd-looking stick, every wadi crossing, every step turns into a potential IED. The boot races through his mind to regurgitate everything he ever learned from SOI or the Fleet, every piece of advice any combat vet ever passed on to him. If the patrol takes fire from the right, does he run to this mound of dirt or that more suspicious-looking pile of dirt? If the crypto goes down on the one-fifty-twos, does he press the "7" button or the "8"? Or does he not press any button and then mess with the dial to get it on load mode? Was he wrong in putting all his tourniquets on the right side of his flak instead of dispersing them on both sides, so if only one arm gets hit he can still access them, but what if both arms are out and his buddy is more than fifty meters away? Each step, hand placement, and prone position is a scientific calculation, mitigating the risk of a pressure plate being in one spot instead of another. Each turn to connect with the grunt behind is on an alternate side, so he is sweeping the whole area by making a connecting file twice, nice and slow, as if to take everything in.

However, the reality of the situation takes over any train of thought. The heat is not only oppressive but penetrates every portion of his body, making him sweat buckets and from places, he didn't even know sweat could come from. That sweet war belt that sounded so smart sounds really stupid now that it's digging into his hips and hindering the movement of his legs. His flak is now cutting into his shoulders, and this is only the beginning of the patrol: there are still four hours and eight klicks to go. Instead of taking calculated steps, he is now trotting forward, somewhat out of breath and anxious for a security halt of some kind, any kind at all, to relieve him from this stupid patrol. Dusk is coming, and he can barely see out of his dark eye pro, so he risks taking it off to see better. He would rather make shapes out in the dark than lose his eyesight from stepping somewhere he didn't want to step. His weapon, previously light and easy to bear, is now a dead weight propped up by the six fully loaded magazine pouches on his chest, his hands just barely holding the thing in place.

At the beginning, he scans every Afghan, every vehicle, every road through his RCO or SDO, but now he merely glances at them to ascertain if it's a threat or not. In fact, he might even drop his rifle to his side, ignoring the tenet that looking aggressive makes one a less likely target. It doesn't matter at this point because all he wants is for this patrol to be over and done. On this patrol, the squad leader is second-in-command to the Lord Almighty. He alone decides when to halt for a quick five-minute rest that never seems like it is enough. The direction and decisions of the entire patrol are made through this squad leader. He makes calls about going left or right, up the hill or round it, sending the Afghans ahead or not. To the boot, these calls seem to be commandments, and he trusts his squad leader to keep him alive, to step where the patrol should step, and to halt where the patrol should halt. But in all honesty and reality, the squad leader is just as preoccupied and stressed out from the patrol as everyone else. He is carrying similar weight and is walking the same line. His decisions are sometimes more arbitrary than tactical. Afterward, the boot tells him, "I feel safe with you, no matter what could go wrong. I know you'll have a solid hand on the situation and know what to do." This is later, after many patrols with that sergeant, and this one is just beginning.

Night approaches, and there are people in the fields. Why are people in their fields at night? Isn't that what they do during the day? The boot is nervous and calls this out to his seniors.

"They work the fields at night when it's sometimes too hot during the day, don't worry about it."

But the night is also soothing because it brings in fresh air that circulates through the front Sapi plate of his plate carrier and around the edges of his Kevlar. The patrol is on the way back to the PB, taking a different route, so there's less of a chance of the Taliban backlaying IEDs. The lights of the PB are on, and by God are they the sweetest sight to behold. Within those lights are chow, the Sat phone, masturbation, and sleep. Glorious sleep: how the boot will never feel the same way about getting enough sleep from that point onward.

Now isn't the time to take it easy. It's said that the most dangerous part of a patrol is the last five steps. Abstract of course, but the meaning is real: not to get complacent because nothing at all has happened. The boot remembers this, and it motivates him to give a shit about the last klick or so. Finally, the PB is within reach of a two-oh-three, and the boot can let his guard down somewhat as the post comes into view. The patrol passes the serpentine made out of Hesco barriers and is almost at the front gate.

Squad leader calls in, "COC, this is Chaos Three, COC this is Chaos Three, permission to EFL, eight packs, one dog." The dog is a $50,000, bomb-sniffing dog that the handler takes out, to search for IED materials.

Barely a second later, "Roger that, Chaos Three, permission granted."

This is more of a formality than an actual response to a request, but it is done for timing, to inform the PB. Radios power down, NVGs are switched off, Thors go from blue to red, weapons aren't condition three yet, but they are lowered. The point man of the patrol gets to the gate and slaps each Marine or Afghan on the shoulder as they go in, counting them. The boot has his shoulder slapped, he steps in the gate and goes condition three, ejecting the round from the chamber, loading it back into the magazine and slaps it back in. Although the boot isn't a combat veteran because the patrol didn't take any fire, he is now something else: he is a grunt, truly earning the title.

Going from my first foot patrol, to my first post standing, without any sleep, and on my first day at Loy Kolay, probably wasn't a physiologically sound idea, but then again, fighting medieval Pashtun tribesmen in sandals with heavy-lift helicopters and twenty-ton tactical vehicles can't be a very feasible one either, but there we were.

I walk into the dimly lit hooch after the debriefing. The entire PB looks like this modern-day Western outpost at night, barely illuminated by just enough lights to see how to get around. Being outside, in the courtyard, or even being in the hooch, with every other American on the PB in there with you – minus the guys on post, and the COC – is an eerie, creepy feeling. Because you know this is it, that these are the only other Marines or Americans there for you: QRF is many klicks and hours away if anything were to happen. We have been on our own before, on field ops, in the massive desert of the stumps, but nothing as isolated and reinforced as this. And every one of us knows precisely just how alone we are. But it is a feeling we come to get used to, and to proudly embrace, at Loy Kolay.

I strip my flak off my sweat-soaked Frog top onto my cot, but leave my kneepad on, as sort of "Yeah, I just did that, first combat foot patrol." I strip my Frog top off as well, slap my headlamp on my forehead, grab my M27 and walk out to the little Hesco furniture area, where Range and Kugler are sitting down, eating. No sooner have I produced some Girl Scout cookies than Martin brushes past me and says, "Vining, you're on post, twenty-one to zero one, with Mauler" as he keeps on going. Martin is completely in his element out here; being the career guy he is, he loves this command role. A look at my watch that is dummy-corded to my Frog trouser cargo pocket tells me it is 2035. Better get going. "Lance Corporal, what do I need on post?"

Range looks over at my bright headlamp, "Well, your flak, weapon, and NVGs obviously. I like to bring up snacks and shit. Make sure you've got a red lens light as well."

Pretty simple, it doesn't sound too difficult right? "Thanks, Lance Corporal." I turn to walk back into the hooch.

"Hey, Vining."

"Yes, Lance Corporal?"

"We're on deployment now. I'm just Range to you. We're in the same danger; that senior shit was done once we stepped off the plane."

"Good to go, Lance … Range."

He nods and turns back to his snack, I keep moving into the dark hooch. That felt good. Very good, coming from Range, as if I had finally earned an element of trust after goofing up so much at Cax.

Flak, pick that up, still smelling of Cordura sweat; war belt, pick that up too, clip it on my waist. Plate carrier goes over my head. I have six magazines, totaling around 180 rounds of 5.56 in my front magazine pouches, then another six magazines on my belt, totaling another 180 rounds on my war belt. The number is "around" because every infantryman knows to only load his magazines to twenty-eight or twenty-nine rounds, due to the possibility of a jam with the issue magazines when fully loaded. Plate carrier Velcro-ed up, left cummerbund first then right, then kangaroo pouch, my Frog shirt still soaking wet from the patrol. I walk out of the now sleeping hooch. Mauler is apparently already up on post. I walk across the open ground of the patrol base, still very unfamiliar in my senses, to the guard tower right next to the main gate. The tower itself is a thirty-foot-tall, whitewashed concrete structure, with a doorway at the bottom, but no door. Inside the doorway, on the left is a metal ladder leading up to a second level. Opposite this one, but on the other hand, is another metal ladder. Both of these metal ladders lead into square cutouts at their respective levels. Climbing up the ladder, with all your gear on, makes a colossal clanking sound, especially if your weapon is on a one-point sling, and that bangs into the ladder as well. Once I get to the actual post floor, at the very top, I hoist myself through the square hole, get on my knees, and pull myself the rest of the way up.

Looking round at the dimly lit enclosure, there is Mauler, my post partner, and Wilbanks and Dejesus, the two post standers that Mauler and I are relieving. In the middle of the floor is this huge table, about chest high, with all sorts of stuff on it, from smoke grenades, a Mark thirty-two grenade launcher, different colors of pyro charges, and a green logbook. Each side of the post room has these huge windows so you can look out in every direction. The window facing north looks over the Hesco serpentine that leads into the PB, and has a Two-Forty mounted on a fixed pedestal, with 200 rounds of 7.62 linked up to it. The west-facing window looks over Route Shiner, the canal along Shiner, and the actual village of Loy Kolay. To the southern end is a mosque, to the northern end a schoolhouse with all the chairs and tables on the roof, and in between are the compounds and dwellings that make up the village, in a crisscross pattern. To the south is the AUP building, a large field behind it, then off in the distance are the bluffs that line the Helmand River. Out the east window is the rest of the PB, with some compounds opposite, and then the Helmand River itself, with a far-off fort-like structure, that just looks absolutely massive from the PB, across the wide river. You can't help but think this is out of some Vietnam war movie, and the only thing that's changed are the uniforms and the local culture.

"Hey there Vining … how was that first patrol? Pop your cherry a little bit?" Wilbanks and his Tennessee drawl come out from the corner of the post.

"It was all right, but a ton hotter and the gear a ton heavier than I expected. Sergeant Mike led it; nothing much happened."

"Yeah … wait till you're on one during the day, leaving at like noon, or early morning. You'll just be fucking dying."

"Remember that patrol up to Aynak, Willy-B? I think Weitoish and Range were on that as well. I just felt like collapsing halfway to the place, like ten klicks out."

"Oh my Gooood, that day was hell. And the fucking Afghans were walking around as if it was nothing, of course; they don't got no flak and carry half the ammo we do." Wilbanks finishes signing out of the logbook, while Mauler takes it over, writing the new post cycle just below.

"See ya later, Vining, I'm gonna go jerk off," says Wilbanks.

Dejesus chimes in, "Yeah you have fun with that pencil dick, Willy-B; I'm gonna go get on the sat-phone and have some phone sex."

Laughing, the two of them clamber down the post ladders, and then across the courtyard back to the hooches, where I watch them disappear into the light of the doorway. I turn to Mauler, now done with the logbook and leaning up against the northward post window with the Two-Forty in the middle: "So how is it?"

He sort of looks outside, obviously pretty tired from whatever he was doing today. "How is what?"

"I dunno. Living here, patrolling, post, daily shit, anything."

Mauler has been at the PB around two weeks longer than me. "Well … living is pretty easy, nothing much to it. We burn our shit every couple of days, take showers and brush our teeth with water bottles, try to stay fit in the jailhouse gym we've got going on. We've got a sat-phone you can use, to call home with every once in a while, but the damn thing seems to be broken half the time, or it just cuts out entirely."

"Seems like a lot to get used to? What about the Afghans?"

"It's not that bad, burning shit can even be fun sometimes. The AUP are an odd bunch, some chill, some alright, and some we just stay away from; that guy in the white man dress is the commander or something. One of them has this really crooked eye, and you can't talk about it in front of him or else he'll know that you're talking about him and he'll get pissed. They are all pretty much garbage on patrol, always stopping to pray, always walking next to each other, holding hands, blaring music out of their boom boxes."

We seem to be doing more for the security of their province than they are themselves. But can you really blame them? They've seen all these American initiatives come and fail, and all these Taliban advances work out, in addition to barely being supported by their own establishment. Why should they sacrifice everything when since the 1979 Soviet invasion, the Afghan rule of thumb has been simply to survive? These guys aren't the A team or the B team; those crews were slaughtered a long time ago. No, they are the survivor team, doing whatever it takes to pull through. For most, fighting for the Islamic Emirate of Afghanistan or for the Taliban is sometimes a simple matter of income or family alliances

"What about the standing post? Up here?"

"Post is pretty straightforward. Four hours on, just about once a day. Make a radio check to the COG or SOG every hour, if they're even paying attention. Basically, you're just looking out at the road, and round the PB, making sure no one is sneaking up. Then if anyone comes to the gate, or a Marine convoy comes rolling through, you call it in, and the COG goes and deals with it. After post, you make sure to refill the generator with fuel … at least two fuel cans fill it up. Make sure you don't fall asleep though, I mean, obviously."

"Anything interesting happen up here? Like, at all?"

Mauler pauses for a second. "Not really man. At first, we thought every car and person was suspicious, a VBIED, or some attack waiting to happen. But really, it's just the villagers doing their thing. Yesterday some old woman came to the gate, wanting to talk to the police. The day before, some kids were asking for fucking chocolate or *ooba*, water."

As I look through the logbook, with a red lens flashlight, I see the earlier log entries: "20110625–1955: Suspicious white Toyota Corolla circling around village, (2) times, called up to COG. 2135: Man walking down Route Shiner, from Field to House, with Shovel. Called up to COG, told to keep an eye out." And on and on.

"And patrolling?"

"I mean, back in the States, we got all this IED training and stuff. Not to say that it isn't valid, but you have to kind of read everything out here. Not every piece of fucking dirt has an IED in it, so you just gotta learn to spot what isn't supposed to be there and how the locals are acting. We also know which areas are pretty bad, and which are alright. You'll get it, after a while, I guess."

Hopefully. Hopefully, it isn't that bad, my life depends on this sort of thing. "And when you aren't patrolling, on post, or working parties?"

Mauler chuckles. "You either sleep, work out, eat, or hang out with everyone at that little smoke pit, the Hesco couches that the Two Three guys set up. Mostly sleep though. You want to get as much as that as possible. You never know when your next patrol or post cycle or working party is going to yoke you up, and you can't plan for it either."

Sleep … I could use some of that good stuff right now, even if it was in my sleeping bag on that creaking rack. I could tell it was going to be loud when I set all my gear on it earlier.

"I got a question, where the heck is Papa Doc, Staff Sergeant, and Toledo?"

"Gowragi."

"What? Goa-what?"

"PB Gowragi, it's about ten klicks that way." Mauler points south. "The rest of third is there, with Staff Sergeant in charge of them, while we have the Sir in charge here. They've got a tiny PB, with some AUP. Some guy from Two Three blew his brains out when they were there before us."

I had heard about that. Lance Corporal Harry Lew, a boot from Hawaii, committed suicide with Two Three in December, several months before we relieved them. Apparently, he was getting hazed, made to dig a fighting hole, because he had fallen asleep four times on post. So he killed himself with his Saw in a fighting hole outside the PB. There was an outcry from a family member who was a congresswoman. I'd like to know what the same government official would be saying if the entire patrol base had gotten wiped out because the Taliban realized that no one was awake on post.

"What about around us? What other PBs are there?"

"Well … you have Spin Ghar to the northwest, that's run by Weapons Company. Then Mamma Khan to the west, some Alpha guys. Then you have Danger to the far north, also Weapons. Then way off into the northeast, past Spin Ghar you have Lamadan, and then this random Police PB, like deep sauce in the desert. And obviously south of here, where you came from, our company PB, Jaker, and beyond all of that, the rest of Charlie's PBs, where first and second platoons are at."

It's about two hours into our post cycle, and we have around two hours left. Mauler sticks to his northern side, sometimes shifting from one elbow to another. To mix it up, I move from the east to the west windows, just to get a better view of the area through NVGs. We've got these enormous thermal PVS28s that turn night into day, highlighting any sort of heat signature: whether it be footprints, an engine, or rats in the courtyard, you'll see it. But nothing is out there, because it's midnight now. Except for the stars, there are stars everywhere, blanketing the sky with bright dots and constellations I never even knew existed. Every so often, a comet shoots across the sky, a beautiful arc of light that you never see in the big cities. The complete lack of lights, the fact that only me, Mauler, the COC radio watch, and the SOG are awake in the compound, leads to the lonesomeness of the place. I haven't even been here a full day, and it feels like we're just so completely alone, in this crazy part of the world, that the very idea would freak you out if you think about it too much. This is going to be a long deployment, and hopefully, we will all go back home.

The workup gave us no degree of uncertainty about the IED threat in Helmand Province. In fact it makes us fear it, far more than any threat from small-arms fire that the Taliban can hit us with. This is because IEDs are the biggest killer of Marines deployed, and the things are just so well emplaced. The Taliban makes an art out of emplacing them and finding better and more varied ways to kill us. With each introduction of a technique from our side, they bring in tactics that place them ahead of the game, leaving us to play constant catch-up. They use remote-operated IEDs, by way of cell phones and washing-machine timers to set them off, and we put in place ECMs that emit a jamming signal that stops it. Now they focus on pressure plates, where you step on two long pieces of wood buried in the dirt; the pieces of wood have metal rods in them that once connected complete the electrical circuit, and then *boom!* there goes your leg. We introduce CMD minesweepers that pick up metal, so then they use the carbon rod cores that you find in D cell batteries. They have kids prying these cores out all day, then taping them to the pressure plates so our metallic sweepers can't pick them up. Then we use CMDs that can detect carbon as well as metal. However, this is a conundrum because every fucking form of life has carbon. Those dead corn stalks you just walked over? Carbon. That freshly plowed field? Carbon. That threatening-looking bubblegum wrapper on the trail ahead? Carbon.

Not only do they have their traditional pressure plates laid in the ground, but they pull this sick trick where they embed the pressure plates in mud hut doorways and windows. So you lean up against a wall in a compound … donskies. They have pressure-release IEDs as well, where they put rocks on top of the release plate. The rock is kicked, and the IED goes off. They watch our movements and know our formations. If one IED sounds bad enough, imagine two or three all chained together to go off at the same time. This is called a daisy chain. Sixth Marines found an IED daisy chain in Marjah laid out fifteen to twenty meters apart, with thirteen IEDs total, in a single-file line. This is according to the exact formation that a textbook squad on patrol would assume. Twelve grunts, and the squad leader. There were even reports that the Taliban was sticking HIV-infected needles around the IEDs, so even though Explosive Ordnance Disposal (EOD) might dismantle them, they might get pricked in the process and suffer a longer-term death.

Then you have the Explosively Formed Projectile (EFPs) or Directional Fragmentation (DF) IEDs. When the Taliban found out that our monster trucks could take the severest of beatings from up to several hundred pounds of HME, they took a cylinder and packed it with a solid metal plate. When the pressure plate is connected, the charge goes off, turning the plate into a solid projectile, melting our vehicle armor and blowing away anybody on the inside. IEDs also aren't just for the ground level. The Taliban would put the pressure plate in the ground, but then have the actual IED placed somewhere at chest height, so you step on the plate, and there goes your upper torso, into pink mist and blood splatter on the other side of you. If all this isn't bad enough, you have the backlaying thing where the Taliban will follow your patrol path, and lay a hasty IED so on the return route that you think is safe because you cleared it, you then get blown up. Or they'll suck you into an L-shaped ambush, and knowing that we are trained to assault through and close with, set their IEDs at the appropriate place, which will blow you up.

Essentially, if you take everything these briefs tell you about IEDs, you'll assume that in going to Helmand, you'll just get blown up. However, the Taliban are human, and humans have faults. In addition, although IEDs are a threat, you still have to carry out the patrol, carry out that village *jirga* meeting, carry out that VCP. You can't let IEDs box you into a corner of no return, because then the enemy has won, and we aren't in the business of losing. You treat every plan, every route, every patrol, every footstep, like a giant game of chess or cat and mouse, overlaid across an entire AO. In the grand scheme of things, every route is different. You plan to take the hard way, you plan to take your patrol through the mud instead of over the canal bridge. If the PB usually sends a patrol into Kosrabad from the south, then this time you take it from the north. The next time you take the longer route from the east, then maybe after that from the west. Now you can rotate back to the south. The same concept with route selection. There is a finite number of routes you can take as you leave the PB, but there is an infinite amount of ways you travel on these routes. This time you walk down the center of the road, next time you walk down the right side, and the time after that you use the left. Maybe the next time you don't even take the road, you trek through the cornfields or the canal.

Another major point is that IEDs aren't just in the middle of nowhere unless some Talib is feeling particularly risky that day. You won't find an IED in the absolute middle of a random field unless you've been crossing that field for some time – or someone else has, and you don't know about it. You won't find an IED in a freshly plowed field, or along the banks of the Helmand River. You won't find an IED inside of the courtyard of a family presently living there: abandoned courtyards on the other hand, yes. But you will find IEDs at junctions, road curves, downhills, shallow canals, shortcuts, doorways, window openings. The more a PB uses these points, the higher the possibility of an IED. Places where the normal human doesn't spend much time looking, or where your attention is diverted. Coming round a bend in the road in a vehicle, don't have good situational awareness on the far side … *Boom!* Gotcha. In addition, the chances increase the closer the environment is to a PB or any ISAF/ANSF operating forces.

Imagine the concentric circles of a nuclear blast diagram, how there is ground zero, and then each outlying concentric circle becomes less deadly until all that is left is fallout, or the risk is very low. Now overlay that system on a PB with that ground zero center on that PB, and every other PB in the area, setting maybe every 400 meters as where it becomes less deadly. Now imagine where all these different circles overlap each other. As an example, if two PBs are five klicks apart, where their concentric danger circles intersect, this is possibly a deadly area, because we have the two forces constantly working these areas. But then go to the opposite end of the spectrum where the concentric circles reach out to several kilometers from the PB, and here the risk is almost nullified unless of course there is extensive coalition activity in that particular area. But if there isn't, I almost bet you there isn't an IED there. Now over all this chessboard of an AO, find every road corner, every shortcut goat trail, every intersection, every blind bend, every bridge, every wadi crossing, every large entryway, and place a red X over it. Now find all the routes most commonly used by ISAF/ANSF, everything from foot patrols to supply routes, and enlarge that red X on all these points. Those spots, the routes most used, and all the tactical points, these are where your heightened sense of awareness comes into play.

We don't actually have this mythical chessboard overlay in the COC, but instead it plays out in our heads, on patrol, or on a security halt. Some parts of the AO are worse than others, and within these parts some villages are worse than others. Within those villages, some roads and trails are worse, and on those roads and trails, one side is worse than the other.

When grunts first get in-country, they imagine everything is an IED. That disturbed earth? IED. That bend in the road? IED. That abandoned motorcycle? IED. This mound of dirt next to me? IED. The eeriest feeling is to pass some feature that you suspect; you just get it in your gut that something is off about it, but it isn't enough to actually investigate or stop the patrol for. So as you pass it, you are subconsciously saying, "Please don't blow up … don't blow up … don't blow up … almost … almost … and yes, it didn't blow up." But eventually, time eats away, and this "every-single-fucking-thing-is-going-to-blow-me-up" syndrome goes away when you realize that 90 percent of the Helmand countryside is like any countryside, harmless. It's just that tiny amount of actual threat that does exist, and that it can't exist every single place because that would be physically impossible, but it can exist regardless.

On the microcosm, at the individual level, there are certain things you just don't do. You just don't kick dirt up, you don't interrogate a ground-sign indicator with your feet, you just don't take a wadi footbridge crossing, you don't take shortcuts, never take shortcuts. When considering a security halt or halting behind cover, you always pick the second-best piece of ground; not the best, because Terry the Taliban might already have scoped that out, and not the worst either because then you're out in the open. In an IED environment, sometimes it is better to take fire in the open while in the prone, than to jump in a ditch for a better position. Every footstep is precisely calculated, every hand placement is done with care. You aren't leaning up against a mud wall, so much as you are simply using it to guide you along. Your zeros, fives, and twenty-fives are your best friend in this war. You scan from right to left, instead of left to right because this method picks up more detail due to the way our brains are wired and how we read, i.e. from left to right.

Then we have this thing called the Thor ECM, an electronic counter-measure man-pack that emits a line-of-sight jamming signal within a fifty- to hundred-meter radius of the pack, therefore protecting a foot patrol from any electronically broadcast median used to set off an IED. It jams the airwaves so when Abdullah is frantically pressing his cell phone, that signal is overridden by the Thor jamming. It comes with three different antennas, a high, medium, and low. The high and medium look like this giant black dildo affixed to a twenty-pound chunk of solid metal, while the low is an array of antennae that stick out at various angles from the device. The system is turned on by pressing buttons on the top of it, or by hand-jamming them in the remote control that is attached to the backpack straps. Holy smokes, is it heavy. The man-pack has this tendency to start off light, and well balanced on your flak while at the PB, but then gains a pound per kilometer of the patrol. And it digs into your shoulders with every step, making crossing a wadi more difficult and laborious than it already is. Sometimes you pass it off between guys on patrol, sometimes you pull a straw out of your left cargo pocket and suck it up. Now we have the CMD mine detector and the sickle. Or the Holley stick. The newer versions are bright orange and collapsible. However, the earlier versions were simply long wooden poles with a farm sickle on the end of them. We usually handed them off to the Terp, the Afghan interpreter, or one of the AUP guys at the start of a patrol. These are used for interrogating a ground-sign indicator. Essentially it allows a grunt to dig something up in the ground, while being a good distance away from a potential IED blast, hopefully while he is in the prone, or in the kneeling, keeping him under the blast cone that will sprout up from the earth should the sickle actually hit something. The RCO and SDO scopes on our weapon systems are also useful for really looking at something from afar because of their magnification capabilities.

The Taliban aren't stupid. Afghans have been playing this game in one form or another since 1979, over the course of multiple generations, from fighting the Soviets, the Northern Alliance, the ANA, and now us. They know a thing or two about setting up a well-coordinated ambush, and how to incorporate that with IEDs. Open up on the Americans from the right side, emplace the IEDs on the left, and either outcome is death. But using everything thus mentioned, the AO chessboard, the individual actions, the Thor, the CMD, the sickle, the RCO and SDO, and most importantly, the Mark One Eyeball, this threat is mitigated. Not closed out, but lessened. Because in the end, this is war, and in war young men die and are maimed, regardless of how sound the plans are or how smart you think you are.

Patrol, post, eat, sleep, repeat. Add in burning faeces, some sat-phone time, jerking off, and messing around with the AUP, and you have the rhythm of PB life. As the hours turn into days, and the days into weeks, time starts becoming routine at PB Loy Kolay. We got our mobile section up and running, so now we have a 4x4 Mrap with a mine roller, along with two Mat-Vs to make up our Chaos 3 mobile section. We even come up with stupid names for the trucks too: *Bang Bus* is the Mrap, in reference to the porn video series of the same name, *Black Hole Sun* is the Mat-V, and our third is *Redneck Ninja*. However, taking this mobile section out is a double-edged sword. Although we have the capability to really project our presence, it leaves the PB barely manned. A minimum mobile mission requires at least nine of us–driver, A-driver, turret gunner for each vehicle, plus some dismounts, which leaves only a couple guys back at the PB, to run the COC, stand post, and be the COG. This would have been fine for a couple of hours, but mobile sections in Helmand don't go out for a couple hours, they go out for days at a time. One does not simply take a leisurely drive down the never-improved-dirt-excuse that is Route Shiner in a tactical vehicle and expect it to take less than several hours for a one-way trip alone.

The terrain we patrol starts becoming familiar. Aynak, Circula, Route Shiner, Route Red, Spin Ghar, Mamma Khan, Gouragi, and hundreds of other seemingly meaningless Afghan village and area names come alive through our walking the very ground that composes them. We begin to understand the land, getting a feel for the local people, talking to them, searching them. But more importantly, we are developing a sort of sixth sense when it comes to security. Some villages we just feel like we are being watched, or trailed. Sometimes a motorcycle drives toward a patrol, then instantly turns around as soon as it sees us, several hundred meters away. Other villages and compounds we know to be somewhat safe, and not harmful. The kids are out playing, asking us for water and pens, weaving in between the patrol. The adults come up to us, or even smile and wave.

"Vining!" Sergeant Mike calls out.

Ugh, I was really enjoying that sleep, I have just gotten off an unusually long patrol to Circula, three hours previously. "Yes, sergeant?"

"You're going to be our generator guy. Go outside; there's some engineer out there who'll show you how to operate the 803."

What the hell is an 803? "Good to go, sergeant, I'll get dressed right now."

Slipping out of my sleeping bag, I grab my Frog trousers and kind of fall into them, stick my feet in my Rat boots, sticking the laces up into the bloused trouser bottoms so I can get away with not tying them. Then toss my still sweaty, wet Frog top on my body, tuck it into my trousers, grab my M27, and walk out of the hooch. Christ, breaking the shade of our building into the searing Afghan sunlight is tortuous, like jumping directly into a giant boiling pot of water. The wicked drumming of the small generator that keeps the PB running is right round the corner, surrounded by sandbags. The heat subsides a bit, due to the presence of the cammie netting covering the space between the COC building and our hooch building. I see that we have had a supply-run stop by our PB, with their Mat-Vs and other gun trucks parked right outside of it. Walking over to the generator, about the size of a convertible Smart car, there is a Marine standing around, with some pretty clean Frogs, like they just got issued to him or something. He even has on an eight-point cover, and, unlike mine, his boots are tied, with his trousers bloused and some sock showing. Himmler would have shed a tear at his appearance.

"Hey, so are you the generator guy they sent me?"

He has on lance corporal rank. I was promoted to lance about a week ago. But guaranteed he is well on his way to picking up corporal, given his MOS.

"Yeah, I guess I am. My sergeant told me to come over here and learn about generators."

"Okay, cool, I'm going to tell you a little about the 803 generator, and how to maintain it."

He kneels down and starts explaining things bit by bit, as well as taking out parts. "Alight, this is your air filter cover; you open it like this. Then you take it out and you knock it all around to get the dust and dirt out. You'll need to replace this once every couple of months. Now, this is your coolant; you never open it while it is running; fill it up with water every week or so, or when it gets used up. Now, this is your oil filter; you unscrew it like this, and take it out like this. You need to replace that about once every two weeks with a new one."

Once every two weeks? Dude, do you realize where we are? We are in the middle of Nawa. Do you see the nearest AutoZone?

But he goes on. "So this is what you do to drain the oil, which you also need to refill with new oil; probably need to do this once a week"

Seriously? Because military grade engine oil is spilling out of the ground here right?

"You take this valve, and you turn it this way; wait for the oil to start creeping out of that little hole." As he does this, he releases the valve and puts a container underneath it, catching all the bad oil. "Now that, you have to collect," he says as it spools into the ground.

"Ummm, why?"

"That's hazmat."

"Hazmat? What? So?"

"Yeah, hazmat – hazardous materials – you can't let it seep out onto the ground."

This guy is literally telling me that I have to collect used generator oil, in the middle of a war zone, now adding to my priorities of keeping my Kevlar on while standing post, in case some Talib shoots at me, or watching out for mounds of dirt while walking down a road in Aynak, or even just making sure to walk around the PB with my weapon in case one of the AUP decides to turn on us and shoot me. No, now I have to take care of hazmat from our generator. Bullshit, I'm letting that stuff go right into the Helmand dirt. I seriously have more important things to take care of. The truth of the matter is that this guy is a Fobbit. He is also a Pog, a Marine whose MOS is anything other than the 03 field. While my concerns are staying alive in Nawa, his interests are keeping his Frog suit clean, and collecting hazmat. Although he went to something called MCT after Boot Camp, Marine Combat Training, qualified on the rifle range, an infantryman he is not. His primary job in the Marine Corps is not to close with and destroy the enemy through fire and maneuver and to repel an enemy assault through fire and close combat. He does not know how to clear a house, keep dispersion on a foot patrol, look for IED indicators, or work a Two-Forty in the turret of a Mat-V. But he has all his MCIs in a row, and will continue doing his MarineNet courses while on deployment, all the while being a good little lance corporal well on his way to picking up corporal.

The other services don't quite have this aversion that the infantry in the Marines do. And this is because of the mantra that we are stuck with: "Every Marine a Rifleman." Which we know is bullshit, every infantryman is a rifleman, every other Marine is anything else. Throughout OIF/OEF, the cultural difference between the infantry and the Pogs has been immensely stark. To the point of us becoming furious at the establishment to even fathom the idea that all Marines are somehow created equal. When we talk about the business of war, the business of risking lives, and putting bullets in skulls, there is a clear distinction in the supposedly all-combat-ready Marine Corps that a disproportionate amount of infantry Marines are conducting this war business beyond the safe security of the FOB or camp, where the Fobbits reign, comfortable with their DFACs – dining facilities – and laundromats. The other disproportionate number is the amount of infantrymen being killed in the war. Who is doing the fighting and dying here? The infantry is shouldering the overwhelming majority of these casualties, not these Pogs and rear-base Fobbits. The same way our modern-day society has zero clue that the war is even being waged, between the ads for old people sleeping pills on CNN and the local news announcements. America isn't at War, the Military is at War, America is at the Mall.

Where was your Pog ass when I was hyping out in Bridgeport on a ten-klick movement in a damn blizzard? What were your deployment complaints when I was burning my own shit and sleeping in a fighting hole? Why are you picking up corporal after a year and a half, with no deployments, when I see battle-hardened senior lance corporals with more combat experience than the whole Air Wing combined? Most Pogs have three things in common across the board, no matter what the MOS. They love the Marine Corps, they are always explaining why they didn't pick "03" or how it was filled up, and they are trying to convince us, that apart from a few minor technicalities, they are just like us and do our job. They love the Corps because they are never bent over by it, they don't know what misery is, an eight-hour-long combat patrol, or being lied to all the time. The Corps rewards them graciously, with gym time, MCIs, low cutting scores, regular work days, and all the Mic-Map pit time enough to look great on that meritorious board. Even on deployment, they are clean and well fed, truly living the life of a twenty-first century Spartan. They live in a world of delusion about what combat is and what warfare entails in general.

However, while all Fobbitts are Pogs, not all Pogs are Fobbitts. There are a number of Pogs who get into firefights and prove their worth alongside us, on our patrols, at our PBs, on our raids. Along with the hundreds of infantrymen who have died in combat, there have been Pogs who have also lost their lives, and absolutely cannot be put down for this.

But in the meantime, it is tough to empathize with this mech teaching me how to maintain our 803 generator on our little patrol base. So I just listen to him, and thank him after he is done. From then on, I'm tending to the generator about once a week, and true to my superstitions, we barely get any generator supplies over the course of the entire deployment, going through around five generators as well, as some broke or even blew up without oil. Along with the iridium sat-phone, which is always breaking down, anything mechanical out here just gets ground down to pieces with continuous usage.

I haven't called Lynn in a while, not since we first got to the PB so I give her a call, sort of to check in. One cool morning off of post, I walk into the COC, sign out the sat-phone, and walk out to the Mat-Vs in the far corner of our little compound. It takes me three tries, and it's almost 10 p.m. in Montreal, but finally, a ringtone.

Ring, ring.

Ring, "Hello?"

"Hey! It's me!"

"Oh my God, I'm so glad you called, I was midway through the shower and heard my cellphone on the outside of it, where I left it."

"Jababy! You wanna go back in and finish your shower? I can call you back, nothing much is going on."

"No, no, of course not, that's silly, not with you on the line. I don't know when you'll get another chance."

"Aaahh. Tank you!"

"Just fo you tho."

"Mmm. So I think you're naked …"

"Maybe, maybe not, maybe I got a towel on."

"Ohh, you playing games with me now. It's okay, I know what you looks like naked."

"He he, well, I know what you look like too, so that's okay then."

I can almost see the smile on the other end of the line. Just talking to her makes me smile. "How's classes going?"

"They're goood … pretty boring as we just started the semester. But I'm really missing you."

"Aahhh, I really miss you too. Like a lot, a lot."

"Me too …I dig my face into your T-shirt just to smell it every day. It smells just like you, when you left. I keep it by my bed every day."

"Ohh, Jababy is smelling up my T-shirt! Dat's the best! I'm looking at our photos we printed; I have them by my rack, posted up on the wall. I also got your notebook that you sent me. I use it for my Pashtu stuff, and I've already read every page you wrote on, like five times."

"Well, that's good! Dat's why I wrote it, just fo my shexy babes! How is everything though? I can't stop thinking of something bad happening to you, every day. I mean, every single time I see Afghanistan come up on Facebook, or the TV, I can't help but think of you."

"Aahh, I know baby. But it really isn't that bad where we're at. Other districts are much worse off than we are. I mean the army is really getting chewed up in the northeast parts of the country. We just do patrols and post, see a lot of the villagers, and sleep. That's about it."

"Ohhokay, if you say so. But you better promise me to do more of that post thing, than that patrolling thing. That sounds dangerous."

"I will baby, I will …"

"Hey, Vining! Paulie said it's your turn to burn the shitter!"

Damned Todd. Always at the worst time.

"Hey, Lynn, I gotta go, gonna go burn some poop. But I love you, okay? I'll try to get a call out this week."

"Ohhh, dat sounds stinky! But I love you too! And thank you so much for calling; that made my day."

"Ahh good! Loves you! Bye!"

And click goes the red button. We could have talked for hours and it wouldn't have felt like enough. Hopefully, I'll still have all my limbs the next time I call her. "Coming Todd! Tell Paulie I'm on it."

Walking back to the COC, I return the Iridium phone to Caldwell, our Comm God and Intel Master. He's playing chess with Weitoish.

"Ahhh, you cocksucker. I didn't need that stupid rook anyways. Good call, Vining?"

"Yeah, sure. If you can call it that. Now I have to burn some turds."

Setting the sat-phone on the center table, Caldwell goes back to his chess game, and the PRC 117 crackles to life, "Chaos Three, this is Six, can you get your actual on the hook."

"Goddammit. Can't the bastards just leave us alone?" Frustrated, Caldwell gets up, picks up the MRE spoon-taped handset, and says, "Roger, wait one … Weitoish, can you get the Sir while I stay here?"

Quickly, I grab a piece of trash paper and a lighter and move onward toward the fecal matter. I walk over to the generator, picking up the poop- and smoke-stained Frog gloves and the shit-stirring engineer stake. Setting the stake next to the AUP guard tower, I grab the cut-in-half empty oil drum and drag it over to the three-sided, cammie-doored shitter by the back gate. Take a look inside, and God almighty, does it stink. The cut-in-half oil drum already in there is filled about half full with shit, piss, and babywipes. Sucking in some less dirty air, I step inside, grab that sucker and haul it out, with all the filthy, gooey mess sloushing around inside. Dragging that over to the open ground, I take the new container and shove it in place, pouring about an inch of gasoline at the bottom to keep some of the flies out. Then, moving over to the full container, I take half a gallon of JP8 and pour it all over the sloushy shit, turning the mess into a floating cesspool. Now I dip the piece of paper into the gasoline jug, and soak it real well. Lighting that sucker with the lighter, I toss it into the cesspool, and slowly the whole thing lights up, shit popping, and dried babywipes crackling. Sticking my M27 on my back, and putting my Oakleys on, I grab the engineering stake, and stir the whole mess around, first counterclockwise, then clockwise. The more I stir, the more black flames spew into my face. As if the morning isn't starting to get hot enough, the flames just made it hotter, and soon I'm sweating through my Frog top, that is also starting to blacken a little from the fire.

Content with the stirring and the progress of the flames, I step back against the perimeter wall, to relax. You don't need to stir the whole time, but you do need to stir enough to really get it all mixed or else only the top layer of shit is going to be burnt, and you won't touch the lower sections. You can see this when you turn it over with the stake, noticing that only the top layer of compacted shit is burnt, while the layers below are still a thick chocolate brown, and not charred like the top.

Leaning against the whitewashed concrete wall, I allow the sweat to dry off of me, letting myself down for a second, M27 by my side. I notice one of the AUP guys come walking toward me from their guard tower. He isn't wearing a uniform, just the traditional Afghan man dress sort of thing, with different textures on it. This AUP seems somewhat off, though. I mean the kid looks younger than me, and I'm certainly one of the younger Americans on the base. He doesn't go on patrols with us, in fact I'm not sure what the heck he does on the base at all. But yet, here he is, with his boyish looks and possibly boyish charm, walking over to my little shit fire. Looking at it, he pinches his nose and points to it, while looking at me.

"Yes kid, it smells like shit, because it is indeed shit burning, no shit right?" Most of the AUP don't get what we are doing every day with these barrels of excrement, because their method of human-waste management is to go outside into the surrounding fields.

The kid walks away, obviously bored with what I am doing. Some of the AUP are actually not too bad, even leading some of our patrols, right up with us, with medium machine guns, going through fields, village compounds, searching people on bikes and in cars, like it's going out of style. Other AUP guys, though, it's give or take. They could be there for us, or they couldn't be. Almost like compelling a lazy, mediocre softball player to get on your team just so you can make the team restrictions for the local league. Last but not least, there are the absolute dirt bags of the AUP. Guys, just like their equivalents in the Marine infantry, who really just shouldn't be there at all. This ratio isn't something that has recently been discovered. Heraclitus of the Greeks, has a two-thousand-year quote that goes, "Out of every one hundred men, ten shouldn't even be there, eighty are just targets, nine are the real fighters, and we are lucky to have them, for they make the battle. Ah, but the one, one is a warrior, and he will bring the others back." I'm not sure who that one warrior is among our AUP, but we have to deal with all three levels, all the time, and consistently. All of these AUP are from Helmand or Kandahar, whereas the ANA are from the other parts of the country most of the time, despite the fact that they speak Dari, and thus can't even communicate in a Pashtu-speaking province. As pointless as that sounds, it is probably better in that case otherwise you'd have Pashtun ANA soldiers possibly fighting their own clansmen in their home districts.

The excrement needs some more stirring, so I make sure it gets stirred up pretty good. An hour later, the flames have disappeared; now all that's left are the caked remnants at the bottom of the barrel. Rolling the drum outside the back gate, I bang it on the concrete trash-collection dugout behind the base, the caked poop that won't burn falling to the bottom. The chore isn't done yet though, because the trash in the dugout has to be burnt as well. But this doesn't take much time, really just soaking the bottom with JP8, then throwing in a piece of lighted paper, and watching the flames streak through the trash like some sort of wicked fire snake. The smoke billows up higher, and I push back from the dugout. I look out over the landscape surrounding our little Helmand home, fields and fields that stretch to the bluffs of the Helmand River in the distance, and of course the sun scorching down on everything. Never mind my Frog top, the very grass seems like it's suffocating beneath the sun's rays.

I bring the drum in, and set it by the shitter. I walk past our interpreter's room, a guy named Nasser who's a local national working for us. He's a Tajik, from the north, but can speak Pashtu. I knock on his door and ask, "Hey Nasser, what's up with that one AUP guy? He looks like a boy? You know who I mean?"

"Hey, Wining. Which one you mean? The young guy? That guy?"

"Yeah, you know what I mean, he looks like a freakin' kid here. Like he isn't even qualified to be a holding a rifle."

"Ohh him. Yeah, he like the commander servant. I hear him every night, all time."

"All the time? What do you mean?"

"Like fucking. Fucking across from my room, every night I hear him with commander."

"Fucking? What the hell? That's nuts man. Never would of imagined that."

"Yes. So in Dari we have word for this. *Bacha Bazi*, we call it … boy play. Very bad, most Afghan don't like it."

Some more small talk and I'm off, back to my rack, the daily chore down. We still have to police call, clean up the kitchen area, and put up some cammie netting. But that's later, after this awesome nap, and horrible First Strike sandwich I'm going to chow down on. "One step at a time, man," I tell myself. "I'll get through this deployment yet." I hope. I really do hope so.

About two weeks later, Haylock comes walking through the hooch door, looking at Todd and me, hanging out by Paulie's rack, watching an episode from *Spartacus*, where some chick is getting her head bashed in against some marble stairs. "When do you guys got post next? Todd? Vining?" He has his M4 in his right hand, radio clipped to the back of his belt, black square handset in his left hand, coiled back to the Motorola Prick-one-fifty-three.

"Sixteen to nineteen tonight," I respond.

"Nineteen to twenty-two," says Todd.

Haylock pauses, does a little thinking. "Cool, you guys are coming with me on a VCP outside the gate. Meet up with me in twenty minutes, all your gear, COC."

"Good to go, Sergeant."

"Roger that, Sergeant."

Haylock turns around and walks out of the hooch. Todd and I look at each other and shrug. "Oh well, so much for *Spartacus*, I'd much rather waste away in the mid–afternoon sun anyways."

We collect up our flaks, Kevlars, and weapons and bring them to the COC. Kugler is already there, sharpening a knife that he had made back home. Haylock is up front, pacing, waiting for us.

"Okay, Vining, Todd, you guys are here. Alright, Kugler, we're just going to do a VCP out front by the bridge. Todd, op check the Thor and bring it out with us; we'll just lay it next to that one compound wall by the road; keep eyes on. Nasser will come out with us for a little bit, but we probably won't need him. We'll be out there until fifteen hundred, then come back in. Any questions?"

"Sergeant, you want me to bring the Hiide as well?" Todd asks.

Haylock thinks for a second and says, "Nah, we won't need it. If we see anyone suspicious, we'll just send them to the gate and search them."

With that, we pull our flaks over our heads, take the Thor, and rack rounds into the chambers of our rifles. Walking toward the gate, Haylock calls out to Caldwell at the COC to call our DFL time, and with that we leave through the small door at the aluminum gate. Slowly making our way across the engineer bridge, fanning out across Route Shiner, for the VCP, with me and Todd on the southern side, and Haylock and Kugler the northern, closer to the bridge.

A white Toyota Corolla comes driving up. I put up my hand for it to stop. It stops. I ask to see the driver's *taskera*, his ID, while Todd searches the trunk and the back seat, and for the millionth time doesn't find anything. We let the car go, and now comes a tractor. Then a truck. Then another white Toyota Corolla. Now some farmers walking down the road; we pat them down and let them keep moving.

So on, and on, a completely typical VCP … until a group of small boys come up to me, asking for the usual, *gallam*, *ooba*, *piesea* – pens, water, candy. I laugh, and make small talk with them in Pashtu, asking them where they are from, or how old they are. Then, something odd happens, and they start talking about a person they have somewhere. It doesn't really make sense, so I call Haylock over, and tell him as much. He doesn't really get it either, and the kids are getting nowhere with us. Some of them then disappear, off into Loy Kolay and we think that's the end of it.

But nope. Winding through the village, we see the same group of kids pushing a wheelbarrow toward us, and what looks to be a … human inside of it. They push it right up to us, and promptly dump an old man onto the road, right next to us. We are completely taken by surprise and literally jump backward.

Haylock yells at the kids, "Hey fuckers! Get back here! You can't just leave this guy here!" Too late, they're gone, running away with the wheelbarrow, leaving us to turn our attention to the guy on the ground. He's not dead, but he's physically disabled, a paraplegic, definitely from birth, judging from the immature development of his spasming-out arms and legs; his face is that of at least a 40-year-old Afghan. And he's now laying in the dust of Shiner, on the side of the road. Me, Haylock, Kugler, and Todd just gather round him, in plain shock. Never in any of our predeployment training were we taught how to deal with a physically handicapped dude being dumped on the side of the road by children. It just wasn't there. I can't understand this guy's jabbering in Pashtu, so Haylock gets on the PB net, and calls for Nasser to come out to us ASAP.

In the meantime, we have no idea how to handle this. Do we move him to the side? Take him into the PB? Give him water? Is it even our place to do anything as foreign forces, or do we tell the AUP? Nasser comes running out and starts talking with him. Through the conversation, Nasser says that the guy wants a ride to Lashkar Gah, about thirty klicks down the road. He doesn't want water, or food, or help, just a ride from any random car traveling on Shiner. Nasser tells him that we can help him with water but he refuses it every time.

Haylock, being the responsible one, sort of snaps out of it and says, "I'm gonna tell the Sir, but we need to get back on security and keep on searching vics and people; this shit will figure itself out."

So we do that, albeit awkwardly because we have this moaning, spasming-out invalid on the side of the road. Eventually, we get pulled back in, I go up on post, and by then, a miracle, someone actually picks him up and he's gone.

Earlier, at the start of the deployment, we had enough guys to man a two-person post. However, now that we have fewer dudes due to the PB personnel rotation, posts are down to one man. One guy is the eyes and ears of the other fifteen, three hours during the day, two at night. Clambering up the post ladders, I check in with the COG, Sergeant Mike. All the equipment accounted for, I lean up against the Two-Forty, looking out across Shiner. Kevlar unstrapped, I gaze out at the road. Random Afghans walking on the road, some boys swimming in the canal, blue-burkha–clad women moving from one compound to another, a tractor chugging over the bridge in front of the PB, a white Toyota Corolla speeding past it, heading south. Some noise in the PB ... what is that? Oh, just Weitoish and Mauler filling up sandbags.

What was going on with that disabled guy? How far removed from our society can this one be that a group of children dump this dude on Shiner, right in front of us, and he practically leaves himself for dead along the road? Is this the extent of a medieval society, one that hasn't changed since Genghis Khan rolled through these parts in the 1200s? One thing for sure, these Pashtuns are an ancient people.

On our patrols, we see that the villagers use the ditches outside their compounds for defecating in. Their fields are a maze of canals and ditches, using the water from the Helmand River to somehow irrigate and grow crops many miles from the main river. Their clothes haven't changed much in centuries. Their houses are made out of dried mud. Even their implements, with the exception of the tractors from England, predate anything that existed in the Americas post-1600s. And yet, these Pashtuns, these simple folk, wiped out a British contingent to a man in 1841 during the First Anglo-Afghan War. With the help of the United States and Pakistan, they forced a Soviet retreat after nine years of war.

Now, with us being in the country since 2001, it seems that no matter how many victories on the battlefield we inflict on the Taliban, external factors outside the battle space always contribute to more Taliban, and an increasing insurgency. Whether it was Operation Red Wing or Operation Anaconda, the army's fight in the Korengal, the British fight in Helmand, the push through Marjah by 6th and 8th Marines, even the 5th Marines in Sangin, as a fighting force, we have proved time and time again that we can defeat this Taliban, but that doesn't matter if young Pashtun men have no aspiration to work for a better country. Interestingly, Afghans have a quaint phrase for this: "The Americans have all the watches but we have all the time."

"Hey Marine!" What? What was that? *"Gallam! Chacul! Piesea!"* Oh, just the neighborhood kid, Ailakula. During the day, he would come round to the post, with his brother Aratulla, asking for pens, knives, or candy. He lived in a compound outside the patrol base, just on the other side of the canal. Sometimes we would throw him what he wanted, but not knives or pens; the Taliban could make blasting caps out of those. He was around eight years old, had a brother, and two sisters. From what I could tell, his father had been killed in previous years, either by the Taliban, or the government. The children were living at home with their mother, being supported by their uncle and other male relatives. But he was always a constant, on post. Other kids came by the PB on occasion, by the canal road, or moving cattle around. Even kids on motorcycles from Jaker with Cold Monster and Pine cigarettes. But none was a fixture like Ailakula, seemingly always there, kind of part of the whole scene, as it were. Sometimes he would get pissed with us, showing the thumbs-down if we didn't throw down some bottles of water or candy. Other times we would have fun, pass the time, from twenty feet in the air, to him on the ground, making funny faces, and doing stupid things, entertaining the kid. Then his older brother would come along and be a little more mature, smiling. Eventually they would leave, going about their chores at home, or in the fields. And through this odd relationship between these Afghan kids, and us, the post standers, some of the complexity of the Afghans gave way to routine, and through the routine, life became bearable.

The boys also had their sister. Her name was Pritchna, and she was around seven or eight years old. I'd see her every so often, but always in the distance, close by their compound. She always wore these shiny, full-length dresses that sparkled all over the place. Women start donning the burkha when they reached reproductive age, or in their mid-teens. She certainly wasn't there yet, so could thus roam free and play with the other children. Every time she'd get close to the post, I'd call out to her in Pashtu, and she'd hightail it back home, scared I was going to kidnap her or something horrible, I assume. Which is pretty sad, because all I wanted to do was talk to her, and see how her life was going. Being a female in Afghanistan is being dealt an extremely raw hand at life, and whenever I could, I tried to do something, anything. Whether that was smiling at Pritchna, saying hello to little girls on the patrols, or even giving out candy to them as well. But they were so wrapped up and protected it was just hard to sort of break that social barrier.

* * *

The low hum of our mighty generator makes the plastic sheeting on the window frames rattle. Miller is on post, Caldwell is in the COC, and the rest of us are all in the hooch, as usual. Nwankwo is messing around on his computer, Weitoish is powdering up his energy drink, getting ready for a gym session. Mauler and Paul are watching another episode of *Dexter*. I'm reading *Catch-22* on my Kindle, I've got post later on that night so I'm resting up for that.

Martin bursts in all of a sudden and says, "Doc, get to the COC. Two Afghans just came in that are all shot up!"

Shot up? What the heck? This is Nawa, nothing happens here. Regardless, we all jump off of our racks and grab our weapons, rushing to the COC building nextdoor. I enter the hallway and as usual the lights are out, but there's a Peck-sixteen light on, casting shadows from the figures at the end of the hallway.

The first thing I hear are the moans. I can barely make out a man on the floor, Afghans and Marines crowded around the dimly lit figure. I get to the end of the hallway and there's this Afghan laying in the middle of it, just moaning away, covered in blood. He's been shot several times, in the arm, shoulder, and stomach. In the other room there's another Afghan, shot through the cheek and also in the stomach. His guts are starting to bulge out from his belly but not so much that it's grotesque, just awkward-looking. It's still not right; your insides should be inside you, not outside you. Martin is there shining the light of his Peck-sixteen on the guy.

"Are you going to do anything?"

Martin shrugs a reply back and the guy continues to moan. By this time we're balls to the wall in doing everything we can in getting these guys to some form of normality, because they are fighting for their lives at this point. They've lost too much blood, so much blood, it's starting to seep out over the floor. The COC is on company tac getting Jaker a 9-Line to get these guys somewhere safe. I'm running back and forth with notes from Doc to the COC. I don't have a pen, where's my pen, stupid boot, people are dying and you don't have a pen to write down what's wrong with them. I look at the Afghan police standing around and blurt out, "*Gallam! Gallam!*" They hurriedly reach in their pockets and produce a pen.

I've written down MIST reports before in training, but that was notional, the words on the paper are meaningless. This time I write, "2 GSW – gut shot and face – barely conscious and losing blood – applied gauze and starting IV." These combinations of letters aren't notional any more, they're the last thing these moaning men will have written down on their behalf while still breathing, if you can even call what they were doing breathing: more like suffocating for air. I run back to the COC and hand Caldwell the notes; he snaps them up without a second glance, reading them into the radio as fast as he can. Dust-off birds are quick, but sometimes not quick enough with lives on the line. The Sir tells Paul, "Get an LZ security team sorted out and form some security for the birds!" Paul rogers up and grabs me, Wietosh, and Kugler to put our gear on. I run back to the hooch, and have trouble tying up my laces on my boots. Dammit, Vining, people are dying and here you are trying to get your boots on. I finish the boots, throw a Frog top on and my flak almost simultaneously; it isn't even tucked in. I grab my M27, Kevlar and off I go. Nwankwo is kneeling over the one guy, along with Sergeant Mike, and Nasser, while Doc Hamaker is working on the other dude.

Nwankwo looks at me frantically and screams, "HOW LONG TILL THE BIRDS COME IN!"

I shout back, "FIVE MINUTES!"

He looks confused for a second then screams back, kneeling, "FIVE MINUTES ISN'T ENOUGH TIME!"

The Afghan is still gasping, croaking for air, even though everyone is looking at him and talking to him, working on him. His eyes are fixated on the ceiling, regardless of the attention being given to him. His mouth suddenly gasps some more and stays open. Silence. He lives no more. Sergeant Mike tells Nasser, "Talk to him, Nasser, Talk to him!" Nasser blurts out some Pashtu, but it's no use. This man won't hear, speak, or know Pashtu any longer. Death isn't the movies. It happens on dusty concrete floors soaked with blood and surrounded by caring people trying to do something, anything, to make a difference. But it still happens, and sometimes there is nothing you can do.

The birds are inbound. Black Hawks, dust-offs, Pedros, whatever you want to call them, they are the angels of the battlefield. I run out of the PB. Paul already has his LZ team set up around the field. Just as I clear the gate I hear them, roaring straight out of the moonlit sky, barely 200 feet off the ground, rotors tilted forward, those beautiful birds. They fly over the PB, do a 180 turn in complete darkness and seemingly at the same time come in to land, barely flaring before they touch down. Dust, straw, chunks of dirt are spewing all over, making a man squint and turn his head away. The birds haven't even settled and one of the crew chiefs comes running out of them to me, because I've got the MIST reports. Dust fills the air and swirls around us. He screams at me over the rotor wash, "What you got man, tell me what's going on!" I tell him what's up: this one has this and that one has that — but surely dead. The aid and litter teams are behind me with the casualties loaded up. "Alright! Worse guy goes in that bird and less bad in that one!"

I turn round and tell the aid and litter teams where to go and they're off to the helos.

The Black Hawks take off, leaving us in a cloud of swirling dust, dirt, twigs, and grass. You can't do anything but look straight down and let it happen to you. The roaring is in the background now, and the LZ team collapses back at the PB, as we all filter in, half walking, half dragging ourselves along. We get back to the hooch and strip our flaks off; no one says anything.

Papa Doc blurts out, "Hey some of you guys, come over here and help me clean up the blood."

Weitoish and I go on over, get rags and paper towels, and slowly work away at the massive puddles of blood on the floor. It's just sitting there like sticky water, acting all innocent. As if someone had set a large water container down and let it just leak out slowly, forming two separate pools. For days afterward I can still make out the drops that dried out on the floor, as if to form some sort of marker, "Remember us, this is where we bleed ourselves to death."

The next day, two Afghans come over to the PB and Nasser gets me to tell them when the bodies of their family members will be arriving back for them. The family members look pretty composed for having their sons killed, no doubt a consequence of this war. I actually think one of the guys is still alive, and tell them so. Then it's confirmed over the radio with Jaker: nope, both died. I come back in the room and tell them yes, both are dead. God, I must have screwed with their emotions for a bit; I feel horrible for it.

* * *

Todd clambers up the metal ladder, his gear smacking the sides of the post wall as he pops through the top, handing me his rifle as he gets onto the floor.

"Good patrol last night, man?"

"Naahh, that was fucking stupid. The Sir just wanted to do a night VCP south on Shiner, waste of my fucking time. And I got soaked coming back, had to break my rifle all the way down to get all the mud out of it."

I can see it too, his boots all crusty with mud caked on them from him probably falling into a wadi. "Damn, that sucks man. At least you'll be here on post when the higher-ups come through today."

"What? What do those fuckers want with us anyways?"

As I turn over the logbook to him, I shrug. "I don't know man. Maybe they want to make sure our boot blouses are up to our knees out here."

Todd chuckles. Before we left the States, First Sergeant had given us a personal class on boot blousing, so I wouldn't put inspecting our trousers past him on a visit to the boonies.

"Well, at least he still believes the bullshit we told him about not being able to cut our hair because it would short-circuit the generator." God, that's some gold right there. Garner told First Sergeant that our hair clippers would short-circuit the generator when we plugged them in. He bought it for a week or two and the PB was able to grow out a little bit.

I start on my way down the ladder. In the distance I can hear the slow rumble on Shiner of Chaos Mobile's convoy from Jaker coming toward us.

"Aahhh seriously? We told him that? What a dumb fuck. The thing can support a PB but not hair clippers? Clowns for leadership, dude."

"Yeah, I thought so too. Fucking idiot."

As I leave the post, I unroll my cuffed sleeves and button them at the end, being the good little Marine I am supposed to portray, and not the savage, shit-burning fuck who wants nothing more than to smoke-check some Taliban. Dropping my flak off by my rack, I join the rest of the guys round the fire pit, waiting for the higher-ups.

First Sergeant and the company commander walk in through the front gate, making a beeline for the COC. Rambo walks by and sort of points to all the trucks outside and put his hands up as a sort of question. All of us just make ugly faces and thumbs-down signs while touching our collars to signify higher rank. He laughs, completely understanding our discontented mood. Chain-of-command hatred is universal.

After a little while, First Sergeant comes out.

"Rah, First Sergeant," we all sort of mumble. Mauler, Paul, and Kugler have been on that night patrol with Todd, and I have just gotten off post, so we aren't exactly the most lively of bunches.

"Good morning, Marines. How's it going at Loy Kolay these days?"

Paul responds: "Just dandy, First Sergeant, we're really getting into the swing of things. Loving life pretty much."

First Sergeant just looks at the guy. Paul knows how to dance that line between sarcasm and being legitimately normal. "Well, that's good to hear, Paul. I hope everyone shares that opinion."

Awkward sort of silence.

"How many of you have done your MCIs for corporal?"

"None of us, chief. Don't exactly have a MCI proctor or computer out here. Kugler says, "The new joins really haven't had that much time, First Sergeant. We don't have any proctors, no way to print out the tests, and our schedules are pretty stacked with patrolling and post."

Thank you, Kugler, thank God.

First Sergeant is obviously not impressed. "We'll accommodate MCIs, I'll get Sergeant Michael to be a proctor, and we can print the tests out at Jaker. Either way, we'll make it work out."

Literally, there is no way around the Corps leadership, even out here on the PB. Can't they just ever leave us alone and let us do our job?

"Sergeant Volpe, where are you living out here?"

Volpe is our official AUP advisor, whose job it is to mentor and teach the AUP. "I've got a room to myself behind the building, First Sergeant; since I got here, while the Two Three guys were still here, I moved in back there."

"Okay, well, you're gonna have to move in with the rest of the PB in that main hooch; we have to have everyone at these PBs all together".

Volpe is one extremely charismatic, anti-authority figure, very ironic considering he was a Sergeant of Marines. It is readily apparent he isn't taking this eviction order well. "First Sergeant, do you live on Jaker with the rest of the guys there?"

An epiphany!

"No, I don't, Sergeant Volpe, I have my own room."

"Just like I have mine?"

You could see the cogs turning in First Sergeant's head with this "Do as I say, not as I do" attitude. "Sergeant Volpe, move into the main hooch, understand?"

"Roger that, First Sergeant"

Caldwell came running out of the COC, "Hey Vining, you mind watching the COC for me? I gotta get something out of the hooch"

"Sure Caldwell."

I thank my lucky stars I'm away from Chaos Eight. There's no one inside the COC, so I lay my M27 on the table and check the radio, see that it's working. All of a sudden I notice the Chaplain walk in. He must have hitched a ride with Chaos Mobile.

"Good morning, Sir! What's going on?"

He still has his flak on. The poor guy, doesn't he know we take those things off whenever possible? "Oh not much, just wanted to come check out the patrol bases. I brought some stuff for you guys." He swings a plastic basket full of various inflated balls and games from the States. "Is there anything you guys wanted out here?"

Ummm, yeah, for you to never come back. "Well, Sir, some satellite internet and working phones would be cool."

He sort of turns his head down. "Sorry, can't do much about that. I got these toys for you guys, though."

Thanks? What am I going to do with a set of plastic horseshoes? I don't even know how to play the damned game. Then I notice he doesn't have a weapon on him. "Sir, where's your weapon?"

He looks up and smiles, "Oh, I don't carry one. That's what RP is for. I'm a noncombatant."

What the hell? Has this kid been anywhere in the AO? Does he have a single clue what is going on? People are shooting and blowing each other up, and he doesn't have a weapon? Of course, I know he is the battalion chaplain and a Geneva Convention–approved noncombatant, but the realization is just too much for me. "Aahhh, gotcha Sir."

He smiles at me again, "Have fun with the toys!" And leaves.

The Sir walks right in. "What's this stuff , Vining?"

"I really don't know, Sir. Just some stuff the Chaplain dropped off for us."

He is just as puzzled. "Well, thanks, I guess. You can go now. I've got the COC. Mobile is on their way out."

Glory Hallelujah. We always get sick of those bastards.

* * *

One September morning I get woken up for post by Martin. It is still dark outside so I get dressed in complete darkness, only turning on my headlamp to not trip over anyone's gear lying in the hallway to the door of the hooch. I look at my watch: five minutes to relieving Miller on post, perfect timing. Flak resting on my shoulders, but cummerbunds not hooked in, I have my M27 in one hand as I walk to the post tower. I clip the single point attachment on the M27 into my centerline sling and climb up the ladder. Miller opens up the hatch for me so I can pop onto the floor.

"Quiet night?" I ask.

"Yeah, nothing. There was an illum mission to the southeast about an hour ago and that's it."

"Cool, you signed out of the logbook?"

"Just a second ... here you go." He hands me the radio.

"COG, COG, this is Post One, radio check, over."

"Gotcha Vining, I'm gonna take a dump."

Miller clambers down the ladder and now I'm alone in the dark. Just me, my thoughts, my red lens headlamp and the logbook.

Dawn approaches in an odd way when you are fully awake for it. Slowly, ever so slowly the darkness is chased by the light, but in a fashion that you can't really put a finger on. You just know that you can see farther now than five minutes ago. September mornings in Helmand are nice if you can catch them. The heat during the day is so humid and oppressive that the mornings and nights are fantastic to be awake for.

But there was something about this particular morning that took me by surprise. It was cooler than usual. Even with a bit of a breeze that you'd never get during the day. When enough light did break the horizon, it shone down on the crops in the fields, casting a sort of ray through and upon them. The crops were waving in the light breeze too. I could easily see across the Helmand River Valley and all the features of the hills there. It was becoming almost supernatural.

And then the Adhan prayer broke the silence, from the Loy Kolay mosque. Of course we had now become completely used to the Azan throughout the deployment. It was the background noise to our patrols and meals. It led the AUP to stop on patrol and pray. Most of the time it was annoying, loud, over bad speakers, and repetitive.

But not … this time. This time, whoever was at the microphone recited that Adhan with such a smooth and tranquil conviction, it was almost as if he weren't human but a sort of natural force that was speaking the words in Arabic. I was leaning on the south-facing windowsill of the tower and just stopped completely. I almost stopped breathing as well. I became lost in the melody of the pitch, riding it as a surfer catching a wave, effortlessly flowing to the next. The cool, breezy light mirrored the beauty of the narration, echoing each word as if confirming its definition. I didn't even know what was being said apart from a few "Allahs" and "Mohammeds," but it didn't matter: this was the most tranquil song, the most detailed speech, the most awesome poem, the most intense video I ever saw in real life.

And then, almost as soon as it started, it stopped. And I was left speechless, my mouth agape. I couldn't explain what I had gone through, no context before or after could have matched what happened. The only conclusion that I could bring forth was that there was something bigger, higher, more in control than anything else I would have known in the world at the time. This was not an accident, a fluke, a coincidence of other worlds. This was deliberate in a way that I could never replicate, no matter how I could have arranged the circumstances in a million different ways.

* * *

Eagle Industries Plate Carrier with no pouches or plates weighs about 5 pounds. CIF issued gray SAPI plates, front, back and sides weigh 10 pounds. Assorted pouches weigh 3 pounds. Six armory issued STANAG magazines loaded to 28 rounds apiece weigh 8 pounds. Three-liter camelback weighs 4 pounds. Kevlar with assorted NVG SL3 gear weighs 3 pounds. PVS14 night vision goggles weigh 2 pounds. M16A4 service rifle with Trijicon RCO, L3 Communications

Peck–Sixteen, and forward grip weighs 10 pounds. Assorted medical gear, extra tourniquets, boots and eye pro weigh around 3 pounds. Optional Thor ECM device weighs 25 pounds of pure steel. Optional Hiide biometric device weighs 3 pounds. Optional CMD detector weighs 5 pounds. Optional assault pack with chow, radio, and extra batteries adds another 20 pounds for a two- or three-day overnight op. Total minimum weight for a typical foot patrol: 50 pounds to be carried anywhere from five to twenty kilometres, from the patrol base and back, every step of the way.

Average temperatures in Helmand Province during the month of September range from 120°F in the day to 70°F at night, just when the Islamic new year of Ramadan occurs in the lunar calendar of 2011. The AUP of course, take advantage of Ramadan so as to not go on patrol with us. To us, we find this ludicrous, that they won't patrol their own AO in their own province but we have to? Of course, to us, we can't conceive of a civil war lasting from 1979 until the present day, or having to deal with seven months of Marines, only to have a completely new contingent arrive when they go.

* * *

Zap cards? Left shoulder pocket, right trouser pocket. Dog tag in left boot? Check. NVGs, with batteries, and spare AAs. Thor, blue light blinking, extra 25-90s. Sickle and CMD, along with three Prick-one-fifty-two green gear radios, and one Prick-one-fifty-three black gear radio. In case one or more go down, of course. Water, filled-up camelback. Water bottles for the AUP? Check. Along with the AUP themselves and their sergeant. Terp? Nasser in tow. Kugler with bomb dog Pete? Got him.

Paulie gets up front in the COC/briefing room. "Alright, fucknuts. We all here? Todd? Vining? Kugler? Nasser? Good." He goes up to the map, pointing at Loy Kolay. "We'll start out here, because there isn't any other fucking place to start from. Exit the back gate, cross Shiner, and walk up this back road here. I wanna stay to the right side; last time we traveled on the left, about a week ago with Mauler. I want to check out these compounds here, talk to them a bit. Then push up to Circula, where we'll chill out for an hour, see what we can hear, and try to ask around for Mohammad … What's his name, Caldwell?" Caldwell, our local Clic guy, and Radio God, replies, "Oh, that cocksucker? Mohammad Tarique Dawud. We think he had something to do with Loylala's beheading."

Paulie spits out some dip. "Gotcha, we'll leave that up to Nasser. Leaving Circula, we'll travel along this canal road, take a right toward Loy Kolay, cross the bridge, and then EFL the north gate, no later than 1800. Any questions?"

Kugler pipes up, "Yeah, when we push up to Circula, you want us maintaining security on that old fort-looking hill thing? Or down by the compounds?" Solid question.

"We'll do both, down by the compounds to talk to people, then up there for the remainder of the time; it's a good overwatch position."

Kugler nods his head in agreement.

"Alright, let's flak up and get this show on the road. Todd and Vining, you guys trade out the Thor; I'll take it if you get worn out. Kugler, you take point with the dog. Remember 'Roll Tide' if you see anything suspicious."

The sounds of Velcro ripping, shoulder straps slapping beaten-down shoulders, and belts being clipped fill the room, followed by the racking of our weapons into condition one. Except for Paul. He is always in condition one.

Caldwell calls us out, to Jaker. "Chaos Main, be advised, Chaos Three is departing friendly lines, four M-Es, one terp, three AUP, and one dog."

Nasser is waiting with the AUP outside, guys named Achmed Jan, Rambo, and Yeah Right You. I shoulder the awkward Thor on my back. "Hey Toddy, can you do me up?" Merely grunting, Todd gets behind me and presses the big squishy button, changing the operating condition from red to blinking blue, now jamming. The thing squishes down on my shoulders that makes it awkward to move.

"Hey, Paul, you mind if I grab a dip from you?"

He looks at me with his M4 two-oh-three in one hand, green gear radio in the other. "Since when did you fucking dip, Vining?" almost not believing himself.

"Since this damned Thor started becoming annoying."

Putting his radio down and grabbing his Grizzly Wintergreen can out of his shoulder pocket, he tosses it to me. "You see, Todd doesn't need a dip when carrying the Thor, because he's a beast as it is." Todd sort of flashes an awkward grin. He is indeed, a beast among men, never complaining about what he is ordered to do.

The patrol walks through the back gate, Kugler leading with the bomb-sniffing dog. Then Rambo, with the PKM, Paul, Nasser, me, Achmed Jan, Todd, and Yeah Right You. We called him Yeah Right You because Todd taught him to look at one of us and scream out, "Yeah, right you!" like some deranged staff NCO.

Spitting out some dip, I step over the rim of the single-person opening in the vehicle gate, onto the packed earth. I stick the inserted magazine of my M27 into the kangaroo pouch of the plate carrier, right hand on the pistol grip, left hand grasping the forward grip just ahead of the magazine. Damn that

Thor. Slowly walking through the soft field, Helmand River far off to my left, Route Shiner and the canal on the right, each step sinks into the moon dust, compounded by the 50-pound weight. Walk ten steps, sweep round, tilt the muzzle, make a connecting file with Achmed Jan, slowly sweep back to front. Walk ten more steps, make the same sweep, only on the opposite side of the first, thus maintaining a 360-degree posture. Repeat for duration of patrol.

Crossing the canal, the heat starts to come on to me. The first globs of sweat appear, beneath the Frog armpits, from the Thor. It starts pouring down my face, permeating my chinstrap, already encrusted with old sweat from many patrols, post cycles, and vehicle convoys. There's not even a breeze to calm it down.

Approaching some compounds, Paulie signals a halt. As if by second nature, we fall upon them, arraying ourselves in a security posture, looking toward all the cardinal directions, giving Paul some comfort in talking with the Afghans present. He speaks into the green gear: "COC, this is Chaos Three, grid four, five, eight, two …"

Slowly, I drop my weight onto my right kneepad on the ground. I press my body up against the mud wall of the compound. It feels cool to the touch, and provides some good cover for the sector I'm covering. The smell of manure is thick in the air, along with fresh fields of wheat off to my side. I look over to Achmed Jan, and he's smoking a cigarette with Yeah Right You, completely oblivious to this security thing. Classy AUP, classy.

Villagers walk by me on the dirt road, some dirty and disheveled from a day of farming, others somewhat clean as they head out, with hoes or shovels on their shoulders.

"*Salaam! … Tsengiya!*" I yell out to them.

"*Jordi, pakhadei!*" they yell back, a common greeting in Pashtu.

Far removed from the patrolling of the initial months in Nawa, we are learning the lay of the land, how people interact with us, what a good or bad road looks like, where we'd probably run into trouble, or not, the good neighborhoods and the bad ones. Whereas previously we were legitimately fearful of every step, now we know better, and we know what to look for instead of guessing the unknown. We still get scared or know something is different, but it is becoming more of a sixth sense.

Paul comes out of the compound with Nasser, yelling out, "Hey, pick up." Into the radio he says, "Oscar Mike, en route to Circula."

The Sir comes back with, "Roger, keep us updated."

Groaning, I ease my way up against the mud wall, hike the Thor round on my shoulders, at least faking myself into thinking that it feels better on my back. Getting back into the single-file formation, the patrol pushes on to Circula.

In the far-off distance a tractor sounds, farmers are working in their fields, looking at us as we pass. The road seems to last a while, just one endless dirt road, with the steps of each guy kicking up dust, remembering to stay on the right side as Paul briefed beforehand. Kugler calls a stop, letting the rest of us know "Roll Tide," or the brevity code for a possible IED up ahead. Todd and I fan out to the sides of the road, covering the flanks while we motion the AUP to cover the side.

Rambo walks up to me. "*Chechsha dah?*" he asks with a sort of twirl of his hand, and an upward motion of his chin.

I point to the front of the patrol, where Paul and Kugler are checking out the ground-sign indicator, Kugler instructing the bomb dog Pete, "Hunt it up!" while motioning forward. "*Zhe fiker kwoom yeo mine laray.* (I think there is a mine)"

Rambo shakes his head and just walks up toward Paul.

"Hey, Paul, Rambo is walking up toward you."

Paulie looks back at Rambo and motions to Nasser. "Tell fucking Rambo that we think there is an IED up front."

Nasser calls out to Rambo and after a brief exchange in Pashtu says back, "He say no bomb!"

Just as Rambo starts walking past Kugler, Kugler says, "What the hell! What don't these guys understand about IEDs?" as he slowly proceeds to get next to a mound of dirt by the road, grabbing Pete with him. Any human can be a minesweeper ... once.

Rambo walks right up to the spot, looks at the ground, stomps on it several times, then looks back at us. "*Zhechazoo, mine nelaray!*" Let's go, there is no bomb.

"Goddammit! Why are these kids so clueless!" yells Paul as he storms ahead, leading the way.

We heave a collective sigh of relief, literally expecting Rambo to have been blown to smithereens. But no, the guy is fine, at the cost of our nerves. At least he already has a tourniquet around his right leg. What made him so sure about his right leg getting blown off instead of his left, I'll never know.

Coming into Circula we push across a road, and see the fortress hillock in the distance. The place looks to be an old outpost that has been eroding away since at least the medieval ages. The actual outpost part stands out against the landscape like the stern of a beached ship, with the village forming the sloping-down portion. All this is around fifty to eighty feet higher than the land around it. Nawa being relatively flat, this allows you to see over the entire landscape in any direction.

Below the hillock are the villagers' fields. As we pass through them, the air gets hotter and stickier than before, from the plants. Moving up the hill, we pass the mud-walled mosque, with various villagers coming and going, all of them looking at us. It appears to be prayer time. Achmed Jan says something to Nasser and Nasser turns to Paul.

"Paul. The AUP ask if they can pray. They can do this?"

Paul looks at his watch. "Yeah, sure, we'll just set up security here. Kugler, Vining, take that corner, Todd, we'll go over here."

Nasser turns to Paul again, "Do you need me? Can I join them?"

Paulie is irritated now. "Yeah man, go ahead." He studies his wrist-mounted GPS, just below his out-turned cuffed sleeves. "COC, this is Chaos Three, be advised, short security halt, compound forty-six in Circula; the AUP are praying."

The Sir comes over the net, "Roger, solid copy on the security halt, break. Any word on Loylala's deal? Over."

Paul again, "That's a negative; we talked to some villagers at the last stop and they had no clue."

The Sir again," Roger, tango. Out."

The fucking Thor is digging into my shoulders, and really bearing down on me. I lumber it off and set it down next to me, while I get in the prone, orientating down the street. The battery level is at forty percent, so I turn it off the jamming mode to increase the battery life. The possibility of there being an RC IED next to a crowded mosque is remote. I set out my bipods and wait for the security halt to be over.

Some children walk past me, probably five to ten years old, a mix of boys and girls. "*Salaam!*" I say to them. Some of them respond but most just smile and giggle. The boys are in their ragged farm clothes for when they help their fathers in the fields. But the girls are dressed in brightly colored, glittery garments. When they became teenagers they will don blue burkhas and become invisible to all but their blood relatives. One of the girls is somewhat shy, so I dig into my drop pouch and pull out some hard candy. I extend my left hand, right hand still on my M27, saying "*Piesea ghari?*" Do you want candy?" She nods and sticks out her little arms and picks the candy out of my hand. Smiling, she runs off to join her friends, the empty candy wrapper falling to the ground.

Just like Pritchna back at the PB, most females in Helmand are regulated to a patriarchal tribal society that sees little need for women's education or welfare. They live these ghost lives behind their burkhas and their compound walls, existing only to bear and rear children. Oftentimes I'd toss a little girl a candy, only to have a boy smack her across the face for it.

Nasser and the AUP return from the mosque, rolling down their trouser legs and fitting their boots on. Kugler rolls his eyes at me, as Paul annoyingly squawks into the green gear, "Oscar Mike to Corona." It annoys all of us. Here we were, thousands of miles from home, risking our lives, while these AUP want to take time out of a combat patrol to go pray, as if we don't have anything else better to do. Whether it's siphoning us for water or gasoline, or electricity, we just feel like we're doing the burden of work, the majority of the time.

Pushing toward the hillock of Circula, we take an overwatch position on top, trying to get a view of the surrounding roads. Looking for a better vantage point, I climb up one of the mounds. Down below, Achmed Jan starts screaming at me in Pashtu.

Nasser yells at me, "Wining! You have to get down from there!"

Why? I can see across half of Nawa from here, an advantageous position to slay bodies from. "Why, Nasser? Is he pissed?"

Achmed Jan starts yelling louder and louder.

"Just do it. I explain to you when you are down."

Fine. Don't want to upset the AUP brethren. Once I'd clambered down, Nasser explains: "Wining, when you are up there, you can see into all the open houses of the village. That's their private lives. Achmed is Pashtun, and he does not want you to see other Pashtuns in the privacy."

Hmmm. "Okay, well, I was just trying to provide security, didn't realize that. Can you let him know?" Nasser nods and talks to the agitated Achmed. A one-hundred–percent tactically correct maneuver can also be the worst cultural move, something that will drive the Afghans to absolute distraction.

From Circula we push east, toward the canal road that crisscrosses the Corona road, and eventually leads to Loy Kolay. Once we get to the canal section, Paulie turns, "Hey, we've got to set up a snap VCP right here for the next hour or so; the Sir wants at least one VCP on this intersection; Todd, Vining, take that northern intersection with Yeah Right You and Achmed Jan. Kugler, you and I will take the south with Rambo. Nasser, you go in between both of us."

I roger up, and set up my Thor in between the two groups, providing as much coverage to both. Todd and I take up positions on either side of the road, waiting for either vehicles or people to pass us by. Some farmers come walking toward us, some with smiling faces, others with eyes of discontent. We stop them, ask them a few questions, where they were going, where they are from, then body-search them from the shoulders down to their calves. Some farmers carry this thing called a *Tawez*, which is essentially a few miniature pages of the Quran wrapped into a tiny bundle about an inch thick and likewise in height. Farmers sometimes sew it into their blouses, in the shoulder area. Normally they carry some canned *naswar*, or Afghan dip, in their front pockets, along with their *taskera*, in addition to maybe cigarettes and a wooden stick used to brush their teeth.

Down at the end of the road, we see a motorcycle approaching. We slow it down with hand motions and our rifles, telling the driver and his passenger to get off the bike so we can *talashey khayom* or search him. However, once we're done with the standard search, the AUP started yelling and screaming at the guy and his friend. They put up a little argument, but to no avail. Todd and I look at each other in astonishment, because right in front of our eyes, the AUP make the men jump into the canal, get soaking wet, and then let them get back on the bike and speed off. After seeing this a few times, I call over to Nasser, and ask him just what the hell is going on.

"So every bike that comes this way, with two or more people on it, they will push them into the river."

What the hell? Why?

"Because the two AUP who were killed a week ago were shot by two Taliban on a bike. So this is to make people not ride bikes like that."

The concept is so bizarre I have no idea where to begin to see the logic in such policing.

The day is getting hot, and we were baking there in the moon dust of the intersection. So hot, my water has turned to a lukewarm mess, scalding to suck on through my camelback hose. Heat like this is enough to push you over the edge at times, making you want to just throw in the towel and be done with any patrol or working party you're on. So it's either that, or the fact that nothing is happening in the AO whatsoever. No pop shots, no sign of the Taliban, nothing. Doing the searches on the cars at the VCP lets me vent my frustration on someone, the Afghans we're searching. I start taking it out on them, ordering them out of their cars, body-patting them down, demanding they open up the truck, the glove compartment, any nook and cranny.

Todd notices and says, "Vining, what the fuck are you doing?"

I look back at him. What's he trying to say? "I'm searching these cars and shit. What do you mean?"

"Yeah, no shit you're searching them: it's like you have a fucking problem with all of them."

"Okay? That's what we're supposed to be doing?"

"We're supposed to be searching them, not fucking ripping them apart. These are just regular poor people, dude; most of them just want to get the hell back home or to their fields. Chill the fuck out, you idiot."

He called me out, and he isn't wrong.

"I guess."

I chill out, feeling stupid about myself, treating all these people like they're all some sort of plague. I realize that the majority of them have nothing to do with the Taliban, and really just want to live their lives in peace. Paulie calls a stop to the VCP, organizing us back into a single file. Todd takes the Thor this time, and I feel really light walking the rest of the way without that fucking thing on my back. But the whole way, I just feel stupid, for Todd putting me in my place.

* * *

Sergeant Mike walked around the corner to where a bunch of us were hanging out at the smoke-pit. He had this devious smile and glow on his face.

Kugler looked up at him, "What's so entertaining there, Sergeant?"

Yeah! What's so funny!

He looked around quickly, speaking in a low voice, "So my buddy from Three Eight sent me this stupid little pinnate, right, and mentioned not to open it around staff NCOs or officers. Inside of it, he stuffed some gas station Jim Beam bottles. I took one of them, poured it into a cup, added some coke to it, then walked into the COC about an hour ago, give it to the Sir, saying, 'Sir, don't thank me or say anything, just drink.' He looked confused, so I walked out. Just now I popped into the COC and he had this shit-eating grin on his face! He figured it out!" Aaahhh got 'em! We all looked at each other over the little fire crackling at our feet, smiling over this hilarious exchange.

The smoke-pit was right outside the main hooch, covered by cammie netting, with the perimeter wall of the PB off to the left, the AUP hooch building in front, and the COC building to the right. Between the COC and hooch buildings was an alleyway filled with the 803 generator and the sandbagged ammunition storage bunker. Oftentimes, we'd congregate here, after post, patrol, working parties, just to chill out. Usually the fire would be going, fueled by bits of trash, planks of wood, or anything else we felt like burning. Although we obviously respected rank, the smoke-pit was where anyone could unwind and relax in each other's company, including the Sir and the sergeants themselves. Many times the AUP would come over as well, and although we couldn't drink with them, we'd share cigarettes, dip, hand-motioned jokes, or clean weapons, cut hair, and eat food. Nasser the Terp would come over as well, adding to the cross-cultural bullshitting, often instigating an argument or something himself. Our rifles were ever-present, either between our legs, or leaning up against the concrete wall or a seat.

Todd turned to Mauler, "Hey Mauler, finish that-them-there story you were telling me about Herring from Alpha."

Mauler chuckled. "Well, apparently Herring was so fucking desperate for a pack of smokes, that one of his buddies at his PB told him that he'd give him a pack if he bit the head off a dead bat lying nearby." What the fuck!

"And he did it! He bit the head off, and got the pack. But then he got rabies, so right now he's at Camp Cup Cake, about to get busted and NJP'ed for destruction of government property!"

Now that was hilarious.

"What an idiot! But props to him if he really needed those smokes, I guess," said Paul.

Miller looked up from finishing the main meal from his MRE. "Ya'll hear what happened to Sergeant Louis?" We all shook our heads. "So apparently he was leading a helo mission from Jaker, and after the briefing, he was so fixated on getting on the bird and getting his counts, that he left his damned rifle back in the briefing room. Didn't realize this until they were on the bird. I guess Gunny Hart was there, and quietly lent him his M4, while Gunny went on the rest of mission with just an M9. Clearing rooms and stuff."

Oh Louis ... he seemed a good enough dude in the company, but I guess he just screwed up there. Poor guy. Caldwell joined us from the COC, as usual, taking his Frog top off and leaving it in the hooch. Todd told some oddball joke about coalmining in Pennsylvania. It wasn't the greatest. Mauler looked over to Caldwell. "Caldwell, tell that joke about the grunt and the insurgent in Fallujah or something." He chuckled.

"You mean the beginning of the invasion?" Drawing a deep breath, he started: "So there's this forward observer on our side, before the invasion in oh three started, looking through a set of binos at the Iraqis on the other side. And he's sitting there for fucking weeks, right. Well, on the other side, he can clearly see an Iraqi soldier staring back at him with binos as well. So essentially the two dudes are just looking at each other, on the line, for weeks. Eventually the American gets bored, and figures he can start a conversation with the guy, right? So while they are looking at each other, he brings his hands up and slowly drops them down, imitating the question of 'Are you a paratrooper?' No response. So then he mimics crawling, asking 'Are you a grunt?' Again no response. Then he imitates a breaststroke action, imitating 'Are you a Frogman or Special Ops?' But still no response. Done with this shit, the American throws his arms down in disgust, at which point the Iraqi runs off the line in a panic. Doesn't make any sense right? But the Iraqi guy goes to his platoon commander and as he is repeating the hand motions, says, 'Sir! Sir! I just got a message from the Americans! They said that when the sun goes down [imitating hands falling], they're going to crawl over to our lines [imitating crawling], fuck us in the ass [imitating breaststroke], and there isn't a Goddamned thing we can do about it [imitating the lost-all-hope arm motion]!"

Dying laughing can't really describe the condition we found ourselves in after the telling. Miller finally got his breath together and said, "That was a good one Caldwell; you don't always come up with really good ones, but that was good!" The rest of us wiped tears from our eyes.

* * *

I wake up to Martin shaking me in my top bunk. "Vining, get up, you're going on the Jaker run today."

What the heck? We already figured out who was going yesterday and I had just gotten off post an hour ago. Oh well. "Good to go, Corporal, when are we leaving?"

Martin yells back from the door, COG radio in his hand, "An hour, you're gunning for *Redneck Ninja*."

Nice. Turret gunner in the rearmost vic, tons of dust to choke on. Groggy-eyed, I roll off the top, landing on my feet. Slip on my Frogs, sling the M27, and walk over to the head with my toiletries. I brush my teeth and make sure to get a good shave in, as higher-ups at Jaker and Geronimo are the worst when it came to shaves. It wouldn't matter if you had just won the Medal of Honor on a patrol, you'd better be shaven once you got back.

I grab my flak and lug it across the yard, to the Mat-V, dropping it in the back passenger seat. Sergeant Mike is running around, and so are the drivers, prepping the trucks, getting things ready. Caldwell is running back and forth between the trucks, doing radio checks on our channel and the company tac. I need to get my gunner's harness on, so I go into the COC, drape the black seatbelt contraption over my shoulder, while picking up a rectangular can of 7.62 ammunition, along with a Two-Forty. Walking out to the truck, I lay the harness next to my flak, then pull myself up, through the side door, into the armored turret, and lay the ammunition next to the gun pintle mount. Then I back out, take the Two-Forty to the front of the truck, and climb up the bumper and engine cover. I rest the gun in the mount, banging the front pintle in, locking the gun in place.

Gun locked in, I get some cereal and milk cartons from the little fridge in the hooch. Bringing it out to the truck, I stand and eat it there with Todd and Doc next to me. We make small talk while we wait to get going. Practically every Thursday, we convoy out down Shiner, to Jaker. There, the Sir meets with all the other officers at a meeting with the CO, while the platoon sergeants have their face to face with First Sergeant. We have odd chores and errands to do while there, wash the trucks, get mail, change out radios or anything else that can only be done at the company PB. Then we'd head over to Geronimo, the battalion FOB, where we'd stock up on class three supplies, actual food that we eat at Loy Kolay, not the UGR-Es or MREs. We might have some more chores there, but then we'd head back to Jaker, pick up the Sir, and back to Loy Kolay. Every week guys would switch out on gunning and driving, to give them a chance to get out of the PB.

Every grunt approaches being a turret gunner differently. Some guys enter from inside the truck, others climb up and in from outside. Some buckle the body harness underneath the flak, so if you're knocked unconscious, it won't accidentally unbuckle while the truck is rolling through the air. Others buckle it over their flak so they can easily get out of it if need be. Some use the gunner's seat, others see it as a sign of laziness and discard it entirely. Some like the joystick to swivel the turret, others prefer the crank. But every turret gunner understands how important the role is. He is essentially the eyes and ears of the heavy, lumbering, noisy truck. He can look out beyond the steel monster and see what the confined driver and VC cannot see, whether that be small-arms fire, a ditch they are about to roll into, or kids approaching asking for pens.

The Sir comes out and does a little finger twirl in the air. Oscar Mike. Drivers hike their way into their seats, VCs into theirs, and turret gunners buckle into the floors of their turret stands. Radio checks from *Bang Bus* go out to see if all the trucks are up and radios working. "*Redneck Ninja* up" … "*Black Holed Son* is up."

Bang Bus leading the way, the convoy rolls out the back gate, like Tetris trucks trying to get out of the small compound, with Martin holding the gate open and waving us through. When we clear the gate I slap the 7.62 belt into the Two-Forty and latch the feed cover down, putting it in condition three. My M27 is right by my side should the Two-Forty ever go down. Then I rotate the turret to the rear, to cover the rearward sector of the convoy.

Shiner is flat in some parts, but downright insane in others. Being in the turret allows you to feel every single bump and pothole that exists, bouncing up and down with each. From Loy Kolay the landscape turns to trees along the canal road, a lone mosque, then alternates between fresh fields and mud compounds.

A white Toyota drives up behind, steadily gaining on us. Three hundred meters … two fifty … two hundred. I yell down to Doc, "Hey we've got a vic from the rear, just FYI."

Doc yells back over the Oshkosh engine, "Gotcha, let me know if anything happens."

One hundred and fifty meters. I get behind the Two-Forty and train it directly on the windshield. Seventy meters … and closing. I drop the Two-Forty, muzzle skyward, eyes still on the car. I grab my M27, point it directly at this dude. Through the horseshoe reticle of my SDO, the driver in his man dress and pakol headgear looks stunned, putting on the brakes immediately, the car spewing dust all over the road. Slowly I drop the M27, then put it beside me. Machine guns get pointed at villagers all day long; that isn't scary. However, a personal rifle means business, and, more importantly, "Back the hell away from our convoy." Suicide bomber or not, we're not going to find out the hard way.

Some more landscape later, our little convoy turns right, passing through the Jaker business district, with all sorts of markets and shops open, people and tractors milling about. Soon PB Jaker comes into view, with its sandbagged post towers, razor-wire–topped double Hesco walls, with an entrance down a narrow alleyway. Over the radio I heard the Sir calling us in, "Chaos Main, this is Chaos Three Actual, request permission to EFL with three trucks, eight M-E, one M-O, and one N-E, over."

About five minutes later, waiting outside the main gate, "Roger, Chaos Three, permission granted." Gates opened up by the grunts on gate guard, I crank my turret around to 12 o'clock, and go condition four with the Two-Forty. Drop down into the truck, unhook the gunner's seat and wait until we are ground-guided into position. The helipad is visible from the vehicle pool, along with most of Charlie's trucks, all over the gravel motor pool, from the rest of the patrol bases, for the CO's meeting.

Doc starts uncuffing his sleeves. "Hey Vining, Todd make sure you guys uncuff your shit, before you leave the truck."

Higher-up territory. "Rah, Doc."

Every time I come to Jaker, I feel bad for my buddies living here. The poor bastards are living directly in the shadow of the CO's and the First Sergeant's wrath. Set times for chow, set times for haircuts, squads rotating in and out of patrolling, post, and resting. It seems like the command treats the guys like dogs, controlling their every move. It isn't the freedom of the patrol base, of us making our own rules and our own standards.

I take my flak off, laying it across the seat of the Mat-V, strip the gunner's harness off, grab my Oaklies and eight point cover, and my M27. "Hey Doc, I'm going to go see my buddy Spencer and go to the Mdub."

"Gotcha, be back here in an hour; we're going to roll to Geronimo for class three supplies."

Giving him a thumbs-up, I cross the gravel lot, past the Hesco barriers, and into one of the troop hooches. Spencer is asleep in his black sleeping bag, on the lower bunk. I shake him up a bit. "Spencer ... Spencer."

Groggily, he rolls over, and opens his eyes, "Oh, hey there, Vining!"

"How's it going man, I just got here with our mobile section."

He gets out of his bag and gives me a hug. "Well, good seeing you, buddy! I was wondering when you'd pop by here." He starts getting on his Frog suit. "I just got off post an hour ago, but I need to eat breakfast because they close the chow hall in twenty minutes, so come along with me."

Ah, off the old post cycle. I feel his pain. Spencer laces his boots up and grabs his M16A4, throwing it across his back, leading us out.

"Man, I didn't know they served breakfast here; must be nice!"

"Yeah, well that's the only thing they serve: the rest of the day is MREs or UGR-Es."

"That's cool. At Loy Kolay we got class three from Geronimo."

"Ah, you bastards at the PBs, it's such a shit show here at Jaker; they treat us like dogs."

"Yeah, I can tell. How long is your post cycle?"

"Oh, six hours, then six hours of rest, then twelve hours on a patrol, then repeat."

"Holy shit, man! That sucks. Like really sucks."

We are now in the line for chow.

"Oh, and they get us with working parties on that six hours of rest, too. So you're lucky if you can fit in three or four hours of sleep."

"Where the hell do you get your sleep then, man?"

"Well, we try to fit it in, during the patrolling ... usually there'll be time there. But if not, you're fucked. Last week I stayed up for forty-eight hours ... can you believe that shit?"

"Yeah, that sucks. Loy Kolay we only have three-hour posts and patrol once every two days or so. It's nice out there, man ... we're on our own."

The Pog chef is slopping soup and potato on our cardboard trays.

"Yeah, y'all undisciplined weirdos."

"You're just jealous!"

We take our seats at the metal tables within the concrete enclosure. Gunny Hart walks by and knees me in the thigh.

"Rah, Gunny! Good morning!"

"I hear you've been sucking off all the corpsmen, Vining. Is that true? Are you being a fag?"

I laugh. "Not at all, Gunny!"

"Yeah, who knows what you queers do out there at Loy Kolay. One of these days we'll catch you losers in a gay orgy!" He keeps on walking, M9 pistol on his thigh.

"Gunny is hilarious, ain't he."

"Yeah, he is. Last week Grotsky freaked out in the MWR because someone told him that his time on the computer was up. Went condition one. Someone told Gunny and he went running over there, drawing his pistol, and says 'Oh yeah! This is going to be fun!'" Spencer makes a hand motion of his hand in the air while waddling back and forth, imitating Gunny Hart.

"Aahh, that's gold right there! I was thought Grotsky was a little bitch. Did you hear him on the company tac the other day? When Karamam's mobile section rolled a vic into a wadi?"

Spencer replied, "No, what happened?"

"They were going back and forth over the net about whether or not some Kevlar was still in the truck. Gunny came over the net and screamed, 'This is Chaos Seven! I don't give a flying fuck about whether a damned Kevlar is fucking missing! I need to know if all the Marines in there are alive!'"

Spencer laughed, "Yep! That's gunny for ya!"

We munch away at the breakfast. Almost done now, higher-ups always want us to get out of the little building to make space for other guys coming in.

"How's your wife? Any word on the kid?"

"She's good. And no, she had an early miscarriage, back in July."

"That's shitty man, I'm sorry."

"It happens, life happens. How about that sweet little thing you got up in that maple-syrup–making place?"

I chuckle.

"You mean Montreal? Lynn is good, haven't talked to her in about two weeks, sat-phone at the PB has been down. I was hoping to Skype her today."

We get up, throw our trays in the garbage bag hanging by the door. "Well, you do that there, Vining. Have a little look-see with your little liberal ball of fun … tell her I give my condolences to her peace-loving Canadian friends."

"That I will, Spencer. That I will. I'll leave you to your Cuban. I'll see ya buddy."

We hug and I head off toward the computer and phone tent they called the MWR. Crunching across the gravel, I notice a sign on the porta-johns: "If there is any graffiti found in here, the heads will be secured. By order of Chaos Company First Sergeant." Secured? Where else would the guys shit? In the burn pit? Whatever, they're lucky they even have porta-johns in the first place.

Entering the MWR tent, the air-conditioning blasts out of a vent. There are four computers and three phones that guys can use to get back home with, arranged on a wraparound set of tables, next to the tent wall. Some books are stacked on a shelf to the left of the doorway, next to one of the company headquarters guys who is giving out passes on the computers. I sign my name, and sit down behind one of the computers, my M27 sandwiched between my legs, muzzle to the ground. The computer thing looks like an alien contraption, the keyboard, screen, how the one is inputted into the other. I almost have no clue what to do, but it slowly comes back to me. Checking Facebook, my email, seeing what's going on back home. Lynn happens to be online, thank God!

Miles: Hey! Babes!!!

Lynn: Omg! jababy! You're online!

Miles: Yes! If only for a while. Can you get on Skype? I can talk there too.

Lynn: Of course!

I sign into Skype, slip the headphones on, and see her come online a second later. I initiate the video call and she picks up.

"Hey! What's up?"

"Nothing! I was just about to go to sleep, but thank God you're online and I caught you."

"Yeah! We're at a rear base sort of thing, with internet."

"Nice! I was really getting worried, I haven't heard from you in like two weeks!"

"Yeah ... our sat-phone crapped out a while back; thing is garbage and we can't get a new one, but I'm glad this Skype call can work!"

"Me too! How've you been? Did you get my care packages? And I sent you like two letters."

"Yes, I did! Thank you so much for the magazines, I've read through *Nat Geo* like five times already, and I'm eating those little snacks you sent me. But I only got one letter so far. I'll let you know when I get the other one."

"Good! And everything else?"

"Eh, just patrolling, lots of post, working with the Afghan police, a tough lot. Not much really, nothing is going on in our AO."

"Jababy, that's a good thing! I don't want you in danger and stuff, although I know you like it."

Story of significant others for all the history of human warfare. "I'll be fine. Thank you, though. How is Montreal? And college?"

"It's going good, starting to get colder every day, but I'm happy with my roommates and friends, our political action club has some events coming up that I'm helping to plan and support, so I'm keeping busy."

Cold ... I wish I knew what that feeling was again. "Nice, nice ... that sounds like everything is going good then. I hope you and Natalie are on friendlier terms?"

"Yes, yes we are, we had a bit of a tiff last …"

"Vining! We're leaving for Geronimo early! Let's go!" Martin is at the door.

"Baby? I have to go, we're leaving early, I'm sorry …"

"Noo, noo, it's okay, it's great that we get to talk to each other! I'm just happy that you're safe."

"Yes, that's right, and you too, I loves you!"

"Love you too!"

I turn in the wooden computer block, and jog over to our trucks. The rest of the guys are already getting flakked up. "Damn Vining, always waiting on you!" Martin is already clipping his Kevlar chinstrap together.

"Sorry about that, Corporal, I thought we were going to be here longer".

"Turd … Get ready, we're taking *Bang Bus* and *Black Holed Sun* to Geronimo for a supply run."

Quickly I put the gunner's harness on, clipping it into the circular buckle at my waist, throw my flak on without Velcroing it, and climb up around the Mat-V into the turret. Finishing off my flak, securing the harness to the turret stand, clipping my Kevlar, I sit in the truck while Doc ground-guides us out. Sergeant Mike and the Sir are staying behind while we go to the battalion FOB at Geronimo, to get a resupply of food and goods with the two trucks.

As soon as the truck clears the gate, I stand up in the turret, and put the Two-Forty in condition three, rounds on feed tray. Driving to Geronimo from Jaker is like a day ride, the area between the two so heavily patrolled by us, the AUP, and the ANA, that you really don't have to worry about much when it comes to IEDs or small-arms fire. The trip is mostly through roads lined with compounds, tall grass and trees, unlike the spacious fields surrounding Shiner. At Geronimo, we encounter desert surrounding the FOB. You can see the base itself from miles around, with the giant observation balloon floating in the air above it. Rolling into it is always the most tedious thing in the world, because you have to wait ten minutes just to get permission to EFL, then you have to roll through the crazy serpentine Hescos the perimeter has going on. Once we get to the motor pool, we park our trucks, leave Todd as a gear guard, and walk over to the chow hall, as not all of us have been quick enough to eat earlier at Jaker.

Jaker is bad when it comes to regulations on the actual base, but at least you know there's a war on. Geronimo is Pog heaven. It has showers, a laundromat, a fully stocked MWR with pool table, a chow hall the size of an indoor basketball court with the high ceiling. About the only thing it doesn't have is any sort of convenience store with AAFES coins as currency. Minus the controlled detonations that take place outside of the FOB, and the firing from the arty on Fiddler's Green, it is entirely possible to live at Geronimo, or Camp Cupcake, for an entire deployment, and never interact with a single Afghan, or realize there's even a war going on.

But the chow hall is nice. Serving ice-cream, cold sodas, grilled sandwiches, even fake beer. We walk in, looking really out of place, with our grimy Frogs, compared to all the other clean Frogs, and cammie-laden figures around us. Except for Martin: his Frogs usually look pretty good. Staff NCOs stare down their noses at us, while we slowly go through the line to pile food on our trays. This is almost a double bonus for me, a small breakfast, and a legitimate lunch. Looking good. Walking back to our tables, we set our food down, and dig in. It tastes great. Although about halfway through, some staff sergeant in cammies walks right up to Doc, and starts lifing him out because his cover is sitting on the table, a typically garrison no-no. The absurdity of the scenario fills me with rage. Does this piece-of-shit staff NCO really consider it his soul-bound duty to make sure dirty covers stay off tables? Does he really have nothing better to do, while forward deployed, to Nawa District? The week before we heard that Garner from PB Mamakhan was asked why he didn't have any boot bands on, while on a foot patrol, by a staff NCO in Charlie. Is that really the most appropriate thing to be going about, while on a foot patrol? Christ, it almost seems the damned establishment is more concerned about pressing uniforms, than slaying bodies. It's enough dealing with the Afghan people and trying to close with the Taliban: we don't need the added bullshit of those above us.

Quickly de-escalating from the Heil-Staff-Sergeant-Hitler, our motley group goes back to the trucks and takes them over to class three, on the supply section of the base. After we load up *Bang Bus* to the brim with canned goods, meats, and cartons of all sorts of goodies, we load back in the trucks, call our DFL to Deadwalker Main, and push back off to Jaker. Halfway there, *Bang Bus*, with Miller driving, comes upon a shepherd with his flock of sheep blocking the entire road. Miller waits for the flock to clear the road, and when it gets to the other side, he starts the lumbering Mrap with mine roller forward, but not before a lone sheep sprints back across the road, in front of the mine roller. It doesn't have a chance, and is cut in half by the 100-pound wheels. As we pass by the flock, I look out my turret and see the poor sucker, dead in the road, with the shepherd shaking his fists at us. Poor guy. Poor sheep.

Back at Jaker, we wait for the Sir and Sergeant Mike to be done with their business with the CO, and First Sergeant. Once complete, we mounted up, and roll out the front gate. I wave at some of my buddies standing post as we drive past. The poor bastards, they probably make them police-call the sand near the chow hall.

Condition three again, and we're out into the Green Zone of Nawa, driving past the markets to Shiner. Once north, and on Shiner, we push northward, rolling over the bumpy potholes, and swerving past tractors driving ahead of us. The sun is lowering in the sky, casting that odd glow over everything, and pushing out shadows longer than they should be pushed out. Facing to the rear in the turret, choking up dust, I am holding on to the turret and the Two-Forty, trying to stay in place, being bumped all over the hatch. Coming up on my left, across the Shiner canal, is a group of burkha-clad women, five of them, almost lost in the mix of the dust and the odd glow of the sunlight. All of them are carrying baskets on their heads, probably coming from the market, being that they don't have any males with them. Of course, all of them have their facemasks down, so they can really only look at the outside world through tiny eye slits, that the outside world can't even look through. All of course, but one … one has her facemask turned back over her head, so her entire face is visible up to her forehead. She is the last of the group, no doubt why she's got away with it. I am astonished. Crazed. An Afghan woman's face … I have never seen one before. We've been in-country for months, and the most I've ever seen are the burkha ghosts on patrol or on post. The next thing she does blows me away. She looks directly at me, the rear turret gunner, and smiles, the biggest smile I have ever seen. She is young, probably around my age, and she looks beautiful. I am so speechless that I can't even wave back or anything. Just completely floored with this performance. Everything I have ever been taught about Afghan women, and experienced, completely contradicts this very moment. And she stays like that, just smiling, until the next curve in the road takes the whole group of women out of my field of view.

Turning onto the engineering bridge that connects Shiner to the PB, our little convoy pulls round to the back gate. Dust still spewing everyone, I swing the two-forty to the 12 o'clock position, and push the feedtray cover up, removing the belt of ammunition. As we are ground-guided into base, I pull the gun down into the truck, and sit in the passenger seat until the truck comes to a standstill. Bringing the machine gun and ammunition to the COC, Nwankwo approaches me: "Vining, go relieve Kugler up on post; he's been up there all day."

I simply nod, keep my flak on, and make my way up to the guard tower. Exchanging the familiar changeover pleasantries with Kugler, he climbs down the ladder, happy to be finally off. I put my Kevlar on, leaving my chinstrap unbuttoned, and lean out one of the post windows. The day is still

Standing outside my barracks on the Charlie Company catwalk are me, Lynn, Spencer, with his wife on the right. Bags are packed and stacked, ready to go. I'm holding a Kindle, while Lynn is holding me. (*Photograph Kay Creech*)

Kevin and Abby Schranz at their wedding after our first deployment. (*Photograph Abby Schranz*)

Waiting at Twentynine Palms in the staging area for Range 400 before the first deployment. In the background is a convoy of seven-tons driving back toward Camp Wilson. We would sleep on the ground next to our packs.

Bang Bus is down. We drove over a culvert that collapsed when our left tire sunk into it from the weight. The front of the MRAP is equipped with a mine roller, a device designed to initiate pressure plates so the main truck doesn't take the blast.

Kneeling down to offer a small girl candy in a village in Nawa. Vining used to always keep extra candy while on patrol and offer it out to children. The rest of the patrol is in the background, talking with several villagers.

Taking a knee at Taylor's Soldier's Cross during the memorial service held in a hangar at the lower base camp at Bridgeport.

Machine-gunners Richardson, Kugler, and Schranz taking a break with Charlie Company at Bridgeport. Note the upright ski poles in the background and enormous "Mickey Mouse" boots under the galoshes.

Crossing a danger area where One Alpha is taking fire from the eastern wadi (left side of picture). Crouching is Hefner; Leonard is about to provide fire. The patrol is running to the parked Mat-V as a halfway point. (*Screen grab from DOD Media, Sergeant Eric Wilterdink*)

Running off the Fifty Threes on the Naw Zad heliborne mission; the platoon is creating a security zone around the bird. Mounted on the Marine in front is the Thor ECM used to mitigate radio-transmitted IED ignition systems. (*Screen grab from HM1 Martin*)

Ayr poses inside his Mat-V. Notice how cramped the vehicle is inside, with barely enough room for weapons and gear. We would often have to spend entire days and nights hunkered in these armored vehicles. (*Photograph Anthony Ayr*)

Sergeant Daniel Vasselian takes a break for a photograph while on patrol. (*Photograph DOD Media, Sgt. Eric Wilterdink*)

What remains of Lance Corporal Erickson's MRAP after it has been hit by a SVBIED. Notice that the gunner's turret is completely severed.

Inside the Bravo Company office on the wall is the whiteboard where Vasselian jotted this motivating phrase the morning of the patrol in which he was killed outside Compound 34 in Whiskey 7 Delta.

Schranz smiling behind his M240 while holding his position at a Hesco fortification. The red tab on his right shoulder is a protruding CAT tourniquet that could be quickly accessed in event of injury.

Kevin's section on the second deployment, at PB Boldak. Kevin is second from right, kneeling with his M240 pointed toward the camera. Sergeant Martin is standing center. The Hesco fortifications behind are what protected many of the bases in Helmand.

The mass grave containing the unidentified remains of Taylor, Vanderwork, Muchnick, Fenn, Wild, Ripperda, and Martino in Arlington National Cemetery (Section 60, Grave 10464). Wild's body is buried off to the left of the picture (Section 60, Grave 10460). (*Photograph Beth Jones*)

Charlie Company veterans gathered around Schranz's mother (at center) during his memorial service in Nashua, NH. At far left in the blues are his brothers.

Vining (right) assists a Free Burma Ranger medic (left), while coordinator Hossanah Valentine ventilates a mortally wounded SDF soldier outside the town of Baghouz, Syria. (*Photograph Free Burma Rangers*)

After Schranz's death, Abby offered Vining the use of his M1 Garand for a historical live-fire recreation for the YouTube series *TFB TV*. Vining is in the orange jacket with the rifle. (*Photograph Marlena Michael Photography*)

hot, but not as bad as when we were at Jaker; that really sucked. Kids are swimming in the Shiner canal, jumping into the murky brown water. A car or two passes by on the road, then a jingle truck slowly snakes its way along the dirt road, some Urdu music blaring out the cab. The sun is just above the horizon, casting a cool glow over the valley, and the compounds. I hear some children's voices below. Looking down, I expect to see Ayakula, but instead it's Pritchna, and a friend, walking past the Hesco, coming up to our post, cautiously.

"*Salaam!*" I figure she'll run, like she always does. But no, to my surprise, she just blushes, smiling up at me. "*Tsyengia yaast?*" How are you?

She looks shier than ever before, but she actually responds, "*Zhe shayam! Taso tsyengia yaast?*"

This is an actual conversation at this point.

"*Zhe haum shayam!*"

And so we talk. I ask her about her family, and she asks me about mine, sort of going back and forth. I throw her a bottle of water, which she promptly drinks and tosses away. Then Ayakula calls to her from the compound, probably telling her to come home for dinner. She responds, looks up at me, and starts running back to her house. I smile, and look away. Progress, has indeed been made.

* * *

"Mauler! Vining" You fuckin' ready yet?" Paulie is at the doorway to the hooch.

"Yes, Paul! We're coming right now, just getting our assault packs!"

Paul is looking at us closely. "Hurry the hell up then! The Sir is waiting on you fuckers for the briefing!"

Quickly we run out, Paul at our heels, across the chillout area to the COC. The Sir, Kugler, Caldwell, Nwankwo, Miller, and Wietosh are all waiting for us.

"Everyone up, Lance Corporal Paul?"

Paul does a final check over. "Yes sir, everyone is here."

After reading a little something in his notebook, the Sir looks up, "Cool, let's get started then." Moving to the huge overlay map at the back wall of the COC, he points to the very northeastern tip. "Listen up, guys, this is going to be the farthest op we've ever done. We're going to be on our own for much of it, so everything is going to have to be screwed on tight for this one. This is probably the only patrol we'll go on where we will be absolutely expecting contact. According to Weapons at Spin Ghar," pointing to PB

Spin Ghar on the map, "as long as we push past the forty-eight easting," pointing to the forty-eight grid line on the map, "and into Trek Nawa, the desert essentially," pointing to the open area at the very top right corner of the map, "actually, most of where we will be patrolling is completely off this map ... over here somewhere," pointing to the actual wall above it. "We'll be taking Vining with the Hiide system, Mauler, Kugler with the two-forty, Caldwell with the Prick-one-seventeen, and Paul leading. The rest of us will be staged back at this AUP outpost, here," also pointing off the map. "We'll be forming up the convoy security while you guys push out into the desert and look around for someone to shoot at you. Any delays either which way, we'll support you with the vics."

Up until this point, we have yet to go through with a mounted/dismounted operation as large as this venture. The concept isn't difficult: drive far out into the desert, dismount, patrol out from there, using the vehicles as a base, sustain ourselves for two days, then come back. For most patrol bases and Fobs, this is a walk in the park. However, for Loy Kolay, with all fifteen of us on it, it will be a complex balancing act of timing, men, and vehicles. Every hour we spend away from the PB, it has to be maintained and guarded by the guys left behind. We can't stretch them too thin either.

"Once we establish contact with this AUP outpost up north, we'll work with them, sending satellite patrols throughout the day, back in these villages, and areas here."

All in the room realize just how wrong things could go on this op: everything from a rolled vehicle, running out of water way out there, being stuck in the desert, and, of course, the small-arms and IED threat.

The Sir ends by going over the many individual details of the operation such as radio freqs, timelines, equipment, and air cover. This all complete, he says, "Alright gents, tomorrow morning, be ready to get this show on the road, zero four DFL."

We all nod in agreement. It is late in the afternoon and there are still a lot of things to get done before we can turn in for the night. I uneasily stand my post that night, thinking about the next day. Filling up the generator, I walk back to the hooch. Caldwell is in the COC, looking at something on the SiprNet. That poor bastard is always in the COC, always up late at night. But our whole patrol base runs on the intel he filters and looks through. Stripping off my Frogs, laying them at the foot of the top bunk, I climb up into it. The smell of the JP8 on my skin doesn't bother me anymore.

Lights. Lights on. Just like in boot camp with the horrendous "Lights! Lights! Lights!" human alarm clock going off. The ceiling is awash in light from the fluorescent bulbs. Martin is saying, "Alright people, you know what needs to be done. DFL is in one hour." Caldwell grabs Mauler and Todd, and has them go out to the trucks with him to troubleshoot comm. It always seems like comm is failing, whenever and for whatever, on foot or in the trucks. I help Paul load some extra 7.62 ammunition into the trucks, for the turret gunners. Everything that we normally take on a mounted mission, plus this time we take more. Whether it be batteries, ammunition, water, MREs, it doesn't matter, because we are going to be out for several days and will have to be self-supporting out in the desert.

Calling everyone back to the COC, the Sir does one final check on comms, trucks, machine guns, Thors and personnel. Then he turns to the map, and traces our route to the AUP patrol base: out the back gate, over the bridge, down Shriner, up Coors, past Spin Ghar, through to Red Dog, and then into the desert. Pushing his finger along the dirt roads and shortcuts, the map depresses with the pressure of his finger, as it draws along the various routes. His eyes are looking intently at the plastic overlay, trying to pierce the material, trying to superimpose himself on those very roads. How many thousands of platoon commanders and patrol leaders the province over have done this same routine, of route selection? And of those thousands of leaders, how many of them would trade everything, from that point on, to go back to that moment in front of that overlay, to take this route instead of that, look at this village instead of that one, interrogate compound 25 instead of 45.

The Sir whips around, looking at all of us. "Let's do this."

About time, it is still dark outside. Not horribly hot yet, but nice and cool. Enough to feel a slight breeze against you as you walk to your truck. I climb up the Mrap ladder, cranking the latch closed behind me, while squeezing the inside combat locks down as well. Kugler is already in there, with his Two-Forty between his legs. He is in his very element, machine gun in tow, ready for a day of lead-slinging and body-slaying. Under the red ceiling light of the Mrap, we look at each other and smile. Bumping fists, I say, "This is it, dude!"

Radio checks, squeaking turrets going chug, chug, chug, the truck lurches forward and we're off. My M27 is between my legs, right hand on the stock, left on my knee. Bouncing over the dirt roads and into holes, the lumbering truck sways back and forth, turning here and there. Out of the rear blast windows, the Mat-V behind us bounces up and down as well, with its headlights drifting aimlessly in the darkness. At times like this, you wonder if an IED is going to turn your world to a hulking mess of steel and collided armor, as your body gets helplessly tossed about the truck like a rag doll. You think, "What will it feel like? Is there anything I can do now to help prevent the pain later?" Eventually you just resign yourself to the fate of surprise, and realize there really isn't a damn thing you can do about it from inside the monster truck.

Halting in the gloom, Martin calls back to us, "We're here!"

Game time.

Kugler and I push out of the Mrap, jumping onto the soft dirt. On a small hill is a whitewashed concrete compound that we have checked out before. The compound has two guard towers, is about a quarter of the size of Loy Kolay, and is run by a small AUP contingent, on the edge of Helmand civilization. To the south is a sprawling village, with random numbers painted on the corrugated-steel and wooden doors of the houses. Later on, we learn this is how Two Three identified compounds when they entered a village for the first time.

The sun is barely breaking the horizon across a small village, a sun rising in the graveyard of empires. No time to commiserate now, though. The trucks park around the patrol base with the turret gunners and drivers staying with them, all the dismounts walking up this steep incline to the patrol base. We greet the AUP commander at the gate. We see there were around ten or fifteen of the AUP along with their single Danger Ranger truck. All have AKs, with maybe a PKM or two in the guard posts. Hindi music blasts out the post windows. The base has a single squat toilet located beneath the southern post. Mauler decides to take a dump while Paul and Kugler laugh and coo at him because he has to complete his deed with the door open.

While the Sir goes into the AUP commander's little office, the rest of us, me, Paul, Mauler, Kugler and Caldwell, sit on the concrete step just outside. The AUP hasn't had much interaction with us, so they are walking around us and our gear, pointing at our Thors, Two-Forties, camelbacks and making all sorts of comments in Pashtu. Once in a while they twirl their hand in the classic, rural Pashtun way, essentially asking us what this or that is for. We attempt to talk to them with the same hand motions and basic words that we know. But how do you explain what an electronic countermeasure is to someone straight out of Hamlet's era? At the end of the day, you really just can't show someone who doesn't grasp electricity how a jamming signal is emitted from such a sold piece of steel.

"Dude, we're on the edge of the world out here," Paul muses.

Kugler pipes up, "Yeah, man, probably the last time these villagers out here saw a white guy was when the Russians were here or something."

"I mean, do you see the desert past all this? It's like there's nothing out there, just straight-up desert." Paul is pretty much right. Beyond the AUP PB, the desert extends over low rolling hills, out into nothingness. Well essentially it is Trek Nawa and then maybe Marjah District, where Weapons and Alpha are operating.

The adrenaline pump from earlier in the morning is wearing off, and I am getting tired in the afternoon sun, with all my gear on. No one has said to take it off, and we don't know when we'll have to leave for a patrol.

But then the Sir comes out. "Alright guys, this is what is happening. Just talked with the commander with Nasser here, and he is willing to give up a couple of his men for our dismounted patrols today and tonight. Tomorrow we'll push out in the trucks, check out more of the villages past that small patch of desert to the north. We'll rotate guys in and out of watching the trucks and patrolling, so everyone gets a chance to rest while the others are out on foot."

Sounds like a solid enough plan.

Standing up, radios are checked and weapons go condition one. The Thor feels just as heavy as ever. I notice Kugler is putting in a fat dip, so I call out to him, "Hey man, mind if I get a pinch?"

He looks up at me, puzzled. "You don't dip Vining."

"Today dude, I do. This Thor sucks."

He finishes placing the one in his mouth, shrugs, and hands the now-clipped can to me. "Have at it. But don't throw up, newbie."

Popping the can, I pinch a solid amount of the miniature leaves between my thumb and index finger, quickly stuffing it in the left side of my mouth, between my cheek and my gum. At first nothing, but then an instant feeling of the nicotine surges through my mouth and quickly overwhelms my face, and then my head. Aaaaahhhhh, this is why they do it. For an instant, the Thor disappears.

Mauler goes down to the trucks and grabs two cases of water for the AUP coming out with us. It is sort of like a bribe, giving them water so they can patrol. They probably could use their own water, but they know they will get extra from us if all they say is no water means no patrolling. What do they need the water for anyways? They literally have nothing on their bodies compared to our flaks, radios, Sapi plates, and a combat load's worth of ammunition.

The patrol leaves friendly lines, and we push through the desert. Unlike Nawa, this is just hill after hill of nothingness, sort of like Twentynine Palms but overseas. It is uncanny, like every hill is hiding something. I know Nawa, and I can tell if something is amiss or not, but this, this moon terrain is the unknown and I don't know the particulars of bad or good signs. But regardless, the patrol pushes on, in our little range file, with the AUP interspaced throughout the line. Eventually a village comes into view, but before it is a large concrete container, about the size of a small swimming pool, like a reservoir. It is surrounded by trees, and right between a couple of dried-out fields. There is no entrance, so it is probably an old water or crop container of some kind, left there for farmers to use.

Puzzled, we scan the insides, and the edges of it, looking for any sign of IEDs, but find nothing. Cautiously, one by one, the patrol jumps into the container. It is absolutely time for a security halt. We have been walking for two straight hours. The Sir is back at the trucks, monitoring communications to our own patrol base, but is having comm issues. Over the radio this sounds hilarious, especially as Caldwell is our RO on this op, and he's standing on the concrete wall, with his 117 on his head, trying to get a strong enough signal to communicate on. Every five seconds the radio blares out with the Sir attempting to say something, but instead getting lost in radio-speak. Back at Loy Kolay, Nwankwo is also trying to get his own speech through the radio, but all we hear is "Radio …broken."

Bursting out laughing, this is probably the funniest thing we've seen since the Taliban got on a captured AUP radio and were shit-talking the AUP, while the AUP were shit-talking the Taliban, all on the same channel.

Paulie says, "The Sir is shitting his pants right now with how pissed he is, and he's probably blaming Caldwell too!"

Caldwell shakes his head. "He's always doing this! Whenever he gets on the radio, he fucks something up, and then blames me somehow. Last time he zeroed out a whole Prick-one-nineteen without even telling me."

Kugler smiles. "Golden man, this is just pure fucking gold!"

The totality of the problem isn't good at all. Middle of the desert, nowhere near any ISAF installation or patrol base, five dismounts, and our comm is shot. That means no medevac, no calling for support, no way for a QRF or quick extract. Alone and unafraid. Literally. But to us, in that moment, we find it entertaining, hilarious even, at the thought that we have practically no communications past the Sir at this moment. We try making a radio check with the Sir, but get nothing back. Because of this, Paul hands me a white star cluster to pop over our position, signifying to any ISAF forces in the area that we are without communications.

Finally, a radio check from the Sir, who can then pass anything back to Loy Kolay. Oscar Mike people. I turn to the AUP guys with us, who really look like they are stationed at some forgotten outpost you see in the old-time Westerns, almost written off the map. The guy has a tired look on his face, and doesn't appear to share our enthusiasm to slay bodies.

I ask him, "*Delta eshta, Taliban cheri day?*"

He responds by telling us to follow him. So we follow him. Usually every Afghan replies with a standard "*Delta Taliban neshta!*" so this is quite welcoming. Such phrases really play havoc with our counterinsurgency efforts among the local populace.

Over dry, cracked fields, past a herd of camels, into one cluster of compounds, then another mud-walled compound, where we stop to drink some *chai* with a family. Then, finally, we come to this T-shaped intersection. The AUP guy I was talking to earlier walks us to what appears to be a giant ditch, on the side of the road. He points inside of it, "*Delta Taliban day.*"

Kugler pushes past on the other side, Paul goes over to the right, Mauler to the left, I to the remaining side, setting my Thor down. Caldwell pulls rear security.

"What the hell are we looking at?" Mauler says to no one in particular.

At the bottom of this ditch are pieces of clothing, and a burnt-out motorcycle. Our AUP looks at us and hand-motions a bomb from the air exploding on the ground.

Paul pipes up, "So we came all this fucking way, just to see some fucked-up bike that got hit by a JDam?"

Looking at it some more, it honestly appears so.

Slowly, the patrol pushes back, back to the patrol base. We take a completely separate route, practically parallel to the one we came in on, 500 meters to the north. Past compounds, fields, and then desert, then to the patrol base where the trucks are still idling in place. The Sir comes out of his truck, immediately wiping sweat off his face from just exiting the thing, and greets Paul. The two of them climb into the back of *Bang Bus*, and go over the patrol and what we've seen. Which is nothing, nothing important.

At *Black Holed Son*, I crank open the back passenger door, jump in the seat, unVelcro my flak but keep it around my body. The air-conditioning feels insanely good.

Todd turns from the driver's seat, "Good walk there, Vining?"

"I guess ... just saw some dude that got blown to bits by a JDam, otherwise pretty boring and uneventful."

He nods, turning back to looking out the windshield. "Typical Nawa brother ... typical Nawa." He gets that right: nothing seems to happen here.

Evening is approaching, and the next dismounted patrol is gearing up to go out. I will stay back with the trucks for this one. Outside the Sir and Paul gather up the guys for the night patrol, completing their PCCs and PCIs. Radio checks confirmed, and the patrol pushes out. After we combat-lock the doors to all the trucks except *Bang Bus*, we watch them disappear into the green night of my NVGs, slowly receding from view over the hill next to the AUP PB. Pulling the feedtray cover up, I feel for the belt of ammunition on the tray of the Two-Forty, brass to the grass, all the way to the right. Satisfied I have a condition three weapon system, I rotate the turret to face the village next to the PB. I focus on the outline of the compounds. A dog walks between them every now and then, a figure comes out, looks to be taking a piss, shakes himself off and goes back inside. Then I wheel the turret round to a different angle so I'm covering as much as possible around the truck. Weitoish is taking in radio checks from the patrol, in addition to our COC back at Loy Kolay.

The night air gets chilly, so I wrap my Gortex jacket around me, making me slightly warmer, but also making me drowsy from the warmth. I take off the jacket, only to get too cold. Putting it back on, I get too warm, and repeat the vicious cycle, while staring through my NVGs and rotating the turret again. Weitoish says something to me. I barely respond. He punches me in the leg to stay awake. I affirmatively respond now. Hour after hour, we sit there, trying to keep each other awake. I see some odd figure down by the canal, shaped like a person, a donkey, or even a combination of the two.

"Weitoish, check this shit man, I think someone is coming onto us ..." I swap with him in the turret and he peers at the object when I point it out to him.

"Vining ... switch with me on radio watch. You literally just confused a bucket of water for an Afghan."

Ouch. Stupid mistake.

"Patrol's heading back now dude."

The sun is now cresting the horizon. The village has woken up hours ago, coming to life for the crops that need to be cajoled from the Helmand sand. Sir is leading the patrol back, somewhat triumphantly, like the good officer he is. Behind him, a single-file column of sorry bastards struggles down the hill, ready to collapse at any moment. The AUP look fine though; they might have even taken a nap on the VCP they took out. After a brief huddle by the trucks, with the Sir dispatching some solid debrief points, the guys split up back to their trucks.

Todd cranks open up the back door of *Bang Bus*, climbing inside, looking completely furious.

"What's up, brother? Fun night?"

"The fucking Sir was a damned idiot, the entire patrol. That fucking bitch didn't even realize what was happening half the damned time." He peels off his flak from his glistening Frog top, a sweet odor filling the inside of the air-conditioned truck. "I was in the rear of the patrol with Paul, and Paul misses a step and falls into a fucking ditch, like ten feet to the bottom.

I go back to help him; meanwhile the Sir doesn't even look back, like he usually does."

This frustrates me. The Sir, like most officers, can analyze a village or the enemy's movements to the minutest detail of scrutiny, come up with the most intricate of plans, but yet be incapable of performing a simple action like scanning behind you on a foot patrol, to make connecting files with the guy behind you. Because, I don't know, he could have fallen into a ten-foot ditch, or have been knifed by some guy in the shadows. Case in point.

"Of course, by the time I help Paul out of the ditch, the patrol is fucking gone, and I've obviously got the damned Thor, so they're pretty much fucked without it. We start walking in the general direction of them, finally getting up to them about 500 meters away, and they're all clusterfucked in a circle, with the Sir asking Paulie, 'Where the hell were you guys?' Paul says, 'Right in that fucking ditch where you bastards left us 500 meters that way.' Of course they got into an argument, with Paul pretty much winning, but the Sir telling him to shut up. So then we push on to the VCP, where this sketch-as-fuck dude comes in; we search him, and he has an Iranian passport, with Pakistani rupees, Nasser tells us he sure as hell isn't from the area, and the AUP even get pissed at him. And what does Sir do? He lets him go. Fucking pussy, dude."

That sucks for Todd. Thank God I wasn't on it though. Misery is always so much more fascinating when looked on from the outside.

After we sweat out the rest of the day, the Sir decides to push out from the PB with all three trucks to probe further into Trek Nawa. Mounting up, I take the turret in *Bang Bus*, leading the way. Over fields, down small alleyways between mud compounds, into the open desert we push forward, not really seeing much of anything. A few white Toyota Corollas drive down this way and that, motorcycles peel in and out of compounds, farmers walk to their fields, but nothing significant stands out. Our little convoy pushes over a smaller dirt road into a village that we haven't even heard of. I'm looking over the road, and see a sort of culvert in the middle.

"Hey careful here, Miller, there looks to be a culvert or something across the road."

Martin yells up to me from the A-driver's seat, "Shut the fuck up, Vining, and let him drive."

I chuckle a bit. "Nah, we'll keep an eye on it, see if it holds the mine roller, appreciate it."

Slowly, slowly, the mine roller goes over the culvert, with no significant change in the ground beneath. Then the front tires roll over it, very slowly. Nothing happens. Solid travels. I focus my mind on this hilltop over to the right: it looks remotely suspicious with a child sitting at the top of it. Always be wary of children on hills, they just might be a King. From the turret stand though, I feel a sort of angle happening with it, as if *Bang Bus* itself is tilting one way. It gradually gets more and more, so I start to subside into the turret.

"What the fu ..."

Crunk! Bam! All 30,000 pounds of *Bang Bus* crash onto the back left wheel, and instead of seeing the road, I instantly see the blue sky, from the front windshield inside the truck.

"Vining! Get the hell down!"

I'm already in though. "I'm already down, Martin!"

Out the back windows of the blast doors, I see nothing but earth. Then I hear some clambering on the right side of the truck, as the Sir all of a sudden appears as if out of nowhere against Martin's A-driver door.

"MARTIN! OPEN THIS FUCKING DOOR! RIGHT NOW!"

Martin tries and tries, but even his jacked arms can't move the 200-pound door, now at an angle to the sky, "I CAN'T, SIR! I LITERALLY CAN'T OPEN IT!"

The Sir is now banging on the door window with the buttstock of his M4, I don't know why. With the angle and my entire world at an oblique angle, I feel if I breathe too hard, it'll be enough to cause the whole truck to roll the rest of the way over.

He circles round and opens the back blast doors, completely level and sunk into the ground by this point. "Vining, Martin, get out of here!"

We don't need him to tell us that. Martin and I crawl out the back, leaving Miller still inside in the driver's seat. Looking back, the whole rear left portion of *Bang Bus* has sunk into the ground up to the spare box containers, with the ladder leading into the blast doors bent upward. Apparently the culvert couldn't withstand the weight of the truck, took the weight up until the rear wheels were clearing it, and then caved in with them. This is why we need Road Safety Standards people.

The Sir and Paul organize a hasty rescue attempt. The sucky thing about this situation is that we are really pushing our AO boundaries, so if stuff went south, the questions afterward from the chain of command would be fast and furious. In addition, calling QRF and a wrecker for something like this would aggravate them further, because they'd have to be going so far out. So in other words, if Sir wants to keep his job, *Bang Bus* had better be pulled out, quick, fast, and in a hurry.

Black Holed Sun and *Redneck Ninja* drive round the wretched culvert, while Martin, Paul, and I take out the towing chains and winches, fastening them onto the front edge of the mine roller also attached to *Bang Bus*.

Once fixed, the two vehicles start backing up, with their *deet … deet … deet* vibrating around us. Some kids have gathered to watch the stuck Americans unfuck themselves from their local uninspected culvert. How dare they not rate those things to withstand an Mrap. They knew we'd probably be in this turf since late 2001. Get with the times!

Bang Bus gets yanked this way and that by *Black Holed Sun* and *Redneck Ninja*, revving up to get halfway out of the culvert, only to sink back in. When everything looks like it is lost, the two trucks gun their engines as much as possible, locking the transfer case into low, and finally spring *Bang Bus* from the confines of the evil culvert. Relief, at last.

These adventures are enough for the day. We have been out for almost two full days at this point. Which isn't a lot, but for the guys back at Loy Kolay it is starting to take its toll. Because the majority of the force is out trying to get shot at in Trek Nawa, the guys back at the PB still have to maintain the post, the COC, and everything else at all times.

Bidding adieu to our water-scrounging AUP counterparts, the lowly force mounts and drives south. Passing the Weapons Company guys at Spin Ghar, we push directly south instead of southeast, mixing up the route a bit.

Randy, our LEP guy, is there to meet us at the back gate. Pushing my turret to 12 o'clock and unloading the belt from the Two-Forty, I crumple into *Black Holed Sun*, Doc next to me fast asleep in the rear passenger seat. I hear the Sir over the company net, "Chaos Main, Chaos Main, PB Loy Kolay, EFL, three trucks, seven ME, one MO, one NE this time, over." Todd eases the truck into the back gate of Loy Kolay, after *Bang Bus*. Martin slowly pushes open the Mat-V door, sinking to the ground. Poor guy, he's had all the motivation sapped out of him. Ground-guiding from Todd, we back up into place and cut the engine.

Pressing myself out of my flak and dismantling the gun, I am relieved we won't have to be living out of the damned trucks for a change. The first thing I want to do is take my socks off and eat anything other than the main meal from an MRE, or a stupid Ranger Bar from a UGR-E.

Kugler walks by. "Do we have a fucking debriefing? We damned well better not."

I shrug, grab the gun and ammo cans, bringing them into the COC where I stack them next to the other 240s.

Weitoish pokes his head in, "Hey, Sir said to just chill out, we'll have the debriefing in two hours from now, at twenty-three hundred."

Thank the Lord.

I bring my flak and pack to my rack, laying them next to it. Sure will be nice sleeping on this thing again. Stripping my Frog top off and grabbing my M27, I find some snack chips left over from the last Jaker run. Outside, I see the rest of the gang sitting around our little fireplace. I take a seat next to Todd and Paul, also shirtless and eating a snack.

Sergeant Mike comes out in his gym clothes. "You boys have fun out there?"

"Nothing but the best fun, Sergeant Mike; we actually won the war out there today. No clue what you losers are even doing here anymore. I'm pretty much ready to hit up the Driftwood next week." You can always count on Paulie to say the dumbest stuff, with a straight face.

Sergeant Mike chuckles, "Yeah, well Bridget would be pissed if I came home next week while she's in Costa Rica. By the way, did you fools stop by Spin Ghar for their internet?"

Kugler shakes his head. "No, we didn't want them to feel like the whiney little bitches they are by having a bunch of real Marines around them, so we decided to forfeit that opportunity and play the bigger guys."

These chips are tasting great at this point, almost as good as chips back home, but for some reason these taste like dust.

"So while you operators were away, like eight dump trucks came and shat gravel all over the yard here. Apparently the BC wants all the PBs covered in gravel before winter starts. Something about the ground becoming less muddy when it rains."

Weitoish looks up, "Rains? It rains in Helmand? We're not talking like firefighting C-130s pouring it out, are we?"

Sergeant Mike isn't impressed. "Either way, we have to spread that crap all over the compound. I figure we have four shovels, and two wheelbarrows. If we organize it into teams, we'll be able to accomplish it in a couple of days. Obviously the AUP fucks aren't going to help out; God forbid they do any manual labor."

Something of a groan from us, the kind where it isn't enough to piss off a superior, but just enough to let the mood be known. I'm lost in a train of thought, as the conversation continues without me. That was a pretty neat op we pulled off, despite the comm issues, the truck living, *Bang Bus* almost rolling over. It is probably the most extensive thing we've done so far, going out a long ways for several days on end, and nothing went wrong. It was good, a solid op for sure. I daze off into the night, looking past the post. I recall very vividly how black the night is past our little island of light that is the patrol base. So very black.

A massive explosion rips through the night, the blackest of nights. There is no flash like you see in Hollywood or on YouTube, just this enormous *boom!* that echoes out from beyond the PB. It is so surreal; if the audio effect wasn't there, we wouldn't have noticed a thing. But we do. For a split second we all perk up, and look at each other.

Then, action! There is no time for indecision. Only result.

No one needs tell us what to do next as we scramble up from our seats, knocking over MRE pieces, bumping into each other and rushing past one another into the hooch. Tripping over beds and things laid on the floor, we grab the cold, sweaty plate carriers and, is if in a race, throw them over our heads and strap them onto our chests, at the same time yanking Kevlars off racks and fastening them to our heads. Ripping out NVGs from pouches and cargo pockets, screwing them onto elbow mounts, then jamming the mount into the connecting rhino mount already on the Kevlar, slapping the thing down, into your fucking face so you squeal in pain but turn on and adjust the infrared intensifier anyways; at the same time crashing into this guy or that halfway across the compound, pulling the charging handle of the rifle to the rear and hearing that round rock into that chamber. No loudspeaker need have uttered that we were under attack right now: it is mutually agreed that we are.

The Sir shows up at the gate alongside us, no Frog top or shirt on. "Haylock! Take Todd, Paul, Wank, and these four AUP, push down Shiner to the south. Martin! Take the rest and those AUP and encircle the PB to the north." He's spitting words into his Prick 152, calling out the DFL, as we're pushing out steadily, weapons up, NVGs scanning the green night ahead of us. For once, the AUP seem just as enthusiastic about closing with this mythical enemy.

Haycock's element moves out of the front gate, and slowly down to the canal alongside Shiner. Mine goes across the field in front of the PB, to the road. The usual night problems associated with NVGs don't seem to exist anymore, now that the threat is too real. We shake out in single-file column, literally prepared to get lit up at any second. Reaching the road, I look into the corn stalks on the opposite side. Anything, anyone could be hiding in there, for all I know. I'm trying to squeeze the darkness out of it into the green being filtered onto my left eye. We're moving again, this time farther down the road, stopping every little while. The night is silent. Nothing moves. Not a person, not an animal, not even the wind. All I hear is the crackling on the Sir's radio, talking about how Paul is going to fire some warning shots into the air because some farmer is trying to run away from him.

* * *

"So we walked over to the mosque today, and asked the people gathering there if they had heard the explosion last night." Sergeant Volpe was just back in from a patrol. "Every single one of them said they hadn't heard it, yet had been hanging around outside at the exact time the IED went off."

Typical of the Afghans in Helmand. It was sort of a defense mechanism for them that had been built up since the Russians invaded in 1979. By disallowing all cooperation, it protects them from both the Taliban, and us. It got even weirder several weeks later, when we responded to an IED two klicks away that had split one of our AUP trucks without touching the occupants. When we got excited about trying to turn the pressure plate over to the bomb labs back on Baghram to find out who planted it, our illustrious AUP commander mentioned matter of factly that, "Oh we know who did it. It was Ghual Mahmud. Lives across the river from Lash Kar Gah; he's an enemy of my family."

* * *

On one of the Jaker runs, the guys get back while I'm on post, doing post things. I get relieved by Mauler and make my way back down to the hooch, stripping off my gear, filling the generator, and getting something to eat.

Here, the Sir comes up to me and says, "Hey Vining, I've got something to tell you, and you'll be going home early as well!"

Oh God, what's this? Going home early wouldn't be too bad. I'd finally be back with Lynn, which is really all I think about when it comes to the States. My parents are cool, but after sixteen years with them, I'm sure they're as sick of me as I am of them, so really Lynn is what I look forward to. But at the same time, the urge to *not* go home is much more. On the face of it, the logistics of running a patrol base depend on every single man, much like a village. With me short, post hours would be longer, guys would have to go on patrol more often. But on the deeper level, it would be leaving my "family," the sick and twisted group of guys whom I'd do anything in the world for.

"Sure, Sir, what's going on?"

The Sir continues, "Well, you've been chosen to work in the armory with Corporal Vannest, as an armory custodian. They need smart guys, because the armory has been pretty shitty, on no account of Yeager and Vahn, just the situation they entered into. They need Marines they know can handle the job, so because of that, you'll be going home advon, and setting up the armory for when we get back."

Fuck. Fuck. Fuck. Double fucked. Vannest? That senior is fucking crazy, and weird, and does an abnormal amount of hazing. But more importantly, an armory custodian? Are you serious? I came into this gun club to stack bodies, not inventory rifles.

Paulie hears word of this, and in one of his random acts of spontaneous showmanship, he shouts out, "Haaah, Vining! You're gonna be working with Vannest! Good fucking luck! Haaah!"

Then Martin comes over and says in a serious tone, "Vining, if you don't accept my rifle, every time, I'm going to fucking throat-punch you through that tiny armory window." Fuck you Martin, you couldn't declare a rifle clean even if it showed up from the factory unfired.

Later on, the Sir catches me in the hallway and asks, "Hey Vining, how do you feel about this new position?"

I respond frankly, "Well, Sir, I'm not liking it, at all."

"Well, I mean, you have to make the most of it. Heck, if you end up hating it that much, just try out for snipers and see where that gets you."

Ah ha! Now that's a brilliant idea. Go into a haze fest that few return from on the "hopes" that you'll make it, and it'll get me out of it. Later that night, I talk to Lynn on the sat-phone, "I've got good news for you [emphasis on her, not me]: I'll be coming back about two weeks early." She's ecstatic. But I'm not, not at all. She senses this, and asks me about it. I say soberly, "I don't want to go back early. I want to stay here with the PB until we get to go back together." She tells me to be happy, at least be happy for her. I am happy for her, I'm extremely happy.

A week passes, and I'm included on the next Thursday Jaker run, to connect with Vannest, Gunny Hart, and begin this armory shit. We get to Jaker after yet another uneventful fucking dust-choking joy ride down Shiner, and I find myself in First Sergeant's office, to fill out various bits of paperwork about the transition. After waiting for a bit, the devil himself graces me with his presence.

"Rah, First Sergeant."

"Good afternoon, Vining."

I sit uncomfortably for a few minutes. Junior enlisted warriors should never have to endure this sort of proximity with their senior NCOs: it's detrimental to their health and can cause them to nail their dicks to a table.

"So, Vining, tell me what you think about going to the armory?"

Moment of truth, fuck. "Well, First Sergeant, to be completely honest, I don't like it; it's not what I signed up for."

After a pause, a lengthy, calculated pause that only First Sergeants seem able to master – I swear to God, they must teach this shit at SNCO school at Quantico – he asks: "You signed up to be a Marine right?"

Bam! Gotcha bitch, no way out of this one without being demoted at least two pay grades below my current one. "Yes, First Sergeant." And with that, like they say on *Animal Planet* after a lion snares a poor gazelle, "This lance corporal is done ..."

My last post is from 2000 to 2300. As usual the night has enveloped the PB and the surrounding countryside; the village of Loy Kolay is quiet, apart from a random car coming down Shiner. I'm thinking to myself how odd this is, that this will be my last post on deployment. I look round the small concrete enclosure and try to take everything in for one last time: the Two-Forty sitting on the pintle mount, the logbook, the M32 grenade launcher, the scrawls on the walls with everything we've written on it. The spare ammunition in the ammo cans, the range cards I've drawn up all over the top part of it. This existence is so ingrained in me that for a moment I can't imagine *not* having to stand post at the PB, like it just doesn't seem right. The PB needs to be guarded, it needs *me* to stand long hours bored out of my mind.

Miller comes clambering up the post ladder, and I turn everything over to him, finishing up my logbook entry. He puts all his stuff down, and takes off his flak, "You excited for tomorrow, Vining? Get to fucking go home!"

I sort of smile in the darkness, "Nah man, not really actually; I don't want to be with the armory, and on advon. I'd much rather come home with everyone together."

Miller chuckles. "Oh well, I know what you mean, man, but hey, make the most out of it, and enjoy the U.S for us when you get back."

I laugh, thinking of Lynn. "Ahh, alright brother, I'll see you later then." I take one last look round the post, still not believing that I'll never be up here again, and then descend the ladder, go to the generator and fill it up, and then cross the PB back to the hooch. I strip off my flak, and see that all my bags are packed, ready to go. I climb into my top rack, and go to sleep.

Early in the morning I wake up, and bring all my bags outside. I shave, because those fuckers on Jaker are anal about that sort of thing. I go round to everyone in the hooch and wake them up individually, saying my goodbyes. I go to the COC, and Sir is in there. I let him know that I'm going out, and he tells me that the convoy from Mamma Khan is on its way. I put on my flak, now a lot lighter because I've stripped all my rounds back to our ammunition supply; hopefully the guys from 2/6 will make use of them when they take over the PB. I load up my LB, and drag my deployment bag with the seabag strapped to it out the front gate, already breaking a sweat in the cool Helmand morning. The trucks from Mamma Khan are approaching in the distance, and eventually they cross over on to Shiner.

Kennington gets out. "Ready to go home, Vaining?"

He helps me put all my stuff in the back of one of their Mat-Vs. With my LB, he throws it up, but it doesn't quite clear the top rim of the cargo area, and it falls back, directly on top of my Kevlar. I hear this crunching sound coming from my spine as the seventy-pound pack lands on top of me. Fuck, that can't be good, but thank God for the Kevlar: survive a deployment only to suffer a spinal fracture from my own LB falling on me.

We get to Jaker with all our gear in Mamma Khan's trucks. Fuck those guys, damn Mamma Khan getting their CARs, the combat action ribbons. They even came up with this stupid hoodie that says "PB Mamma Khan, WE GOT OURS." As if they pushed Sangin or something. Bitch, that was one measly gunfight that you just so happened to get caught in the middle of – an ambush by the Taliban on a civilian truck convoy. All the talk at Jaker is about the guys who pissed hot, and their current predicament. They have had their weapons taken away from them, are made to live in a separate tent, and can't talk to anyone at their own PB, while of course doing all the PB working parties.

I link up with Vannest, and my hatred for him grows. Deep down he is actually a kind guy, and a loving one too: last I heard he was having a kid. But this doesn't stop my hatred for him now, and the way he treats me like a child. Hey, I know we've only got one combat pump a piece, and neither of us saw anything significant. My hatred reaches epic proportions until he NDs into his leg with his 1911 back home, gets fucked by the command for living off base, and then gets T-boned by a car on Lejeune Boulevard. Then my hatred somewhat levels off to discontent, and nowadays I could not frankly care less about him.

But at this moment the struggle is real: between his belittling remarks, and his racist overtones, he is quite the despicable NCO. And my boss. So that entails an awful amount of suck. For me that is, not him. We load up in a large convoy going to Geronimo, good old Camp Cup Cake. We get our deployment bags and LBs all loaded up, and head over to Geronimo, where things are infinitely more ridiculous than Jaker. At this point, the entire company advon is formed up. We are comprised of around twenty Marines with Gunny Hart as our leader. Most of the guys in the group are having babies born soon, or just had babies born so they get an early ticket punched to go back. Other guys like me and Vannest are there to facilitate the return of the company, basically open up the offices back at Lejeune. Along with this element from Charlie, each company has a similar advon element they are sending back to do the exact same thing. On Geronimo we get our gear sorted out, sleeping arrangements set up, and wait patiently for a Fifty-Three flight to come take us to Leatherneck.

This will be a first time for many of us, as the battalion came into Helmand via Dywer, the desert base in Garmsir District. But in the meantime, Gunny Hart hooks us up with a pistol qual – a USMC Pistol Qualification – as armorers are supposed to have one, to have an M9, to guard the armory, which is all part of the of the whole "We're doing things right in the armory this time." Big mistake, chain of command, no one wants to be there in the first place. So we get this pistol qual, which in 2011 the Marine Corps qual course is still a joke, so both of us score High Expert. I'd say this is the only thing Vannest is an expert in, but that would be harsh.

Eventually we get a locked-on date for the fifty-threes to pick us up, and we're going in heavy, meaning that we're dragging all our gear with us, the entire time back. The fifty-threes are slated for something like 0200, and so the battalion advon stages its gear outside of the Geronimo LZ. We wait for hours for the birds to come, and then hear that they are inbound. The birds come in, and there is this terrific sandstorm that they whip up, the blades looking like they're cutting chunks out of the darkness as specks of sand shine bright where the edges of the blades are whirling. I've never seen anything like it. We load up the Fifty-Threes, all our packs and gear down the middle, us compressed on the sides like sardines. The poor things can probably barely move. Regardless, they take off, and we're moving across the Helmand desert. I can make out villages, and lights on the ground, as I'm sitting right at the back and can look out from the open tailgate. Eventually everything just turns to straight barren desert, so we must be getting close to Leatherneck.

The perimeter fence of Bastion is now coming into view and the bird slows down, landing on the tarmac. Leatherneck is like being in a Pog wonderland. Hot showers, pizza huts, barbers, PXs, gyms, enough food to feed Ethiopia, even an entire bus system that takes you all over British Bastion and American Leatherneck. It is surreal, entirely surreal. Marines, soldiers are walking around as if there isn't a war on or something. As if grunts aren't sucking it up on patrol or post, just miles from where Leatherneck stands. Heck, even the weapons-carry conditions on Camp Lejeune Forward are reminiscent of Twentynine Palms. You aren't allowed to walk around with a magazine inserted in your weapon. There are concrete posts with Ivan targets in them, to simulate a guard being inside. Are we even in Afghanistan anymore? (About a year later, when the attacks on Bastion happened and two Air Wingers were killed, I shook my head in disgust. What the hell did the base command even expect, with the entire base walking around with unloaded weapons? Even worse were the news reports of the attack, "Camp Bastion attacked, Prince Harry is okay." Who cares about Prince Harry when we've got two dead Marines?)

We then take a C-17 Globemaster out of Leatherneck that then takes us to Manas in Kyrgyzstan. There we sleep in those stupid hangars where they leave the damned lights on 24/7. Leaving Afghanistan feels surreal as well, similar to leaving my last post at Loy Kolay, like it wasn't supposed to be happening or something. In Manas we board commercial 747s that stop in Frankfurt, which is awesome because we get to get beer, many of us being underage but it doesn't matter. After about two beers, most of us are done for, practically drunk without any for so long. We board the plane a rowdy bunch, yelling and hollering, and telling the lamest jokes, laughing about some of the deployments, all of us passing out as soon as the plane is in the air and on the way to the U.S.

The first U.S. stop is Bangor, Maine, to refuel. Somewhat home, but then the plane takes off again for Cherry Point, where we unload everything onto seven-tons and get into those nice tour buses to get back to Lejeune. Some of the motorcycle vet groups in the area get together and provide a front escort for us, American flags waving on the highway. One of the first things that strikes me looking out at the North Carolina countryside is the sheer amount of green everywhere. Green trees, green grass, green fields. Just fucking Green all over the place. I had almost forgotten that the color exists.

At Lejeune the welcoming party at the CP mostly comprises the RBE. These guys were left behind when we deployed, full of broke dicks, med holds, guys soon getting out, or guys who had been sent back for one reason or another from deployment, wounded guys as well. In addition to this, all the families are there. My mother is there to greet me, and it's great seeing her again; she gives me this big old hug. Another mother takes a picture of us together, me in my cammies and day pack, holding my mother, small in comparison. She's full of smiles in the picture, happy that her son is back from war. But my face is indifferent. I look at it now, and I see the look of not wanting to be back, not ready to return to civilized society. I've changed in that picture, I've weathered and aged from when I was a 19-year-old before we deployed. I just look pure tired. Since then, I've seen things, and done things that I had never before done in my life, and that I would never forget. I still have that look in me today.

My mother hands me my charged phone that I left behind. Immediately I dial Lynn's number, in Canada. I hear her pick up and I say, "Lynn! Lynn! I'm back, I'm home now!"

"Oh my God, I'm so happy, I'm so relieved. You're home now!"

"Yes, yes, I am, hard to believe, but I love you, and I'll see you in a few days. Me and Mom are going to pick you up at the airport."

We get some admin stuff out of the way, turning in weapons, setting up the armory. We've since moved armories from before the deployment, into much larger bays, much nicer as well. It won't alter the misery of waiting in line, but, oh well. But here is where the transition starts occurring to me. Every time I leave the house where my mother and I are staying, I'm looking round for my rifle. I find myself sitting somewhere and then getting this odd urge that something is wrong, very wrong. I realize that I'm not in Helmand anymore, and I don't need my rifle at that moment. Sounds annoy me as well, I jump at a loud noise, and quickly turn round to see where it came from. But I realize it's a drill, or some door slamming.

Girls, girls everywhere, of all shapes and sizes, all types of hair: blonde, black, red, tied up, or flowing in the wind. Perfume too, they smell so sweet when I pass them, a smell I forgot existed.

Lynn comes down from Canada, and we go to the Jacksonville airport to pick her up. Boots in Alphas are walking out of the doors. I chuckle to myself, remembering when I was, just a little over a year and a half ago, waiting to embark on this grand infantry adventure. On my insistence, we're something like two hours early for the flight: I want to make Goddamned sure we pick her up, because this has been seven months in the waiting. I find a kids' lounge in the airport while Mom reads one of her books.

I look through my phone, calling up old buddies, and telling them that I'm back, my various family members as well. Soon Lynn's plane comes in to land and I'm ecstatic. I'm waiting right outside the security clearance, where the passengers come through. The boots, the typical wives and weirdos coming to J-Vegas start streaming out of the gates, and I'm looking for Lynn. Finally I see her, coming through the small Albert J. Ellis receiving area. I smile, and she smiles. She comes to me and we hug, and we kiss. It's not very climactic: we're just so happy to be alive and together. I grab her bags, and get in a taxi back to the house in J-ville where we're staying. We have a sort of dinner with my mom, and then she goes to her room and we go to ours. Clean up the room a bit, with all my gear in it, and now hers as well. The lights are switched off, and we get on the mattress on the floor. We're kissing ferociously now, grabbing at each other's bodies. Sweaty breasts swishing over my chest, a soft neck open for kissing, butt cheeks being grasped, fingers intertwined in ecstasy, waists bumping against each other, forehead digging into my chest, and lush lips soaking my face. These are things I've forgotten even existed. Warm, wet, and throbbing describes the motions of the night, clawing and feasting upon each other like never before. Like the seven months was nothing but a little fun in the sun, moving from one previous predeployment night to this in a heartbeat.

She falls asleep before me. Jetlag is still deeply embedded in my bones. I stay up for a little bit, with my arms around her, cuddling her, in disbelief that this is happening right now. The damned jetlag still hasn't worn off. Car beams illuminate the room. I can hear some cricket chirping. Tonight is not the night where I get woken up for post. Not anymore.

Finally, I am home. But am I really?

Chapter 3

The Illustrious Terminal Lance Corporal

Driving down the road in my humvee, searching vehicles and Iraqis.
Staying in my rack and watching "One Tree Hill," so I'm never gonna get
  a confirmed kill.
Reporting contact even if we don't get it, Just so that we can get our combat
  action ribbon.
It's a Fucked up arrangement! Our PPE prevents proper engagement.
Its an OIF seven or seventeen, It doesn't really matter I'm OFP.
The War is already over so let's go home. I can't wait to go on leave so I can
  get stoned.
And MO, MO I got PTSD. Sick and tired of hearing my Staff Sergeant
  scream.
But I would rather run over an IED, than ever have to hear the BC speak
  to me.
And hey ya'll know I'm just a Lance Coolie, and I hate everybody in the
  COC.
First Sergeant, he would never give me a chance, that's why I'm getting out
  as a terminal lance.
Sing EAS baby, you can't stop time! Uncle Sam's getting his, so I'm getting
  mine.
FUSCMC, you can suck my Cock! Can't wait to be another homeboy back
  in the block, yeah.

The EAS Song, Taylor Satterfield, 1st LAR

There is a special kind of relationship that men in mortal danger develop with each other. It happens when men are actually put to the test, for each other; something that even many a spousal relationship will perhaps never go through in a lifetime of marriage. You would think that this bond would be something eternal, something untouched for the remainder of their lives. Because at the small-unit level, the cogs and wheels that make up this extremely well-oiled killing machine are usually so completely tight-knit, that it appears as if this bond will last forever. You can tell by how that guy carries his rifle, cocks his Kevlar, or takes a knee, just who on your patrol base that is. You'll get in fights with these same guys, sometimes a vicious bloodbath, but then you'll still stammer out that you've got their back no matter what at the end of the day.

So at the end of a deployment, you have this amazing band of brothers, who will do anything for each other. But then everyone comes home. And for the first week or two of being home, things will stay the same. You won't be going on any foot patrols or standing any posts with each other anymore. But you still have each other's backs, and you're still trading stories like you were on deployment.

However, after this, life happens. Platoons get reorganized, guys get sent off to new units and schools, new cars and marriages, new social groups and cliques. And everything that once was turns into ancient history. A company or platoon returning from a pump will be completely unrecognizable within months or even weeks of returning from some of the most harrowing experiences these grunts will experience in their entire lives. It will still have the same numerical value. Third platoon, Charlie Company, 1st Battalion, 9th Marines will still be Third Platoon, Charlie Company of the 1st Battalion, 9th Marines. But it will never be the same as it was between the months of June and December 2011. New leadership, new boots, new squad leaders from other units, new shitbags and new cocksuckers.

This is of course inevitable. Life has to go on, the organization has to adapt and change. People can't stay dormant in the same positions forever, careers have to evolve and guys gotta get out, boots have to check in. It is in this environment that this unbreakable bond that was been forged through blood, sweat, and tears in foreign lands might begin to falter. Sometimes it doesn't falter, and guys stick it out for each other and stay by each other's sides until the big man calls them home; help each other in times of need, give the shirts off their backs, without hesitating to drive many long hours and miles to see each other.

However, the exact opposite of this happens as well. Backstabbing, playing the hatred game, screwing guys over in the States, even after leaving the service when everyone is playing civilian again: some of this animosity continues. But these are the two extremes. In this post-deployment dwell time, a good number simply go about their way. They might see each other from time to time, in various circumstances. They might trade a few low shots at each other, like the time Todd and Haylock played silly games with the AUP, or when Sergeant Mike got shots of liquor in through the APO mail.

But that'll be it, and they'll soon be on their way. We often talk of brotherhood and camaraderie, and how much we are there for each other, and how much we need to support each other in the fight against reintegration, suicide, or PTSD. At one point, that amazing gem of human existence is real and raw. We felt it on our patrols, working on wounded brothers, and in taking turns on watch at night. It is one of the more real human connections we feel over the course of a lifetime. But that was then, and it existed solely because of that context, and that moment. At the end of the day, we are only human, and whether or not we decide to build on that relationship is up to the individual, and cannot be applied universally.

I was hanging out at the Bricks, drinking with some of the seniors, Paulie, Range, Kugler, to name a few. Before the deployment, these guys were hazing the dogshit out of us, the boots. But in the end, they take care of you, like an older brother. However, after deployment you are technically a senior now because you've deployed. But you'll always be "their" boot and they'll always be your "senior." No matter where either of you goes in life, no matter your future status as a rock star, sergeant major, or lowlife, this relationship will always remain. A good senior will take care of you, train you right, haze you just enough, make sure you do everything you're supposed to do, and ideally, you'll become equals because you'll have "grown up" in the Marine Corps under him. But he'll still be your senior.

A bad senior will screw you over, get you in trouble, not cover for you when you fuck up, and haze you nonstop without warning. You'll hate him with all your guts, probably even beat him up when he's not around his peers or your other seniors. But he's still your senior, no matter what happens. This also goes for Marines who aren't even in your platoon or company, although it mostly stays within the company. Similar to the idea that it takes a village to raise a child, it takes a company of seniors to churn out their replacements. Your sergeants and platoon sergeants are there for you as well, but they are far removed from everyday contact. They stay in the office, or go home at the end of the day. They are still there for you when shit gets rough, or fuck you over if they are horrible leaders. But your relationship with them is completely different from the seniors that watch over you in the barracks and live with you, probably even have you as a roommate – a very bad situation.

Although my squad leaders and platoon sergeants were in charge of me, that's all they were, squad leaders and platoon sergeants. They weren't my corporal and lance corporal seniors whom I dealt with almost all the time. So there I was with Paulie, and a Sergeant Rice, one of his peers. We were drinking in Paul's room and having an alright time, getting drunker by the minute and talking about the deployment. Something came up about how close Paul and I had become, and how it was a little different for Rice and his boots. Of course, we'd become close, we lived within one hundred meters of each other for an entire seven months, our lives depended on how much effort we put in. We shared post schedules, patrol rosters, COC watches, meals, and everything in between. The conversation came to a point where I looked Paul straight in the face and said, "If Paul had ever gotten hit and was laying out in a field somewhere, I would have run out under fire to get him, even if it meant me taking a bullet or an IED." Paul stared at me for a brief second, and said, "Vining, I would have done the exact same thing."

That moment meant more to me than anything else that had transpired since I got in. I had gotten certificates of commendation, two meritorious promotions, a meritorious mast, words of praise from my higher-ups. I had been responsible for being a tactical interpreter, a Hiide operator, and had even led a few patrols. But none of these achievements came even close to that one moment where I declared that brotherhood, of putting my life on the line for Paul, and him for me. ISAF's mission, America's stance in the war on terror, fighting for freedom, and being a Marine, meant absolutely nothing compared to me being able to confidently and truthfully say I'd have put my life down for Paul, and vice versa.

One Nine checked out on some much-deserved post-deployment leave. Up to that point we hadn't had much interaction with civilian society, just on the 96s and weekends. With the "Just got back from Afghanistan" still fresh on our lips when asked, getting some leave was great. I knew, we all knew getting home would be different for us, in different ways. The damned officers gave us their stupid "Don't beat your wives" speech before we left country, and we had to take the pathetic "Post-Deployment Health Assessments" with questions like, "How often did you feel you were in danger?", "Do you think of intending harm on other people?" and other questions with completely the wrong wording to ask someone just back from Helmand without them being a complete idiot, answering it wrongly and getting flagged for the psych ward.

Mentally I didn't think it was that big of a change coming home, apart from everything actually working, toilets flushing, not carrying my weapon everywhere. Physically, I jumped at the sound of gunshots on PT Road, from the pistol range on the New River. On leave I was walking home on New Year's Eve with Lynn and a civilian friend. We were crossing a foot bridge when all of a sudden *pop ... pop... pop, pop, pop, pop, pop.* I immediately dropped and my mind turned to Nawa. I grabbed a hold of both of them and pushed them to the ground, acting, not thinking, the primal animal part of my brain with all the sirens going off, leaving no room for the logical human thinking section to contemplate the circumstances and link fireworks with

New Year's Eve. Where's the nearest weapon? The best cover? Someone get out their cellphone and dial 911. After about five seconds, my friend put his hand on my shoulder and said, "It's alright man, you're back home, those are just fireworks." Slowly, I raised myself up, along with Lynn and him. I breathed a sigh of relief. Holy shit, did that just happen? Physically, I might have started the readjustment process, but mentally, it would take much, much longer.

Back in Lejeune, the battalion was starting to get the gears working in a new direction. The daily work of peacetime started invading our lives, as the work days got longer and the field ops started coming down the line. Guys were already getting cut orders for new units, while our seniors, the corporals and lance corporals with their two deployments, started the long checkout process. And how agonizing it was, in a way that only the Fleet could make it. All over the horror stories started coming in. Staff NCOs and officers lifing out grunts who had done their time: "You're a fucking Marine until your very EAS date", "You're a piece of shit for not reenlisting", "You'll be nothing on the outside; you don't know how good you have it here in the Fleet", "What are you going to do? Work at McDonalds?" There was nothing these guys could contribute to the battalion that their boots hadn't already somehow gathered or figured out by now.

Many of these guys were anxious to start their new post-Marine Corps lives, at college, in some industry. But no, the system was so bent over backward fingering itself, it was criminal to even consider pushing an early-out package. What the hell are you going to do with one to three months in the Fleet, in a Victor unit anyways? That had no word on any deployment? Nothing is your answer, but yet our staff NCOs and officers pushed for guys to draw all their turned-in Cif gear for a field op when their EAS was a week away, or refused to sign off checkout papers for one reason or another. It was ludicrous enough for two of our lieutenants to petition a number of generals and get a *Marine Corps Times* article out, about how ridiculous exiting the Fleet was. There were no more combat deployments, our government was in a recession, the drawdowns were being felt, and we had a pathetic Air Winger commandant who took away our rolled sleeves.

In the midst of this, I started getting angry. Just a little at first, but this soon mounted into a fury I didn't know where it came from. The smallest things sent me into a blind rage; it didn't matter what it was: something at the base commissary not being there, or having to go to the CP at noon. At the same time, I steadily began missing the simple life in Helmand. Everything in the United States was so unnecessarily complicated: bills, new car, Lynn's emotions, new commands, racist Vannest in the armory. I began missing every single thing about Loy Kolay, no matter how pathetic or mundane it was. Just standing post on a scorching hot August day seemed better than being in the States. I wanted back, I wanted in again, I wanted that life. Slowly, I became envious of other units leaving for Helmand, other guys on Facebook mentioning they were going over. I wanted to be in their boots, I needed to be in their boots, my sanity back home was falling apart just thinking about what I was missing out on.

Luckily, something came up that helped. Being in the armory was terrible, but the battalion scout sniper platoon was holding an indoctrination screening, essentially a week-long haze-fest tryout, to see if you had what it took to be a part of them. I tried out for it, being that I always found snipers fascinating. Miraculously I made it, earning the title of Pig, Professionally Instructed Gunman. As opposed to Hog, Hunter of Gunman, or a school-trained Scout Sniper. Everyone in a Sniper platoon is a Pig until they go through sniper school, at which point they became a sniper, or a Hog. Being in the platoon was a whole new world, essentially an infantry culture shock. Everything was done different from the line companies, and to a much higher standard. Lynn made cute faces at me on Skype about me being her "Shhnipa" and "You gonna shoot me? Don't shoot me, I looooove you." I laughed. I loved her too, and couldn't wait until the next leave block where we could curl up in a bed somewhere.

A Pig or a Hog has to be able to stalk a target, carry massive amounts of surveillance equipment in addition to the forties (M40A5 Sniper Rifles), call in airstrikes and artillery, effectively work in a small team, understand how to camouflage both himself and his equipment, engage targets accurately out to a klick away, and be an all-around expert when it comes to any other infantry task. It was almost like the line companies were the high-school junior varsity, and the sniper platoon the collegiate pros, performing much riskier tasks to a much higher standard. I had to completely unlearn every tactical subject from the line company, to replace it with new knowledge from snipers.

This being the case, a sniper platoon is a highly interesting social demographic. Snipers usually attract the top-performing grunts in the battalion, no matter their previous specialty or billet. So what you have is a collection of the fastest, smartest, and strongest infantrymen a battalion can offer. This turns into a constant game of dog eat dog, each member continually proving his worth to the platoon at every possibility. No position is secure, and there is no room for error. Just as easily as a grunt can get to snipers through passing an indoc, so can he get kicked back to the line company he just came from if he shows that he can't hack it in the platoon.

Being in the platoon certainly helped. But only when we finally had three things confirmed to us was I finally at some sort of peace. One Nine, the "break glass in case of fire" battalion, was getting deactivated along with the other two 9th Marines battalions, i.e. Two Nine and Three Nine. However, not before the battalion went on one more Afghan pump, and a trip to Bridgeport, California, for cold weather training. And we would be getting a new BC. I cared less about the other two, but knowing that we were slated for another combat deployment made me ecstatic. Lynn wasn't very happy, but I could put all my discontent with the Fleet on hold. As long as the endgame led back to Helmand, almost anything was worth it when it came to the amount of bullshit the higher-ups were throwing at us. I came into the military looking to do a job as an infantryman, and I'd be damned if I was going to spend seven months on a ship or in Okinawa.

Snipers fell under the command of Weapons Company, with the 81mm mortars, machine-gun platoon, and CAAT platoon. This way I got to move around the battalion and to interact with guys I had last seen at SOI or boot camp. It is possible to be in a company in an infantry battalion and never really access a social group outside of it in another company. There isn't really a need to, to begin with. In addition, even if another company lives on the other side of the barracks, they might as well be living on the other side of the base: the connection just sometimes never materializes.

Moving into Weapons I ran into a boot camp buddy, David, who was one of the mortarmen. In addition to David, two other buddies from SOI were in Mortars as well, Vanderwork, and Herring. Herring was a hilarious clown, the same guy who ate a bat on deployment for a pack of cigarettes and contracted rabies. I was always running into him and making some stupid joke or another. David had a marriage that was falling apart: he'd show me pictures and texts from girls he was talking to at the time, and then right after he'd show me videos of his little girl.

"Does Vicky know about any of this, dude?"

David would look up from his phone, "Of course she does. Heck, she does it too. We're moving toward a divorce anyway, it's pretty much over, man."

That was sad to me; they had been together before boot camp. Instead of being the exception to the rule, David's predicament was actually the norm in J-Vegas, and if anything it was a product of the environment. It was horrible for both of them.

Every military base has its own environmental culture. It's hard not to when you have over 50,000 servicemen stationed there. Just as the suburbs around Washington DC conform to the government atmosphere, and Seattle to Boeing and Microsoft, the Jacksonville area conforms to the Marines at

Lejeune, New River, Johnson, and Geiger. J-ville isn't a special case at all: Fayetteville (sometimes nicknamed Fayettnam) around Fort Bragg and Ocean Side near Camp Pendleton are far worse. These are economic platforms that feed off the military with great business plans, from knowing exactly when Marines get paid, to capturing the need for daycare establishments, car dealerships, and barber shops. Marines need a place to get their hair cut every Sunday (the lifers get theirs on Saturday, maybe even Friday after work, when they get their kids a high reg as well), married Marines need places to live, and boots need overpriced Mustangs to buy. It's a product of the environment.

But that doesn't mean we have to hate it any less. It's no coincidence that the best businesses in Jacksonville are barber shops, strip clubs, car dealerships, tattoo parlors, and bars. In Jacksonville, everyone you meet has some connection with the Marine Corps, either by being in it, married to a Marine, offspring of a Marine, or whatever. Essentially, don't wear a white T-shirt when you leave base.

Marriage though: problems that result from Marine marriages will never end. The military even buys into this, by making it easy for Marines to get married. Why shouldn't you? You get paid more, get to own your own apartment or house, get to set your own rules (outside of base), don't have to do Sunday morning police calls in front of the barracks either. And to a teenager fresh out of high school, this is tantalizing bait. They can finally call themselves independent, with their own home, paying their own bills, starting a family. So much of this is living in a fake world. How are you truly independent if it's the military that gives you the extra money to live on your own and support your wife? From boot camp onward, boots are told, "Don't get married, it's the worst thing you can do to yourself." But the incentives are so great that a number of grunts arrange contract marriages, that consist of guys having an actual courthouse marriage with a woman they know or don't know, and where they split the Basic Allowance for Housing (BAH) money between them. The command absolutely realizes this but whose business is it to investigate if two people are actually in a legitimate marriage? The concept of marriage is so vague and confusing to begin with. To be fair there are a lot of marriages that do work out, couples that do stay together until death do them part, that raise children in a military community.

The military has statistics galore for the divorce rates among active duty members, which are pretty abysmal. However, these statistics don't include the failed marriages after these guys get out. Now, there are two things going on here. First of all, people put the blame of a failed marriage on the service, deployments, constantly being in the field, and so on, so of course the military plays a part in the reason for a divorce. Another way to look at it is via a time machine. A marriage that fails in the military was probably going to fail outside of it anyways, had the husband never enlisted. All the military did was speed up the time it took to fail, by putting that stress and challenge on the newlywed couple. In other words, if a typical civilian marriage only lasts five or ten years, that same marriage would probably only last a year or two in the service. Second, the reason for these marriages happening to begin with has to do with the incentives and the kinds of guys involved. As an example, you don't see this alarming divorce rate among officers, partly because the officers tend to be a lot more mature and educated, whereas with the enlisted, you have a completely different dynamic.

Oftentimes these enlisted marriages result from a high school romance. Leaving for boot camp is the first test, which in the eyes of teenagers means that if they can last three months apart, then of course it's a dead ringer for a good marriage. The wives moving to Jacksonville is also an allure; a lot of these girls are from small towns across the U.S., and getting married to a Marine is almost a triple advantage for them. It gets them away from their small-town environment, it moves them into a big city with all its amenities, and their husbands have an extremely steady job and a source of income (at least for four years, which is forever at that age).

For the Marine, it gets him out of barracks, to become a man so to speak, what with owning a vehicle and a house and doing adult things. A huge factor often overlooked is that they'll get hazed less if they live "out in town." This is one of the primary motivations for a brand-new 03 who is getting his dick beaten into the dirt every time he's in his room. This happened to Spencer when he was a boot. One of the seniors even called him back on duty, and hazed by him making him scuzz the third-deck storage room on his hands and knees for hours, all night even. But at least he didn't have to deal with this type of threat all the time like we in the barracks had to, because he was married and out in town.

So the boot proposes to his high-school flame, she of course says yes, he moves her out to J-ville, gets her enrolled in Deers for Tricare, gets the base decal on the car and they even get an apartment for a price that has absolutely nothing to do with the amount he gets in BAH every month. Then the problems begin. The car breaks down because he bought it off his parents, the traffic on Lejeune Boulevard makes him late for work and he gets hazed for an hour, the new wife slips into depression because although she's in this huge city with so much to do (compared to before), she can't make friends or hang out with anyone. Money problems start piling up because the Marine doesn't know how to handle bills and the wife doesn't know how to spend wisely on grocery shopping. He goes to a loan shark and gets a "payday loan," sometimes even resorts to borrowing money from his buddies on the premise that "I'll have more money by payday" without telling them that they are tenth on the list. They see a Rottweiler puppy for sale on the street, buy it for $500 and then have to have it put it down for another $500 because it contracts parvo virus.

He can't handle his wife not understanding that he can't go with her to the clinic for the ultrasound because he has a field op, and she can't handle him because he comes home at such random, sporadic times that she has no idea when to cook dinner or even when to be home to unlock the door. Oh, and guess what, he's going on a combat deployment and might not come back so let's at least get a baby out of this. Then he starts drinking and she starts cheating or they're both making accounts on Plenty of Fish or Tinder. I've personally seen these online accounts where women are openly cheating on their husbands. One of my friends even slept with a woman who was married, and who just took all the pictures and connections down while he was on deployment. There is some animosity toward wives who cheat, especially while her husband is on deployment. But in all honesty it happens to both husbands and wives.

While all this piles up, it gets compounded by the command not caring that half the unit is married, or by disputes within Jacksonville. This is when the spousal abuse occurs and then triple homicides when the husband blasts the guy she was cheating with him on, blasts her, and then blasts himself for good measure. Or he just kills the guy and then kills himself, leaving his now-widow alive. Or he gets in a heated debate with a staff NCO at a bar, takes it outside and knocks him out; the SNCO's head hits the curb, he goes into a coma and dies.

One of the boots in Bravo Company was a prime example. His wife was sleeping with guys in his own platoon – she later divorced him and married one – and they had a newborn baby that many say wasn't even his. By himself, the kid was all right, he paid attention, followed orders, got along with everyone else. He was really small and scrawny, but he pulled his own weight. But his marriage impacted everything he did. He was constantly getting pulled out of field ops to deal with legal issues (about the only thing you can get out of a field op for, that or dental appointment), constantly away during working hours attending to this matter or that while his squad was training or learning new things.

Garrison life started becoming stupid. Stupid for me, stupid for all of us in all the line companies. To have a weapons MOS involves some inherent belligerence in the first place. So when you get an entire company of belligerent senior terminal lances, the bullshit rises to ridiculous proportions. The rules, the regulations, the uniforms, the officers, the staff NCOs, the inspections, the bullshit working parties, the Chuck Fridays, the pathetic field ops. None of it made sense, none of it seemed worthwhile. Behind all the reasoning were lifers talking about how it all made us who we were, to allow us to close with the enemy … maybe if we were closing with the chow line on Leatherneck or Dwyer, but not an actual enemy with IEDs and rifles. None of it seemed to contribute to how we made war overseas, none of it seemed to tie up with how we went on patrol, how we stood post, how we conducted a mobile convoy.

This salt dog, this terminal lance corporal mentality permeated all of us back from deployment. A lot of us, especially from Charlie Company, hadn't even earned our combat action ribbons, and we still felt like this. That was another point of contention. Despite all our patrolling, post standing, and everything else, many of us hadn't gotten in a gunfight. We weren't proud of this fact. We wanted that title, that white elephant of the job. And although we had done our jobs on deployment, we still didn't have the CAR, so what were we? Were we fake grunts or something else pathetic?

Regardless, our disdain for the chain of command, and everything on Lejeune grew. We lowered our trouser blousings, left our sleeves uncuffed, wore field boots and field cammies, to act as a calling card to other seniors in our position that we felt just like they did. During this period, it really dawned on many of us in the battalion, my generation of guys, that we far referred to be Marine infantrymen than Marines. An infantryman did what we did, lived in the suck, went on patrol, stood post, and wanted to go back to that. He also engaged in mortal combat with his enemies, but that wasn't our fault it hadn't happened to us, as we sure as hell wanted it. But a Marine, a straight and true Marine, did not necessarily know what we knew: he lived for the promotion and MCIs, had 300 PFT and CFT scores, loved the organization because it was kind to him, in more ways than one. We distanced ourselves from this state of mind, wanted nothing to do with it, wanting only to return to where we felt most comfortable, and safe, with each other, back in Helmand.

The more discontented I became, the more I took it out on everyone around me, especially on Lynn. The very environment of J-ville seemed to propagate this discontent, to encourage it, to ensure that that side of my teenage immaturity never advanced. It was hard for a young person to maintain any sense of morality or a straight compass in that town, what with argument after argument, over the dumbest things.

What had once seemed like a bedrock of a foundation now started to sprout cracks. Maybe because we were really starting to get to know each other through spending more time together. What made it worse was the extreme long-distance aspect of it, involving a flight, a car ride, a train, sometimes all of them in a single leave period. Previously we were so worried about deploying, going to EMV, or even just getting leave to begin with.

But now that I was back in the States for a stable amount of time, we had time to really decompress. Lynn came down to J-Ville one time and we stayed at Spencer's house, which ended up being a terrible idea because Spencer didn't like her. I made stupid decisions that I never would have made today. My fascination with firearms came to a head in the George Zimmerman case when I took Zimmerman's side and she took Trevon Martin's. We argued over who was right for hours, and to what end? If I could time travel, I would have simply said, "I don't know enough about the case to make a judgement here." Boom. End of story, but instead I had a to be an immature little lance corporal. When I visited her in Montreal, her roommate got bad vibes from me for being gay. At the time I was homophobic to some degree, but this eventually changed over time. Lynn saw this for what it was: immaturity.

When we would actually meet up during leave blocks or libo periods, we'd try to push these issues away but they would eventually force themselves back up in small ways. It seemed like the harder we tried to enjoy and love each other, something would inevitably pop up and then it would be arguments for hours. I remember very distinctly the time that I asked Lynn if I was still "perfect" when in bed. She leaned over and said, " Yes you are, but there are some things ...," or when I made a pathetically stupid and immature comment about the little bit of weight she had put on while at college. Or when I went into another room to work on MarineNet Humvee courses because our argument had gotten so ridiculous.

But then things would be on the upswing, such as when Fleet Week happened. Every Memorial Day a battalion of Marines loads up in ships at Norfolk and sails to New York City where an entire week of debauchery takes place. Walking around in Chucks never felt so good. We set up static weapons displays in front of Citi Field where the beautiful women of New York stopped to unload phone numbers. A New Jersey golf course had an open tab all night where a Medal of Honor recipient encouraged us to stack more bodies. I had a restaurant bill charged "0.00 Dollars" with "Captain, USMC 1965–1968" signed at the bottom. At the end of it, some Com Pog from 6th Marines went UA to go bang some hookup in Long Island and we had to do a shipwide accountability formation to find out who was missing. The entire event was so epic and out of this world that I am still in complete disbelief that it happened and that it continues to happen every year. I might just go back some day for the vibe alone.

During the week we had Cinderella rules where we weren't allowed to stay out past midnight. I was able to convince the Company Gunny to allow me to stay out overnight because he was a raging alcoholic that made calling him during his stupors a cinch. Lynn was able to come down and stay in her friend's apartment in lower Manhattan during that week. This was one of those short respites where we reverted to that sort of fairytale condition of things being great again. Except when I allowed an Army bandswoman to flirt with me. That was stupid.

* * *

I was sitting in the duty hut one day with Corporal Ripperda. The poor guy was one of the seniors who was trying to get out. He had been on the Meu, and was in Weapons while they were out in Trek Nawa, constantly getting into firefights. Ripperda was one of the most chill, laid-back guys in all of Weapons. All he wanted to do was get out, and build sailboats back home. While chatting, I got a text from Taylor, an Alpha company mortarman I had come in the Fleet with: "Hey Vining! Want to go watch the newest Harry Potter at the base theater?" Uhh, straight out of bootville, bootnation, population one, but Harry Potter sounded great that afternoon. When I was done talking to Rip I asked my roommate, Thompson, who was playing some stupid *Call of Duty* game, if he wanted to come. Thompson looked up, game on pause, and said, "Harry Potter? Duh! Let me get my stuff on."

We all piled into Taylor's car, anxious for the movie.

"Hey man, I haven't seen you for a while, brother, not since SOI!"

"Yeah thanks! You too Thompson! I heard you're getting married soon?"

"Yep, I go on leave for that next weekend; she's in Missouri. You've got a fiancée, right?"

"Abby, yeah, good to hear that, man!"

"When you guys getting married?"

"Funny story man, we were going to get married in Ohio, during June, but now we have that Kuwait deployment, so it looks like we'll have to postpone until after Bridgeport. Ahhh shucks, right?"

"Fuck dude, that's too bad man, pretty shitty if you ask me!" I added.

Taylor sort of blushed at the cuss words. The poor kid could never bring himself to swear, despite his job occupation. The car pulled up to the base theater, by the Lejeune water tower. We all got out.

"Hey man, I heard you ghosted a dude on deployment with your truck! Is that true or just whatever?"

Taylor looked around, as if we had brought up something really explicit. "Um, yeah that's true. I don't like to talk about it much. I haven't even told my family yet. But yes, we ran him down during one of our firefights, and my staff sergeant told me to ram his motorcycle around a curve. I hit him and he went flying off the bike. Staff Sergeant got out and shot him in the head with his M4 right there."

"Damn man! That's savage as fuck right there. Should be proud of it!"

"Freaking T! I remember hearing about that from the Alpha guys when we went out and supported them at that one PB."

No more was said as we got into the theater and took our seats. Harry Potter was glorious.

After the movie and some more small talk, Taylor dropped us off at Weapons barracks.

"Hey Vining, you still down to come with me to church tomorrow? We'll get a Monster on the way there, just like before."

"Of course man, meet at the chicken shack around zero seven?"

"Sounds good to me, see you there, man!"

Taylor went off to his room while Thompson parked his car in the HP 185 barracks parking lot. "Going to church with T, eh?"

"Yeah man, he invited me a couple of weeks ago and I went with him; pretty cool people there."

Thompson nodded.

"Dude, Taylor is such a unicorn out here man. You literally don't find guys like him in the grunts. Just a straight-up, overall good kid, good human being at that."

"I agree man, I wish we would hang out more often, you know."

Thompson un-paused his *Call of Duty* and I jumped onto the top rack, phoning Lynn in Canada about the latest Harry Potter movie. The evening came upon us and we stepped outside to enjoy the sunset, far off in the west.

One of the other guys in Snipers, George, comes in and starts chatting with Thompson.

He looked at me. "What was the deal with Rowley getting shot, and Vinyard waxing a whole van of Taliban dudes?"

He laughed. "Everyone keeps mixing those two stories up. It just started as a rumor sometime during the deployment."

"Well, enlighten me, will you!"

"So Rowley's team was crossing a field one day, and they started taking fire from the other side of it. The whole team ran back to the edge of the field, except for Rowley: he got shot through the knee and went down. Vinyard turned out and saw this, ran back to Rowley, helping him up and bringing him over to the edge. When he got there, he provided covering fire, while they patched Rowley up, and got him flown out on the Black Hawk".

"That's how Vinyard got the Nam with the V? I thought I heard something about Reimink helping out?"

"That fucking squishy-face bully? Fuck him, he's the worst NCO we've ever had."

"Well? What happened?"

"He helped return fire a bit, but he really didn't do anything. Then when they got back to Alpha's company PB, he got everyone in the same tent, and told the whole team to write their after-action testimony one way, to make it look like Reimink had been a freakin' hero the whole time. It was nuts; when they read the two citations, one for Reimink, and one for Vinyard, they sounded like two completely different accounts of the same action."

"And the machine-gunning of the van?"

"That was Whitehead. Completely different. Whitehead was on post at one of the Weapons Company PBs, and the dudes from the PB were out in the field police-calling. A Taliban van drove up next to them and just started unloading on the patrol. Whitehead just so happened to be on post and had a clear view of the van, so he lit those idiots up with his two-forty."

We were being kind of loud, and the sergeant living next door, Sergeant Bishop, poked his head out of his door. This guy was a legend among One Nine. His nickname was "The Butcher" because he had it tattooed across his back. Supposedly, he had adopted a small puppy in Iraq, and lost his head when someone killed it (or it was the other way around). When One Nine was on the Meu, he used to sit next to the ship's kitchen, every morning, and read his book. If those kitchen doors didn't open at exactly zero five, he'd be banging on them, telling the sailors to get out with the food. One of the guys in the platoon, Jankxter, was a machine-gunner in Bravo at the time, and had to stand post on the two-forties topside of the ship every morning. This one morning, Jankster and some buddies walked up to the kitchen at around 0430, asking if they could get some early chow for their post. The sailors politely refused, saying that the food just wasn't ready yet. When Bishop asked them what was going on they replied, "Well, sergeant, we were just trying to get some early chow for post topside, but they won't give it to us." Bishop slammed his book down and yelled out, "Oh, hell! NO!" He ran straight into the kitchen and smashed every sailor he could into walls and tables. Eventually one of the chiefs led him out of the kitchen, hand on his back. Bishop looked at the Bravo guys and shrugged, saying, "Sorry guys, I tried my best."

Bishop looked out at us, kind of sideways, then slowly said, "Sometimes … I just want to kill you guys … not all the time … but sometimes." Then he slowly receded into his room, and quietly closed the door.

George, Thompson and I looked at each other and half smiled, realizing it was time to go back inside. We had to get up early for PT the next day anyways. Apparently the Sir was joining us, but we knew he never would.

* * *

One of the Hogs in the platoon was having a going-away party and I was semi-volen-told to be the DD for the night. I didn't mind really; I liked all the guys in the platoon who we were going out with. And I got some gear in payment, which is always useful. The drinking begins at his camper truck off the Piney Green Gate and twists its way into several strip clubs in J-Vegas. I've never really been to one of these, so I accept some of the dances for the novelty of it, or so I think. Lynn doesn't think it's really funny the next day when I tell her. In fact she thinks it's so stupid of me that she signs off the Skype call immediately.

This starts a new round of arguing that is at a new level of vicious debate that we haven't seen before. Every small problem and previous argument resurfaces, and it is too much. Lynn offers that we take a week off and think of other things for a while. I fight it. I fight it hard for an hour or so on the Skype call in my barracks room. I don't want to do it, but it seems like she does. Fine, I say, let's do it. The conversation signs of and I immediately get a phone call with her crying bitterly: "Why did you say that! You weren't supposed to say that!" I'm shocked, honestly, I probably shouldn't have uttered those stupid words.

What do I do? How do I act? How was I supposed to respond? I could call in a polar mission, program a Prick-one-fifty-three, speed reload my M27 in split seconds, hike for eternity, burn feces all day long. But I had never been trained for this near ambush of the heart, never rehearsed a contact drill for this battlefield scenario, didn't pick up the TM on "How to Fix a Failing Relationship Due to your Pathetic Immaturity as a Man." I was clueless, useless, and completely unprepared to repair this shattered dream.

* * *

After being released from a lazy Wednesday afternoon, I went up to the third deck, unlocked my door, tossed my top across the little desk and let myself down into my rack. I didn't even bother texting Lynn because I was sick of the stalemate. Opening up my laptop, laying it across my lap, I logged into Facebook to see the latest. I noticed a new message, from my high school buddy Koeller. Last I heard of him he was in Afghan with the 75th, the Army's elite Ranger Regiment. Clicking on the message, it said that he was back home. Pretty good, he didn't seem to have gotten hit on his deployment at all. Looking up his phone number, I called it and he picked up within four rings, sounding all groggy.

"Heyyyy buddy, glad to know you're back."

"Yeah man, thanks. We just got back from Bagram four days ago … still getting used to the time zone shit … you know how it is."

"Indeed I do, brother, indeed I do. So tell me man, how was a Ranger pump? I'm interested to hear about it."

"Oh it was alright, man. We just did four months in–country, rotating out with another Ranger company from second; essentially we're a countrywide asset, as an Isaf strike force. They give us capture or kill missions, and we infil in with birds, usually at night, do our shit and get back."

"Any wounded? Killed?"

"No, thank God, no. We had some guys get hit, but our medics were right on that shit, and they were actually back out with us the next mission most of the time."

Good. That was good. It's good not to lose guys.

"Good man, I'm glad for you. We had some guys get shot and blown up, but no KIAs or amputees. Really lucky for Helmand, essentially."

"Yeah, likewise man."

"So, Pashtu *poueshey* at all?" I chuckled.

"What? What's that?"

"Oh, wondering if you picked up any Pashtu while there?"

"No, no just a few words to corral our prisoners on the bird, but that's it. Didn't really interact with Afghans a lot."

"Gotcha … Where were you based at?"

"Bagram, the regiment has their own little section of the base dedicated just to us, fenced in so nobody can snoop around or anything."

"So the deployment was essentially staying at Bagram, and then doing these helo missions every week or something?"

"Yeah, pretty much. Rangers don't do that kiss babies and shake hands bullshit, or whatever that hearts and minds crap is. We straight up wreck shit in Trashcanistan."

"Well, yeah … you guys are a Jsoc asset right? Supporting Isaf and stuff."

"Exactly man"

"How are your folks? Still in Philly?"

"They're good man. I haven't gotten to see them yet; we're about to check out on post-deployment leave, then we'll get right back into the training cycle for the next pump."

"Well, that's good man. Yeah, I've been there, done that, know how it feels."

"Yep. Not really looking forward to it just yet. Well, hey buddy, I have to hit the gym; my roommate is egging me on right now."

"Sure thing, man. Keep in touch alright, don't be a stranger."

"Will do, dude. Take care."

"See ya!"

Hanging up, I thought about what my Ranger buddy had told me. Although both us of were in-country for our respective roles as infantrymen, him more advanced, it seemed as if we came away with two completely different experiences. Sure, his Ranger company absolutely contributed to Isaf's mission there; I'm sure they bagged more Taliban leaders and networks than all of One Nine ever did on our deployment. His single platoon probably saw more combat than all of Charlie combined, despite our best efforts patrolling and closing with. However, there was just something missing that I couldn't pinpoint. After several minutes I figured it out.

Although that Ranger company was physically in the geographical boundaries of Afghanistan, were they really *in* the country? Did they know the Pashtu words for, "Please stop, I'd like to search your vehicle" or how to say "Shut up!" playfully with the AUP? How many Pritchnas, and Aakulas did they toss water to, or listen to as they walked by their posts? Although they went on these capture or kill missions, did actually *feel* the lay of the land, the names of the villages and routes, the atmosphere of the people, the rounding of certain curves or the steepness of certain hills; that this shop happened to stay open on Jummah, or that guy was the local teamaker? Or were these landmarks just lost in a numerical mix of grid coordinates, target reference points, LZs, and avenues of approach?

It almost seemed the polar opposite of the Pogs we so despised in the metropolitan bases in the far rear, except they were at the opposite end of the spectrum. Both Pogs and the Rangers were physically in-country, but not really *in* it at the same time. Granted, the Rangers took enormous risks with life and limb on their capture or kill missions. There are many Rangers who have lost their lives, limbs, and livelihoods directly because of their role in the war.

You can risk your life anywhere. You can risk your life in downtown Detroit, or swimming through the Florida Everglades if you really want to. But to actually know a people, a culture, a language like Pashtu', to see their struggles, feel their pain, know their names and watch their movements through this thing called life ... that, you cannot do anywhere, or at anytime. We may not have stacked bodies and rolled up on compound doors after an early morning helo infil, but I got to understand and observe a small part of Afghanistan, unlike many Americans before me and after me, and I got to put a face to a name. I will never trade that for any amount of heavy combat.

* * *

Lynn texts me, tells me to get on Skype.

"Okay, are we really doing this?"

"I guess we are."

We both take deep breaths. And it is over. The conversation ends.

STUPID! STUPID! STUPID! STUPID! HOW COULD I BE SO STUPID! SO PATHETICALLY STUPID! I scream at myself years later. So absolutely and pathetically idiotic. Why! WHY! WHY! Why did I let her go like that! I look through our old Facebook messages, our old emails, our old texts. It is so entirely, blatantly obvious the level of my incompetency, immaturity, and pathetic approaches to EVERYTHING. How could I ever be so completely dumb and uncalculated? Cringe factor to the tenth power as I read every word and sentence that I sent to her for some completely unknown reason. Why in the world was I like that! Why did I have to be such a fool to let her leave, to not compromise, to keep treading the line

Lynn says to me through her tears, "Promise me you'll never treat another girl like this again."

Although I thought I could keep that promise, it embarrasses me that I'd have to tell her today I was never able to keep it. The last promise I made to her, just like every other promise I made to her, was ultimately broken.

I told myself I couldn't care less, and hooked up with a GWU chick in DC the next weekend. The truth couldn't have been further from the center. Just as I plowed into her while we were in that small dorm room, so too was I burying every emotion and experience I had ever had with Lynn. I was psychologically trying to evade the pain by not realizing just how important it had been to me. Forget, I wanted to forget, I didn't want to remember. I didn't want to think about what she sacrificed for me, what I sacrificed for her. I wanted it to go away, be gone, have my mind be wiped, *Men in Black* style, with those memory-wiping sticks. I wanted to forget the time that we stayed at that apartment outside of Central Park and made love for the first time. I wanted to forget the time I completely snuck out of our SOI schoolhouse barracks lockdown so I could be with her when she came down to J-ville. I wanted to forget when I arranged with her parents to get into her room while they distracted her with some computer problem so I could surprise her when she came back. Or when I went to see her in Canada for post-deployment and didn't tell anyone in the chain of command. I wanted to forget the death letter I typed out where I told her I wanted to marry her if I came back alive. I wanted to forget the stupid picture of us kissing in the snow in New York City that my friend Beretta took. When she came all the way to China with me to meet my parents in Beijing. Pain, pain, pain. That's all I could conjure up after the breakup.

A boy enlists in the infantry, and he goes to war, where he seemingly matures. He does, in many respects. He has seen death, taken responsibilities far above his peer group, done a service few in his country will ever replicate or outdo in their adult lives. But does this make him an adult? In many ways it does and in many ways it still doesn't. He doesn't get why the LGBTQ community should be treated equally, or how the complexities of Afghanistan are far beyond any ISAF ability to solve.

A girl goes to college, and she might be able to elaborate on abortion, same-sex marriage, or foreign policy. She'll take all sorts of classes, and see the theory about how our society is this way or that, from an extremely rationalized point of view. And she will have matured by becoming a learned woman. But she won't have matured like that boy did, in the primal and wild sense of the word. She won't see the on-the-ground reason why her idea of economic prosperity won't work, and he won't see how embracing a human being – no matter their sexual orientation – makes a difference when all he knows is men trying to kill other men, without any sort of emotional connection between them.

Thus, our relationship, so seemingly strong with a two-and-a-half-year timespan, a coincidence meeting on the Jersey Shore, surviving a deployment, crumbled to bits when it came down to the nuts and bolts of it. We were like two phones trying to ring each other on a different number.

Bad news followed more bad news. The next week I was dropped from the Scout Sniper Basic Course, failing Land Navigation. My childhood dream had fallen into my lap and I let it roll away. Thereafter I got kicked out of Snipers, due to my inability to work with others in the platoon, and my lackadaisical, terminal lance, salt dog attitude. You can't have that in Snipers, with small teams counting on the superhuman ability of everyone else to pull through.

Lost, I step outside my barracks room and walk to the middle corridor where the central staircase and laundry machines are located. Previously I would have called Lynn in this sort of situation. And so I pick up my iPhone 3 ... and dial Lynn. She answers. Very calmly.

"Hey .... what's up."

"Hey Lynn ... I failed Sniper School."

Long pause.

"I know that was very important to you."

"Yeah ... it was ... How are you?"

Another long pause, this time much longer than the first. I can hear her choking up on the other end, like she can barely speak through the tears. She hangs up. Texts me. Says not to call her again and make her hear my voice again. I don't know what to do. My heart is filled with lead.

Years later, sleeping in a bunk bed in northern Iraq while with the Free Burma Rangers, I have a dream. The dream is so vivid I know it to be true. I'm in a garden with other people. I can't really recognize the other people. But I can recognize Lynn. She is as vivid as I can ever remember, with her shoulder-length dark hair, shorter figure, quirky facial gestures. She looks neither happy nor sad; just in a kind of neutral state. But there she is, leaning up against a tree in this cool garden. I'm less than a yard from her and so are all these other people who are there for some reason. I call to her, "Lynn! Hey, it's me, Miles." She doesn't answer. In fact, she looks away, looks at the ground, anywhere but at me. The other people don't really pay attention or care about what is going on; they are content with each other, having a jolly time chatting away. But not me. I want to talk to Lynn, have her say something, anything, I don't know what. So I keep calling to her, moving myself into different frames. Maybe she'll notice me and look up, smile, say something silly, that what we went through was really too bad, and we should be friends again. But no, nothing at all, nothing comes through and I'm desperate. I have this feeling that if she doesn't say anything now, I'll be gone and she'll be gone, and I won't ever hear from her again. This is my one chance, right here in this dream, to hear from her.

The garden slowly fades, the bushes turn into curtains, the tree she is leaning up against turns into the corner post of the bunk bed. I'm under soft covers and alone. I want the dream to come back so I can see her one more time.

So often I look back at Lynn and I and try to rationalize the breakup. Oh, it wouldn't have worked in the long run: I was too conservative, she was too liberal. I wanted to be overseas, she wanted a real job in a big city in the U.S. I wanted to keep my guns, she would have never lived with one in the house.

But this is all some sort of coverup I tell myself, to stay sane. Love isn't rational or the answer to a long-winded, multiple-choice question on a mid-term quiz. Real love is raw and without a hierarchy. It doesn't conform to any man-made structure of ideals or perfection. It flows like water around enormous obstacles in life, engulfing and dodging in every which direction. It doesn't fit like pieces to a puzzle with a designated geometric dimension. We don't fall in love because "it makes sense" like one would shovel a snow-filled driveway because "it makes sense."

While I was deployed I asked Lynn to buy a notebook and just write on the top of every page, then send it to me in Afghanistan. She did so and I barely wrote in it because I didn't want to trivialize what was written at the top. On one particular page she wrote, "Our love is proof that there is something bigger in the universe for us, that we aren't just meant to exist here and then die." I still have the notebook.

Sent to Bravo, I found myself in a company I didn't care for, and a platoon I didn't know. The boots were all new to the battalion, and the entire company had less than twenty seniors who had been in Afghan, the rest getting out or transferring to Alpha for the Kuwait security mission, or Charlie. I didn't realize it yet, but I was slowly sinking into depression.

One night I found myself in Alpha's barracks, as Taylor passed me. "Hey Vining, what's up buddy!"

"Oh, nothing much, just dealing with Bravo, you know ..."

"Yeah, that must be rough, all those new guys. Well, hey, I got my Kimber 1911 in, I wanted to show it to you sometime."

"Oh, show it? Let's shoot it! I just got my Springfield 1911 in the other day."

"That'll be sick!"

"Yeah, man! How does this weekend sound?"

"Uh no, Abby is gonna be down! But how about the first weekend we get back from Bridgeport?"

"Deal, brother, I'll hold you to it! I got to go, though. I'll see you later, Tee!"

"You too, Vining!"

Things couldn't be that bad, right? A shooting date after some training in the tundra?

Dead Walkers who took their lives

Sergeant Levi Lopez (Bravo Company), Lance Corporal Gregory Postiglione (Charlie Company), Lance Corporal Mathew Koppers (Charlie Company)

Chapter 4

We Are the Dead

We are the Dead. Short days ago
We lived, felt dawn, saw sunset glow,
Loved and were loved, and now we lie
In Flanders fields.

Take up our quarrel with the foe:
To you from failing hands we throw
The torch; be yours to hold it high.
If ye break faith with us who die
We shall not sleep, though poppies grow
In Flanders fields.

In Flanders Fields, John McCrae

One grizzly cold morning in January we get first platoon formed up outside the bricks. Corporals Dom and Gonzalez are walking around, checking out the platoon, making sure everyone is doing alright, and ensuring their fireteam leaders have accountability of their guys. Kind of hard to miss accountability if you're a boot living in the Bricks: there really isn't anywhere else to be unless you got left behind last night by your boys. We're waiting for Sergeant Mendenhall, the platoon sergeant, to show up and take his own accountability of the squads so that he can pass that on up to First Sergeant. But heck, is it cold, cold enough to be much more than really uncomfortable.

Smith, a boot from the back of the formation, blurts out in his perfect deadpan sarcasm, "And today it's negative five in Bridgeport, just to put things in perspective, gents."

It must be something like 25° at Lejeune, and hearing that Bridgeport is in the negatives is a tremendous blow to our morale. Never mind that Bridgeport is going to be filled with snow, wind, and mountains. The Marine Corps Mountain Warfare Training Center (MWTC) was established shortly after the Korean War. This was when Marines were hit with some of the lowest temperatures the U.S. military has ever gone to war in, in addition to being completely unprepared for an all-out winter assault. The infantry battalions came out on top, with Chesty leading a fighting retreat to the sea, but only after severe losses. This was one of those "never again" situations where the service looked hard at how to prepare itself for future winter warfare, in a mountainous environment.

But we don't understand much about Bridgeport at all. Since the beginning of OIF/OEF, the normal rotations that take battalions to places like Bridgeport, Okie, and other such illustrious destinations have been curtailed due to the war effort. The entire focus of the Fleet is on the Iraq pumps that really took their toll from 2004 to 2008, and then the Afghan pumps from 2009 to 2013. Anything else is focused on the MEUs in the Atlantic and Pacific, and toward the end of Afghan, the UDP to Okinawa. Bridgeport was nonexistent, and would only come up if some salty SNCO brought it up in reference to the cold. SNCOs were the only Marines we came across who had either heard of Bridgeport or had even been there. Certainly not a lance coolie or NCO thing to do.

Major McNulty replaces our beloved Lieutenant Colonel Zagurski, and we keep the same sergeant major, Sergeant Major Tracy, also quite admired by many of us. We've never heard of either of these two leaders screwing guys over in an unfair sense, and they seem to on our side much of the time. But McNulty is a different beast. When I was in Snipers, we had a Ranger Ruck March challenge where you had to make twelve and half miles in three hours, with full kit. More than walking, you have to run lengths of it in order to pass. But about midway through this endurance hike, I'm trudging along, doing my best, and sucking in air, with my head pointed at the ground. From behind me I hear a guy fast approaching; he doesn't sound like a human, but maybe a demon out of breath, and is really pushing it. I look back at the ground, and see these unbloused cammies. I continue looking up, and up, until I get to his face as he comes abreast of me. And sure enough, it's McNulty, staring right back at me for a second, before he keeps on trucking ahead of me. Doesn't even say anything, just trucks his way along, beating me to the finish line. This guy is subhuman, a beast.

As soon as he takes over the battalion, literally from the change-of-command ceremony, McNulty announces that not only are we going to be doing a series of ridiculously long hikes, but we are also going to be going to Bridgeport. Later on, he reminds us that when he took command he promised us Bridgeport, and sure enough we get Bridgeport. And this is how the beast got the name "McNutso," in addition to his official wall portrait of him, with the most intense eyeballs you've ever seen, trying to stare into your soul. It's almost as if Darth Vader took off his mask and put on a set of Alphas. One day this guy ran by Charlie Company in line at the armory, stopped, looked inside at the grunts behind the fence cleaning weapons, ran back to the battalion CP, and promptly ordered Charlie's chain of command to start on a ten-kay hike. Just like that: Marines are being unproductive, go hiking.

The battalion then embarks on this massive twenty-five-mile hike, that eventually a number of guys fall out on. This is after a series of hikes leading up to the 25 to get us in shape for the 25. The route is so long, that instead of starting at the CP or the Bricks, we get bussed out to one of the training areas in Lejeune and start the hike from there. The loadout actually isn't that bad, just flaks and assault packs, and the hike itself isn't entirely arduous, just mind-numbingly boring and repetitive. But we hike all day, and eventually end up at Onslow Beach, where we are told we will be finishing. But no, once we get to the beach, it appears that we are several hundred yards short of the goal of 25 miles. So what do we do? Walk up and down the beach, of course, until we get that mileage in.

Come January 2013, the battalion starts the admin and supply work for Bridgeport. Each company rotates into C-tep, drawing cold-weather gear. Huge white Mickey Mouse boots, thick brown socks, polymer leg gaiters, Nalgene bottles with metal cups and their mesh Molle containers, and of course the infamous happy suits. These suits are a three-piece combination: a thick jacket, thick pants that can be unzipped off without taking off your boots, and then the booties for your cold feet. We got so much cold weather gear that they give us a deployment bag to stuff it all into as well. This is where some of the uncertainty starts to creep in. Of course, we know it's going to be cold, but seeing all the gear in the flesh gives us extra goosebumps, as if to say, "We've never worked with this sort of thing … what did we just get ourselves into …" Complicating this mess is the fact that the battalion is more or less completely boot. Weapons, Charlie, and Bravo companies pretty much only have seniors for fireteam leaders and above, with entire squads of just boots.

The battalion gets a 96 liberty before we push out to Bridgeport. Sort of a last chance to collect ourselves before we face this odd unknown. We cannot even comprehend the misery that is about to befall our poor selves. So on the day off, we get all our gear out, deployment bags, main packs, and one seabag per fireteam. Draw weapons, and stage for the buses. The buses take us to Cherry Point, where we get the flight manifests in order, load up the planes, and off we fly to Marsh Air Base in northern California. We deplane, get all of our gear on the tour buses that await us, check our EDL, and then we begin the long drive to Bridgeport. Night falls, and most everybody sleeps on the bus.

We don't notice the drop in temperature, really a descent into hell. Soon we are winding down roads surrounded by bare hills that rise on either side of the road. Eventually the signs start popping up – MARINE CORPS MOUNTAIN WARFARE TRAINING CENTER – and we pull into this shabby establishment. I look out the left side of the bus, and I see these hills in the distance that don't look so large; this place can't be that bad. File off the bus, and heck, it is cold, brown bear warming layer cold. And it just bites into you, from every direction, and eats its way into your ears and nostrils. Beanies come out, and hands go in the pockets. Probably the only Marine Corps establishment where cold hands stuffed in warm pockets is permissible, just. It becomes hard to breathe, because of our elevation at some 7,000 feet above sea level.

Bridgeport hooches are warm, I'll give the training center that. They are divided into four open squad bays, with a central corridor separating them, and a common head also in the center, with open showers. Everyone in the four squad bays shares this common head. At the entrance, there is a foyer with double doors leading into the warm corridor. This is where trash, gas tanks, and MRE boxes are piled up, ready to use. Each squad bay is large enough to fit a T/O platoon, with bunk beds lining either side of it. Down the center of these squad bays are lockers, about two per bunk bed. But as if going to Bridgeport isn't a sick enough joke, all the lockers are different sizes. Some are large enough to fit your main pack, deployment bag, and seabag, with a top shelf for small things, while others serve a better purpose of just barely fitting some hockey sticks lined up vertically.

I wake up in the morning, sleeping in because the main element hasn't gotten here yet. I go shave, put on some cammies and walk outside to go to the chow hall with some buddies. I look up at where those nice little hills I saw at night were, and instead I'm greeted by mountains. Huge mountains! But that is one of the evil tricks Bridgeport plays on you. Take that hill, that gentle rolling hill over there. Wait no, this isn't gentle, this thing goes straight up, completely vertical! And it isn't rolling: it gains several hundred feet in elevation.

Adding to the sick joke, the Bridgeport chow hall is the best chow hall in the Marine Corps, hands down. The place is huge for an installation of its size. And the diversity, oh, the diversity! You can have apple, blueberry, orange, juices, vanilla mix, and all the brands of soda. Desserts are a different item on several refrigerated shelves that you get to pick from, constantly being restocked and refilled. The salad bar is huge, and you get to pick whatever you want from it. Main lines are the same, with all sorts of food and no limit on how much you can take. Leagues ahead of the chicken shack back at

Lejeune. Then you have this killer view of the snow-capped mountains and countryside that just extends for miles. And on good, clear days, you can see the tallest of the mountains far off in the distance.

Soon we get our mountain warfare gear. Ancient skis from the 1970s, ski poles, snowshoes with metal cleats, skins for our skis, gas burners so we can boil water, heavy-duty tents to sleep in. But where does all the commonly used gear go? To add to the sick joke, they have this thing called the MCWIK – Mountain Cold Weather Infantry Kit – which is a sled, with a zippered canvas top, and two poles with a belt. This evil contraption is strapped to a designated poor soul's waist, often the biggest guy in the platoon or squad, but no one can haul it for long as misery is best when shared.

We get all this extra gear, on top of the cold weather gear we already have, on top of all our normal CIF issued stuff. We get down to marking everything with duct tape, specifically our names and platoon. Then we tie five-fifty cord around the laces of our Mickey Mouse boots so that they don't become completely separated from the skis when we do fall off of them. Apart from a select few in the battalion with prior experience, no one of course knows how to ski.

Acclimatization usually takes a month or two for the average human being at these heights. We only have a week before we start the first exercise, of spending two weeks up on the mountain. During this time we do PT in the morning and take various classes that the "Red Hats" give, called Pre-Environmental Training, or PET. These are Marines permanently stationed at MWTC, in an instructing capacity. They are the subject-matter experts on all things cold weather- and mountain-related. They are called red hats because they wear these red beanies everywhere they go. Make no mistake, these fellows are conniving and all in on the sick joke that Bridgeport is. You'll be dying on your skis with your full gear on, crashing into snowbanks left and right, while these guys seem to be floating by on their overseas precision-made equipment, saying, "Look at me! Shit's not that hard." In addition to the various snowshoe and entry-level cold weather classes, we have all sorts of briefs on what not to do in the mountain. Don't dig holes, don't smoke, don't carve crap onto Native American trees, don't cut wood, don't start fires unless in a survival situation, shit in buckets, and piss on piss trees.

McNutso has a comprehensive briefing for all NCOs and above in the large auditorium. Here he introduces his favorite mantra of "Check, check, and recheck" for which we are all make fun of him afterward. He emphasizes the strong need for leaders to be there for their guys. And for the most part, he is correct. The odd thing about Bridgeport, and cold weather fighting/

training isn't so much the actual temperature, but is in fact the psychology of how much the cold affects us. Within this cold weather environment, simple things become difficult and complex tasks become impossible. Something about the constant cold makes guys completely shut down, lose their minds, go suicidal. Some even "cocoon," when guys have nothing wrong with them physically or mentally, but their mind has completely shut down, and they are in priority M-E mode entirely, often sitting in a corner and complaining of cold hands and feet, not being able to feel their toes or fingers. An absolute test of leadership, Bridgeport separates the men from the boys. You don't doing anything differently in a mountainous environment when it comes to infantry tactics. Hiking places, setting up a defense, conducting an attack, it's more or less the same set of procedures as anywhere. But the actual conduct of absolutely everything is infinitely more complicated than on Lejeune, or even in Helmand for that matter. Just getting out of your sleeping bag, and putting on a fresh pair of socks, then putting on your white Mickey Mouse boots, and tying them, takes up a good ten minutes because your fingers are bitterly cold, your face is about to fall off, and the drift coming in through the tent flap is chilling your entire body. Never mind a complex task like setting up a tent or plugging digits on a PRC 117. These are the sorts of things that McNutso warns us about, and we have no clue what we are about to get into.

The day we start our ascent is all-or-nothing time. We spend the previous night prepping, ripping apart white cold weather MREs, making our gear as small and tight as possible. Team leaders are moving between their guys, checking that this item has been marked in a certain way, or that every third man has this piece or that. Making sure that no one is wearing any woolen material like your skivvy shirt. You always think to prepare in the past tense, and as a leader you do, but yet everything gets pushed to the present, like several hours before a movement. Oh, this just got passed from battalion/company to do this thing or that thing. We have to pack our main packs this way or that, put our skis in on either side of the pack. Before you know it, the time is 02, and we have to wake up at 04 for the hike.

"First platoon, form it up outside!" yells Sergeant Mendenhall.

Rush, rush, rush, squad leaders pushing their team leaders, team leaders pushing their guys. Where the heck are Ward and Smith, always late to everything. We get outside, packs laden with awkward skis, clanging into each other. Bravo and Weapons are formed up together for the long hike, in two columns, typical admin march. They tell us this will be the longest hike we do, at something like seven or ten kilometers. Final EDL, and then we wait around for a bit. It has started snowing, just a little bit though, nothing too much. Just enough to make the eyebrows tickle.

"Stepppppinnnnnnnng!" goes down the line, and we're off, to begin this winter wonderland adventure.

For the first kilometer, through MWTC, and working our way up the back mountain path, it isn't that bad. It's uphill, and we start warming up because Bob the sun is out, and the pace is manageable. Then guys start dropping. Like flies. Huffman is the first to go. He just stops, held up by the guys in front and behind; his eyes are closed, and the poor kid is gasping for air. I run over and grab him by the chest. "Huffy, talk to me Huffy, TALK TO ME!" Nothing, this kid is a goner, he is overheating. Torres goes down as well. The kid just drops to the side of the road, almost passes out. It is a frantic move, ripping off his pack, his Gortex, letting all the heat out before his brain starts cooking. And it continues like this throughout the march. Sergeant Mendenhall drops twice: the one second he's standing there, the next his entire body impacts the road, his M4 stock hitting his forehead. The second time, I'm behind him, and he stops for a second, wavers, then topples over on his left. I run up to him with my pack on.

Zhao the corpsman is also there: "What's your first name? Where are you at right now?"

Mendenhall stammers out, "Z … Z … Zach, I don't know."

Gonzales comes up; he's the new platoon sergeant. Mendenhall is going back down the mountain. LeMasters, or LeMac as they call him, goes out during a short halt. The second you stop moving, you start freezing, so you learn to get out that happy jacket and throw it on during these things. LeMac either doesn't get the memo or isn't thinking, which is all of us really, not thinking at that point. LeMac starts shivering, almost going into shock; the kid has hypothermia. Quickly we strip him down to his boxers, and get another kid, Simmons, in his boxers as well, putting the two of them in a sleeping bag so LeMac doesn't get any worse. The safety vehicle, a Norwegian tracked thing called a BV, pulls up and wheels him out of there. Pickney, one of my M27 gunners, goes down as well. They say he was frothing at the mouth when they threw him into the safety vic.

Bravo Company clears the last small hill, where we pull up. Stragglers start coming in and we count our losses. All in all, 1st Platoon is down to less than twenty-five guys. If a unit is decimated, it means more than 10 percent of the unit are casualties. We are practically combat ineffective at this point. Because darkness is coming, we fix together a giant tent made out of tarps, held up by ski poles. Under this we try to sleep, freezing, absolutely freezing. The feet are the worst. You can warm up your torso with the happy jacket, your head with your beanie, your arms can wrap around your chest, but your feet are the farthest extremity from your heart, so the blood struggles to circulate to your feet.

The next day, and for the next two weeks, we are up on the mountain, digging fighting positions in the snow, defensive perimeters, and learning how to ski, which no one really masters, and everyone eats powder at every attempt. We boil snow to make water, which takes hours if not done right. We learn how to set in our tents, cover them with snow to keep the heat in, and build deep holes in the snow, which we sleep in. We crap in plastic bags that are emplaced in yellow buckets, because California is environmentally like that. Every few days we move to a fresh location, where new training and classes are held.

McNutso comes out and gives us a pep talk about our state of affairs. "You guys are lucky; people pay thousands of dollars to do what you are doing right now, and not only are you getting it for free, but you're being paid to do it!" He doesn't mention that the entire battalion has had over 350 casualties, from hypothermia, overheating, broken bones, guys getting suicidal, frostbite, and a range of high-altitude conditions. Each time we talk to the corpsmen, the numbers go up by the day: 100, then 150, then 200, then 250. We conjure up some rumor mill that says if the battalion gets to 400, they'll take us off the mountain, or if it gets below negative 25 they'll take us off the mountain. Negative 25 is where all of our gear is rated to, so theoretically we can't possibly operate in that temperature range due to the limitations of our gear.

But the snow! Oh, behold the snow! It entraps you as you walk to take a piss without your snowshoes on, it freezes you when you fall off your skis and you're covered by it, and it warms your tent by providing shelter against the wind. You will sit there, for hours, scooping up chunks of snow and dropping it into your heated cup to melt. But fire watch has to tend to it all night, and somehow down the line it gets forgotten, and you have no water in the morning when you go on that practice ski run. Oftentimes you get so thirsty or bored that you start eating the stuff, and it feels good as it melts on your tongue. Not only is this incredibly unhealthy, but it is a sign of closing in and breaking down mentally. You lose half your gear in it because you'll wake up in the morning and if you forgot to put a tarp over your main pack, then the whole thing is covered in an inch of snow from the night before. Your weapons, skis, and snowshoes all have metal on them; they get cold with the snowfall, and now you have the first stages of frostbite just from touching the metal in sub-zero. Then it is everywhere: you look at the mountains, it covers them; you look under the trees, it is there; you look across the valley, and everything is one blanket of snow.

One morning, we get a runner from battalion. One of our guys, Ryan, has to be pulled out of the field. Instantly. To get back to the east coast, this straight from the sergeant major. We are confused. Rumors float around, something about a family member of his assaulting his wife back in J-ville, and several legal charges or something. It's all odd to us. However, it doesn't come as a surprise; the kid is having endless trouble back home with his marriage situation anyways.

Eventually, we reach the end of our two weeks' PET, and we hike back down the mountain. This is a glorious hike because we know we are going back into those warm hooches where we left off. The snow even senses our presence, and it appears to melt as we get lower. Downhill the rest of the way, many of us are triumphant in spirit, stripped down to our Gortex trousers, and bottom-warming layers. We walk into MWTC from the northwest, along the horse pens and the airfield, until we break up into our hooches. There we do an EDL, stash our gear under our racks and wherever else we can squeeze them into. Then we take showers, and we can feel the coldness of the mountain leaving our skin as the seething hot water washes over us. Get into cammies, and a trip to the chow hall in formation is in order. Rest my son, that mountain sucked. I can't believe the amount of suck that happened at Bastogne, where they didn't have the luxury of lightweight thermals and hot showers down the mountain.

But the sick joke isn't over yet. After about three days, we prep to go right back up the mountain. This time, it is for the Fex, the field exercise. Here, instead of the red hats leading us along, they will sit back and observe us, grading our every movement and technique. The plan is to move the entire battalion up the mountain in a matter of hours, using BVs. The problem is that there are not enough BVs for the whole battalion; there are not even enough BVs for one company. So this involves several trips per company, multiplied by four total company forays. The hurry-up-and-wait game is overblown into proportion, and instead of leaving at around 0900, our BVs aren't ready to pick us up until maybe 2000, in complete darkness. In addition to this cluster mess, a full-blown snowstorm is in effect the night we get up on the mountain, limiting visibility to forty feet or so. Then some of the scout skiers, specially trained and equipped grunts that can cover vast distances across snow, get bogged down in the snowstorm, some of them requiring a medevac. On top of this, one of the BVs starts smoking from the inside when a wire catches fire, and the whole crew has to come tumbling out, some of them being treated for burns (they eventually still get sent up the mountain).

The Fex goes along smoother than PET. For the most part, we spend the days sitting in defensive positions, until we get told to pack up, cover up the track plan, and push on to the next defensive position. We never get used to the misery of the cold; we sort of just learn to deal with it. It never becomes tolerable. Similar to how people might look at pictures of polar bears or seals and claim that with their skin and coats they are so warm. I think the animals are just tolerably miserable, and not entirely cozy to begin with. The end of the Fex is Bravo Company going on the offensive, taking a small mountaintop where an element from our OpFor (Fox Two Nine) is in position. After being mercilessly cut down by blanks in an open field – we were crossing it and then got stuck in it with our snowshoes – after firing a barrage of blanks ourselves, we finally take the objective and set up camp around it. The peak isn't too bad, because it starts warming up, enough for base-warming layers. And we can see the scenic treetops all around us, the valley off in the distance. Finally the Fex comes to a close and we are done. The closing statement of the sick joke is that the BVs are late, and we almost spend the night out in the snow. But sure enough, the BVs come out at around 03 and take us back. Bridgeport is over. Thank God.

Down at lower base camp, the battalion begins to turn everything in. All the extra cold-weather equipment needs to be put together, cleaned out, sorted through, and stacked for the final turn-in. The only problem is that a quarter of everything is back on the mountainside, because of one reason or another. So we send guys back up there in the cold to go looking for this lost gear. Some of it comes back, some of it will probably always be up there. The end result is everything is turned in, and we're ready for our next adventure, Hawthorne.

While in between PET and Fex, I'm at the PX and the battalion Gunner is behind me. He's a tall, serious-looking man, with all his time in the Corps blatantly showing in his textured face, and slow manner of speech, very precise and carefully worded as well. He is a Gunner, essentially a certified, experienced expert on all the weapons the battalion employs. He spent his enlisted time with different Victor units, going to Iraq and Afghanistan, before becoming a warrant officer. These officers almost seem to have the best of both worlds. They have the experience and common sense of the black-spray-paint NCOs, the authority and prestige of an officer, yet none of the overwhelming responsibility that either carries. Because I'd talked with him several times previously, I turn and say hello to him, but more importantly because I know he has the answer, I ask him, "Sir, what's the deal with going to Hawthorne in Nevada?"

The Gunner replies, "It's a bonus thing for battalions. Come to Bridgeport for the mountain warfare side, then go to Hawthorne for some more practical training along the lines that is more relevant to Afghanistan and Iraq." Makes Marine Corps sense, and that's all that's important.

The drive to Hawthorne is on the typical white school buses that the Marine Corps always has sitting around somewhere. We pile up our main packs and flaks on the seven-tons, then fit into the buses for a comfy ride to another middle-of-nowhere destination. And indeed it is. Hawthorne Army Ammunition Depot is absolutely in the middle of the Nevada desert. The place doesn't even have that many soldiers on it, just a whole lot of contractors guarding one of the largest ammunition depots in the country. But it has tons of empty space and makes for great training, gents, great training. The whole location looks straight out of a *The Hills Have Eyes* set. Even the populated portion of the base, with the old army houses and abandoned buildings, still has posters from the 1970s and 1980s on their corkboards. Regardless, it's good training, gents, good training.

The training evolution is divided up between three stages, or a round robin as we call it. Each line company goes to one location of the three, does about two days' worth of training, and then rotates out to the next stage, and so on. One stage is a company live-fire attack, another an MOUT (Military Operations on Urbanized Terrain) town evaluation, and the final one is IED training. Bravo's first stage is the company live-fire, both night and day attacks, in addition to rehearsals. It isn't a bad range as live-fire ranges go, but it is extremely long, almost as long as Range 400, the infantry granddaddy of all live-fire ranges. We do it as a company live-fire, and it goes alright, but we're all a little rusty on the traditional infantry role because we've gotten used to Bridgeport. But in addition to the heat, it feels good doing something normal again. Oh, Lord, the heat: it feels orgasmic just being around it, and not having to worry about which one of your three pairs of gloves is the soggiest. One thing that gets us though, is that we're using pyrotechnic charges, 5-star clusters that have dates of manufacture on them older than some of our parents.

After the company live-fire range, we rotate to MOUT-Town, while Charlie Company does the live-fire range. The MOUT drill is a number of conex boxes arranged in a hamlet; I can't even say a city. Here we work on room-clearing as a team, squad, and platoon but otherwise actually get to take a breather from everything. After our two days we move on to the final station, which is the IED lane-clearing role. Switching with Alpha, we get out of the seven-tons, and Alpha jumps right on them, a very quick switch. I remember seeing Muchnick, and maybe Taylor, but didn't think anything of it as we passed. I wish I had seen them or made contact with them in some way. It was the last time I would be seeing them alive.

The IED lane-clearing consists of a mounted IED attack, and a foot patrol IED attack, in addition to an actual IED indicator lane where we walk through an area that has a number of indicators like pressure plates, ant trails, pressure releases, tree-mounted IEDs, wires coming out of the ground, and EFPs. Pretty good training. But here I am tasked out as a Humvee driver, as I have my license (I lost my spot as a squad leader in the live exercise, due to my incompetence as a leader). It's a nice turn of events when you're a driver: you just have yourself and the truck to worry about. The trips get you away from the platoon, and whatever police call or nonsense the company feels it's necessary to inflict on the Marines. As a driver we have to ferry chain-of-command members back and forth, pick up water and chow, in addition to driving the Humvees for the mounted IED lane. One night we drive back to the live-fire range, where Alpha is, and one of our A-drivers has been smashed into by a Humvee. He isn't the brightest match in the box. He was ground-guiding the driver into a Hesco but omitted to tell the driver to stop the truck, and got jammed between the Humvee and the Hesco. Eventually, the truck backed off, but Craig was left with a crushed something in his body, and had to be evacuated.

The rotation comes to a close, with only Alpha still at Hawthorne. We close out with a pizza party, ordering pizza in the field; the store apparently has to get a whole van to cart the damned things to us. Hundreds of dollars' worth of pizza, and it's glorious, every bite of it, even if it's cold by the time the delivery guy finds us. Finally, it is time to go home. We still have almost a week before our expected flights will take us back to Cherry Point. The buses take us on the two-hour ride back to Bridgeport. We arrive in the evening, and pull all our dusty gear off the seven-tons, get our final EDLs and pull into our racks. Charge up cellphones on daisy-chain chargers, take showers, set up firewatch, and chill out.

After a while of settling in, a sick rumor starts around the hooch, in whispers, something about an accident in Alpha Company. Corpsmen seem to be walking back and forth for some reason. Then word gets passed, "All Bravo Company get outside." What's going on? This has to be serious now. We gather outside, in one large group, leaders getting their head checks, from team leaders to platoon sergeants.

"Second Platoon is up."

"Third's good"

"First is up"

"Weapons? Headquarters?"

"Roger, First Sergeant, Weapons is up."

The CO, Captain Plasencia comes out from the double doors. School circle. "Gents, I have gathered you all out here for a reason. I don't want to waste your time. Alpha Company has suffered a fatality at Hawthorne while doing their live-fire range. We don't know anything else at this point, but anyone who has deployed knows that we will have to go into 'River City' so that means we'll be collecting all your cellphones, and we'll hand them back out when River City has lifted."

What … the … heck … just … happened?

* * *

The next morning, a staff sergeant comes in to our squad bay and asks briskly, "Hey, who here is a Humvee driver?" I volunteer instantly. As soon as those words had come out of his mouth, I immediately started thinking of my friends in the Alpha mortar section: Taylor, Herring, Fenn, Kline, and then, "Not Taylor, not Taylor; it can't be him."

We're still in River City because they have confiscated all our cellphones. River City is put in place mainly overseas when Marines are killed, to ensure the families don't learn about their sons getting blown apart on national TV. It lasts until the family is properly notified, which can be anywhere between several hours and several days. Frequently Pogs or civilians gripe about not being able to use the internet, which pisses grunts off as a comrade is dead and all these people are doing is complaining about not getting on the Wi-Fi.

CNN is on and it's already across the news: "7 Marines killed in Nevada During Training." That hits us as a huge surprise, jumping from one fatality to seven. We know it was a mortar accident and this makes it even worse. The M224 mortar system is organic to an infantry company, light artillery, as it were. It can reach out to several thousand meters and has a kill radius of fifteen meters, and a casualty range of fifty-plus. The way a mortar team works is three men are on a gun, all within touching distance. One man holds the base plate, another drops the round, while a third stands at the rear directing the team. To have a mortar detonate in the tube is a mortarman's worst nightmare.

Our task is to go back to Hawthorne to pick up the personal effects of the casualties, killed and wounded. One of the supply staff sergeants and his aide come with us, to account for the equipment. We flak up and take two Humvees to the fuel farm at Bridgeport for the two-hour trip. I know the aide from my first deployment; he was a lance who deployed to Kuwait with Alpha. I turn and ask, "What are the names? Do you know them?" Still in the mindset of "Not Taylor, not Taylor, not Taylor, he's too good to go, he's better than most of us in any field, he's about to get married, and he's a Goddamn virgin, for crying out loud."

The aide looks at the staff sergeant uneasily. They know the names but cannot tell until River City is lifted. The staff sergeant knows who I am. "It's alright, you can tell him; he knows not to be stupid." The tension grows; a knot forming in my stomach, half wanting to know the names and half not ever wanting to know, not ever wanting to find out how fellow grunts had been ripped apart limb from limb due to a 60mm mortar round.

The lance takes a deep breath and says, "Alright."

Here it comes.

"Vanderwork ... Muchnick ..."

Wow, Vanderwork? He was about to get married; I had just met his fiancée before Bridgeport, and Muchnick? That party animal, are you serious?

"Martino ... Ripperda ..."

Who is Martino? Ripperda had two months left in the Corps, an older corporal, almost thirty. I talked to him at length one time on duty about his sailing ambitions and his tough time getting out of the Corps.

"Fenn ... Wild ..."

Wild I didn't know too well, and Fenn had a daughter but was in the middle of a divorce. I was in boot camp, SOI, and entered the fleet with Fenn while he went to Weapons and me to Charlie.

The second the name Taylor comes out of his mouth, tears started streaming down my face. And they kept streaming, unto this day. When I see a bright ginger kid, or a compact Kimber 1911, look down at my black memorial bracelet, or see a church on the side of the road, I think of Joshua Taylor.

Months later, an Irish girl I'm talking to is scrolling through my Facebook page, looking at all my photos, all my friends, the usual thing that young people do these days to get acquainted with each other on social media. All of a sudden she pipes up, "Who's this Joshua Taylor guy? He looks like a really handsome and proper Marine!" She doesn't know about Hawthorne or Taylor, she had just seen his profile picture on Facebook, an account owned by a man will who will no longer enter in his username and password. But I smile, and I realize, it's just another one of the small things Taylor has brought into this world: he's still impacting people. Even if it's just by his reddish hair and good looks.

Before the memorial service at Bridgeport, and again at CAX I gather my boots around and tell them, "I hope you never have to hear a seven-gun salute, or get in your blues for your friend's funeral. Never have to touch a coffin that has your friend's mangled corpse in it and say, 'This is it brother, rest easy.' Never have to hold his loved ones because they are never going to hold him anymore. Never have to know that a man is ten times better than you'll ever be: that if you were a quarter of the man he was you'd be successful. That this man is now gone, gone forever, that the best thing you can do is live out his life through yours, to honor him on Memorial Day and Veterans Day, to tell others his story …"

We roll into Alpha's staging area, and the mood is dead, just like the seven grunts. NCIS and EOD are already there, their vehicles parked at the side, to investigate ground zero. The packs are already lined up for us to load in the barn-door trunks of the Humvees, dead in one and wounded in the other. Off to one side is the mortar section, now barely a squad, their flaks and assault packs smeared with dried blood. I pass Alpha's gunny, a list in his hand with "KIA" at the top, listing my friends, my brothers, my fellow grunts, men I have grown up with in the Marine Corps, went to boot camp and SOI with, deployed with. Over by the packs of the dead a small group huddles round Taylor's pack, all grabbing at the straps as if to try and feel him and bring back alive by touching some of his gear. Kline is there, with a bandage on his head from horsing around back in Bridgeport: that injury prevented him from running Range 500, and saved him from being on that gun line. He is crying, the guys round the pack are crying, all of Alpha is crying. I put my hand on his shoulder, trying to reassure him. "Not here man, not in training, this isn't the way to go out." And that's the worst part of it all.

As grunts we sign up for the firefights, for the rush, to kill people, to sling lead. We know we face death and injury, we know we face turning into pink mist, and gunshot wounds to the face. We train for it, we try to mitigate it but at the end of the day, even if we do our jobs perfectly, textbook patrolling, actions under fire, we can still die, no matter how much braver you are than Dakota Meyer. We know this and expect it overseas, in mortal combat with our enemies, even fantasize about it: "I'm going out of this world like I came, screaming and covered with blood, in a pile of spent brass." But not here, not in training, not in some desert in Nevada. This is America; this is the land we patrol mindlessly to come home to, stand thousands of hours of post to see again. For girlfriends and wives, bar-hopping and alcohol, watching TV and feeling normal. Training isn't where you die, where you get ripped apart, lose limbs and die slowly. This isn't a warrior's death; this isn't supposed to happen. But it happened, and we are reminded every time we think about the guys we lost.

Bridgeport was a horrible experience, the cold and snow the most miserable times of my life. But we'd all go through a thousand Bridgeports if Fenn was still be around to play with Nyka, Taylor to marry Abby, Ripperda to own a sailing boat, Martino to have his two kids to raise, Vanderwork to take weekends off at Onslow beach, Muchnick to bang scores of beautiful women, Wild to become a firefighter.

McNutso came out during the memorial service taking all the blame off himself, saying that he had taken every measure he could to ensure this shouldn't have happened. We rolled our eyes and hated him for it. You stupid son of a bitch, it was your fault we went to that winter wonderland to ski for free, your fault we went to Hawthorne, where Twentynine Palms has more terrain character. We were using pyro charges with "1971" stamped as the manufacturing date; no wonder the round blew up in the tube. Some of the mortars had cracks in them from going from a cold environment to a warm one, like how rocks crack from rapid changes in temperature. The medevac bird took over an hour to get to Hawthorne from Reno: dust-off flights in Afghanistan take less than that.

The Marine Corps published a report saying it was a double feed in the tube. This can happen when the sixty is being fired handheld with a round already at the base of the tube, and the trigger is pulled, but another round has been dropped without any knowledge of the first round. The first round is fired and hits the primer of the second, thus detonating in the tube. But these weren't boots brand new to the Fleet; although one, Martino, was, but he wasn't on the tube that blew. The rest were combat veterans, all had two deployments under their belts, and most had been on the Advanced Mortar Leaders Course. These guys knew their mortars backward; they could have executed a flawless fire mission blindfold and under fire. The report labeled it human error, even pointing to Vanderwork as the culprit behind firing the trigger, explaining that there was a double feed, with the second mortar round found 100 meters away, unexploded. This is easy for an organization like the Marines, label it human error and all we have to do is fire some officers. God forbid it's the weapon's fault, then those juicy defense contracts fizzle out. Death demands accountability. To this day many of us are still bitter about the entire episode.

As a result, the command was shuffled up. The BC, Gunner and Alpha CO got relieved and their careers were done for. We didn't mind the BC going, good riddance even. Alpha never liked their CO, but the Gunner was a good officer, knew his stuff and had deployed with us before. But he was the designated weapons guru for the battalion and ultimately responsible for every weapons system employed, from our M16A4 service rifles and Two-Forty medium machine guns to the larger 81mm mortars and Javelin missile systems in Weapons Company.

Some of the story that filtered back was that Alpha was running their night live-fire attack. They were almost done with the exercise; in fact, some of their forward elements were at the end of the range, when they were told to index and admin-column back. Taylor's gun team, consisting of Mason Vanderwork and Josh Martino somehow got confused in the low-light confusion while firing from the handheld position. This is where the loader drops the round in the tube, and the firer grasps a handle at the base of the mortar, clutching an oversize trigger, that then fires the mortar like a firearm, a firing pin through the hole. However, the tube was double-loaded with two mortar rounds. The first one hit the base of the second one, and exploded in the tube. The second one was propelled 100 meters away and did not explode. Martino, Vanderwork, and Taylor were killed instantly, limbs torn off, faces gone, their flaks completely shredded. Roger Muchnick, David Fenn II, and William Wild were nearby on another gun team; they died from their injuries within two hours: lost limbs, all with massive blood loss. The more they kept working on Muchnick, the more entry and exit wounds they found on him. Fenn died on the medevac helicopter. Aaron Ripperda didn't even have to be there that night; he was helping out the range PSO (Position Safety Officer) because he was a mortarman himself from Weapons Company, but he was standing behind the gun team when it happened, as PSOs normally do.

There were seven other casualties, some critical that occurred from the same blast. Doc Ian Mclannahan was one of them with his entire lower jaw blown off. On his own, he inserted a nasopharyngeal airway tube down his nose and throat, thus clearing himself an area and allowing him to continue breathing. Not only did he have the presence of mind to do this, but he was waving oncoming first responders onto the more seriously injured grunts that were dying.

One of the boots in the mortar section had constantly been getting hazed for doing boot things the previous couple of weeks, and was known as the bitch of the mortar section. However, that night, he sustained a savage hole in his hand from the shrapnel, but didn't tell a soul because he wanted to stay and help the wounded. It wasn't until the light of morning that someone noticed his hand and said: "Holy shit, you need a fucking corpsman." That boot earned his right to be in Alpha weapons platoon.

Warrant Officer West was the battalion aide-de-camp, sort of like the third-highest-ranking officer in the battalion after the BC and the XO. He was hit in his legs, and wheelchair-confined for many months afterward. But as he lay on the ground suffering, he kept his composure, and cracked jokes to all the wounded, maintaining some semblance of morale. Lance Corporal Hand was a boot NBC specialist in the battalion, and was almost killed when shrapnel came within a fraction of severing his femoral artery. But he survived.

Returning to Bridgeport was a silent ride. Nothing but me, my A-driver, and all the KIA packs in the Humvee. We get back to the hooches, unload the packs and the staff sergeant takes care of the rest. I walk in with my flak still on. No one at MWTC knows any of the details of what even happened. Ponte and Homar see me, as does Dom.

"Who are they, man? I know you can't tell anyone but tell us," says Gonzales.

"Well, there's Taylor ... Muchnick ... Ripperda ... Vanderwork ... Fenn ... Martino ... and Wild ... fuck man."

Silence. Gonzales shakes his head at each name, slams a locker and walks off.

Dom asks, "Vanderwork, he was from Weapons Company, right?"

"Yeah, he was in my squad on deployment. Fuck, Vanderwork, he was such a sweet kid."

Later on that afternoon, we form up for chow. The day is dark, and everyone in the battalion along the way has this disgusted look on their face, especially the seniors who served with the killed, but also the younger guys, those who didn't know them; all just have this dark look of foreboding.

A platoon from Charlie Company is passing, and I see Stinson in the front rank. I tell Gonzales, "Hey I'm going to step over here for a while, if you don't mind." Gonzales nods.

"Hey Stinson! Come over here for a second man."

Stinson looks at me and grins a bit, "Yeah Vining, what's up man?" He separates from the formation and walks with me over by a few staged conex boxes.

"Stinson man, I have to tell you something. Fenn man ... Fenn ..."

Fenn was with Stinson and me in our boot camp platoon and in our SOI class. Taylor, Muchnick, and Vanderwork were also in our SOI class.

"No ... no ... noooooooooo ... not Fenn, man ... not Fenn."

"Yes, Fenn, man, I was over there today in a Humvee picking up all their gear to bring back here. Taylor, Vanderwork as well."

"Taylor? Vanderwork? Fucking hell, man ..." He starts crying a bit, wiping away the tears. I hold him tight and pat him on the back; I'm crying a bit as well.

I see Hillard, one of my buddies from Charlie at the smoke-pit. I heard that he was working on the wounded during the incident. His eyes are fixed on some spot on the ground, not really taking anything in around him.

"Hillard, man."

He looks up at me, and we hug each other. Slowly, his story comes out: "I was a PSO down with second platoon in a ravine when it happened, and I checked out Harris first and then went ... on from there I went across the hill after they called over the radios for the combat lifesaver and Dmoc guys to come to the mortar position. The first person I came to was Davies … he told me to go help someone else … he was good … then I came up to Miles …. Harris checked him out … he was stable. I wanna say Joseph Zoeller was working on Muchnick. The next person I came to was Vanderwork. I started talking to him but I didn't have a light … shook him, and realized he was dead …he was laying on his stomach, and I realized his head was gone. Tried to help Doc Mclannahan … after that I remember helping move the dead and helping guys getting on the helos."

* * *

There is a ramp ceremony the day after at the Reno airport. A number of us get on buses to attend. We drive out there and wait around a bit. Then we all line up in the cold, in two columns leading up to the open ramp of a C-130. Soon enough, the hearses arrive and stage at the end of our column. We salute, and an honor guard made up of National Guardsmen takes the flag-draped coffins, one by one into the aircraft. There are eight coffins: seven bodies, and one unidentified remains. This eighth coffin is later interred at Arlington while the bodies are sent home: Taylor to Marietta, Ohio; Fenn to Clearwater, Florida; Vanderwork is cremated, his remains to the beach in North Carolina; Wild to Arlington; Ripperda to Highland, Illinois; and Martino to Debois, Pennsylvania.

The coffins are loaded up, the crew start going through their takeoff procedures, to take the bodies to Dover Air Force Base in Delaware, where all military KIA are processed, bodies fixed up and sent to their families. Most will have a closed-casket funeral because the damage is so severe. We all fall back to the glass building where we watch the C-130 rev its engines and take off. Many of us have a teary eye.

Bridgeport and Hawthorne complete, we settle to the tasks of going home to Lejeune. Packing bags, gear inspections, EDLs, field daying the hooches. Finally the buses arrive and we stuff our seabags, main packs, and deployment bags in the holds, board the buses and tune out to our iPods. We leave at night, just like when we came. On the way out, we see a solitary coyote about to get run over, but he darts away as the buses near. Somewhat of a natural finishing touch. On to March Air Base, board the civilian planes, then on to Cherry Point. The planes land, we get off, go through the process of getting all our gear, then get on the tour buses that take us home to Lejeune. The sweet humidity of North Carolina engenders a newly acquired admiration compared to the cold of Bridgeport. I'm coughing up a lung, later diagnosed as bronchitis. But finally, after this winter wonderland and the Hawthorne nightmare, we are home. Minus our seven dead, and seven wounded.

Many moons past my EAS, I visit this mass grave in Arlington, several graves away from Wild's plot. It is a bright sunny day in Northern Virginia, I'm in a good mood with my girlfriend, but as we round the corner and find the large stone, I see all their names etched on it, and I tear up. Something about seeing all their names on there like that, etched for eternity, just gets to you somehow. I don't know how Vietnam vets deal with that on their wall.

Dead Walkers who took their lives

Corporal Julian Ortiz (Weapons Company)

Chapter 5

Burn Burn

"The things you've done, the things you've seen, the things you've touched, the things you've smelt, isn't normal. We were placed in a situation that we all signed up for, to be able to close with and engage the enemy. That's what we're trained for, and that's what we've wanted to do, and we've done it. And fortunately we've returned. However, our friends who've never returned, they don't want to see you giving up the lives that they fought for, they didn't die for the Queen, they didn't die for our country, they died for you. They died for me. They died for the opo who was standing beside them, the one who was willing to go into that compound with them, and kill the enemy. He was the one who died for you."

Sam Benson, Ranger Company, Royal Irish Regiment,
2 Para Battle Group

Her moans matched the rhythmic splash of the Atlantic Ocean waves against the Wilmington shoreline, accelerated only by my thrusts into the 19-year-old UNCW freshman, and muffled by my sloppy kisses. My hormone-fueled task completed, I collapsed on top of her, only to continue with the kissing and another round of fucking, right underneath the midnight moon and a lifeguard shack on the Wrightsville Beach. As long as they were of age and single, it didn't matter to me. Having a warm vagina beats my hands any weekend of any week, and I was swimming in hookups. Fat, skinny, single moms, Wilmington girls, northern Virginia and DC girls, black, white, Mexican, my only real restriction being anything in Jacksonville and married was off limits. I used Tinder, Plenty of Fish, and OKCupid like it was going out of style, and all at once. Done with one, I'd be moving on to the next one, while at the same time texting another to get prepped for when I came back home on Libo. For one, I certainly wasn't alone when it came to the procreation game. The practice isn't limited to grunts either, but Pogs as well. Girls don't know the difference, or care for that matter: it's all Marine to them. You can take that title a long ways if you want to. Part of this is young men doing what young men do. However, for myself, another part of it was Lynn. The emotional side of me was in such shock from the breakup, that my mind coped with it like a sort of trauma, tucking it away in the only way I could, in the far corners of my mind, and piling woman after woman on top of it, imagining that each of them was somehow going to bring me back to what I had with her.

This was greatly helped by the Fleet, in that it gave zero time to decompress, to process exactly what had just happened, by piling on tasks, MarineNet courses, training boots, the next deployment, prepping for Bridgeport. Dealing with the deaths of the Hawthorne guys didn't help much either. Although I was physically at Taylor's and Fenn's burials, I wasn't there emotionally. In the midst of trying to get over it, I fucked more random women, and drank more nights away, and went on more field ops with Bravo Company, my new home after leaving Snipers. It worked. It worked so well I pretty much forgot about Lynn, only to have it slap me in the face after I got out. But relationship problems weren't my only woe. Failing Sniper School, getting kicked out of the platoon I had worked so hard to get into, being transferred to a company I had no ties to, with no friends either, and then the whole Bridgeport–Hawthorne fiasco, with our seven dead as the lava icing on the volcano disaster of an eruption that once was my peaceful green pasture.

The Marine Corps, the face of my beloved infantry was also changing. Amos, a Pog Air Winger, had replaced Conway as commandant. For the first time in its history, the Marine Corps, primarily a fighting force, was being led by a non-trigger-puller. Away went the rolled sleeves, and the hazing in the barracks. The same hazing that had formed myself and my generation of boots was now getting grunts in trouble left and right. Rolled sleeves were gone too, making us look exactly like the army, and Lord knows no Marine wants to look like the army.

This led me to become a prisoner of precedent. Like a toddler, if it couldn't be done the way I was used to, or my way, then it couldn't be done at all. Whether it was field ops, training, or deploying, instead of adapting and overcoming, I organizationally just died. When we went to Cax we wore cammies instead of Frog suits. We only practiced direct assaults and defensives on our live-fire maneuver ranges. There were no role players, there were no kill houses full of amputees to provide realism. Apart from a counter-IED class or two, there were no actual IED lanes and scenarios. Everything was just a check in the box to deploy, like a conventional battalion going on a UDP, not a complex Afghan combat deployment.

Even the issued gear from CIF was different. The Eagle Industries plate carrier and older MTV turtle flak jacket were now gone, replaced by a newer, slicker plate carrier. No more were the days of single-point slings, or three-pointers for that matter, just the Blue Force issued two-point catastrophe. Newer, lightweight helmets complemented the tan main packs and assault packs that replaced the digital-green older versions. All this as if to underscore every other change that was happening. Once we actually got in-theater, even all the minor things were different as well. Rules of Engagement seemed almost to have been written by the Taliban themselves. In 2011, if a car got within a hundred meters and wasn't stopping, we were cleared to light it up. Now we had to wave some stupid, bright-colored flags, then shoot a pen flare, then shoot some pyro, then fire warning shots, and finally unload on the vehicle. Going outside the wire now included some sort of under-armor-style blast-resistant boxers, and then, on top of that, these literal cammo-patterned diapers that wrapped around our groins, and which were made of Kevlar, to help dissipate any sort of blast. The things might have been able to save lives, but they sure did look stupid, and were the most uncomfortable things to wear.

I fucking hate Leatherneck. Not past tense; I still hate it. I fucking hated that bloated base in the barren wasteland. I hate how there are numerous Pogs and wooks and REMFs who are now out, now at home doing whatever, going around saying that they're "Afghanistan Veterans." Bitch please. Camp Leatherneck/Bastion was mini-America. I understand that my deployment existed because of that place, but that's because BLS needed babysitting. Throughout this story I will make it abundantly clear how much I hate everything about Camp Lejeune (FWD), but hopefully you get a sense of where I'm coming from. The complete op tempo and mood was 180° different from 2011. In 2011 we were on the offense, we were actively trying to go after the Taliban wherever we could. Just two years later, in 2013, everything was a rearguard action. From dismantling the base, to handing over security to the ANA, everything was focused on leaving. Even the number of Marines on the base was constantly dwindling through quotas that had to be met, every month. Some nights, we'd see convoys stretching for miles, of retrograding 3/7 Marines bringing in Fobs and PBs from Sangin or Musa Qala.

Our own missions were limited to hitting enemy targets via helos, deep in Taliban-controlled territory, that we had apparently already handed over to ANA and AUP forces several months or years prior. Yet this was now enemy territory. See the irony? And this was outside the largest ISAF location in Helmand. Never mind those far-off regions mentioned earlier. Into this mess was me, an extremely confused senior lance corporal, for whom everything was changing around him, and he didn't know why. But what he did know was that he wanted combat.

The plane landed at night. The familiar feeling of hot air blasting into the cargo bay as the doors lowered was welcomed. After the mad scramble to grab packs from the pallet in the bay, everybody formed up outside on the tarmac. We herded onto ragged buses, being driven by hajjis, probably local contractors. It was a pitch-black night, except for the eerie streetlights. They glowed a dull yellow, each orb surrounded by swarms of bugs. "We're here," I thought. It was so much like Dwyer the last deployment. The dry heat was blasting us; Manas was temperate and now we were crammed like sardines on a shitty bus with hajji music blasting, rifles and gear jabbing us, the smell of old, stale seats in our nostrils. I hated those stupid buses. After a nice little tour of the base, we were unloaded at customs. We meandered a bit, saw Gunny Fatshit, and did another working party. It was middle of the night but we were pounding water, drinking gallons.

Oh, and a traumatic event happened to me. Right after being dumped off, someone's slung rifle swung into my leg. No big deal, right? Well I had a Rip It energy drink in my cargo pocket and that sucker exploded. Cursing, I could only let it soak into my pant leg and socks. I didn't have any water at the time and I was too tired to care. Eventually we got dumped at a barren spot near the temporary personnel housing. Our main packs were being brought up in a semi-trailer. This was a wholly disorganized event. No one knew where we were supposed to be staying, and even after being told we had no idea to get there. Our company was now a hobo-train, wandering down unfamiliar paths, darkened alleys, all while carrying a giant rolling suitcase, a seabag, main ruck sack, and assault pack. It was a mess and one of those unavoidable components of moving masses of men around the globe. I do not miss that at all. I remember meandering around, and trying to figure out where our advon was billeted. The "permanent personnel" were quartered in double-stacked hooches with catwalks, looking like modest apartments. But we, the interloping infantry, were billeted nearer to the Jordanian and Georgian troops. After all, we wouldn't want to upset the gentle countenances of the permanent personnel. So eventually we found our little set of dormitories, one-floor prefabs with a dozen or so squad-size rooms, but a huge improvement in quality of life for homeless fighters.

Previously, on Camp Dwyer in 2011 we had company-sized tents with cots, and that was considered luxurious compared to even the year before. Yet now we were in an actual structure with a couple of AC units mounted on the walls, with Wi-Fi, bunk beds, lights, outlets, damn near a hotel room! I was not expecting that at all. Because of how the company was strung out, and the fact that nobody had a clue how to organize and house us, everyone kind of piled into the first available room. I wasn't thrilled because I was in the same room as one of the white-trash-tragedies of the platoon, a bunch of boots too. At least Rick Perry and I think Nick too were in my room. We had to pile in a dozen dudes, and all of our gear. We were gypsies packed like sardines. I had a top rack, because, fuck me, right? At least I had an outlet so I was happy.

On our last deployment, Charlie Company deployed with four rifle platoons. This just meant that weapons platoon ditched crew serves and served as a rifle platoon with organic systems. However, this was due to our last AOR not requiring rockets, Two-Forties, DMRs, or mortars. The more traditional deployment would have the three rifle platoons with weapons platoon Marines as attachments with weapon systems. We had yet to receive word as to how the company would be organized. I don't really recall too much grief from everyone, but I was furious. I was a senior lance corporal. I was severely allergic to bullshit and lack of knowledge. How did they expect to fight in a week when they didn't have a basic TO sorted out? "Yup, we're pretty much fucked," I mused.

The next few days were a blur. We did the mandatory "Welcome to Afghanistan" classes and training. We acquainted ourselves with the local terrain – chow halls, PXs, MWRs – and grew accustomed to the heat once more. Thankfully, this was late-September heat in the open desert. Still hotter than damn-near anywhere in the States but it was nothing like the humidity and heat of our last deployment. The highest I personally saw was in August 2011, with 90 percent humidity and 125°F. It got hotter but that's just what I saw. Another key aspect of the local area was the human terrain: Pogs galore, immaculate uniforms, brand-new rifles, wookies, too many smiles. I despised them. You'd never think you were in a war zone by their appearance and demeanor.

At this time in the deployment, one of those formative periods comes upon certain grunts. Within the infantry, you're a boot until you deploy. I was fortunate. My boot-hood lasted about half a year and then *bam!* I was deployed. But for guys who always had to be at parade rest, were always being hazed, and always being reminded that, why yes, you are indeed the lowest piece of shit in the history of existence – well, now they were free! They could become beautiful butterflies, on the way to becoming crusty salt dogs. But they had to walk a fine line. My own former boots, guys I had worked with a lot, Cox and Bradley for example, were okay for boots. They weren't full on waterbrains but Bradley was always a smartass when he wasn't causing too much trouble. And Austin and I were good from being in the same team so much.

Pop culture paints the picture of a "troop" leaving home at a convenient part of the plot, going to war where they are immediately thrown into an ambush on day one and shit goes down. Nowadays, it takes a while for anything to get accomplished, and spare time needs filling. We eventually spent about a week on Camp Leatherneck getting all the pieces together. We had to zero our rifles, so we hiked to the range in gear – obviously the wrong one first because Higher never deigns to inform one of relevant information such as location. We did medevac drills, had classes on counter-IED equipment, and Law of War. Because we were in the corrupt Hamid Karzai's Afghanistan, we were being told how to conduct a pacifist war so as not to offend the locals. Because if we offended the locals then the dictator Karzai would be able to bitch to Centcom and hinder our efforts to fight his war for him. Thus, we attended lectures and PowerPoints on how to be mindful when we called in ordinance because we were being pinned down or being blown up by patches of dirt near "unaware" locals.

I don't think the average American is aware of just how much we were trained to civilly conduct warfare; I reckon everyone thinks we just go over and blow shit up with no consequences. People call the Second World War the "Good War", but the U.S. firebombed and leveled cities in Europe and Japan. But in the 2000s if U.S. troops killed an Afghan who was driving full speed toward a patrol, Karzai would pitch a fit and declare the Americans murderers who deserved Afghan prison time. Apart from the classes and standard schedules, the biggest pastime was bullshitting and killing time. The gym rats, most of the seniors and a lot of the boots, immediately began scoping out their new lairs. I mostly hung out with my buddies and read. I had packed a few books and was busying myself with *I Hope They Serve Beer in Hell* by Tucker Max. I had always been meaning to read it and it provided a nice distraction from the heavier stuff I had brought along. I felt bad because I cackle like a witch, and that book was just too funny for me. At night, people would be on their phones, sleeping, heading out to take a piss or what have you, and I would be laying on my poncho liner, shaking the rack and stifling my schoolgirl-like giggles and hyena barks. Pretty sure I apologized a lot until I finished that book.

One of the biggest and best pastimes of my people – lowly enlisted infantry scum – was to bullshit. We'd gather around anything conducive to said activities and discuss matters of the days. Cubicle workers have their water bubblers, grunts have the sacred smoke-pit. Especially for me and Kurt, that was our kind of decompress time. "Hey man, you want to go smoke?" Translated: "Yo, dude I'm kinda worried about 'X', mind hearing me out?" Or just time to relax. Me and him would go out and discuss how much this shit was starting to hit us again. We had both been to Afghan last time, but we were younger and more gung-ho then. Now, we were excited for an actual kinetic deployment.

After Bridgeport, I became a team leader of four boots who came into the platoon: Hefner, Weider, Ayr, and Weaver. Hefner was a Tennessee boy, very rough around the edges, but could be a solid worker when he wasn't dodging out of things to do. He had a wife back home as well, one of those high-school sweetheart deals. Weaver was also a Tennessee boy, who could be a pig when it came down to cleanliness, but he knew his job and was dedicated to it. At heart he was still a kid, wanting to get drunk with the boys on weekends. Weider was one of the boots who came in with kids, a baby daughter with a girl from high school. Getting Weider for any actual training was tough because he was always being slaved off to drive seven-tons, Humvees, or Mraps. Being pretty skinny must have helped him getting into those tactical vehicle seats. Then we had Ayr, the platoon RO, our comm monkey, more or less attached to my team for admin reasons. Small and blond, but he could mess you up in seconds, always talking trash – he was from Brooklyn – and he also had a high-school sweetheart thing going on.

When we touched down at Leatherneck, Bravo Company was designated the battalion heliborne company. Charlie was sent out to rot at Patrol Base Boldak, located about twenty klicks from Leatherneck. Alpha Company took over the local security mission, which consisted of aggressively patrolling around the trifecta of bases known as Bastion-Leatherneck-Schroback, or BLS. Weapons Company got completely screwed and was sent down to Camp Dywer in Garmsir District, mostly to be the security element to protect the UAV operations against Pakistan there. The heliborne role consisted of having three platoons in a rotation, one as the raid force, one as the QRF for the raid force, and the final one as the QRF for all of Helmand Province.

Platoons would rotate in and out of these roles as missions were completed. The actual raids were pulling some real weight as well. In addition to a complete infantry platoon with weapons attachments, we brought along EOD guys, Marine listening terps, forward observers, counter-ED dogs, all to support an Afghan Special Forces component known as 444, or just "Triple Four," that had British Parachute Regiment mentors, or "handlers" as they were called. The Brits, along with the Afghans were absolutely great, always looking to get into a good bit of fighting wherever we went. What would start out as a single platoon, usually ended up in almost a hundred-strong raid force, with all the attachments. We would take four Ospreys or four CH-47s out of Bastion. The mission of the raid force was to approach some of the hornets' nests in Helmand, get in the thick of it, and interrupt enemy operations. This meant either suspected caches of weapons, HME-manufacturing facilities, or known Taliban hideouts from Now Zad to Musa Qala. Usually we would hit a village, insert in some open fields beyond the village, and patrol in, encircling and securing it, then letting EOD blow up whatever they needed to destroy, or having our TSE teams take detainees.

Our first helo mission is to a village in the Helmand district of Musa Qala, some 100 klicks northeast of BLS. Musa Qala ranks up there with Sangin, Marjah, and Now Zad for the ferocity of fighting between the Taliban and the Marines. Pitting IED warfare against drones, both sides have taken extreme losses in some of the heaviest fighting Marine infantry has experienced during the global war on terror. However, at this stage of the war, there is much less Marine interaction in these districts, thus the IED threat is considerably diminished because of the lack of active patrolling. But the Taliban are there, make no mistake.

During the prepping stages for Musa Qala, the raid force gets out at night and we do helo drills, practicing getting out of the fifty-threes, immediately moving left, setting up a circular perimeter around the bird. Again, and again, Sergeant Early make us go through different scenarios, taking contact off the bat, reacting to contact, moving and communicating.

Ayr gets pegged as a notional casualty, gunshot wound to the chest and the arm. We push up security while Hefner, Weaver, Weider and I break out the pole-less litter and bring him over to the side of the field. Weaver applies a notional tourniquet, chest seal, and looks for exit wounds. Meanwhile Early tells Ryan – the kid who had to leave Bridgeport early for some sort of domestic matter – to call in the 9-Line. Ryan has since learned pretty much nothing about his job in the infantry, because he has been so saturated with taking care of his dysfunctional family that he can't perform a simple infantry skill, like calling in a medevac.

"COC, this is … ummm, what are we again?"

Early stares at him in the dark, senior eyes burning holes in this life boot. "What we've always been Ryan. Bad One One."

"Oh, that's right, sergeant. COC, this is Bad One One, stand by for 9-Line, over." Ummm. "One patient, badly injured …"

"What the fuck is that? Is that even how the format goes? Hef, give him the card."

Hefner rips out his zap card, with the full format of the 9-Line on it, helping Ryan along with the process. Halfway through, realizing this kid has probably never seen a 9-Line reporting format before, Early says, "Stop. Just fucking stop." Early has this crazy method of making you feel like the world's most despised creature, without raising his voice at you. "Ayr has just bled out. Why? Because you just let him down, because you don't know your job. Something as simple as calling this shit in, and you don't know it, and we're supposed to depend on you?" The tension is high. This kid is already in Afghanistan, and he doesn't know his job because he's been too busy working out the drama of a failed marriage to be with the platoon, and being yanked back from Bridgeport to deal with an assault charge. I guess you have to take care of your family first, but in neglecting the guys you go to war with, then that family won't be having a warm body coming home.

"Ayr, stick with him, and have him write it all down. Then I want you to write that reporting format fifty times before you go to sleep tonight. I better see it slid underneath the NCO door when I wake up tomorrow. Got it?"

"Yes, sergeant."

Ryan was on the first flight home to the States. Never left the wire. Never got his CAR, or an Afghan Campaign ribbon. A nice kid, but hell, did he have his priorities backward.

Done with the drill, the platoon walks back to the hooches. On the way, we hear some yelling behind us, turning round only to see a minibus with all of third squad under Sergeant Vasselian flying by us.

V yells out, "See ya at the hooch, suckers!" God, he's such a riot at times.

Arriving at our T-Wall-encircled company enclosure, the platoon separates into our hooches, minus third of course, those losers already at the chow hall. These hooches are sheet-metal rooms all connected to each other. Each room has six bunk beds; it can technically fit twelve Marines, but only houses six, with guys using the top bunk as storage space. Each Marine has a sort of personal arrangement within his bunk, stringing up tarps and packs to make a little castle. V has the most elaborate setup, constructing an entire wooden enclosure around his rack in the NCO room, complete with a door, and foldout pictures of naked women tacked to it. He even has nails to set his Frog suit and rifle on. After numerous briefs, checks, and more rehearsals, the game is on.

I am the lead CMD searcher for the security north section and am a little nervous about sweeping, having not done it since the last deployment. The mission starts out at zero dark retarded, and we fly in under cover of darkness. Birds touch us down in the middle of some fields to the northwest of the village and we fan out to get our security perimeter. Almost immediately out of the helo, the ground seems to be this dry, pasty muck that you sink into with each step. With all our gear on, and NVGs illuminating the area around us, we fan out. The birds take off, leaving behind their thick cloud of moon dust that permeates everything, and all you can do is keep your head tucked in to avoid swallowing half of it. Eventually they are gone, and all is silent. Alone and unafraid, right? Definitely alone, but you have to be kidding yourself if you're unafraid.

You're in Musa Qala District, Helmand Province, with only a hundred other souls to count on, many miles away from the rear and the facilities of medevac or air support. You aren't even getting shot at yet, but you have to take that fear and stuff it somewhere behind the scheme of attack, your particular role in the grand plan, and your sector of fire through your four-power RCO. It's a cliché to say that the training kicks in, but more importantly all the other stuff kicks in, and that is what you have to focus on to get through it.

Radio checks pierce the calm of the morning gloom. "Bad Six, Bad Six, this is One Alpha Actual, radio check over."

"Roger One Alpha, I got you Lima Charlie. You got security north in place yet?" Time is ticking, and we have to be Oscar Mike to get in place for the actual raid.

Shinohara calls out to me, "Vining, lead the way with the CMD."

I reply, "Roger, en route." I yank the CMD out of my drop pouch, pop open the elbow support, twist the handle into the user position, and extend the actual rods that are connected to the flat detector. I place the straightened detector on the ground so that it is level with the ground. Too much forward, and the detector head scrapes the ground. Too much rearward and the detector isn't even flush with the surface and you'll get a bad reading. The flip is switched to the ON position, and the BIT test is run. After a couple of beeps, the system checks out and now you have to do the soil composition test. This is important because the system is designed to build an index of the elements in a certain area in order to pick out the carbon and the metal pieces in the soil. However, the problem is that every field, every piece of desert, every compound is different. Different rocks, different types of soil, different types of mud houses. So to alleviate this, you do your soil composition test on every subsequent patrol or mission ... practically every time you pull out the CMD for that matter. This is done by pulling back on the toggle switch, waiting until you hear a constant beep, so that when you release it, it becomes a steady beep. Now for two laborious minutes, you sweep a square meter in front of you, nice, slow sweeps with the detector head about two inches off the ground, nice, even sweeps overlapping each other, left to right, right to left, and moving forward at a less than normal pace. You can't go too fast because you'll start missing spots, but you can't be too slow because then the patrol isn't getting anywhere, and you're leading the patrol pace by being the point man. So you have to find this happy medium of going at the right pace where you can still sweep effectively and pick up as much as possible, but you can't treat every single metallic or carbon hit as an IED, because a) you'd be there all day waiting for EOD, and b) the patrol leader has compounds to search and people to kill. So like playing criminal forensics in real time, you have to take everything in, and make a spot decision. The morning was still dark, but not dark enough to require NVGs, as the ambient moonlight was good enough to see where we were going. I lead the patrol through the LZ and toward the village of Barrack, the field dirt being hard to get into.

I start off on a farmer's trail on the side of the field, but then realize that's a really boot move, and so move off into the actual field, where progress is harder, but the threat is much less. Williams is behind me with his M27 and Thor pack, slowly walking at my pace as well. I hit a metallic signature with my CMD along the side of the field. I sweep left, its high, I sweep right, its high. I pause. Does this signature mean I have to hold up the entire patrol to investigate? Or is it not worth it, and we push forward, possibly endangering everyone behind me? I stare at the spot on the ground, looking for ground indicators that might show a sign of an IED. Seconds turn into hours. Mostly because this is the first time I'm back in-country, first combat patrol of the deployment, and first CMD find.

Williams whispers from behind, "Tapped Keg?" This is the brevity code for an IED find, where we have to start the 5 Cs of Call, Clear, Confirm, Cordon, and Control. No. This isn't the day I lead my patrol onto a homemade charge of explosives. We're at the edge of a soft dirt field, near nowhere strategic, along no well-traveled route, or previous traveled route. The landing zone is randomly selected, and it isn't like the Taliban were at the brief this morning when we were given the eight-digit grid. I take out my bottle of shaving cream, and draw a large circle around the metallic hit, to mark it, and let everyone behind me know not to bother with what lies in the ground. Oscar Mike, motherfucker, today is not the day.

We keep pushing, over fields, canals, and curves. Slowly we make our way toward the village, and slowly the sun starts coming up. We see more of the area around us, compounds, huts, some Afghans here and there, out for a morning stroll, of course. Soon, Cobras are circling above, as a sort of escort and overwatch. They start shooting rockets at the hillside beyond the village. More just to scare whoever is on the other side and let them know that we have brought the big guns. We get up to the village itself, and Triple Four enters, leading the way via searching compounds. Our security section gets up into the first compound and Shino tells me to sweep the area around this massive crater. Weider has the other CMD, so we both get to sweeping the area, over and into the crater. The spot is clear, or at least clear to us. We set in, and we wait.

The raid is pretty uneventful thus far, nothing has happened yet. All of a sudden I see some kids at the top of the hill from where we are setting in our security. First Sergeant Schooster is with us, and asks me to go up there with Weider and talk to them, see if we can get anything from them. So Weider and I push out to about halfway up the hill and call some kids down to us. Two little boys come marching down and in my best Pashtu I ask them about the area, their families, if any Taliban are around. Of course there aren't any Taliban in the area, "*Taliban neshete!*" say the kids. The effort is fruitless, and we return to our positions.

Then of nowhere, this donkey, laden with Afghan saddlebags comes waltzing down the hill, almost to our position, stopping twenty meters from us, just standing there. What is this? A suicide donkey about to blow us up? I take out my slingshot and make the attempt to hit it with stones and ward it away. It's a failure, so Shino takes the slingshot from me and eventually gets it with a few good hits. But here we are, in the middle of Musa Qala, looking for the Taliban, and we're concerned that a donkey is going to blow us all to hell. After a time, word is passed along to get in the crater. I don't know why we are getting in the crater but we all get in it, about fifteen guys from the security section.

Time ticks by, and I still don't know why we're in this crater. Then, from the direction we came in from, the exact direction I cleared on the way up, this massive explosion takes place, about fifty meters from the crater we are all huddling in. My heart drops like a lead weight. Someone stepped on a pressure plate that I cleared over, and I'm to blame for it. But nobody around me is surprised that this earth-shuddering explosion just took place, in fact everyone was expecting it to happen. Because it is a controlled det on the IED-making compound that Triple Four found. I keep my sentiments to myself, and I remind myself to take sweeping more seriously next time.

A Marine infantryman is a jack of all trades. He fights a three-block war, he drives tactical vehicles, he delivers humanitarian aid to the oppressed, he is a MCMAP student, and he volunteers at the Special Olympics to time races. But above all these, he is a fighter and he kills for his paycheck. His job description is "To locate, close with, and destroy the enemy through fire and maneuver." If he fails this, then what is he? Is he not an infantryman? Is he just another Marine? A mechanic fixes vehicles, a corpsman administers first aid, but an infantryman kills. And if he does not engage in mortal combat, then has he fulfilled his basic billet description? Ask a Marine infantryman from the 1990s what he did in his service. He probably went on WestPACS and Med floats, had the time of his life partying at Libo ports, but did he fire his weapon in anger? Did he take fire and return fire? Did he low-crawl to a better piece of cover? He probably did none of that. That doesn't make him any less of an infantryman; it wasn't his fault we weren't in a full-scale war during the 1990s – barring Gulf War I, of course. But he wanted it, and he would have jumped at the chance to prove himself given the opportunity. An infantryman can run a hundred live-fire ranges in his career. He can assault Range 410 Alpha at Twentynine Palms, or do IPBC at Fort Pickett in textbook fashion. Controlling his team well, putting plastic Ivan targets down, calling in notional 9-Lines and even assaulting through the objective. But has he seen combat? Does he know the difference between a *whiz* and a *crack*? Does he actually understand the difference bounding overwatch makes while on a foot patrol? Does he know what it truly means to sprint for your life because PKM rounds are kicking up all around you? Does he know that positive identification fills an admin role when you need to return fire? He doesn't know these things until he has taken that test, and passed it. Most infantrymen do pass it, and it's because of the training and indoctrination that they go through. Some don't. Some curl up into a ball and some jump into the safety of an Mrap when rounds come over their heads. But we don't know these things unless we've been there, and it's completely arbitrary who will freak out and who will keep their calm.

Sometimes it's the oddballs that you don't expect who truly pull through; lot of times it's the complete shitbags in the rear that pull through under fire and prove their worth. But in the big Marine Corps, they're still seen as shitbags because their boot blouses are just a little too low. Where were you staff sergeant, when I was wearing unauthorized boots with no boot bands and *still* took the fight to the enemy? Many a grunt will end his term of service honorably, and to this day wonder aloud, "What would I have done? How would I have acted? Would I have froze, in front of all my brothers?" This is the biggest fear, of not just combat, of any challenge as a grunt. Letting your buddies down, especially when you're needed most and not putting forth what you can contribute. And it doesn't make one grunt lesser than another because one has seen combat and the other hasn't. It's luck of the draw. But for those that have, the first time is comparable to the first day on a big job, or maybe even a first date. It doesn't make much sense what goes where or why, but there's a path to it that is eventually adhered to and eventually you get that path down and then it becomes second nature.

After the controlled det went off, our raid force pushed through the village and eventually wound up huddled up, doing our EDLs and accountability, waiting for the birds to come in at the LZ. I personally was inputting some

Afghans into the SEEK biometric system. The rounds always come at the most inconvenient time, when you're recalling a fond night with that one girl, or mid-sentence in a conversation, or taking a piss against an Afghan hut. Just as I was about to hand-type some biographical information about some guy's tribe, the *whizzes* came over, a couple bursts of PKM fire directed at our element from some 700 meters away. It was effective fire in that it got our heads down, but it wasn't entirely accurate. This is an important side note to an infantryman: Marines can maneuver under ineffective fire, but you can't move a damn inch under effective fire. Ineffective fire means the enemy is shooting at you but isn't hitting where he's aiming at, the rounds going wide or all over the place. Most importantly, they sound like a high-shriek whistle. This is because they are ten or more feet away from you and you are semi-safe. Effective fire is a *crack* and those bullets are traveling right by your face and in your direct vicinity. You're dead unless you move or fire back. I was in a slight depression behind the gun teams. The *whizzes* came over and I sort of calmly glanced up and said in my mind, "So this is it, this is what it feels like to be under enemy fire, this is what it feels like when someone is trying to end your life, because they're not shooting paintballs at us." That, that feeling right there is the true substance of combat. Someone, somewhere wants you to die. A painful or quick death is irrelevant, but they want those bullets to penetrate your body and kill you. Life is not the same after that revelation and it becomes even more so when the role is switched and you try to end theirs. These two revelations, of other people trying to actively kill you, and you trying to actively kill them, leaves no one untouched once it occurs. Because from that point on, the phrase "one bullet away" becomes very real and you have a different perspective on life in general.

It's also euphoric, you feel alive as you have never felt before, precisely because you're so close to death. It's a high better than heroin, and it's the ultimate adrenaline rush. And this is what constitutes our grunt mentality, that high is what we yearn for, that rush of kill or be killed. This is why we separate ourselves from the rest of the Marine Corps, because we have a personal interaction with death that most Marines will never begin to understand throughout their entire careers. And this is why we are proud of being infantrymen. I glanced back at the Afghan I was talking to and calmly said in Pashtu, "*Zah, zah,*" which means "Go, go" and pointed to his house behind him – we were in his compound. The guy didn't have to be told twice.

Sergeant Brightwell was on the gun teams like a man ablaze, "GUNS! Get the Goddamn guns up! Set those tripods up! Lock the Ts and Es in!" This is a prime example of Marine Corps leadership. It's swift, and direct, and it gets people moving. Because if these commands aren't called out, then people die because of their inaction. Leadership in combat is simple, "Follow me" sometimes being the only thing a leader says. This is not only needed, but required if a unit is to have a chance at surviving an engagement. There's no room for contemplation, no room for discussion. It's *act* because if you don't, you're dead, and dead Marines aren't useful.

To this day, whenever an 03 sees another Marine in a service uniform, regardless of job description, the first thing we look for is a combat action ribbon, or CAR. Now obviously there's a lot of bullshit CAR write-ups, from being on a Meuw, on ship, and getting it while the ground force was actually under fire on land. Then there have been cases where maybe a single vehicle in a convoy was hit, and all of a sudden everyone on that log train receives it. But for the most part, CARs are earned. It's really the first and only thing an 03 looks at in a stack, then looking for an Afghan or Iraq campaign ribbon. In some cases, a Desert Storm or Kuwaiti Liberation medal.

The gun teams got their two-forties talking, and the snipers set up on the rooftop of the mud hut, and started getting shots off and scoping the cliffs from where we were getting hit. Our other element was further down, actually downrange of our fire. The CO called back and told the gun teams to cease fire because of the proximity of their own rounds to the CO's element. We consolidated up, got a head count and eventually the 22s showed up and we ran out into the field next to our compound and left Musa Qala for Leatherneck. A good number of our cherries had been popped that day.

The funny thing about fear in situations like this, is that it occupies minds in different ways. I found myself to be very scared before a firefight, and even more fearful after a fight when I realized what I had been through. But I wasn't scared during the actual gunfight. A prominent military psychologist who researches how we kill and how that mentally affects us, made a very similar point. Throughout his interviews with veterans, he found that fear still occupied their minds during the fighting, but it wasn't fear of death or injury, but a fear of not doing their jobs, and letting their brothers down. Throughout various firefights and patrols along possible IED-laid routes, I can certainly identify with this sort of fear. Being killed or injured becomes an objectified action. You don't pause during a gunfight to have an epiphany and realize that you could die; you pause to look for better cover, or a better vantage point to fire back from. The end result of you not finding a good spot, or you not running like hell across a danger area, might cause you to get shot or blown up, and you become a hindrance to your boys.

When we finally got all sorted back at Leatherneck, 1st Platoon took seven-tons back to the company COC building, where we turned in all the mission-essential gear, and completed the debriefing. From there, we made our way back to the hooches, stripped off our flaks, and stuffed them underneath our bunks, with the air-conditioning at full blast. Some guys took showers, others stayed in their racks, relaxing, while others went to the Green Bean coffee shop, or the USO, to just hang out. Literally, not several hours ago, we were under enemy machine-gun fire, while in one of the more volatile districts of Helmand Province, one known for violence, Musa Qala. But yet, here we were, letting warm water run over our bodies, and sucking down on sweet Mochas. If we wanted to, we could go to a DFAC, get a full meal, and chow down on some strawberry ice-cream with whipped cream toppings. In fact, we could have even gone to the Indian-run MWR, and flirted with Army girls, maybe even checked out the CrossFit gym right next door. Similar to how everything about this deployment seemed to be changing, so was the way we went about the business of war, maybe comparable to the B-17 crews from World War Two, being completely terrified over Germany while on missions from England, but then coming back and getting down with partying Brits in Piccadilly Circus that weekend, only to get blown out of the sky the next. This was to continue throughout the entire deployment, this almost, very surreal sort of existence, even to the point of coming back to our hooches and hopping on Wi-Fi with our phones after a patrol. A sort of War 2.0 if you like.

The guys in the platoon were going nuts back at the hooches though. Like some triumphant sports team after a victory, their purpose for becoming infantrymen had been solidified. They had taken enemy fire, and although most of us hadn't returned fire on this occasion, we had seen the white buffalo and had not broken. We stayed up half the night, putting on DVD after DVD of war movies to further confirm our belief that we were finally not some infantry wannabes: we were the real deal.

"Man, I was walking along one of them lines in the fields, and all I heard were those rounds coming over. Even though I had a Thor on my back, that bitch felt like two pounds, and I just shot across the field to those compounds," said Williams.

"I was up on that one hilltop with snipers, and we took fire when we peaked our heads out … it was like Crack! Crack! Like splitting the fucking air. I've never dropped like a sack of potatoes in my life so quick," said Ward.

"Did anyone see Sergeant V out there today? The guy was screaming like he was having the time of his life! He was returning fire with his M4, like he was crazed or something. He loves this shit," added Zhao.

When the chatter died down, and the lights were turned off in the hooch, I snuggled up in my sleeping bag, content with myself. Though I hadn't been in a gunfight in Nawa, I certainly got mine this time round. That lethal cocktail of adrenaline and danger was addictive. It was exhilarating. And I loved it. I drank the shit out of that Kool-Aid.

Second platoon of Charlie Company had already gone out and gotten into a scrap in south Showal. SAF and an RPG. No casualties, and no vics hit or anything. Memorable event that was and us giving shit to Woolbright for not shooting anyone – not his fault, at least he didn't freeze up – and apparently Gresham was pissing when they shot at his truck with an RPG. Apparently it was pretty close. I bet he pissed himself, oh right, never mind.

Pretty soon after that my squad had its first dismounted patrol. We were gonna walk over to H-Bad – Hyderabad, Gerishk District – and see what happened. I really don't think it was anything other than a contact patrol. This was early October so we had a full squad. Keel, Husky, myself as team leaders. I, being a lowly lance, was designated third team. Martin was squad leader. I had Klossing with the Mk. 12, Cox had the IAR, and I had the Two-Forty. Cox and I switched off throughout the patrol though. Since it was early in the deployment, and we were going on foot into an area 2/2 Golf hadn't really covered, we had a big group. Snipers was with us which was cool. But while they had a purpose and use, we had a fuckin' circus-tent's worth of clowns as well. Random SNCOs from who knows where, CAR-hunting Pogs tagging along, the freakin' BC, and loathingly, Fat Sausage. We probably had twenty-five motherfuckers on this patrol, only eleven of whom were second platoon.

We were tailend Charlie, but I insisted on taking out the gun because of my pride in being a machine-gunner. Poor Klossing was the squad HIIDE operator so he was always running the length patrol to enrol locals. But he handled it fine and then later he was put in first team so he didn't have to go running all over Afghanistan. Since it was our first venture into an area guaranteed to be eventful, we all had daypacks full of ammo, water, batteries, flares, signal panels, radios, C-IED measures, and since my team had the Two-Forty, we carried a thousand rounds. I still had the stupid, fucking MDO, a useless extraneous weight, mounted; we didn't use the nutsacks until later patrols, meaning we had nice long contact belts. I had a Prick-one-fifty-two, a Two-Forty, heavy back pack, camelback inside the pack, pockets full of random shit, and I was still getting used to the new blast diapers. The big problem we had moving out was the fact that we had way too many people for the mission at hand. It was a simple contact patrol a few klicks out, and yet we had enough guys to storm Suribachi. Comms were a constant problem, predictably. Snipers were moving all over the place. We were new to the AO. October is only half as bad as the summer heat, but then again summer heat in Afghanistan is the heat of hell. First Sergeant was dicking around, harassing the Marines, and generally wandering around being useless. Cox, Klossing, and I were at the end of the tac column, so we thought we'd be left alone. But of course not, because I have terrible luck with higher-ups. Fat Sausage was on my and Cox's ass the entire time as we had the Two-Forty. He kept bitching us out for carrying the Two-Forty like a machine gun – weird right? – instead of like his cute M4. Cox had the gun and had it on his shoulder. FS approached him, IN H-BAD …. IN THE OPEN … AS WE WERE MOVING INTO A HOSTILE FUCKING AREA, BUT HEY! FIRST SERGEANT KNOWS BEST. He threatened to take the gun from Cox, which in hindsight I should have just responded with, "Go ahead First Sergeant, it's all yours" and watch his fat ass fall out. So at this point I had the gun, baby-carrying it on my mags, making me want to puke (foretelling!). We had already been out for a few hours. The summer heat hadn't dissipated yet. We had crested the hill over in H-Bad proper, in this open field which would become very familiar to Charlie Company for the duration of the deployment. The summer harvest had been collected, so the fields surrounding the compounds were bare except for stubs of poppy plants. Goat droppings were all over the place. As the last element, being my team, moved into the open, we started taking fire. One shooter it sounded like maybe.

"Here we go," I thought, rounds snapping overhead, the disturbing *whirr* and *whizzes* of ricochets.

Everybody drops. We get fire going downrange, cherries popping. I sight in on the compound we are taking fire from, like 500 to 600 meters away. I see shimmers of heatwaves through the scope. I sight in a doorway. Racking back, I let it rip … ish. *Boom!* goes the gun. The machine gun. As in automatic, as in it should be ripping. I'm shooting between some Leatherneck guests, so I have to move up because the dust I've kicked up is covering one of them, a staff sergeant. I take a knee, encumbered like Atlas because of my pack. I get up – *snap, snap, snap* – and never mind, I guess I'll move later. I lay back down and start shooting at the compound; looking through the MDO, I see I'm hitting the corner and door. Heaving up, I move a little closer along the bare field. Fire is sporadic, but accurate enough to keep us pinned. You can tell because every time someone gets up to move, a burst goes right overhead. Being on the periphery of the patrol, I holler at Cox to watch the six and Klossing to watch the nine. We hear one or two shots from that direction but can't see where from exactly. While we are all laid out and about to pick up again, we hear that we got a wounded Afghan up. Apparently some dude on a bike was a little too close and wouldn't stop:

Sergeant Gunn shot one round and took out the tire and the ricochet hit the guy in the leg. Nothing serious; Keel put a tourniquet on him and it got taken off before we left.

But I get ahead of myself. So while we are more or less static in the field, sort of consolidated, me panting and heaving with all my shit, I notice that I'm laying in nothing but goat pellets, inescapable in the field, just fucking everywhere. "So, this is how this deployment's gonna be," I muse. "It's gonna be 'shit' or 'shot.'" While laying in goat shit, fucking around with my links and gun, feeling my back contort between the ceramic Sapis and my heavy pack, I notice I can't stop my leg from jumping around like it's cool. My firefight adrenaline mark is my bumping leg. Every time the adrenaline flows, the leg goes jumping.

We move up more and finally get out of the field. There is a string of compounds to the north running east–west and we're going up to check out a compound for a future PB op. We get up there and the first team starts sweeping and checking it out. This is another great moment. So by this time we're gassed. Okay, maybe just me, but I am pretty sure everyone is sucking wind. And now the compound is clear, but we remain outside. There is a nice little depression with a raised dirt lip. Great defensive position. Gives us eyes to the south where we took most of the fire from. Cox and I are chilling with some of the snipers and we get word that first platoon is gonna come up with the wounded guy. "Cool, that means we'll get picked up, no more walking?" Wait, this is Charlie Company. We walked in so they know we'll walk out … Fuck us, right? Directly north of the strip of compounds are low, bare, rocky hillocks. We get set up by Martin to provide overwatch. At this point I have switched with Cox so I have the IAR again. I end up spending most of the time just chilling alone on this little hill; I am far NE guy so I am tasked with road duty.

Now let me first explain a little tidbit. Afghans can sometimes seem stupid. We have just been in a pretty decent little TIC (Troops in Contact). Word to the unaware: firefights are loud. You can hear them from a good distance away, especially considering the multiple firing points from both sides. Yet these dumbasses always seem annoyed and oblivious whenever we tried to keep them away from a fight. Add this to the threat of VBIED's and S-Vests and you get a sense of the tension.

Finally the convoy from first platoon showed up, me on the lookout for Dan Yeager in the turret so I could be a goon and hopefully make someone laugh. Sadly, I think his truck was closer to the cemetery, farther west of me. So what was our general attitude by this point? Well, Marines, grunts in particular, need to bitch. We don't care when people shoot at us, we just get pissed. But then we get even madder when we feel screwed over, or feel like what we're doing is pointless. Marine infantry is taught with a version of *auftragstaktik*, to be aware of what the mission is. Being more intelligent troops, we get pissed off when we see things being executed in a fashion divergent from the best path. All that aside, I was sitting watching from my little spot on top of an exposed hill, watching 1st Platoon do their thing. I held on to hope that they would offer us a ride. I don't think they even bothered because they probably didn't want Fat Sausage bugging them.

So away they drove and that meant for me that I had to get my pack and begin kicking rocks again. We got formed up and began trudging. The last three in the patrol were me, Cox (Two-Forty), and Klossing (DMR). Just as we picked up, I saw a Mazda Bongo truck hauling balls toward us, 150 meters tops. Being a veteran of Viet-Nawa, I stepped into the road and yelled, "*Woahdrega!*" while holding out my hand. Lieutenant Garbade hollered out, "STOP THAT MOTHERFUCKER!" as he and Klossing begin hammering the car with probably thirty rounds or so. The truck stopped, and out of the cab stepped a man who looked at us all confused like, doing the ubiquitous hand twirl of the Pashtun people. Motherfucker, we almost killed your ass and you seem mildly annoyed. Try that in America and see what happens! Later, Klossing explained that the reason he didn't kill the driver was because he was aiming at the left seat, where the driver sits in US-styled cars. The windshield looked like a sieve. I'm pretty sure the Sir was hitting the grill. We didn't check it out because we were already pushing the timeline and the dude was okay, so he chilled by his car smoking and we moved out.

The adrenaline rush came back as we began to move out again. Just as my team got into this intersection – south-running road, go figure – some ass-hat with a PKM sends a pretty accurate burst between the three of us. The rest of the patrol was clearing the next couple of compounds, expecting things to be over by now. Nope! As mentioned, rounds don't go *whizz*, or whistle. They *snap* if they're near you or *whirr* if they ricochet. Well, in this particular instance, these rounds made my ears ring and the *whirring* was rather pronounced. I wish I could have seen myself from a different perspective then, because I was dancing like Michael J. Fox's marionette, as I started shooting from the hip all the way until it was in my shoulder.

To tell you the truth, I was walking my rounds up. "Oh, you're a machine-gunner, that's what you do, right?" Yes, however I wasn't doing it right. My first hip rounds were about fifteen meters in front of me! But by the time I was in the knee I had a good idea where the fire was coming from and was actually hitting a doorway in a compound across the field. First and second team along with snipers moved up and cleared another compound. Staff Sergeant was up with either them or the first team, not too sure who. But as my guys were set up and waiting for more fire, I heard one of the funniest things over my 152: "Cronos Two, Cronos Eight, be advised. I saw a motherfucker on a bike with an AK. I took a shot but I think I missed the bitch." Between the phrasing and Fat Sausage's voice I nearly fucking keeled over from laughing. Now mind you, this was just minutes after my team and I almost got shwacked. You gotta just laugh sometimes.

So finally we just picked up to move. We were already late, everyone was gassed, and we were still about a mile out. Truthfully, I just guessed that. My memory makes me think we were five klicks out at least but apparently Google Maps called me a liar. At most it was two klicks. A little over a mile. But it was a fair trot, rough terrain, new AO, and, oh yeah! it was hot as balls. As we are beginning to hump out of the strip of compounds, we took another series of bursts. By now I was getting pissed. We had been told we were gonna get helos and I was looking up and trying to see or hear them. Finally we got told they were en route. Some British Lynx helicopter was overhead. "Fuckin' finally!" Truth be told, by this point I was furious with the Taliban. We'd had our fun: they shot, we shot, good game, go home! At last we cleared the cemetery. By this point the patrol was split for whatever reason. My team was up front.

The Prick-one-fifty-two crackled, "Hey everybody, stand by for Hellfire. Sixty seconds."

Hell yeah, brother! Let's do this! Now that we had greater standoff, we began moving up to get a good view. Because incoming be damned, I want some good TV! We waited. We waited. And we waited. Finally the field between us and the Taliban firing points started erupting. I think it was a GAU-18, the helo .50 cal. I remember thinking that it was the coolest thing to see a hundred-square-meter area get chewed up like that, There are so many moments of surrealism in war. Childlike sublimity, fright, excitement, immaturity, a thousand other feelings. It hits me every now and then. I'll think about what I was doing, or what we were talking about and it just blows my mind. I just can't believe this shit sometimes.

* * *

The various districts in Helmand where we pulled our weight all have a particular flair and flavor from the stories and tales that came out of them. Sangin was by far the worst: Three-Five got that reputation down pat with their horrendous casualties rates compared to other battalions. Marjah received a lot of media hype, mostly for Operation Mustarak that the 6th Marines took part in. But make no mistake, Marjah was almost as dangerous as Sangin was in the heyday of operations in the 2009/10 timeframe. Musa Qala, Kajaki Dam, and Now Zad all occupy similar frames of mind, with Musa Qala boasting the hardest fighting out of the three. All three of these districts are open, with lots of flat ground and desert, with mountains and valleys separating the various villages and farmlands. Nad-i-Ali falls into this category as well, but develops some vegetation as you move eastward into the district, toward the Helmand River.

This is where Bastion-Leatherneck-Shrobak (BLS) is located, and most of the Marines coming to Helmand would depart from there to their PBs, COPs, and FOBs. Moving south, we had Nawa and Trek Nawa. Nawa is directly on the Helmand River, where PB Loy Kolay, PB Jaker, and FOB Geronimo (or Camp Cup Cake) were located. There wasn't any desert in Nawa, but lots of vegetation, tons of canals and irrigation ditches leading from the Helmand River. However, as you moved west, toward Marjah, you would run into Trek Nawa, which is all desert. The farthest tactical extent of this AO was the Sistani Gap, where we had a PB or two. South of Nawa was Garmsir District, where battalions from the 8th and 3rd Regiments were sometimes based.

Garmsir literally means "heat" or "hot." The district is more or less where the green fields of Nawa end, and some more of that desert begins. This is also where Camp Dywer was located. The camp acted as a southern logistical and command hub for the south of Helmand, while Leatherneck acted as the northern hub. After most of us had withdrawn from the PBs and FOBs, Dywer took on the role of being a drone base for Predator drones into Pakistan. South of Garmsir is wide open desert until Helmand ends and where the Baluchistan Province of Pakistan begins.

This was mostly the territory of the LAR (Light Armored Reconnaissance), and the Afghan border police. Our second helo raid was into a village called Barrak, in Now Zad District. The target was an opium- and IED-producing facility in the middle of the village. The overall intent of these helo missions was to have Afghan 444 Special Forces lead the way with their British Parachute Regiment handlers. We were there for the support side of things, holding security, bringing up the air assets, EOD guys, Radio Battalion terps, CMDs, dog teams, and LEP police personnel. Essentially we would provide a zone of comfort around which the Paras and 444 could clear out compounds and yoke up prisoners. The coordination for all this was immense, the supporting elements taking up the size of platoon, in addition to the rifle platoon which actually acted as the security.

After the Paras/444 element, the entire raid force would number ninety-six troops, requiring four helos to take us from Bastion airfield to the target village. Bravo Company had the air mission One-Nine. We were the raid force, QRF for the raid force, and in addition QRF for all of Helmand, or Regional Command South West (RC SW). Alpha had the BLS security role, working the main gate and doing the surrounding area patrolling.

Later on, Three-Six stole our helo missions and we switched to the outlying base security role that Alpha was previously providing, while Alpha themselves turned entirely to the main gate security; Charlie and Weapons stayed the same. The overall concept behind this was that One-Nine would provide a complex layer of security for BLS, from the far-reaching AO of Boldak, to us constantly patrolling out to twenty kilometers, to Alpha manning the main gate and running internal security patrols within the outlying perimeter of Leatherneck. All this was tied in with the Jordanians helping the main gate, the Georgians, Triple Canopy contractors, and British troops staffing the perimeter posts, and the various balloons and ISR drones constantly looking down on us. But the helo missions themselves were extremely complex in coordination, involving days of briefings, drills, rehearsals and classes. Going from slick drills to gear-mounted, then to mocking up the raid in a full dress rehearsal on one of the LSAs (Logistics Support Area) on the base, using it as the village we be assaulting.

On the morning of the Now Zad raid we flakked up, and went to the company COC area where we began the mission prep. Drawing radios, Thors, CMDs, op-checking them, and pulling spare batteries. Making sure GPSs were turned on and working, getting the right crypto loaded on the 152s and 117s. Sat com organized as well. Then the whole raid force, from the lowest grunt to all the supporting elements gathered round the mega terrain model and the full briefing began. From start to finish, unit leaders took on their various roles in the gameplan, walking through which element would complete which action, and what they would be calling in over the radio, phase lines, codewords. Marines got quizzed toward the end. "Hefner, if we take casualties at this compound, where are they going to be moved to?", "Weaver, if comm goes down, what are the secondary and tertiary comm plans?" Watches and radio time hacks were made. The radio hacks were necessary because all the frequency hopping crypto needed to be on the exact same net so that they could all talk to each other. Several seconds off, either late or early, and you have serious comm issues.

"First platoon, ON THE TRUCKS!"

It's just about go time now; you can't really turn back from the airfield when you get to this point, and in the opposite regard you can't come back here if you forgot anything. Swear to God, you don't forget anything, like a GPS, or a weapon. The drive from the COC on Leatherneck, all the way through Bastion and finally to the airfield is only about thirty minutes, even taking the shorter route round the western end of the airfield, by the base perimeter. But it makes for some quality nap time, especially since you didn't sleep at all the night prior because half the damned room was up prepping for this thing. The buses drop everyone off at the base of the monster dirt mound on which the Air Wing hangars are located. Shinohara gets an EDL of everything going on the mission, from compasses to Two-Forties with the attachments. We move in formation toward the hanger where we lay everything in stick order, specifically by individual Marine's name. This is so we have a particular movement onto the ramp of the helos that allows us to exit the helos in a particular order that is conducive to the first movement or linkup while on the ground.

Here we also get our Afghan Triple Four guys and Brits assigned to the sticks, so they make up about a quarter of the raid. And now we wait. On our gear, while the birds start revving up. I don't know what it is about the helos, but they just sit idling for incredibly long periods of time. They are off in the distance, about 200 meters from the hangars, inside their protective concrete enclosures. So we sleep, dip, or read magazines that someone thought was smart to bring. At this point we've done so much prepping for the mission, there is nothing left to prep. Just the waiting. The darkness turns to twilight, and then the twilight turns to day and still we wait.

"Flak up!" says someone, and so it begins.

Our gear goes on, not to be taken off until the mission is complete. Ballistic diapers start being clipped on (our ballistic underwear was put on prior to arriving at the flight line). Many of the injuries from IEDs ended up in tearing out the groin area. So to replace the oddly shaped groin protector of Iraq days, the military has come up with ballistic underarmor, like Spandex, that we wear in place of boxers. The garment might work, but holy hell, does it make you sweat buckets, and keeps all that sweat in. The diaper is made out of actual Kevlar, and covers your crotch and the lower portion of your buckets. This is usually clipped through your belt loops to keep it up, or if you're particularly high speed you attach it to your flak or war belt so all you have to do is roll it down and clip it on the sides once you put your flak on. Although the combination of this protection might be a lifesaver, it is the most annoying garment I've ever worn, and forever ruins all types of moto pictures, making us look like some sort of superman with just the red underwear on.

It's time to go, and we file off by stick to our respective CH-53s. We usually do these missions in either Fifty-Threes or Ospreys; it seems the Air Wing has enough different birds for each mission. The Fifty-Threes are great because they are so large and roomy on the inside that it feels like a flying bus. The Ospreys are somewhat odd because on the outside they seem just as large as the Fifty-Threes, but in actuality the inside is very small compared to a Fifty-Three. This is because the landing gear and all the mechanics for the propellers take up a lot of space. They also do this scary dip maneuver after taking off, when the propellers switch from helicopter mode to airplane mode, and the entire airframe drops several meters in flight, almost as if the thing is about to go down, but then jumps right back up as the propellers are pushed forward. We make our way across the tarmac to the birds. The closer we get, the hotter it becomes, and the force from the rotors turning is like an ever-flowing strong wind that pushes into our faces and bodies, stronger as we approach the bird.

We step onto the ramp, and there is a commotion, with everyone trying to get their packs off and bumping into each other as we try to get our seats as quickly as possible. Buckle up, or at least try to, make the crew chief think you're buckled as he goes down the line of Marines and checks that everyone has a seat and is in it. Here we wait maybe twenty minutes or so; the platoon commanders are given a headset so they can talk to the pilots over the intercom. And then the word comes round that we are taking off, and off we go, into the feisty wild blue yonder.

For Musa Qala the flight was pretty high until we got to the target village. This was probably because of the large amount of hills in Musa Qala preventing low-level flight. But not for the Now Zad mission. Now Zad is mostly desert and we climb to a high altitude for a little bit, but once we enter the district, the birds drop low, like brushing-treetops low. We receive some intel prior to the mission that the Taliban know we're coming so this might have been factored in. Just like the Black Hawks coming in and abruptly landing, these Fifty-Three pilots aren't playing any games either, and set down outside the village of Barrack.

As soon as the bird touches down, we're standing up and ready to move, the bird still settling on the ground. The first man pushes out through the ramp, making a sharp left turn so as to not get chopped by the tail rotor. We all pick up and follow him, running a wide arc around the helo until a full circle of security is established. Here you can't really provide much security so you just keep your head down in the prone, weapon facing outboard. The thick moon dust is too much to work with, so you wait until the bird picks up and leaves. The leadership then goes through their radio checks. I have a

Prick-one-fifty-two stuck in my dump pouch so I turn it on, and switch to our platoon channel where all the linkup and moving-out chatter is going on.

I pop my CMD out, get the soil comp test down, and get ready to move out. Point Man. I pick up, and move out, toward the village we are meant to hit. I know from the rehearsal that us being security north, we have to hit the northernmost edge of the village, and provide cover northward, or the mountains in this case, in order to protect the main effort of the mission that is going directly into the village. We start crossing the open fields, mostly dirt at this point. We bisect paths with another security element, somewhat comically forming an X as the patrols converge and diverge. At this point I'm not too concerned about IEDs: wide open ground doesn't lend itself to picking a point where to vaporize a Marine and hopefully his buddy with bad dispersion. But as we near the village, we encounter paths, compounds, recently plowed fields. All these aren't necessarily bad places to be, but given a number of other factors, they can be prime IED-laying land. So we skirt the footpaths, traveling on the sides instead of on them.

We cross fields instead of taking shortcuts, all the while I am laying out a path with the CMD and my bottle of shaving cream, marking off corners and different directions to go, circling metallic or high carbon indicators along the way. We eventually get into the village proper, where the Triple Four guys and the Brits are doing their thing, going from house to house, searching. Afghans come out to greet us, but not many. The Taliban have apparently spread the word that if you don't want to be in a gunfight, you had best get out of Dodge because bullets don't discriminate. Now we are stopping every forty meters of travel. Patrol, stop, get our bearings, connecting files, linkups, then keep pushing on until the same thing happens again. Loaded down with packs, Thors, ammunition, and water, you play this little mental game in your head where you concentrate on the next security halt to get comfortable. Each security halt seems like mini-paradise because you are covered down and taking a break.

Then the call goes out to keep pushing, and you labor yourself up to one knee, then the next one, then one foot, and then the next one. Now you're on your feet and you keep moving, to that next security halt behind whatever piece of cover is next available. We come about halfway through the village, then hit the road that straddles the northern end. This road has the village on one side, a hedgerow that runs next to it, then open fields on the other side of that. Here we fan out, rear man on the far side of the road, me as point at the other end of it. Now we wait, for the other forces in the village to catch up to what they are doing.

ICOM chatter comes through and is passed over the radio, then from man to man: "The Taliban have announced 'Begin the work' over their radios." How crazy is it that? For the first time in the history of armed conflict, we have a real-time idea of exactly when the enemy is about to commit to action. As promised, not ten minutes later, automatic fire comes from the other side of the village, the southern side.

All of a sudden the oddest of radio exchanges comes over the company net from the EOD component: "Hey, my teammate just got shot in the head, but he is okay." It transpires that the EOD guys went to the rear of a compound, out through a small opening to see what was on the other side of it. As they positioned in the back entryway, the one EOD was looking out, and a single round comes flying in, and pops his MICH helmet enough to make it jump in place. They run like hell back to where they came from, which is the open area in the compound. All this gets caught on the one guy's helmet cam and eventually becomes a YouTube sensation two years later. But at this point in the mission we are all like, "Fuck, one of our guys just got hit, we're in it now."

But Oscar Mike, right? We keep pushing a little farther on down the dividing road where eventually we halt our limit of advance and take up security positions to the north and the south. Weaver and I move onto the other side of a building where we find this giant ditch and get settled in it, me facing north, and Weaver facing south, with a large compound directly in front of us and across a road, obscuring anything to our east. Here we wait, keep up on the radio traffic, and attempt to scope out our sectors of fire for anything unusual. All the action is going on to the south, and I glance that way every once in a while to see what's happening. Mostly Triple Four guys trading fire with the Taliban along with our guys, and a lot of running in between positions and spots of cover. The Sir is behind us in the compound working out the radio and keeping everything coordinated at his platoon level.

All of a sudden, as I'm looking north, I hear automatic fire, and I see puffs of smoke pop up in those fields beyond that dividing road. Immediately I turn to the south where I assume the fire is coming from. Unbeknown to me, the fire is actually coming from the north and is directed at us: it can't have been coming from the south because I hadn't heard any *whizzes* prior to impact. Although I am a senior, this is only my second time being shot at, and I am still getting down that whole direction piece of figuring out where shots are coming from. But as soon as I face south, it feels like the individual molecules of oxygen are splitting apart: *crack, crack, crack, crack*. This is the second burst, right on Weaver and me with the air exploding, the ground is chopping up left and right, with impacts spraying dirt on us. I push myself down into the ditch as low as I can. This is accurate suppressive fire and the only thing you can do is press your head into that sweet earth and hope you just don't die.

After the firing stops, I hear the Sir from directly behind me. "Holy Shit!" I turn and look at him, the expression on his face is one of a ghost. "Vining, Weaver, you guys almost fucking died!"

Me and Weaver sort of look at each other, and back to him, as if to say, "Yeah, Sir? You really think so?"

At this point I'm still thinking the fire has come from the south, so I pick up and run crouched to the other side of the compound where the ditch is. Weaver stays with the Sir. I fling myself down next to Doc Zhao and Williams, both orientated north. They're locked on to that sector because they realize that the fire came from there.

"Guys, they shot at us from the south!"

Doc Zhao says, "No you idiot, they've got a PKM or something over there in that compound and they hit us from there!"

I'm puzzled, "You sure, Doc?"

"Yes Vining! The rounds were impacting the wall right behind us and almost mercked the AIR-O and his radio operator."

Hmmmm. "Well where'd they just go then?"

"They ran behind that wall!"

And so ends the debate about where the rounds were coming from. So we peer through our RCOs, looking at that exact compound. Looking for more of an excuse to pull the trigger instead of actual intent to commit violence. We see a little kid playing around outside the compound, about 400 to 500 meters away, a long shot but very capable of being made with our M4s. Eventually we see the fucker who shot at us stroll out of the compound with no weapon, and he just looks at us. Then he saunters back behind the compound, as if all he's doing is checking out his garden, instead of admiring the work he just completed. This is the difference between the early parts of the deployment and the later parts of it. If this helo mission were held at the end of the deployment, we would have absolutely opened fire, regardless if we had seen a target or not. The Taliban are human as well, and if we can put our rounds next to them they get spooked just like us. To officers we would have said we saw someone with a PKM or AK, but in reality we would have seen nothing. You can't just sit there and get shot at, and not do anything about it.

Eventually it starts getting really dark, and our NVGs come out of their dummy corded pouches and we clip them to our helmets, op-checking them for brightness and ambient light. One by one we peel off from behind the dirt mound and run to the wall behind us, the one covering the other while the runner turns and covers the next runner when he is set. In this fashion we pull back to the safety of far wall.

The raid force finds an IED and opium cache, and EOD blows it in place, creating a large cloud of dust. We push on, in the dark, working our way through the various alleys of the village until we get to the linkup point for the entire raid force. Here we align ourselves in sticks so we can make movement out to the LZ. I run into Early and we chitchat about the mission; he's exhausted and leaning up against a dirt hedgerow at the linkup position. He was on security south with the Paras and Triple Four guys, getting into a good gunfight of their own. Later on he tells me that when they were taking fire, he and Jeremy, a Para, were taking cover behind some dirt, and Early turned to Jeremy and said, "You know, man, if this was two hundred years ago, we'd be shooting at each other." Jeremy replied in a British accent, "You know, mate, I think you're right about that one!" The oddest things we say when at war ...

The entire raid forces pushes out toward the LZ. At night, in pitch darkness. It isn't half as sexy as it sounds. In fact it sucks, because I'm asked to CMD, lead, and direct the stick with a GPS. Eventually my blundering gets to be counterproductive and Shinohara uses the GPS to guide me to the LZ. We walk for what seems an eternity, because the threat is very still active, and if the Taliban were feeling smart that day, they could have backlaid our paths to the LZ. Spotting an IED in the day is hard enough; spotting one at night is like sunbathing on the moon.

Eventually we get to the grid where the LZ is supposed to be, and we set down, forming a security perimeter. We're tired, we're hungry, it's starting to get chilly, and all the adrenaline from earlier in the day is now gone with the sunlight. Birds are twenty mikes out, but now we have a problem. The grid that the pilots give us is completely different from the grid where they're supposed to be at. Or maybe it's the other way around and we have bootenants – green officers – for land nav. Either way, we now have to pick up and move to this new grid location which is 300 meters to our southwest. So we start trekking, but this is through some freshly plowed fields, nice and thick with the muck of the earth. We get to this new position, and finally see the birds inbound, but the bastards are still farther off than they should be.

They must be on that Blue Force tracker mindset or something. So we push off and start running for the birds, more just out of time's sake than any sort of tactical necessity. Finally, we get on the ramps, and NCOs are there to do the head counts, making sure everyone that needs to be on is actually on. Counts are up, everyone does a quick gear and EDL check, word gets passed, platoon commanders put on the intercom headsets, crew chiefs get on the rear-mounted fifties, and we're off, into the silent night. Shinohara tries to hang an American flag out of the open ramp, but gets flat-out denied by the crew chief, something about it accidentally getting sucked into the rotors and killing us all. Tough times. Leatherneck is off in the distance, and as we get closer, the lights become brighter and brighter.

Lord, is it a huge complex lit up at night. The Fifty-Threes touch down and we clamber off, the giant mechanical monsters slowly shutting down as we make our way off to the hangars. Here a full EDL is taken, but the night certainly isn't ended yet. Waiting around for the buses, I see the shot EOD guy, and he's still rattled from getting popped in the dome. I see his MICH helmet, and sure enough, it's torn up from where the 7.62 round pierced the top. Too bad he won't be getting a new one, as the EOD guys routinely purchase their own MICHs. The buses arrive, we load up, and are taken back to the COC. Here gear is turned back in to the armory, radios are powered off, batteries are accounted for, and everyone gathers round for the debriefing, chow in hand.

The CO walks the entire force through the raid, discussing every major action, and how it all worked out. Our Sir and the AIR-O mention the burst that almost took out me and Weaver, but there are far too many close calls that day for us to stand out. The debriefing is done, we pack up, and make our way back to the hooches where we rack out, and that is some great sleep. Weaver walks by, and I call out, "Hey, remember that time we almost fucking died?" Both of us laugh, and give each other a high-five. Life is good when you're still alive.

Back in my rack, I hop on my iPhone. The room is dark, and it's cold, almost midnight. Hefner, Zhao, Ayr, and Tomassi have all gone to sleep behind their privacy blankets on their bottom racks. Clicking the Home button, I swipe right. Then clicking on the Safari app, I tap Accept on the Sniper Hill terms and agreement usage policy. *Boom!* online, welcome Facebook, Whatsapp, and iMessage. I see Alice is still online right now.

You: Heyaaa.

Alice: Oh hello :) How was your day?

You: Eh, helo raid, almost died, can't complain.

Alice: OMG, are you okay???? Seriously tell me!

You: Yeah I'm fine, I guess, I'll tell it to you on Skype though ;)

Alice: Fine, but you have to tell me, I get really scared about you when I don't hear from you for a long time.

You: I know, it's okay though, I'll be fine, we always seem to make it out all right.

Alice: That's good : D. Did you get my pics earlier?

You: Mmmm I did, I actually looked at them before we left, the ones with no bra yeah?

Alice: Mmmm :) I sent you some more too : P

You: I'll go take a look then shall I …

I'd been talking Alice up since the beginning of the deployment, a girl from Ireland. Then Mary came online, another Irish girl. Same conversation. Then Zoe came online as well, from the U.S. Same conversation. Then Agatha, a South African chick with ass for days, came online. Same conversation. Then a British chick I knew from Bastion, in the British Army. Not the same conversation, but it was getting there.

All these girls, being on deployment while single was like having five girlfriends at once. Can't talk to one of them? Switch to another one, instantly. Morals, you ask? Where is the morality in me almost getting shot and blown up every few weeks? Why get one set of nude pictures when I could get five, at once? I didn't care that I was playing their emotions, what was important was that I was living from patrol to patrol. Being on BLS was safer than being in Detroit on a good day, but it was the patrols that took us beyond the wire where the balance was tipped.

It was beyond the morality of war though. There was something inside of me that wasn't centered or screwed on tight. Maybe it came from being somewhat isolated in school, a lack of spiritual conviction, or still trying to get over Lynn. Maybe some of my depression at where I was in life. Whatever it was though, I knew it was wrong, but talked to all these girls anyways.

* * *

Not two months into the deployment, we go into River City, a base-wide media blackout, with all nonessential communication closed off. MWRs, USOs, call centers are all closed down. The reason for this is that an ISAF member has been killed in action, and it's a race to notify the next of kin in the United States. Every time it happens we're asking questions as to who it is. Is the guy from One Nine? Is he another Marine? Is he British? There is a sort of common dread shared by all the grunts, because we know it could only have happened outside the wire. Of course, the civilians and Pogs on the base couldn't care less. They don't have a stake in who leaves the wire and who doesn't.

In this case, it's one of ours. Lance Corporal Christopher Grant from Alpha Company was point man on a dismounted foot patrol as they walked into a group of compounds. A suicide bomber made a beeline straight for him and before anyone could get a round off, it went off next to Grant. Grant was one of Alpha's boot drops before Bridgeport. He was from Louisiana.

One Nine held a memorial service for Grant in Alpha's vehicle lot. The CO went up and told some story about how Grant was fire support during Cax, where he kept his M27 running during an attack and held up a heavy rate of fire. It sounded stupid, a typical officer thing. The guy had died; no one wanted to hear about some training attack that Grant probably didn't care much for anyways. They should have let one of Grants friends own the memorial service, and not this pathetic captain.

Not because of Grant, but probably due to the strain that Alpha was under, the battle space got moved around. Alpha was completing both the base security mission, and the internal guard mission at the main gate, while also guarding contractors who trained Afghan soldiers over on Shrobak. These three tasks were really stretching the company thin, and hurting efficiency where they didn't need being hurt. Thus, Alpha was retasked with only the internal base security mission, Bravo took over the external patrolling mission, while Three-Six, took over the ROC helo mission. Up to this point, Three-Six was mostly in Sangin, primarily closing down FOBs and PBs. We'd see their convoys coming into Leatherneck all the time, vehicles for days, with everything coming in from the outside. Charlie Company stayed where they were on PB Boldak, and Weapons was still stuck in Taliban resort area Garmsir, standing post at Dywer, watching over Predator drones.

Although less sexy, the new mission still had us in the fight. If anything, we were guaranteed more of a fight right outside Leatherneck than in some far-off district where nothing might have been going on. But switching from a heliborne force to a mounted one was a reversal of gears. Alpha turned over all their trucks, Mat-Vs and Mraps. Our platoons split into two-vehicle sections each, an Alpha and a Bravo. Thus 1st Platoon split with One Alpha under the Sir, with Sergeant V as the section leader, Krystal and Leonard as the NCOs. One Bravo was under the platoon sergeant, with Herrington and Early being the NCOs really running the game. In addition the Weapons Platoon was dissolved, with all the machine-gunners becoming turret gunners, and mortarmen/assaultmen becoming either drivers or dismounts for these sections.

Prepping the trucks was the name of the game for about a week. Working all day and into the night, each vehicle section had three to four trucks apiece, usually one 4x4 Mrap, accompanied by however many Mat-Vs, with a mine roller with the lead vic, almost always an Mrap. Everything had to be done to Bravo's SOP: 400 rounds of 7.62 in the turret for a Two-Forty, another 400 strapped down to the deck of the truck (so they don't go flying around and hit someone in the face during an IED blast). Green, white, and red smoke in the turret, stretcher ziptied to the side of the trucks, along with a medical kit on the outside. Logos for each truck painted on the side, PRC 119s locked down in the radio brackets, headsets set up for the vehicle commanders. Triangular towbars strapped to the front of the trucks with ratchet straps, and chains, and extra meals with water in all of the spare compartments. And much, much more, each truck configured to look like the next, with us stealing and taking any available supplies from all over the place, Motor T, other disabled trucks, and so on.

Trucks were named according to their placement within the section. One One was the lead Mrap, One Two the second Mat-V, One Three the third truck, and so one. Bravo section had a similar numbering system as well. Each truck was assigned one driver, one vehicle commander, a turret gunner, and at least two dismounts in the back of the truck. This way, we could have two elements out of a single section while on patrol, a dismount and a mounted section. We could take all the dismounts and vehicle commanders out, then leave the trucks behind with the Sir controlling them as a sort of bounding overwatch, while the dismounts went about their foot patrol.

The company plan was to have a four-day platoon rotation. One platoon was designated QRF, living at the company vehicle lot, in large tents and cots. This was to be the mobile QRF for both Bravo Company, and One Nine as a whole. Within that QRF, only one section would stage their trucks and sleep in the tents for two days, while the other section would be on standby in the hooches, and would take over the next two days of QRF. If things really got bad, then another section could be drawn up for QRF. This way, there was always a mounted section ready to leave the wire, no matter what the situation. Another platoon was to be on its patrolling cycle, actively going outside the wire every day, on combat patrols, with the purpose of finding and fixing the Taliban in the area around BLS. Then the final platoon was to be the guard platoon, standing post at the company lot, in addition to their NCOs being the SOG of the company itself. After four days, these roles round-robin'ed with each other, which continued until the end of the deployment.

Sergeant V gathered One Alpha section together before we moved out to our trucks. "Hey, One Alpha, EDL."

On cue, we all yelled, "Dump 'em out!" while pulling out our NVGs, optics, and weapons. Dump 'em out was something Sergeant V had started in Cali during CAX: the platoon was moving kind of slow when Staff Sergeant was calling for EDLs, so Sergeant V came up with everyone yelling in unison, "Dump 'em out!" for the prosperous occasion when a female might walk by, undo her top and show us her tits. Sergeant V would say, "Ahh, she didn't do it that time! Better luck next time, First!" Corny and juvenile as it was, the phrase stuck, and it did get us moving when it came to getting EDLs done.

We were amping up for our first large-scale patrol. One Alpha and One Bravo were being sent into an area southwest of BLS that the battalion hadn't paid much attention to. Really it was a collection of villages and compounds that, although might not have posed a threat, were an unknown quantity to us. Briefings were made; we found out the op was to comprise several overnights. Each day we'd be checking out a new group of villages and during the night we'd set up OPs and Indian-wagon-circle it up. I became a turret gunner behind the Two-Forty in One Alpha.

EDLs and final checks done, both sections proceeded to push out. Just getting to the south gate of Leatherneck seemed to take an eternity, bumming along all the way. As a turret gunner I put the Two-Forty in condition four, and sat out the ride in the gunner's seat. This time round, we actually had gunners' seats, unlike the first deployment where only our Mrap had them. Every truck also had an actual working foldable sunshade, in addition to a joystick-operated control lever that moved the turret around. I missed my crank, and the ensuing *crrr, crrrr, crrr* that came with it when I rotated the heavy turret. Hefner and Weaver sat scrunched up in the passenger seats below me, on my left and right, as I was orientated with the gun at 12 o'clock.

Once we got to the south gate, manned by Bosnian soldiers, the Sir called in the DFL with the pack count, and we were off. Between Leatherneck and the villages was nothing but rocky, bumpy desert. Standing in the turret, with one gloved hand on the turret rip, the other on the stock of the 240, I couldn't believe the terrain we were driving through. I thought I knew about vehicle operations from the first pump, but noooo, this was a whole other monster, almost knocking me straight up several times from all the banging around, my gunner's seatbelt barely holding me in place. From the outside, the enormous vehicle seemed to conquer the ground, but on the inside, it was an impossible task just staying in one place. It took us around two hours to get to this southwestern AO where we were to operate over the next few days.

As we drew closer to the first village, a lone white Toyota Corolla appeared to be coming our way. Leonard yelled up to me, "Hey, make sure you don't let that fucker get close to us." Eyes still on the truck. "Roger!" I yelled back, over the sound of the gigantic Mat-V engine. He kept driving toward us, so I started the pathetic escalation of force we had had hammered into us ever since we started this. First, I waved a large orange air panel. Nope, didn't stop. Then I took the pen flare mounted on my rifle, pointed it in the general direction, and popped the knurled knob, igniting the little sucker like a firecracker, zooming after this car. Nope, still didn't stop. Taking a white pyro charge tube, I turned the lid on the bottom, aimed it in the air over the guy, and popped it using the opposing palm. *Wheeeeeeew*, all over the general area. The car turned down a different road, oblivious to all the ROE procedures I had just gone through. Thanks battalion; shit really works, doesn't it.

The Sir came over the radio, "Dirty, Meat Hammer, come in, over."

"One Actual, this is Dirty, send your traffic, over." Dirty was, of course, Sergeant V, Meat Hammer was Corporal Krystal.

"One One, One Two, we're going to push up to the north side of that hilltop. One Three and One Four, push up to the south side. We'll provide bounding overwatch while the dismounts roll through the village below us."

Sergeant V then came over the net, "Alright dismounts, get out, form up by One One."

Below me, Hef and Lane unbuckled their seatbelts, Hef taking the Thor out with him. The poor guys, they'd been napping up until then. "Good luck guys!" They were too busy to hear me, this being their first dismounted patrol after the heliborne operations. With mounted and dismounted operations, all we had were our ground assets, the dismounts supported by the gunners in the vehicles. Air cover might come out, but it wasn't guaranteed like it was with the helo ops.

After the dismounts formed up in their single-file patrol, V took them off into the village, moving from compound to compound. From our overwatch position, I could see them through the binoculars issued to turret gunners, primarily for gaining PID at that stage of the war. Every so often I'd track them through their patrol, taking security halts, and then move back to manning my sector, scanning it with the MDO on top of the Two-Forty, also for PID. Every time the patrol made significant gains through the village, we would push up and move to a better position to see them, halt for an hour, then move up again. Each time I coordinated with the other truck, to make sure we had our 180s covered with the turrets. Being buttoned down in those things, it would have been easy for anyone to walk up to your truck, and toss a well-placed grenade into the turret hatch if you weren't keeping your eyes open.

The day had started out cold, but it somehow got worse, with the wind ripping into my face, and through every crevice. I had my happy suit on, and my facemask wrapped round my face, but I wasn't able to move at all; being stuck up in the turret, I couldn't generate any heat. At least the dismounts were moving around, going from compound to compound, working around V's schedule. So I alternated positions in the turret, getting closer to the heat of the Mat-V, putting my butt on the rear of the hatch, while straddling the entire hatch itself, anything to just move about and get the blood flowing differently before that too became painful. I went through UGR-E after UGR-E, ripping the damned things open, looking for the First Strike Bars, and the peanut-butter-flavored wraps, then discarding the rest of the package inside the truck.

Villagers, Marines, I kept an eye on both. V took the patrol and went to go check out an isolated compound. After a few minutes of searching it, V came on the radio abruptly and said, "Christ! There's a fucking liger in here!" A little while later, I looked over to the compound, and all I saw was this short guy in Frogs, running out at speed, panting into the radio, "It's fucking chasing me!" Ayr, the driver, and I just laughed out loud. Here was this slayer of bodies, this war machine, being chased down by a huge dog, almost the size of him.

The Sir ordered the dismounts to come back into the trucks, and with that Hef and Lane popped open the side doors of the Mat-V, and dropped onto the seats. "Any fun, guys?" Both of them sort of just looked up at me, and turned away. They were dog tired, having been patrolling, holding security and searching compounds all day.

V yelled up at me, "Vining! Take that fucking happy jacket off! The damned CO is out here, don't you know?" I knew, and I knew better, but I was cold up in that turret.

"One One's up."

"One Three's good."

"One Four is ready to roll."

The Sir rogers up, "Hey, Lima Charlie, One Alpha, follow us in, One Two. We're going back to the rally point for the night. Vehicles revved up, following one another, gunners orientated in alternative outboard positions, as dismounts started falling asleep in the back, with the trucks rolling and bumping through the gullies. Eventually we sighted One Bravo's trucks, arranged in an Indian circle. All four of their trucks, including the CO's 6x6 Mrap, were nose to tail, with their turrets pointing out like a porcupine. The One Bravo guys were arranged around a fire in the center, burning their day's MRE trash. But we pushed past them about a klick and set up a wagon train of our own.

V came over the radio and called out all our sectors of fire, making sure the turret gunners interlocked with each other. I cranked my turret to the south, orientating it in the direction we had came from, now a mass of rolling desert hills. The desert out here isn't like the Sahara with its soft sand dunes but more like the surface of the moon, a lonely landscape, with no end in sight.

"Each vic holds their own watch tonight. Try to have the dismounts on first or last in the order of watch so they get some rest for tomorrow's patrolling."

I set up the watch for my truck, Lane taking the first two hours in the turret, me the next two, then Ayr, then Hefner, which would bring us to 04, when we wanted to start pushing for the day. Our Mrap sent up the G-boss infrared and thermal camera, about twenty feet into the air, with some of the dismounts watching that and on radio watch with Bravo Main back on Leatherneck.

Lane got up in the turret, while Ayr tried to sleep in the driver's seat, but the damn thing was so uncomfortable. I wasn't faring too well in the back left seat with absolutely zero room to stretch my legs, all scrunched up, feet on top of my flak jacket below the seat. Hef was eating an MRE next to me, the heated Chili Mac main meal smelling pretty good from where I was scrunched up. The cabin was lit up by the blue lens of the cabin lights, so we weren't completely giving our position away with the white light. (Lights had been changed from red to blue, because you can't see blood underneath a red lamp.)

The VC door was creaked open, and V got in. He stuffed his hand into his cargo pocket and pulled out the personal electronic device he was supposed to have left behind on Leatherneck, his iPod. Toss that rule: we all brought our iPods out on patrol.

"Hef, how's it going, buddy?"

"Going all raaaght, sergeant. I wish we could have done more than just patrol today, but, oh well."

"Yeah, that happens. I like getting out there, and even if you're not getting into a firefight or something, you're talking to the Afghan people."

Hef was surprised. "Really, sergeant? Even though they smell all crazy and don't clean themselves? I saw you today with them elder or something."

"You're getting a little taste of their culture. Sitting down, having a cup of *chai* with the locals. Just realizing that most of them are normal people, trying to have a normal life just like my family and yours back home. They're not all bad people. I like to sit and talk with them, just like to get a little taste of what they go through every day."

"I guess that makes sense. It's just so damned cold these days, you know."

"You got that fuckin' right," added Lane, who was especially cold in the turret. Poor bastard didn't even have a happy jacket. V had an earbud in one ear, tuning out to something on his iPod. The command had strictly forbidden any personal electronic devices to be taken outside the wire, and one of the Docs from Snipers had already gotten ninja-punched for it. But we didn't care; we all brought stuff out anyways. GoPros, Contours, cameras, iPhones, MP3 players, just as long as the Sir didn't see them, and you weren't zoning out on watch while outside the wire.

"Hey, Sergeant V," said Hefner.

V looked up. "What's up?" He had this really thick Boston accent.

"What do you like about all this so much? I always see you so cheery?"

"Fuck, Hef. Getting all philosophical on me. What are ya, from Havaad? … I don't know, it's that adrenaline rush, you can't really describe it but nothing beats it. This is the best thing I ever did, and I can't seeing myself do anything else. I love being deployed, I love being infantry, it's a pride thing. Growing up, I've always wanted to be infantry. It's very hard to explain … I love it, I can't get enough of it."

"Is that why you came here after OCS? And you didn't get out?"

"After my third deployment, I figured out I was getting out from there, but then I got spit orders. And at the same time, I was thinking, 'Oh God, another deployment, it's more miserable.' But you know, it's that feeling of 'I'm top dog in the area,' It's that feeling of, you know, I'm on top of the world in a way. But at the bottom of a bucket as well. It is very haaad to explain how it's a good time."

"When did you come in?"

"I joined in o'six, got into the Fleet in early o'seven and did a workup for Iraq. I was pretty immature. But I mean, I still am, I am still a very immature person. I had great senior Marines, some of them were on our ass every two seconds. I liked it … me and my peers were brought up well … it was tough love. And it molded me into the Marine I am today. Their hatred for the Taliban over here, who're killing innocent people, killing Marines. They wanted to instill that hatred for them in me."

"So what do you want to do when you get out?"

"I plan on coming right back here, but not as combat forces, but as an instructor in contracting. I want to open up my own bar back in Massachusetts. I think of bar names, and I got my blueprints all drawn up. But I plan on coming right back here. I love it more than anything."

We fell silent, all tired by this point. V turned back to his earbud, and fell asleep in the VC seat. An hour passed and Lane tapped me on the shoulder.

"You're up." I nodded, stretched a little from the no sleep that I had gotten, and cranked open the Mat-V door, putting my flak on, then my happy suit, and stuffing an MRE into my cargo pocket. Lane dropped into my seat, closing the door behind me.

I walked over the front of the truck, now very cold from the biting wind. Stepping up on the bumper, I hoisted myself onto the fiberglass hood, up to the windshield, stepping on it to the roof of the truck, then squeezing myself into the turret. Finally I was behind the gun, so I checked the condition, belt on feed tray, bolt forward, weapon on fire, slamming the feed tray cover closed.

Looking out over the bluish-black desert, I could see the faint glow of BLS behind us, to the north. The rest of the area was just a rolling black sea of desert, with nothing out there. Every ten to twenty minutes I would hold up the UTMs and look around the wagon circle, occasionally seeing a Marine get out to take a piss, or some small desert animal scurrying away. It had been a very long time since I had done this sort of thing before. The last time I had stood on turret watch at night, I was still with Lynn, the Hawthorne guys were still alive and laughing, Post and Koppers were still alive, and I had no clue how much I hated garrison Marine Corps. The desert reflected all of this back to me, and more, much more, while the gentle idling of the trucks threatened to rock me to sleep, with Lane's snoring punctuating the entire scene. Another barren, empty night in Helmand was passing me by, just like the hollowness inside me.

Oftentimes after I got out, I still find myself in that lonely turret, with only the ability to move my position left and right, or my Two-Forty up and down, looking at the barren wasteland of life around me, also pondering Lynn and why things didn't work out when in my heart of hearts I wanted them so badly to. It's still just as lonely in that cold, windy turret.

Over the next two days, we repeated the cycle. Mount up, push to a new village, dismount, overwatch vics, patrol through village, remount, move to next village, then wagon circle up. The overwhelming consensus was that there was nothing there for us, the villagers were peaceful, or at least this was the side that they wanted us to see. One of our terps, however, did find an AK wrapped up in a tire inner tube, halfway buried in a field. Nothing too interesting or revealing really.

Driving back, over the surface-of-the-moon-on-earth, first platoon debriefed, parked the trucks, turned in all our essential gear, and moved into our first post cycle. Although we were new to these types of mounted operations, we were slowly getting the hang of them.

Two weeks later, Bravo section came back from patrolling in the eastern wadi. This part of the AO was starting to become a hotbed of Taliban activity. Look east from BLS, and northeast from Charlie's base at PB Boldak, there ran two large wadi systems. These wadis weren't like the ditches of Nawa, but instead were more like dry riverbeds. Of these two, you had the western, and the eastern wadis. Past the eastern wadi lay the rest of the Nadi Ali district, with the typical green vegetation and fields of Nawa, until the Helmand River. The western wadi wasn't so much of a problem, but the eastern wadi was where you went to play ball, with bullets. Here Alpha had lost Chris Grant to a suicide bomber, and all the TICs and IED finds took place here.

The guys from One Bravo were freaking elevated. They had gotten into a running gun battle for half of their whole patrol in the eastern wadi. A lot of close calls but obviously no one had gotten hit. We were tickled with jealousy, those freaking gunslingers them! Somehow rumor got around, from the Sir that we were going right into Whiskey 7 Delta the next day. Afghanistan is divided into a series of sections by the intelligence community. These sections are based on the various villages and districts, known as GRGs, or Gridded Reference Graphics. This system even goes down to individual compounds, labeling them as little yellow numbers on a map. Thus instead of calling over the radio a complex grid that someone will have to look up, you simply say "Foxtrot 8, compound 45, we're taking fire from that compound." The AO around Leatherneck had particular meanings to us. We knew that if we did anything in the western or southern areas, absolutely nothing would happen. You could set up a week-long OP and sunbathe on the top of your vehicles where the flies would be more of an issue than the Taliban. However, the farther east you pushed, the more you were looking for a fight. Especially along the eastern wadi that marked the edge of our AO, you were almost guaranteed to get hit with something: an IED, indirect fire, or effective small-arms fire. Unless it was raining then the Taliban wouldn't come out to play. Whiskey 7 Delta was one of these regions.

We had an inkling we were going to be sent there the next day as Alpha section's patrolling cycle was in full swing. So early the next morning we got up at around 05 and made our way to the company lot. Sergeant V opened up the briefing talking about where Bravo section had gotten hit and where we would mostly likely be hit from. We all knew it wasn't a question of if we were going to take fire, but where and when. But just like any other mission we went about our way and started prepping the trucks and revving up the engines, doing all the system checks.

During all this, V took a white erase-board marker and scrawled in his chicken script on the platoon board, "1st PLT going out to pick a fight." I took one look at it in the platoon office and shook my head, "Freakin' V," I told myself.

A bit later, V called me over and said, "Hey man, we have to drop a pack because of all these fuckin' comm issues. Prince is going to come along and make sure the radios are working. Do you want to sit this one out?"

What? Me? Sit this one out? Was that even an option these days? "Fuck no, I want to go on this, but if you pick me then I guess I'll just do that."

He gave me his little cocky half-smile and said, "Yeah man, let some of the young guys get out there. Just get your stuff and go back to the hooch, and try not to yoked up for some stupid working party."

I grabbed my flak and my weapon and started making my way back to the hooch. I got in my rack and masturbated for a while before nodding off to sleep. Later on, I did get yoked up for a working party, as our Pog Commandant, Sergeant Major, and Dakota Meyer were visiting the base and the PMO needed road guards for his convoy. So I put on a stupid road guard vest and stood at the corner of an intersection for the whole day. I wondered how the patrol was going but figured the guys would be alright; it wasn't their first rodeo, they'd know how to handle it. Towards evening, I started seeing Bravo guys coming back and they looked pretty miserable, barely glancing at me. Then I saw the same guys walking back toward the lot and I figured something was up, maybe some stupid EDL or something.

One grunt had the presence of mind to stop and ask me, "Have you heard yet?"

I was puzzled, "Heard what? I've been standing here all damned day."

"Sergeant V's dead. One Alpha was in contact and he got shot through the chest … they medevac'ed him to Bastion but there was nothing they could do."

I was shocked … how could V get hit? He loved this shit.

One Alpha had pushed down to Whiskey 7 Delta and dismounted at the northern portion of the GRG area. Almost as soon as the boys had left the trucks, they started taking fire. The rest of the day was just one huge movement from and to contact. Pushing across fields, to compounds, returning fire, running at a dead pace. Krystal was urging Hef and Lane, panting, "I know you're tired, but you need to keep running" as they were taking effective fire. Hef saw a guy running across an open field and fired at him, some 400 meters away. The trucks were pushed back a bit, not in sufficient range to provide overwatch covering, so they didn't. V was making fun of Hef and Lane as they crossed another field, saying how silly they looked with machine-gun rounds kicking up behind them. Entering a mosque, some young Afghan gave V a half-smile; then they found an Icom radio on him. V punched him across the face and used the terp to question him but to no avail.

Moving on to compound 34, the patrol split into Krystal's element and V's element, bounding each other as they advanced. V took a single step outside the entrance to the compound, to make connecting files with Krystal. At that point, Lane described hearing a single impact, but unlike a round hitting a mud wall or the ground, it sounded like it was smacking into meat. V dropped, with Hef and one of the snipers, Cox, pulling him in. Doc Zhao ripped open his plate carrier, Frog suit, and immediately started a needle decompression that filled up with blood, before stabbing V with another. It was no use: V was dead before he hit the ground, the round going under one armpit and out the other. Cox and Hef jumped outside, immediately returning fire at the treeline where they figured the shot had come from. Hef unloaded with his M27, growing angrier with every round he discharged. Cox picked up V's M4/203 and fired every single one of V's 40mm grenades at the treeline.

The Sir started spinning up the 9-Line, while Leonard, now the section leader, ran over to another Mat-V and cut away a rigid litter zip-tied to the side of the gun truck, screaming at Watson the driver for a knife. Watson remembers hearing that V was hit over the platoon net and thinking, "He'll be fine, he's probably just a little grazed or something, that's V for you." But then Leonard slammed open the vehicle commanders door and screamed at him for the knife, and Watson realized something was really wrong.

The Brits came in low with their Chinooks, loading up V on the stretcher, while the section kept returning fire and taking effective fire at the same time. After V got lifted back to Bastion Role Three hospital, where he would be pronounced dead, the section kept fighting, from compound to compound, returning fire and trading rounds with the Taliban. Until it finally got dark and all the compounds had been cleared,

One Alpha loaded up and headed home, minus one pack. One Bravo followed suit, from their overwatch position nearby. That night, after we got back from the ramp ceremony, everyone in the room was talking about the mission; they couldn't shut up about it. I got in my bed and put on my music, just wanting to shut them all out. I wasn't there with them, with the very guys I had trained throughout the workup with, when he was killed. I should have been on that mission, I was on that mission and V took me off. I look back on it now and play the what-if game. Hefner later recalled:

After me and Lane linked back up with everyone, we started patrolling down a road with berms on both sides. We started receiving sniper fire. He was snapping rounds pretty accurately over our heads. So we had to stay low. We then entered a compound that had no men in it. It was connected to another compound and we jumped over the wall into it. Inside that compound there were several older men in that compound. V tells us to start searching them. I search one of them that had the most Afghani on him that I have ever saw on a person there. Also two cell phones and an MP3 player. I was pretty certain that bitch was a Taliban leader. So I told him to sit down and went to tell V about him. After I told him, Krystal's element radioed asking for a connecting file so they knew for sure what compound we were in. We were right by the doorway that just had a blanket for the door. I told him I would do it and started lifting up the blanket to exit. V told me no that he was going to do it. I asked him if he was sure. He said, "Yeah man, that sniper is out there."

Once he exited I heard a shot that sounded like nothing I've ever heard. It didn't sound like it hit a wall or the ground, it was hitting human flesh and bone. Krystal's element started running over saying, "He's hit! He's hit!" I thought who the fuck is hit? So I lifted up the quilt and helped drag the body in. I realized it was V. I thought, he's fine, it's fucking V, he's a bad ass. He's been there, done that. Then I went right back out the door and almost had a burst take my head off so I ducked back in and that's when I really saw V. They had his flak off and Zhao was taking his Frog top off. I saw the blood, not gushing out or trickling out, but kind of just a slow pour. I saw how pale his skin had gotten. And how his body was limp as Zhao was trying to position him. Then I remember looking at his face and saw how his eyes were rolled in the back of his head. He was dead. I knew it. He was dead before he hit the ground. The only word that can describe the way I felt in that moment was fuck. Like FUCK! There is no WAY. Then I was filled with rage and wanted to kill every single fucking person in that goddamn village. I wanted to slaughter and cause them as much pain as possible.

That day will haunt me for the rest of my life. V walked out that door and took that risk so HIS Marine would not have to. He was a great leader and mentor and not a day goes by that I don't think of him and how he was always just trying to pick a fight …

Maybe if I had been there I could have shot back better than everybody else, maybe I could have seen where the rounds where coming from better than anybody else and I could have unloaded an entire magazine to make sure V hadn't have gotten killed. I'd unload a million magazines if that had meant he hadn't have gotten killed. Or maybe I would have gotten shot and killed, maybe it would have been me going home as the sole passenger of a C-130. Or maybe more of my buddies would have gotten hit getting to my dead body, or maybe I would have been wounded and they would have gotten killed getting to me. I don't know how fate works, but V changed it that morning in Helmand Province. First with me, then with Hefner. I later blamed my own incompetence. If I had only accepted the rank of corporal, if I hadn't been so damned self-centered and figured everything was about me. If I had put aside my hatred for the platoon and just played the game. If I had been a corporal, I would have probably been out on the ground with them because I would have been bringing an asset to them.

V was the one guy in the platoon who told me to my face, "Vining, you're fucking stupid for not picking up; what the fuck is wrong with you." Maybe he was right, maybe subconsciously his soul knew he was going to go and he was reaching out to me, to try and save him and keep him alive. I don't know, I'll never know. I'm not the one who got shot through the chest, just above my Sapi plate.

That night, as the rest of the guys in the room were talking and arguing about the patrol that day and what happened, I buried my face in my pillow, facing the wall of the conex box. I should have been there with them. Every second of that patrol.

Second platoon took over from our patrolling cycle, and apparently got in some deep sauce with the Taliban in the eastern wadi, slaying some bodies. But it didn't matter how many bodies we stacked and how much lead we slung, none of it was going to bring V back. The CO tried to make us feel better about it, but it was just hollow to us. The NCOs did get together and smash V's iPhone to bits, a promise they had made to each other if any of the others were killed in action. V would have gotten a kick out of it. The next patrolling cycle we went on, Bravo had both sections conduct an overnight overwatch. These missions literally turned out to be the most boring thing you could ever do outside of BLS.

The entire mission set was to leave at dusk or near dusk, drive a section out to some random spot in the middle of the desert, set up in a wagon circle with all the turrets facing outboard, send up the G-boss tower and observe the desert until first light. After a completely uneventful night, the section would then drive back to BLS, via the long, winding north gate, park the trucks in the motor pool, only to have to do it again the next night.

We get out in our wagon circle, and set up fire watch, all three trucks with turret watch, and one guy on radio watch in the Mrap with the G-boss thermal viewer. Hefner, Lane, Zhao, and I set up in the middle of all this, sleeping systems sprawled out underneath the desert night, trucks around us with diesel engines idling. Although the ground is rocky, our Iso mats are smooth and keep us from being poked in the back. The stars are insane, blanketing the entire sky with shades of sparkling bright white dots. From one black Afghan desert horizon all the way to other one. You feel endless, at night, between the stars and the desert floor.

Hefner asks Lane, "Hey there, Lane, you're a big boy, ain't ya?"

Before Lane can answer, Zhao says, "Yeah, but big for nothing; you can't run!"

We chuckle. Lane doesn't. One time in MOUT town at Lejeune, Lane silently smacked a piece of buttered MRE bread out of another kid's hand as he was about to eat it. The other kid, Smith, was pissed. Retribution was swift ...

"You know, apparently my girlfriend was with her mother in the car one time," Lane tries to deflect the insult. "And her mom looked sideways at her and said, 'So you and Lane have been dating for a while, eh?' And she was like, 'Well, yeah ...' Then her mom said, 'You guys have been having sex?' ... 'Yes, Mom...'" Lane pauses as he imitates the mom looking down at her daughter. "'He must wreck you ...'"

We burst out laughing. For a while we talk about nonsensical issues, how far the moon is from the world, why Stanley cups have to be so expensive, and how we can to get Zhao to lose his virginity on post-deployment leave. As the night goes on and different guys go up in the turrets to stand post, one by one we fall asleep until the conversation eventually dies a natural death underneath the blanket of stars above us.

I get woken up for my watch, which is the last one of the list, just before the sun starts coming up. Sitting in the turret with my happy jacket on, the idea of some sort of rising-sun moto picture comes to mind. The more I think about it, the more attractive the concept sounds. The sun is now above the horizon and you can see the entire desert, rays splitting over the rocks and gullies. But who to take it? Zhao of course! This is probably the best idea I've had the whole deployment. I go to wake up Zhao.

"What the fuck, Vining! You want me to take a stupid picture of you?"

"Yes, yes of course, dude. Get out of your warm sleeping bag; it's going to be totally worth it."

He tells me to get lost. I don't mind too much. But to my actual amazement, he comes over several minutes later. "Okay Vining, now you woke me up, I'll take your stupid picture!"

Finally, Operation Moto–Pic is about to commence. I think just standing there and looking out into the rising sun would look kind of neat. One of those horizon portraits, you know. Zhao takes it. I look at it on the camera, and it looks neat. When we get back to Leatherneck later that day, I take another look at it on the computer screen. It's certainly an interesting portrait; with my back turned to the camera, the rising sun in the background, I cannot deny this. I keep returning to this picture. Not only on the deployment but in the future as well. Something about it speaks to me in ways that I cannot explain. I certainly wasn't thinking any prophetic thoughts while standing there on that Afghan plain. But in a philosophical way, what am I looking for? Why is my pose shrugged? As if I'm tired from the war, tired from the deployment, tired from everything. But I'm ready, with my M203 mounted on my M4 and fully flakked up on patrol. As I circle back to this photograph, more unanswered questions keep arising: What am I looking for? Is it Lynn off in the sunrise, as if she is going to materialize in the desert? Am I looking for my future at college afterward? What I'm going to do next? Am I looking at myself in a decade, wishing I was able to teleport back to this very moment in time? I don't know. But I still look at the picture today, and every time I look at it I think something different.

Maybe a day or two later, I walk into the USO, sign out a wooden phone block, and get in the privacy booth. Some kid in cammies down the line is threatening his spouse with murder if she sells another one of his game consoles: "You FUCKING BITCH! I can't believe you would do that to me! I'm going to KILL YOU WHEN I GET BACK!" While a Triple Canopy contractor perimeter guard chick is getting her finances sorted out back home, I settle into one near the end, by the computers. I don't really know who to call though, kind of just want to touch base back home. There's no Lynn on the other end anxiously waiting for me either. Those days are over. But there is Alice, Agatha, and Zoe. I settle the muzzle of my M4 on the floor while taking a seat, and hooking my leg over the pistol grip. Then I punch in my home number, in Washington, DC.

Ring, ring.

Ring, ring.

"Hello, this is Kirby."

"Hey, Dad."

"Oh, hi Miles, wasn't expecting a call from you at this hour."

"Well, I'm sorry … I can call back … later if you want."

"No, no, no, it's alright, Mommy is asleep right now. You've got a couple things in the mail, some gun magazines, and then something about a USAA debit card. Does that ring a bell to you at all?"

Who's going to be getting V's mail now?

"Umm. Thanks. Just keep the card, I don't really need it out here. I've got my Wells Fargo one."

"Okay, I'll make sure to set it in your stuff then."

"Cool …"

Long pause.

"My section leader was killed last week."

Another long pause.

"I'm sorry to hear that, Miles. Did you know him?"

Did I know him? What kind of a question is that? I probably wouldn't be trying to reach out to someone if it had been the base CO that had gotten whacked, would I?

"Yeah, I did know him … he was my boss."

Another long, awkward pause.

"Was he killed in combat?"

No, he was stampeded by a herd of elephants. What else is the leading cause of death among infantrymen in Helmand Province?

"Yeah. The section was in a firefight. I wasn't there; he took me off. He got shot through the chest."

Everything just felt hollow.

"I'm very sorry to hear that, Miles."

Enough of this bullshit.

"I have to go, Dad. I love you."

"I love you too."

"Bye."

Click.

* * *

Fuck. Goddamn NVGs. Fuck. Ow. FUCK! Okay, I swear to God I am going to ban fucking night patrols; this is some serious bullshit! Ohhhh nooo guys, the Taliban are totally out here at 2 in the FUCKIN' MORNING IN GODDAMN FEBRUARY! Oh wait, no. The fuck they aren't beca … AW SHIT! Great … of course I slipped. Of course I'm fucking covered in fucking hajji shit trench mud … just three klicks left …

We are in Habibabad. Our company already knew just a couple weeks in that this is one of the hot villages in our AO. 2/2 didn't patrol here much; it is Taliban town. My platoon's first dismounted patrol there saw us take contact five or six times in just a few hours. So we go out to conduct a patrol base op. I am a .50 gunner in an Mrap with Swygart as my VC, and we have the back full of snipers. I am all keyed up to go slay bodies. Wanting to make sure the snipers, whom I don't know well, know I'm not a boot so I am yelling back in Pashto to the locals and try to appear nonchalant and all-knowing up in the turret.

After a day of driving around aimlessly, accidentally leaving the AO, and our trucks being stoned by snotty Afghan brats, we finally get to the cluster of compounds we will take over for the op. It comprises two abandoned compounds and a little shack on the backside of a hill between a main road with shops and a cemetery a few hundred meters away. Dismounts get out and began sweeping and searching the compounds. It is a favored tactic of the insurgents in our area to put IEDs all over these compounds. 2/2 had a couple casualties this way.

My buddy Dakin is chilling by the shack, kneeling with a hand on his Two-Forty and looking out south. Out of nowhere comes the cracking of a burst. Looking straight at Dakin, I see dirt kick up right next to him. He lays down and gets ripping with a strong burst. I look across the open field to the south and see a compound with a ditch and a treeline. "There!" I go condition one. Adrenaline's pumping. The heavy metallic machine in my hands is ready. "CONTACT SOUTH!" I shout just as the radio fills with similar calls. I'm ready. SAWs, Two-Forties, rifles all begin their discordant song. I press down on the dainty butterfly. Images go through my head of my rounds tearing chunks from compounds, cutting down trees, disintegrating delicate bags of flesh.

I hear instead a slow *thuk, thuk … thud*.

FUCK! "GUN DOWN!" I scream. Racking back, I try again. A desultory, solitary *thud* answers me. "FUCK FUCK FUCK FUCK!" The firefight is in full force now, everybody is shooting south or east, trucks are moving into better position, and our guys are getting prone or into cover from the incoming rounds. And here I am futilely battling my own weapon. I check the headspace and timing; it's GO for both. I check ammo. It's in the right way. I call for diesel to pour on. One of the snipers, Thompson, hands it up. I douse the gun and rack it okay. I put out a couple more bursts and then some dickhead hajji takes a shot at me. Close enough for me to think it hit the turret. Close enough for the *snap* to make my left ear ring.

"Swag," I shout down, "those assholes shot at me!"

By now the firing has died down a little but I still shoot back and hit one of the trees near the hajji, dead center. Since I'm using API, the impact flashes with a little *pop*.

Then I hear on the radio, "Light up the treeline!"

Rounds stitch up the compound and all around the ditch and trees. Whoops! That's just my API flashing, I think. Oh well. The firing ceases.

We hold and check for targets. I see some van hauling ass toward us. I wave my cute little flag to get his attention. Nothing, go figure. It's like 300 meters away so I pop a flare at the driver. He stops, and he and the passenger just look at me befuddled while I wave-motion him away. After some stellar communications skills on my part, he gets the message and backs off. That or someone shot a warning shot at him. I can't remember clearly. We hear that the Taliban have backed off and egressed from their positions. So one of the trucks moves up and the VC, Tim, confirms one dead guy in white hanging off a rooftop. Good shooting, Dakin! Klossing, one of the DMs, says he hit a shooter in the treeline a couple times and saw him drop.

So at least two dead fuckers and no one hurt on our end. We fucking rule. While we're waiting for word, I see something that just fuckin' gets to me. Gresham is peeking round the corner of the shack, looking south through his RCO. Then fuckin' Lieutenant Fairy Dust comes up to him and looks too. What's so bothersome, you might ask? Simple: his ejection port cover is closed. Seems minor, I look nitpicky I know. But the thing is, I know he was on the ground. We took pretty good contact for a while, and Gresham's ejection port is open from firing. I know Fairy Dust was just chilling in a compound, waiting to see if things died down enough for him to go get his CAR. To quote Sergeant Steiner, "I hate all officers ..."

Regardless of our skirmish victory, the location is deemed untenable and it's too risky to stay. We load up, high-five and drive off. I am last vic so I see that no sooner have we moved than locals swarm to collect our brass and other scraps. Like Goddam vultures.

As I'm returning to the hooches, Leonard comes up to me with a sheet of paper. "Vining, we found your laundry slip in V's shoulder pocket when we went through his stuff. Any idea how that got there?"

Of course. Because I had taken his laundry to the Nigerian contractor-run laundromat a couple days before that patrol. "Yeah, it's because I helped him take his stuff over there once, and I must have exchanged mine with his when it happened. No big deal, I'll go get it when we leave the lot."

Leonard hands me the slip. "Alright, just drop it off on his rack when you get it. We have to send all his shit home."

He turns around and walks into the NCO room. I stuff it in my pocket. Biking to the laundry section, I lock my bike up outside, by the wooden pole, enter through the front door of the tent, and get in line. This shouldn't be a big deal, right? Just hand them the two slips, mine, and his, and they'll just give the completed laundry bags to me? Can't be that difficult, we do this all the time. I get up to the counter, this kind-looking Nigerian dude behind it. Behind him is this dry erase board with a motivational quote of the day written on it, a really neat individual touch done by them. I slide the two slips over, and lean back against my M4. The guy goes back, fetches my bag, brings it up, makes me sign for it. Then he takes V's slip, goes back, finds it, and brings it back to the counter. "Where is this man?"

What do I say? "He's not here right now. I'm just fetching it for him."

Gives me a puzzled look. "Okay, if he is not here right now, can he just come back later? We need to match his name here to his ID card."

Dammit. "Okay, well he won't be here for a long time actually, can I just pick it up for him? I've done this before, I think."

This guy is getting confused. "No, we need this guy, 'Vass…..liaaaan?' Can he come and get it? The slip needs to match with his ID card."

I've had enough. "Look man, he is dead! He was killed several days ago, on a patrol, remember? The River City we were all in? That's why!"

The Nigerian literally takes a step back with his mouth agape. "Oh … oh my God. I am so sorry, so sorry, may he rest in peace. I'm so sorry, I'll just get it for you."

That's kind of what I was trying to get across but he couldn't catch my drift. I didn't mean to be rude or off-centered; he honestly seemed like a good man. I turn with Vasselian's clean laundry bag and brush past all the absent-minded Pogs and civilians, leave the tent, get on my bike, and cycle back to the hooches, dropping the bag off with Leonard.

* * *

One afternoon on QRF rotation we hear a faint explosion, not loud at all but it comes from the southern portion of Leatherneck. Explosions are such a common occurrence at Leatherneck because of all the EOD controlled detonations of bad ammunition that they are rarely worth a second thought. But this one is different; it came from the south whereas the controlled dets are announced beforehand and come from the north. We kind of look at each other and say, "Well, that don't sound good."

A second later Sergeant Leonard runs in yelling, "QRF mount up!"

Obviously somebody needs us and in a bad way.

Scrabbling as fast as we can, we mount up. Frog top on, lacing boots up, throwing a flak over my head and Velcroing it together, NVGs, extra batteries got them, rack a round in my M4, check my 203 HE grenades and throw my extra gear pack in the truck along with my helmet. Rev the trucks up and do all the system checks, lights, CTIS, ECMs turned on, Blue Force trackers signed into. Stuff some MREs under the seats because you never know how long you're going to be out there. Place the ammo cans in the turret mounts, lock the guns in and wipe them down real quick with CLP, clip that gunner's harness in. Switch the truck Prick-one-fifty-two radios on and get solid comm checks with the other trucks and then turn the dismount radios on and get checks with them back to the COC. Op-check the Thor and CMD metal detectors, extra batteries for them too … we don't know if we're dismounting or not either. Stash those sickle sticks and unbutton shoulder pockets to leave the tourniquets hanging out in case you need them real quick in a massive trauma hurry. The whole time this is going on you want to know the details, what's happening, to form a mental picture of what we're getting into.

Could just be some idiot patrol broke a mine roller and needs a wrecker; easy day. Or someone's in contact and needs another vehicle element to bail them out on the eastern wadi. Either way they need you there. Running to the pisser for a last minute piss I catch up to the LEP, Mr Gibbs, "Hey sir, what's going on? You know anything?"

He pauses for a second and replies "Yeah, Motor T got hit with an SBVIED, three guys medevac'ed, two urgent."

Damn, an SBVIED? Those things are no joke, especially if it blew right next to one of our trucks. But two urgent? At least there're no dead so far; get them back to the Bastion Role Three as soon as possible … those docs are amazing and they'll be able to fix them up and get them out to Ramstein or Bethesda within days. I think as far back as World War Two guys have always held out that if casualties can at least make it back to a larger, rearward aid station, they'll make it. And why wouldn't they? The aid stations in the rear have all the amenities and surgical expertise of a hospital and they're amazing at what they do. Get them there in that golden hour and they'll be fine. They might be missing limbs or an eye but they'll live and that is the most important part.

This isn't Hawthorne where the nearest hospital is forty minutes away by helo but Bastion, a brisk five-minute ride on an emergency American dust-off or British Chinook Tricky (medevac) flight. We link up with EOD at the back gate of Leatherneck, make sure our comms are good with them and then we depart friendly lines out to the site of the convoy. Going out the back gate always is a burden because of the terrain: it's popping you out right into the desert. Whereas going out the north gate brings you to Highway One, which is a hardball so at least you get to have an easy journey before heading south and into the AO. After a bumpy ride of about twenty minutes, we arrive at the blast site. EOD guys head up to the site while my truck pulls security. I get out with my corpsman buddy Zhao and we set up a roadblock consisting of traffic cones and sea wire. In the distance, I see some sort of a block or building and a number of Marines wandering around it. I look through my RCO but I still can't really make it out, even through four-power magnification.

Leonard gets on the net and says, "Hey One Alpha, send Vining over here so we can talk to the people here."

So I trek over to where all the Marines are. At this point, we don't know if it was an IED or a suicide vehicle that hit the Mrap; we just know that Motor T got hit while on a supply run from PB Boldak. In fact, from where we are we can actually see the easternmost portions of Leatherneck, and the G-boss tower of Boldak. That's how close the convoy was to both the bases. But we still assume it was an IED, so I make my way over very cautiously, staying in the tracks of previous vehicles as the road hasn't been cleared as yet.

The building that I couldn't make out turns out to be a 6x6 Mrap, laying on its left side, and the huge circular gap in the middle of it turns out to be the hole where the turret used to be. I get up to the vehicle and things are just a complete mess. The hull is mostly intact but all the windows on the right side are completely blown out. The massive tires are a hundred meters away and turned inside out from the explosion. The engine block is completely blown away and almost every single item inside the truck has been blown out the back and is laying in pieces all around it. The turret itself is laying on its side, twenty meters from the truck. I peer inside the turret hole and everything inside is strewn all over. Outside the vehicle are trails of the gunner's blood and mucus.

One of my Motor T buddies comes over, really calm with himself. He is a sergeant, and a Pog, usually the worst possible combination, but he's cool, a good guy. Completely casual he relates how he found Erickson propped up against the mud, how the Navy medical senior chief in the back had his legs all fucked up, how Erickson's face was completely mashed in, but still breathing somehow. The explosion was so big that he felt his own truck had been hit, even though he was two trucks ahead of Erickson's. Just like us, they swept their way over to the truck, thinking it was an IED of some sort, so were on the lookout for secondaries. He walks off and we go on about our business.

A few minutes later, I hear sobbing, uncontrollable sobbing. I look over and it's the Motor T gunny with his hand on the sergeant's shoulders, trying to comfort him, trying to tell him there's nothing they can do for Erickson, that he was pronounced dead at the Bastion Role Three. The well that the Mrap crushed is connected to a compound right next to it. The family, minus the women, are outside, squatting on the edge of it, looking at us. I start talking to them in Pashtu about what happened. They tell me a little but then start asking for compensation for their damaged well. I give them this long stare, thinking, "One of our guys is fucking dead and all you want is compensation for your damned well?" I almost tell them as much, but catch myself.

We all just kind of stand around it for a bit, in total shock at the utter devastation. When you spend so much time inside an Mrap or Mat-V, you get accustomed to believing that it'll protect you from just about anything. Well at least an Mrap will. Mat-Vs have a nasty habit of splitting right down the middle and turning into a catastrophic kill, meaning five dead Marines going home in steel containers, later flag-draped pine boxes lowered into the ground with weeping mothers staining the ground with their tears. We know our vehicles aren't completely invincible, but to see one like Erickson's so torn up and mangled plants a little thought in the back of your brain housing group: this could easily happen to you next time you're out on a mounted op.

The recovery operation took over six hours. EOD guys combed the area and did their post-blast analysis from which they deduced that the vehicle used had to have had over 500 pounds of explosives. We searched the area, looking for pieces of the Mrap to bring back and throw in the vehicle. The heavy parts such as the tires we just left them. EOD got all the ammunition that was in the truck, put it in a pile far away from the vehicle and blew it in place for fear the ammunition had become unstable from the IED blast. We heard over the radio that the ramp ceremony was going on back at Bastion.

Krystal, in his twisted humor, said, "Thank God we don't have to be at that. It was so cold that last time we were there for V's." Some of us laughed, me included, because although it was true, it didn't make the joke any sicker.

Then the wreckers came out and started the dirty work of lifting the entire vehicle onto the flatbed of an LVSR. Hoisting a forty-ton tactical vehicle is not joke, and requires a considerable amount of skill on the part of Motor T. We went searching for remnants of the suicide vehicle in the field next to the Mrap. Hefner actually found the driver's jawbone, so we plastic-bagged it for evidence collection. His Tennessee accent was unmistakable, "Hey guys! I fauund the motherfucker's jaaaw! I gawt his jaaw!" With everything cleaned up and completed, we mounted back up in the vehicles and headed back to base. Doc, the Sir, Hanney, and Watson were in my vic where I left them earlier to talk to the local villagers.

Doc asked, "What happened man?" Their only frame of reference was the turned-over Mrap, as seen from their vantage point 300 meters away on security.

I told him, "Fuck man, that whole truck was fucked. The turret was completely blown off, the tires were 100 meters away, and I saw the gunner's blood and mucus in front of where the truck stopped, apparently his whole fucking face was mashed in. Chief broke both his knees, and the A driver broke his arm."

The rest of the trip back to Leatherneck was in silence, as we rolled through the south gate and back to our spot on QRF at the company lot.

What happened was when the log run left Boldak, a white Toyota Corolla started trailing it. As the convoy got about a kilometer away from Boldak, it sped up to the rear truck and the driver detonated his 500 pounds of explosive right alongside it. The force of the explosion completely disintegrated the car but flipped the 40,000-pound Mrap onto its side and perpendicular to the road, flattening a local Afghan well. The vehicle commander had his left shoulder broken, the Navy chief who was in the back broke both his legs and the turret gunner had his face mashed in because the entire turret assembly flew off and took him with it. Ironically, the driver, whose widow was digging up dirt, was perfectly fine, even walking around the blast site as we were cleaning it up. It was the turret gunner's first deployment: Lance Corporal Caleb Erickson from Michigan was killed on February 28, 2014. Some of us blamed our restrictive ROEs for allowing this to happen. If this had been 2011, that car would have been shot up when it passed the 100-meter mark. But even then, there is no guarantee that would have made a difference.

* * *

Second platoon was on QRF cycle at Boldak. I'd like to recall the time as us almost being relieved, like 11 p.m. or so. You know, everyone was all ready to get in their bags and go to sleep, strip the trucks, relax or whatever. But fuckin' snipers decided to have some fun and shoot a couple IED emplacers. Cool cool, good job, snipers. But hey, they gotta check out the bodies and the bodies needed to be picked up. So in the middle of the night we piled into our trucks and headed out. Thankfully the snipers were just in north Showal so at least they were close. We pulled up and set the vehicles in a cordon. Thankfully no one was trying to be Ricky Recon because everybody had white lights on. We saw a bunch of Marines walking around a field next to a compound, with some going into the compound and a bunch of locals zip-tied in front of it. Sweet, job done, time to take a nap in the truck. Nope! Martin called over the radio for first squad to dismount and assist in sweeping and what not. "Goddamn it." Man. I hated when I could have stayed in the truck and had to get out and, ugh, work. Come on, let me nap, man! So we got out, and our squad took security around the compound. Stalin and someone else went north, Cox and I looked after the locals. Man, this part was one of those crazy moments. He and I were yelling at these people who were freaking out; we had one old guy and a couple teenagers all zip-tied. "*Chup shaw! Woahdrega! Aramsha, motherfuckers!*"

All the time they were freaking out at the guy with his head blown apart and this other guy who was all fucked up from getting shot. Middle of the night and all of a sudden their day already started off shitty. Me and Cox had our lasers and lights on and were moving them from person to person, shouting at them to just shut the fuck up. Meanwhile Martin had me moving back and forth to grab CMDs and shit from Stalin; the path I took was right next to the dead IED emplacer. An old guy, he was sprawled out on the path next to the compound, dead as fuck. His head was missing a lot from a 7.62 doing its job. I walked through the blood and it didn't bother me. This other guy was in the field in front of his house; Doc Shang was checking him out. He was hit in the pelvis or stomach; apparently he got hit from a kilometer out, at night. What a shitty way to get hit, huh fucker? He was puking up stuff and moaning like it was his job. We, being the sick bastards we are, were pissed off at the snipers for not finishing him off before we got there. "Come on, you guys have suppressors. You should have just taken him out!" Most unfortunately for us though, was that since this guy was wounded, he'd get sent to the hospital at Bastion, which meant Charlie Company would have to babysit him when we were there … fucking bullshit.

Being on QRF was always entertaining. If we had to respond to a section in contact, that was a bonus; if nothing happened, then we had two nights filled with movie-watching and otherwise hanging out on our own at the company lot. Staff NCOs could put us on working parties, but we could never be involved in something major, like individually counting thousands of rounds of ammunition or rearranging some stupid conex box locker that Gunny needed remodeling, like the sections on the post cycle were sometimes yoked up to do. We might get corralled into maybe cleaning up a single room, or police-calling the lot, but other than that we were left ourselves. We'd usually eat pretty good too, with a constant supply of pies and fruits being deposited in the tent, outside of the usual chow hall trips to the DFAC, where we would mount up, park the trucks outside the DFAC, leave a gear guard, eat, and then return to the company lot. As an NCO, I could even get on the NIPRNet with my CAC access and diligently complete my MarineNet corporal's course. I'm still not sure how that translated into me becoming a better leader, but I'm sure someone at Quantico could shit me a solid explanation.

Laptops were hooked up to the projector in the briefing room, which was also used to show PowerPoint patrol briefs. But more importantly, we used it to watch pirated movies and DVDs, sometimes even the latest releases.

If we couldn't watch movies there, then we'd crowd around a laptop in the QRF tent on someone's rack and watch them there. Some of the guys were bastards and wouldn't give up their laptop for the good of the cause, but who were we to tell them how to properly use their laptops?

Masturbation was done in the porta-johns bordering the Hesco barrier, lifing was done in the jailhouse gym that Motor T owned. When it started getting cold, the QRF tent was the place to be, because of the heating vents hooked up to it. Otherwise, you were bundled up in whatever warming layers you had brought from the hooches.

Hanney and Farmer were our two machine-gunners. Farmer was the One-Two driver, while Hanney was usually either a turret gunner for One-Three, which was Krystal's truck, aka Team Meat Hammer, or as a dismount machine-gunner with us. Hanney was constantly making fun of Farmer for being slow, from Tennessee, and not being able to actually "gun" because he was a driver, while Farmer was always dissing Haney for being from New York, accidentally getting Burgess shot on one of the helo missions, and being an otherwise bleeding-heart dumb Yankee. The conversation between them was just pure infantry gold at times.

"Hey, does everyone remember watching Stump's helmet cam video of Farmer? Where Stump asked Farmer to simply call in a radio check while they were getting shot at, and Farmer's hick voice spouts out, straight from a reenactment of Forest Gump, 'Saaaargeent, I doooonooooo muuuuuch abuuut raedeos,' and then Stump just tells him to fuck off and he low-crawls back to the gun."

"Hah, hah, hah. Very funny Hanney, tell me about that time you got Burgess shot in the gut on the Mamma Carres mission?"

"Burgess got himself fucking shot, because he moved from the position I left him in; he was fine there."

"Yeah, whatever Hanney, quit lyin'; we all know you never liked the kid to begin with."

"Fuck you, Farmer." The two were tussling about on the cot, the rest of us dying laughing.

Krystal looked over from his laptop, "What the fuck are you two doing? You're going to break the cot."

"Nothing, corporal."

They released each other and went back to their old spots on the cot. Lane came in and sat down next to Hanney. Somehow sex became the topic of conversation. Hanney recounted of story of personal victory. "When I was at college this chick I had known from down the dorm hall banged on my door one night and I answered it, saying, 'What the hell do you want,

I've got football practice tomorrow at five in the morning,' and she was like 'Tom, can we fuck?' I was all sleepy-eyed and shit, and said, 'Yeah, why not,' ... easiest lay in the world."

Farmer looked at him, "Yeah right, you didn't get laid, football got you laid, you stupid fuck."

"Whatever Farmer! At least I'm not banging my cousin or whatever the hell you inbreds do down in Tennessee."

Hefner chuckled, "Hey now, Jack! We ain't all like that back home; it's just in east Tennessee where Farmer is from!"

Doc Zhao sort of smiled at this Southern dig as well, looking up from his iPad.

Hef said, "What are you looking at, Zhao? At least we're not all virgins like your China ass."

Zhao came over to us, iPad in one hand, an earbud in one ear with another in his free hand. "Yeah? Yeah? Yeah? Who cares? Who fucking cares, you stupid bitch."

We all looked up, Hef saying, "Whoa Zhao, calm down, I was just stating a fact, you know, it's an American thing."

Zhao eyes burned through Hef. "Yeah ... yeah ... next time we get shot at, I'm going to yell at the Taliban and say, 'Shoot Hefner! I feel like tying a tourniquet down extra tight today!' Idiot." He shook his head and sat down on his cot again.

Hef looked at me I shrugged and went back to reading *Shantaram*. "Guy can be bipolar as fuck, dude."

* * *

One Two is landing in waves, coming to relieve us. When One Two's deployment is over, they will be the last Marine infantry battalion to leave Helmand Province. Pretty prophetic stuff, really, if you consider we've been slinging lead in Helmand since 2008. However the relief-in-place process needs to happen so we have to interface with the guys from One Two as they come in. My section takes a section from One Two out beyond the west side of the base as a sort of practice patrol with them. That particular side of the base is completely safe, as nothing ever happens of substantial value and we even stay inside the farthest tank ditch for most of the patrol. But as we step off, the One Two point man is having some trouble with the CMD sweeper.

"Have you done your soil comp test, man?" I ask.

He pauses. "Umm, what's that?"

Oh Lord, only the most basic thing you ever learn when being taught CMDs. Boot Town here, population one, about to be dead. I take the CMD and work as point man for the rest of the patrol, leading us inside the berm.

During the patrol the One Two section leader sees a live cannon round that appears to have been unexploded from a Cobra. He gets excited and thinks we need to call EOD to take care of it. We're so confused because we know exactly what it is, and realize there are no IEDs here. Krystal walks up to it, picks it up, and tosses it.

The One Two guy goes nuts, and says, "You ought to put that thing up your ass!"

Clown ... but hey, we all started somewhere when it comes to deployment.

* * *

Ayr came into the hooch in cammies. Hef looked at him from the movie he was watching on his bunk and said, "What are you in stupid cammies for?"

Ayr took his eight-point cover off, letting it fly onto his bed. "We're ending patrolling this week man. I was just working with the Sir to turn in all of our section's radios. No need to wear Frogs anymore."

This was it. The end.

We were only supposed to have been in-country seven months, September to March. However, we got extended into May. I didn't think I could ever get used to Leatherneck, but it turned into a bit of home for us. Gear inspections, armory turn-ins, washing trucks, cleaning hooches, canceling BLS accounts, mailing stuff home, everything needed to happen before we could hop a ride on that big freedom bird. After a solid week of preparation, the day finally came. Buses showed up outside the hooches, the whole company hollering and yipping away, as we dragged our deployment bags and seabags into the cargo holds.

One final EDL outside the hooches, as the platoon sergeant yelled out, "EDL first!"

"Dump 'em out!" came back.

Loading up the buses, they took us to the airfield on Bastion where they did customs. This was nice, because it meant we didn't have to do customs anywhere along the way. Rumor had it that we were stopping in Romania this time, instead of Manas, in Kyrgyzstan. Somewhat of a change of pace.

Customs over with, the extreme long waiting over with as well, we single-filed out to the C-17 sitting on the runway, covers stashed away, assault packs on our chests and weapons by our sides. Taking our seats, anxious to finally leave, we waited what seemed like another hour on the plane, while the crew went through all their preflight checks, and control tower procedures. Finally, we got word that we were about to take off. Sitting in those cushy seats, in oddly fitting cammies, the plane roared straight up, into the air.

I remembered coming onto Leatherneck, in the C-17, eight months previously. I remembered the uneasy looks on all the boots' faces – not boots anymore – zero clue of what to expect on their first deployment. Early and Harrington were cracking some stupid joke to each other, about how going into Iraq was so much better than Afghan. I remembered looking over at V, sitting in one of the side jump seats of the aircraft, his M4 broken apart, and cleaning it while tuning out to his music through his earbuds. Would he have been proud the way we had turned out after him? What would he be saying if he were on this flight with us? Would he be cracking some stupid V joke, or be dipping into an empty water bottle, watching *The Evil Within* on his laptop? Would he chuckle at the fact that we still yelled out "Dump 'em out" when EDLs were called?

That had been a long time ago.

Dead Walkers killed in action

Lance Corporal Christopher Grant (Alpha Company)
Sergeant Daniel Vasselian (Bravo Company)
Lance Corporal Caleb Erickson (H&S Company)

Dead Walkers who took their lives

Lance Corporal Jason S. Roth (Bravo Company)

Chapter 6

For Lack Of War

"They are blessed with that experience for a year, and then they come home, and they are just back in society like the rest of us are, not knowing who they can count on, not knowing who loves them, who they can love, not knowing exactly what anyone they know would do for them if it came down to it. That is terrifying. Compared to that, war, psychologically, in some ways, is easy, compared to that kind of alienation."

Sebastian Junger

The seabag drag from Leatherneck, to Romania, to Cherry Point and finally to Lejeune, was just like any other deployment – slow, boring and anxiously waiting to get home. Romania was completely unlike Manas in that it actually had an environment about it, it was green, the first time we'd seen that much greenery in months, and it was beautiful to our desert eyes. Also, unlike Manas, we actually slept in concrete rooms, with lights we could turn off and be surrounded by beautiful Romanian women. Smelling perfume again was a glorious experience.

The command organized a little drinking, and of course, we blew that out of proportion. Guys were fighting each other, and a stupid lockdown was arranged, but, oh well, we got our drink on after eight months in the desert. Got back to Cherry Point, unloaded our bags and onto the bus to Lejeune. The first deployment we had a motorcycle escort, American flags and all, it was a fantastic sight to see, leading us all the way to A street where the battalion headquarters was. This time we didn't have anything, apart from the seven-tons waiting to pick up our gear. I don't blame the motorcycle guys. It was almost midnight by the time we were on Highway 24, otherwise known as "Freedom Way" for all the grunts that traveled down that road in buses, for some of them that ride being the last one they'd have on a U.S. hardball. Heck, this time we didn't even have a cruise book put together for the pump.

Back to Lejeune and the world is a blur, getting the battalion organized, checked back in, TMO returned, weapons cleaned, rosters filled, gear sorted. Soon we are on a 96 Libo, that magical of all Marine Corps words.

I go up to Indiana with my father, to check out the college I'll be attending post-EAS. I talk to an Iranian teacher there, and she asks me if I have ever been to Afghanistan after I mention some phrases in Pashtu. Straight-faced, I look into her eyes and say, "I was there a week ago." My internal dialogue is saying, "I wish I was still there."

Back to Lejeune, and it's time for me to check out of the unit, and the Marines. This day literally could not have come soon enough. That magical DD214 is ever-looming, ever-present in my eyes, throughout the whole signature checkout list, Supply, Chaplain, Admin, First Sergeant, CO, Post Office, the list goes on and on. The battalion career counselor asks me a simple question, "Do you want to reenlist?" And I give him a simple answer, "No." Why don't I want to reenlist? Because we aren't at war, you stupid career-monger. We're pulling out of Afghanistan. What other combat deployments can I jump on? I came in for the war, the war is what I got, and now, I'm gone. I don't want to be treated like someone's little five-year-old child either, constantly being monitored and checked. I want to live someplace where I won't be screamed at for walking and talking on my phone, or being called a little bitch for sticking my hands in my pockets.

There's a small glitch in the plan, however. I check out on terminal leave on Monday. But the battalion is holding a memorial service for V, Erickson, and Grant on Wednesday. Their families are coming down. Do I stay? Or do I check out on terminal? I stay. Something in me realizes the memorial service is worth going to. So I get my 214, and I kind of illegally stay in the barracks for two days. Oh well, what are they going to do? Kick me off base? Thanks, guys, was going that way anyway.

The stay is worth it, the memorial service is entirely fitting. All first platoon is there, One Alpha and One Bravo are reunited there for V's part of the service. But afterward, we go to Marston Pavilion, a popular venue on the New River. V's widow is there, his father and his younger brother Joey are there, along with assorted cousins and family members. At ease isn't even an appropriate phrase for describing the mood. Just being there with the family, making jokes about V, remembering his smile, and his stupid "Dump 'em outs" after an EDL, his silly Viking-inspired bicycle helmet. The family even went so far as getting black T-shirts printed with an American flag, and a "V" across it, giving them out to all of us. I still have it.

None of them are in tears or distraught. They just seem happy to be around the men that were last around V. It makes for a really joyful event, everyone mingling, introducing themselves, talking about their personal interaction with V and how he made their lives miserable, hilarious, or both at the same time. His mother gets to meet Doc Zhao, who worked on him while Hef and

Cox returned fire. Leonard comes up with this odd gift, a sort of ring. He presents it to V's brother, Joey, "Joey, this is something that we all put in to get, a ring, with a steel knuckle on the outside, and a bottle opener on the inside. Because V was always about picking fights, and drinkin' beers." Joey laughs it off, accepts it and says how thankful he is that we all came out to this.

But before we end, I call all the One Alpha guys together, and tell them I want a picture with all of us; we haven't really ever taken a picture of One Alpha all together, so this looks like a great time. I throw up the terminal lance sign, Krystal just looks at me and slaps it away. I start laughing with the rest. Later on, the picture actually turns out to be pretty good. A bunch of young guys with skin-tight, rolled sleeves, sharp low regs, all looking smart, especially me, obviously, with my hands on my hips. Often I find myself looking back at that picture, as if in some Harry Potter book where the characters can look into a photograph and actually jump into it for a brief moment in time.

Time is of the essence; V's family has to drive back to Massachusetts, first platoon has to get back to work, probably doing something stupid like cleaning the third deck, and I have to leave base and get home. I say my goodbyes, give my hugs out. I single out Weaver, Hef, Early, and Zhao to pay particular attention to but I say goodbye to everyone.

To Weaver, for one last time, "Hey man, remember that time we almost fucking died?" He laughs; gets us every time.

Leonard takes advantage of the opportunity, "Christ, Vining, get out of here! You're finally out! Stop making us all jealous!"

They are laughing, I'm laughing too. I walk to my car, get in the driver's seat, toss my desert cover on top of the dashboard, just below the bottom of the windshield where it belongs. I close my door, rain is starting to come down. I start unbuttoning my blouse, just out of habit. But then I stop. I rebutton the buttons I just undid. A realization hits me. This is going to be the last time, I ever wear this uniform, in this capacity. As I start up the car, back out, and drive off base, past the E-Club, past Lejeune High School, another realization hits me. Despite any bad blood I've ever had with first platoon, with training boots, hating change, dealing with Bravo Company, and being on Leatherneck; despite all that, the fact of the matter is that I was with a group of guys, that I could trust with everything I had. The thought that never again would I ever be in this sort of setting was so upsetting, that having anything else was truly, and absolutely frightening. The rain pelting on the roof of my car was like the tears that rolled down my face on that ride back off base.

Six hours later, through North Carolina, up Interstate 95, slowly through Virginia, I got back home to my family's row house in DC. My parents welcomed me, thanked me for being alive, and I thanked them for enduring another one of my deployments. I was happy to see them and glad to be home, and especially alive. This is something that civilians don't seem to understand about the vitality between life and death. Whenever we hear of a casualty, our first questions are whether they made it or not, no matter how significant the injuries are. You can live without legs, you can live without all your limbs, you can live without half your face, you can even live halfway mentally challenged. But you cannot live if you're dead. You cannot feel the sunshine and look at pretty women on a busy street. You cannot look through Facebook newsfeeds and sleep through Sunday mornings. You cannot because you're dead; you are gone. Taylor, Fenn, Ripperda, Martino, Wild, Muchnick, Vanderwork, Grant, Vasselian, and Erickson can't do these these things anymore because they're dead; they no longer exist. They will always live in our hearts and in their families' hearts and will have influence far beyond the grave. But they cannot take trips to the beach, and puke all over downtown Atlanta. They cannot because they are dead. And this puzzles us when civilians say how someone got hurt in a terrible way. Grunts pause and say, "Hold on a second, are they alive? Are they conscious? If so then it doesn't matter; they could be gone, like my friends on deployment, like my friends at Hawthorne."

This was my mentality when I came home, of death and life and what to make of it. For eight straight months, I had lived in a kill-or-be-killed environment. I had championed the deaths of our enemies and mourned those of our own. And was neutral when it came to civilians. Every action we took minimized the risk of death, but there was still the glaringly obvious conclusion that you could be dead too, no matter how well you planned and executed your five-paragraph order. With this permeating my every action and inaction, I came home, to a society that doesn't consider turning into pink mist if they walk on one side of the street or the other.

My parents beckoned me upstairs, and said, "Look, there's a surprise waiting for you." I opened the door, and there was a kitten, barely three weeks old, staring up at me. "We rescued him from New York; he was found in a gutter about to cash in on life, and we took him to a vet and got him fixed up."

I thanked my parents and they left me in the room with the kitten. I slid down to the floor and picked up this tiny animal, this miraculous thing of life that was full of love. And I just sat there, playing with it and petting it. At that moment I felt a love for this kitten that overcame all the threatening emotions I was experiencing. This kitten didn't know what death was, didn't know that an Mrap steering wheel column can be forced straight through your Sapi plates and into your chest from an IED explosion. This kitten was new at life, with none of the animosity that comes with it. He was pure, and I was holding him, and somehow I was pure with him. I just felt all my emotion drain from me, by somehow connecting with this little life form. Now, in retrospect, I realize that being home and alone with that kitten was the first time I also actually slowed down. Just wholly put on the brakes and took a step out from this wild thing of deployment, getting out, or whatever you want to call it.

From DC I went on my terminal leave. I went to Ireland via the gracious secret of the Air Force's Space Available (MAC) flight program. Alice was waiting for me in Dublin. I had built her up entirely during the deployment, while at the same time I broke several other hearts. I was selfish, entirely selfish. In Dublin, I was in this odd world of still feeling like I needed to go somewhere, do something, join something before realizing I actually had nowhere to be at all. Looking through videos that Alice took in Dublin, I see myself spaced out, completely lost in some sort of fourth dimension. Whether it was walking down a street, maybe thinking about V or Taylor, or staring at the woods while on the Serpentine lake with her. Literally just looking into nothingness, until she calls me back and I only marginally turn.

Lynn started coming back to me in my thoughts. Three times I called Alice "Lynn": after sex, at a nightclub, and walking down the street. She obviously wasn't too impressed. I was going through a sort of unprocessing, and unpacking. The breakup with Lynn had been so swift and had happened so radically that my emotional side had thrown it to the basement of my soul. There had been no time to bring it to the forefront. Because I had Bridgeport to get through, and I had a deployment to prep for. To help with the sealing of the basement, I busied myself with all those girls I banged and the Fleet. Only by finally isolating myself from that environment was I able to break through that cement seal, and bring those painful memories to light. This was only the beginning.

As much as I told Alice that Lynn was behind me, the more she kept coming out. Of course, Lynn had already gotten over me. She said as much in the one email I got back from her, after the many I had sent to her since Bridgeport. But I hadn't. One of the Charlie guys told me that his sister had died while he was deployed and he had merely shoved it to the back of his mind, and only when he had actually left the Marines did the full realization that his very own sister had passed away completely catch up and floor him with the full effect.

None of this was apparent to me, and none of it was explained either. It didn't make sense why I was calling my new girlfriend an old girlfriend's name. Regardless, into the civilian world I plunged. Odd sights, odd situations, I felt like a child in the outside world for the first time, being exposed to all these peculiar things in civilized society. The questions I got asked as well: "How could you shoot at people?", "I don't believe in what you were doing, invading foreign countries", "Your deployments must have been horrible, I'm so glad you came home alive", "You're a veteran? You look too young to be a veteran", "Have you killed anyone?", "Did you get shot at?", "Were you scared?" Answering them almost became as ludicrous as the questions themselves.

Even the vernacular I used set me apart and alienated me. Some pimply faced freshman looked at me and said I look like a certain famous musician. Without skipping a beat, I responded, "Who is that? Some hippie fucking faggot?" Maybe because I was busy worrying about turning into pink mist while this kid was busy worrying about his first prom date. I called my friends "fags," and if something was stupid, I called it "gay" or "that fucking cocksucker," and more obscene, politically incorrect vernacular. Enough to make civilized society shocked at what they would hear. It doesn't need us spitting the rough and ready grammar that we use, daily, to deal with the lives we previously led.

Coming back from Dublin, I went straight to college in Indiana, absolutely convinced that every college student and professor I met was going to be a liberal, tree-hugging peace activist. The reality was that although there were a number of these types around, not everyone was like this, and I found pockets of conservatism, even some vets. However, the only vets I could really associate with were other Marine or Army infantry guys. They got it, they came from the same suck, the same community, and they missed it. Every damn day. However, around a year or so later, I started running into 03s who got out after me. They were in infantry battalions, but because they had enlisted after me, they had not been to Afghanistan, only Meuws, or UDPs, because they were just a few grades behind my generation, and hadn't gotten the opportunity. But the problem was that it was hard connecting with any of them.

The college world starts to take its toll. Slowly but surely I started spiraling down into a sort of hatred of anything and everything civilian. That fuckstick walking down the middle of the road wearing his headphones? That girl walking around with the zippers of her backpack undone? That stupid college professor who claims to know what stress is like, in front of an audience? One of my classes opens up with a woman who had previously been a man and had gotten a sex change. She opens her deep-voiced mouth, and I physically cringe in my seat, shrinking into it as if taking fire.

Everything just seems phony, a stupid excuse for an existence. I try crossing the road, a car comes toward me, I put my hand up at it. Expecting it to stop. Why? Because I have a fully automatic light machine gun, a squad of grunts behind me, and I'm on a VCP. This guy doesn't stop, he's getting lit up. But no, he keeps coming and coming, and finally, he passes by me completely, leaving me behind and confused. Why didn't he stop? Why didn't I shoot him before he exploded his suicide vehicle? I'm not in Helmand anymore …

I have this sort of inner rage that boils throughout the day. Small things completely set me off, kicking and screaming at things, stairs, people, anything. One day I almost collide head on with a kid with his earbuds in crossing a street and I scream into his face with a rising intonation: "Why don't YOU FUCKING LOOK!" Someone asks me what there is to do in DC. I quietly think, "You could visit my dead friends in Arlington." This new lifestyle lacks all sort of purpose, any condition of meaning. What does it accomplish to complete a homework assignment? On deployment, I stood post, or I went on patrol, back in the rear, I trained for those things. But doing a homework assignment? Taking a test? That isn't life or death responsibility, that's a waste of time, a meaningless measure of nothingness that has zero quantitative value to me; it doesn't kill the enemy or help a village. Sometimes all I can do is trump into my dorm room, throw my bag on the bed, sit in my chair and put in a fat dip, then get blackout drunk later. Every day. I'm going through more dip than I went through in the service.

Quickly I learn to shut up about my service, to be quiet about what I have done. Sometimes people catch me off guard, and they ask me if I miss being in, or if I miss being deployed. I find myself answering with, "Every Goddamn Day." Yet I don't know why, I just know I can't deal with this civilian bullshit, day in and day out. I'll be sitting at my desk when something will remind me of deployment … YouTube video, a word, an attitude, or even just a glance at my black bracelet with five names on it: Taylor Fenn Ripperda Vasselian Erickson. I'll look off into the distance, at the trees or something, and if I try hard enough, I'll recreate the cool concrete on post, or the uncomfortable jostling of a Mat-V. I think of Pritchna; she's probably wearing a burkha right now. Auakula and his brother Aratura, possibly fighting for the Taliban because they have no other choice, or maybe even farming the same fields we left them with.

Guys from the Fleet, I go on Facebook and see where they are now, who they're marrying, or what schools they're at. I watch our homemade deployment videos, shaky footage of us pouring water on each other or getting shot at. Memorial Days become somewhat hard to understand. A community and a country trying to justify our deaths as if they're for these vague notions of "Freedom isn't Free" or NASCAR races. All I can muster in my mind is just hollowness, the complete hollow emptiness these events seem to propagate. There's nothing personal about it, not like kneeling down next to Fenn's Soldier's Cross at Bridgeport or drinking a Monster at Taylor's grave. On the news, first Iraq then Afghanistan seem to be collapsing, falling to the enemy we spent so many years fighting. What did we end up even fighting for, then?

My girlfriend takes me to the Indy 500 at Speedway, Indiana. The second I'm in front of the stadium and feel the music, the yelling, the drunken debauchery, the crowds, I freak out like I've never done before. I'm having a legitimate nervous breakdown, and my hands are shaking. I'm in control of nothing, I don't have my firearm, these strange young people are screaming, "U.S.A.! U.S.A.! U.S.A.!" I swear to myself, "Can a single one of these idiots name a single American who has been killed in action? One? Just one man or one woman who has been killed in Iraq and Afghanistan." They continue screaming, and I grip my face, contorting it this way and that way, furious and scared all at the same time, while white-knuckling the tent poles on the muddy field I somehow convince myself to spend the night in. A fat body in our group flicks my girlfriend's cap up, so I get in close to him and tell him to not do that again. He mouths back a pathetic answer, and I want to beat him to a bloody pulp mixed in with the mud of the stadium. I'm filled with rage at him, at these people around me, at this stupid excuse to remember the dead. Damn Memorial Day. I don't need a single combined day once a year to know that V was smoked on December 23, I don't need some government holiday to remember that Taylor and six others were blown to smithereens on March 18. Or why my eyes fill to the brim with tears when I check my phone and see those dates when they seem to slap me in the face.

Anyone who thinks we fight for the red, white, and blue is borderline psychotic. That might have gotten us in the door, and images of 9/11 might have reminded us boots why we we were doing what we did. But the only American flag in that first firefight at Musa Qala was forty miles away, flapping in the breeze on Leatherneck. We fight for each other, and we die for each other; you can't get any more truthful than that. They don't get it, nor will they ever get it. Do they even want to get it? How is a bubbly college kid supposed to understand what it's like to burn human feces in an oil drum and do your laundry in a bucket? How can I relate to a lovely middle-aged lady behind a storefront counter about what it's like to run across a field while under PKM fire, carrying a full combat load and being the point man?

How do I tell the grumpy old man in the corner of a restaurant that we actually believed in what we were accomplishing in Iraq and Afghanistan but the political establishment bent both the local peoples and us over with its greed? The fact is, I can't.

These people cannot relate to anything we've been through. And I don't want them to know either. I don't want them to know what it's like to watch someone die from a gunshot wound, have your boss shot through the chest or to take indirect fire. I want that burden to be on me and those other grunts who share it. Because somehow, in some sick way, that's a reward, that the people of this country have a choice not to be involved in the protection that is afforded them. So when these prepubescent kids are asking me what I did before college, I give them the answer of having transferred from a school in Pennsylvania. I skip the entire Marine Corps experience because they won't understand it, and neither do I expect them to understand it. Which is why I feel comfortable around other veterans now that I'm out. They get it, we know where we've all come from. Why we joined, why we yearned for a combat deployment, why we think that picture of a dead Taliban fighter is absolutely hilarious, and it'd be even funnier if some grunts were pissing on him. That is us, that is our burden to share and withhold. But they also know the pain involved, of those mind-numbing patrols, horrible chains of command, and what it's like to be at a memorial service and meet the family of the men you would have easily traded places with in a heartbeat had you the chance.

During my first semester at college, I went to the local cafeteria, like any other day. Usually I don't wear anything Marine Corps-related because I don't want people bugging me about it. But on this particular day, I was low on laundry and threw on my Sergeant V T-shirt. As I took my food to the checkout lane, the cashier, a lovely girl, looked at my shirt and asked, "Is that an A on your shirt?" I looked down, looked up, and said, "Umm, no, it's a V, it's for one of my former bosses, guy named Vasselian …" In that moment, I raced for something, anything to say. What was I to say? "Yeah, he was my mobile section leader, he got shot through the chest and died on a patrol that he himself told me not to go on, he was an amazing man, always had a Red Bull and made fun of you whether you liked it or not. But most of all, he was a true warrior, you know like the Vikings, or the Spartans, he loved a good fight. Yearned to kill the Taliban and defend the Afghan people who had nothing to do with it. You should look him up, and read about him. Read about men like him who gave their lives so that I might buy this garbage food and pay you money with which you'll go home and blow on TV shows or nights out and not have to worry about a tyrant in charge or a repressive country, or just being free in general."? Was I supposed to say that? To this young lady who was just doing her thing and having a beautiful day as it was? How could I tell her that my T-shirt was a memorial to a fallen hero? So I stuttered, looked away and said, "Yeah, you know, yeah, have a nice day." As if she could read my mind, tear it apart, see how I felt. Maybe my DD214 or my CAR would have helped her with that.

I dump Alice from a thousand miles away for another girl, a completely wrong move, handled in the worst possible way. During one snowing winter day, this new girlfriend comments that the snow looks nice, and I instantly snap, "Shut up, don't say stuff like that." I wasn't thinking of her, I was thinking of Bridgeport.

Then I go on a summer program and experience some depression. In a state I've never been to, and a city I never knew existed, I spend the good part of summer. No friends, no meaningful social contact, not even any vet connections. Zhao actually comes up and visits me, while he is stationed at the Naval Hospital in Lejeune, and that actually helps a lot. But I take my depression out on the girlfriend, over Skype. And after multiple weeks of this, she tells me to "Talk to your mom, talk to a shrink, talk to your friends, but don't talk to me because you're making me depressed."

Really? At the moment I need you the most, you aren't going to be there for me? What if Leonard and Zhao hadn't had the sense to fire those 203s? What if Nwankwo hadn't given up his water during that patrol? If she wasn't going to be there for me, then I wouldn't be there for her. I fly up an old-time bang buddy, and we spend the next week at my apartment smashing. Later on, I dump her, and I go out with the friend, whom I then dump several months later. I can't hold on to anything emotional, and I always revert to Lynn, while leapfrogging from woman to woman, never suffering myself in the process. Every warm body after her is just my substitute for her not being there.

On my first December break home from college, my parents instruct me in no uncertain terms that I've got too much junk, and some of it needs to go because it's taking up space. In return, I tell them that I'm stocking up for the second American revolution because I've got enough military gear to outfit a decent fireteam of Three-Percenters. In reality, the massive amount of gear I have is due to the stockpile that most grunts find themselves with. Due to the need to scavenge discarded equipment to do your job and to go out and buy things that help you at your job but the Marine Corps won't issue you. Ironic isn't it? We send you on a deployment that has significant national security ramifications, international repercussions, you might not even come back from it alive as an 0311 and oh, by the way, we're only giving the minimal amount needed to barely accomplish the mission, but we're still expecting nothing but outstanding performance. Good luck, and here's some extra ear pro.

In actuality I'm a gear queer, meaning a grunt who is obsessed with different pouches and pieces of equipment to the point of blowing a good amount of his salary on such items. Regardless, I now have almost three full plastic tubs of uniforms, pouches, vests, and other things that I acquired while I was in. I pick up my plate carrier, the same one that I used on my two deployments, most of my field ops, and in Bridgeport. It still stinks of dried sweat and is pretty much held together with 550 cord. The side Sapi carriers are colored whitish with the leftover salt residue. Stains cover the entire thing from top to bottom. The camelback holder affixed to the rear portion has actually been in Fallujah and was used by a senior before me on my second deployment. This line of genealogy is impressive, but at the end of the day, it's just a camelback holder. There's a full-length mirror in the room, and I decide to put it on for old times' sake. Last time I wore this plate carrier was on my final patrol in Helmand while showing guys from One Two how not to act like total boots while outside the wire.

I pull the carrier over my head and feel the soft shoulder straps fall on my shoulders. God, how those sucked after a long post cycle or on the final steps of a mission. I got a pair of front and back Sapis from a buddy who found them left behind on Jaker, the side Sapis I traded an iPod for while on Leatherneck. I buckle the waist belt; it still fits my waist, but just barely. I wrestle the cummerbunds around my belly after what seems like an eternity because of some the weight I've gained while at college. But eventually, they buckle underneath the front flap, where the Velcro barely holds itself together after being ripped off after so many hikes. The Mich helmet I got from a senior as well, complete with a much-coveted Norotos diamond plate and mount. I actually lost the elbow mount after a late night patrol, pulled a huge fit and eventually got a mount sent out to me through Fedex within a week via Leatherneck. The Mich still has the little American flag I fitted inside of it, complete with my handwritten names of the Marines we lost – Vasselian, Grant, and Erickson. The helmet pads are still shaped to my skull, so it fits just right.

But a helmet never fits "just right" because there is nothing right about wearing a helmet in the first place. It adds weight to your head, makes everything awkward, is a pain to lose, and gives you actual headaches. It provides protection against shrapnel, blows to the head, and could possibly deflect a round, but God forbid a 7.62 round hits it dead on because then it's pretty useless. I strap the helmet on, and I'm complete, minus the Frog suit,

M4 and grenade launcher, 180 rounds of ammunition, six HE grenades, water, twenty-pound Thor, 90° heat or negative 10° cold, and of course the fear of turning into pink mist from an IED or getting shot at in general. I look at myself in the mirror and contemplate.

I'm staring into it, but who is staring back? This used to be me, this used to be my entire existence. I used to live this, day in and day out, I used to wear this as part of my job description. Closing with and destroying the enemy wasn't apart of some printed mission statement, but the very core of my existence. Not anymore, now I'm a part of an alien civilian world that I'm still not prepared to accept and be mentored in. I'm surrounded by people who don't know and don't care how many of my friends are no longer with us, how many of my friends are still facing their demons at twenty-two a day. This is no longer me, but I miss it, and I miss it every goddamn second of every goddamn day.

As I go through my stuff, sorting and organizing, throwing things out, I realize I not only have another plate carrier but also enough gear to completely outfit it. So I start with the camelback and loop it through the Molle down the center of the rear portion. You need it in the center because the sides offer spots for other stuff you put on your back – radio antennae pouches, pyro pouches facing upside down so you can unclip them so that white star cluster can fall right into your hand. I stick a bladder into it and loop it through the shoulder straps, so it's always where I need it to be – in front of my face. Officers tend to loop it under the armpit, which seems to be a trend they learn at IOC. My magazine pouches go in front, on the carrier flap that holds the cummerbund in place. Holding two magazines apiece, they hold up to 180 rounds at belly level, ready for a quick reload, but you always take the magazine farthest away on your right side if you're right handed so if you really need a magazine quick, fast, and in a hurry, the most readily available ones are there on the left side.

Above them goes my admin pouch, which holds my GPS, pens, and pencils, my reporting formats such as my 9-Line medevac sheet or Call for Fire. Right underneath my face, ready for use just like my hydration hose. Next up is my individual first aid kit, on my right side so I can access it with my right hand if I ever need it. But what if it is my right arm that gets shot or blown off, then what? Such is the use of a belt, where you can twist it around with your left hand to get to it. Then I have my dump pouch, which is used for anything other than magazines: if you're a hard-ass NCO you'll punish guys for putting anything other than used magazines in it. I find a Velcro name tape and affix it to my drag handle, then I find a subdued American flag which I affix to my admin pouch. That completes my second plate carrier.

But this one I don't put on or try on for size. It has no intrinsic value to me. It is just some extra gear. It wasn't on that 25 K we did at Lejeune. It wasn't on me when I clambered up that guard tower for my first post cycle at Loy Kolay. It wasn't with me when it came over the net that Alonso was a double amputee and it wasn't on me when I knelt down to give a little Afghan girl some chocolates. But it's ready, ready for what, though? The second American revolution?

Like me, its use is meaningless in this post-Marine Corps world. Its side carriers won't be scraping against the cool Afghan dirt as I press for cover, its front won't be covered in MRE crumbs as I sit out a night-long overwatch position in a claustrophobic M-ATV. It has yet to be proven, to be tested, to be taken out on patrol, and like me in this new world, it probably won't be. My older one is indicative of a time when meaning was pumped into my life, when I took immense pride in my suffering and joy, when I felt the most alive. When I knew I could count on every guy in my own mobile section or patrol base to be there for me. This new one I don't even bother to try on, because it doesn't mean anything to me.

Whenever I'm at family gatherings or catch up with family members, they're always asking about my college, my degree and my classes, how I'm finding it. I'm polite and cordial, I answer all of them in a mannerly fashion and talk about my ups and downs while at college and all these things going on.

But behind all the cordial bullshit, I'm screaming, "I don't care about this fucking college stuff, I don't give a damn about my classes and degree. It doesn't give me meaning, it doesn't give me purpose, it doesn't define my very act of being alive and contributing to something important. It doesn't make me feel alive like I felt while in a firefight. Ask me about my deployments, ask me about my views on Afghanistan, ask me about my dead friends."

They're all asking about my new plate carrier. All I care about is my old one.

* * *

Although I went to Taylor's funeral, paid my respects and said my goodbyes, it still was not closure. Despite the viewing and the actual ceremony being private, it still was a group sort of thing. His family, of course was there, a lot of Alpha was there, the BC was even there. But it wasn't between him and me, it was between him and us. After the funeral, I felt like I needed my own closure, between Taylor and me. Especially after his gravestone was set in, I wanted to be there, to kneel down in front of it, touch the marker with my hands and have that connection with him, once more. Opportunities came up, I went off to college, kept delaying it. Being in Indiana, Ohio was more or less on the way to and from home in DC, but things kept getting in the way.

Finally, around Spring Break, I get myself out there with my girlfriend at the time. We get into town and have an amazing welcome with his mother, Abby, and an Alpha guy who has come out as well. By complete chance, it happens on the day he was killed, March 18. We sit around and talk of Taylor, all his funny stories, his love of Harry Potter, his religious identity. Halfway through, his mom starts tearing up, not too much but just a little bit. She eventually says, "Thank you all so much for coming, means a lot to us." She excuses herself to the bathroom. She comes back, and we finish dinner.

The next day, we drive over to the cemetery. Taylor's marker is instantly visible from the street. Every single person who walks by can see it perfectly. I get out of the car and walk up to it. There is a random woman walking around the marker as well. I've never seen her before, but I'm polite and courteous.

She notices me, and says, "Do you know this man?"

I pause. Cannot believe this is happening. "Why, yes ma'am, I served with him."

I tell her about Taylor, about him being perfect and having a fiancée, and Hawthorne.

Then she tells me this, "I've walked by this marker every day for the past month, and it just spoke to me; my son died in November, and I've been looking for a marker for him. But every single time I walk by here, for some reason his marker just speaks to me."

I nod and I smile, and I tear up. Just as with my ex talking about his Facebook profile picture, Taylor is still reaching out to people, even in death. Still trying to impress people with the need to be a good person, showing up his smile and red hair.

After she leaves I put in a dip, get a bottle, because I won't spit on this hallowed ground. And I sit, cross-legged, in front of his marker. I pop open two Monster energy drinks, one for him and one for me. I sit his on his grave, because he won't be drinking Monster anymore. And I cry. My tears fill up my eyes and choke my vision. The Grizzly Wintergreen is all loose in my mouth from all the tears, I don't know why I'm crying so much; his death is in the past, the shock is gone, but I still mourn. And this is my mourning, my moment of being with him again. I ponder relentlessly over why a guy like him, so pure and helpful, and a genuinely good person, had to get blown to bits at a spot in the desert most people in Nevada don't even know exists.

I leave, and I am back in Indiana, I feel a little better, just a little bit. Something has come off my chest. Now, every time I drive through Ohio or West Virginia, and I see the big green signs with the blocky white font of MARIETTA OH on the side of the interstate, I sort of turn inward and smile. I'm remembering Taylor, for Taylor, and not for his death. I remember the quiet redhead with the big smile, who took me to his church, and convinced Thompson and me to drag ourselves to the base theater to watch Harry Potter.

Much later on, my reserve infantry battalion was going to Bridgeport for their annual training. While everyone in the unit was busy hyping themselves up about it, I was openly dreading it. The physical pain from the mountains and cold, and the emotional pain from the Hawthorne deaths loomed over me and crept up on me the closer we got to the date. I could have opted out of it, I was on my IRR contract time, so I was literally a phone call away from quitting the unit, no questions asked. But something about the dough (two grand for two active duty weeks), or the chance to play Marine again just got to me, and so there I was on a C–130 leaving the Terrible Haute Indiana airport, dipping and jamming out with my newfound friend Siedel from Hawaii's Two Three.

As expected, being around lower base camp was just a kick in the gut mentally. There was the hooch we were in when River City went into effect. That was where I told Stinson about Fenn being gone. This corner was the last time I remember seeing Taylor alive. That gas station was where I was told the names of all the seven. Just everywhere I went I was reminded by the sights and smells of how much I hated being there. But luckily, being in a reserve unit, they didn't spend much time at lower base, and we were hiking up the mountain mere days after we got there. And that changed everything. As a buddy of mine said, "Tell your guys that once they stop sucking wind, stand up and take a look around at the freakin' beautiful landscape." And he was right.

With the snow and the cold, Bridgeport's landscape in the winter is a scene out of hell. But in the summer it has some of the most fantastic scenery I have ever experienced in my life. Now there's a difference between hiking up a 10,000-foot mountain and checking out the view, and in flying over that 10,000-foot mountain and also checking out the landscape. The first view is ever more amazing because you've earned that right to set your foot on top of that mountain from climbing the thing. But something else happened that summer, something much deeper and more serene than any change in scenery. Every time I took it all in, I thought of the Hawthorne guys, and their deaths, and how they were killed in 2013. But then I had an internal dialogue with myself where I was able to make a sort of peace with it. It went something like: yes, those deaths were horrible, and they hurt everyone around them, and those Marines were such amazing human beings who should not have been killed in training. But seeing the difference between the hell of winter and the summer, was almost as if God was saying: "All that is true, but there is a beauty in the world that surpasses all evil." Life goes on with their memory in it; their loss was horrible, and although this amazing thing called life and living doesn't make their deaths worth it, it makes living bearable and worthwhile. That from the hellhole that we associated with Hawthorne comes this life of Bridgeport in the summer. And through all of that I was able to make a mental break. In that I was able to make peace with myself that yes, those deaths were horrible, and they affected us deeply, but they happened, and we have this thing called life that needs to be lived and treasured, if not for our selfish sake then for the Marines who died.

Dead Walkers who took their lives

Corporal Christopher Stull (Alpha Company), Lance Corporal Frank DiBattiste (Bravo Company), Lance Corporal Austin Arnold (Bravo Company), Corporal Zachary Solomons (Charlie Company), Lance Corporal Casey Ryan Campana (Charlie Company), Corporal Kevin Schranz (Charlie Company), Lance Corporal Ryan Robert Smith (Charlie Company), Corporal Mario Kletzke (Charlie Company), HM3 Stiles (Charlie Company), Sergeant Christopher Hirsch (H&S Company), Sergeant Guppy Higginbottom (H&S Company), Staff Sergeant Dennis "Goose" Gosnell (Weapons Company)

Dead Walkers killed at the Chattanooga, TN Reserve Station

Sergeant Carson Holmquist (Weapons Company)

Chapter 7

From Dust to Dust

There were times I really felt that I was really losing my mind
You'll be criticized by people that just wouldn't last a day
And every other month another friend will pass away
Tryna to keep you positive about your time here in the Corps
Because we lose more to suicide than we do to the War.

Young Fitzy, 'Welcome to the Infantry'

In my second year at university, while on a typical school day, I stopped in at the Veteran's Support office for a quiet place to sit down and do my homework. I get on Facebook, as every 20-something these days does. The first post I see is something from Schranz, what appears to be a call for help, if not a suicide note. He talks about wanting to call it quits, saying goodbye, telling people to look after his wife, Abby, saying something about taking the coward's way out, and so on. I'm puzzled by this because I can't understand it; you don't usually see someone's last words on Facebook, and I figured this wasn't any different.

But I'm concerned, like many Charlie guys who posted on his page, telling him to pull through, telling him their phone numbers. I post on it as well; in addition, I write a post, tagging him and some other Charlie guys in it, saying that we need to help him out. Immediately I also call him and send him a text. He doesn't answer, but I tell him that I'm only in Indiana and his place in Ohio isn't too far away, I don't care about skipping school to go hang out with him. Later on, I message White, one of the Charlie guys that I came in with and he tells me that apparently he had a gun to his head but the police showed up in time; he's in the emergency room and will eventually go to go to a VA clinic afterward. "Phew," a huge sigh of relief. Just like in-country when a wounded Marine reaches Germany or Bagram alive, we know the chances of something happening are now slim, as the golden hour has been reached and it'll be okay.

I'm kicking myself in the dick for not hanging out with him sooner, as we were going to collaborate on a book together, to put all our experiences on paper. This was several months ago before he moved out to Ohio with his wife's family from New Hampshire. A little bit later on, I'm in my internship building when I get a message from Range on Facebook. The senior I certainly respected the most and was my team leader for much of my time in Charlie, Range is the real deal, he tells it like it is. A split personality to the max, but he takes care of the Marines in his charge. So the message he sends me says this, "Call me Brother," and he provides his new number.

Immediately I give him a call, figuring that everything is okay with Schranz, that maybe Range just wants to give me an update. It might be a little more serious, but nothing more. I'm hoping against hope that nothing has happened. So as I wait for his rings, I start walking away from my desk, and he picks up.

"Hey man, have you heard about Schranz yet?"

"Yeah, he's doing all right, the police got there in time."

"No man, the police did get there in time, but he went out the back of his house and killed himself." Right there, I stop in my tracks. A dead stop. The tears well up and I can't believe what I'm hearing.

Just like with Taylor, the second the words are put together in my brain, I just start losing it. Not Schranz, he was doing great. Got out on an honorable, using the GI Bill, settling down in Ohio, had a really cool wife, the guy was upbeat about everything. I go back to his Facebook page, and the proof is right there: the guy was posting smiley faces and silly comments up to twelve hours before he pulled the trigger. And I hadn't even seen him since he got out, living in Indiana. Sometime either that week or before, I had given some thought about going out to see him, telling myself, yeah, I'll pick out one of these weekends and get out there. Then telling myself, eh, he's probably far too busy to spend a weekend with me.

Unfortunately, neither of the two versions are correct as to the actual details; both got mixed up in rumor and confusion. This is the correct one, as relayed to me by his wife, Abby Schranz:

When Kevin was at home that morning after I left for work, he wrote me a letter (the detectives found it on him) and made a few videos (I found them on his phone later). He drove out to the railroad tracks. He made me a video there and sent it to me along with a text message. He also texted Kugler and his friend Christopher. He left instructions of how he wanted his funeral like. Kugler and I did our best to follow those wishes and everything in Ohio was entirely for him. He called the police himself. He told them his name, location, and what he was about to do. He shot himself in the forehead immediately after calling them with his 1911. (The detectives didn't tell me this at the time, but it was pretty obvious when I saw his body.)

I start calling all the Charlie guys I still have numbers for. Some answer, some have changed their phones, most are busy. But all have the same response as me, thinking that everything was going to be okay. The truth of what happened is somehow the story got misconstrued, and it came out that he was still alive. Schranz was dead by the time I read his suicide note on Facebook. One-Nine has suffered at least five suicides from the generation of 03s that I was with. Four of them are from Charlie Company. Koppers and "Post" Postiglione were the first ones we had to deal with.

A month before Schranz took his life, a senior to my seniors, Casey Campana, took his own life as well. Both Koppers and Post were part of the "cartel" ring on Jaker that was smoking opium and hash on post. They were busted by one of the COGs that found a stash of hash in one of the posts there. In total there were around seven or so grunts who got kicked out for it. When that happens, some guys can't see a way forward. They can't ever get a federal job, the GI Bill means nothing to them at that point, they can't purchase a firearm for the rest of their lives. Some of them work their way out of it and find success in the civilian sector, some even manage to attend college and end up with long lives and happy families.

And it's sad, unfortunate, because Koppers, Post, Callahan, King, Todd were all great guys. They served their country on multiple deployments, some of them proved themselves while in-country. They made some bad decisions that got them forced out, but that cannot count against what they accomplished. Within all these suicides, you would think that the Marine Corps would be in an absolute outcry over the sheer numbers of guys taking themselves out. The officers and staff NCOs really only care about the guys on active duty in a state of depression. All the propaganda that the PR machine puts out revolves around the fact that there is a stigma about suicide and not having a career for reporting depression.

These same officers and staff NCOs don't care about the guys who get out and kill themselves. Schranz, Koppers, Postiglione, the list goes on and on, not just from One Nine but with many other battalions, some much harder hit like Three Five or Two Six, the Marjah and Sangin vets. We've literally heard these higher-ups talk about how these deaths are irrelevant because they happened once these guys got out, and not while they were in, as if the service had nothing to do with their complete alienation in civilian society. Just like everything else, at the end of the day, the only people that give a damn about us are the guys we served with and went to war with.

Ortiz was a 31' from Weapons Company. He was trying to get out, while at the same time dealing with a failing marriage. The command was screwing him left and right, things at home weren't the best, and none of his friends were there because we went off to Bridgeport. So one night he took his personal rifle into the woods, called everyone he wanted to say goodbye to, and then called the police, telling them where to find his body. Then shot himself in the head. Eerily similar to what happened to Schranz. Mathew Koppers was an 11' in Charlie Company. I didn't know him too well because I was in third platoon and he was in second. But he was one of those seniors who mostly kept to himself, didn't mess with the boots too much, was more concerned with his personal life than anything the Marine Corps could do for him. My most significant interaction with him was through the Mrap course we did at the beginning of the first deployment that I eventually dropped on request due to my inability to drive a heavy truck. He was one of the drivers who went through the course, kind of helping the beginner drivers along. Even then he mostly kept to his rack in our free time, next to Brouneus, or Old Sloth as he was known because of his age. Koppers would sit on his rack and watch movies while the rest of us boots chatted about all the excitement we thought we were having in the rear on Dywer. Over the deployment, Koppers went on to PB Jaker where he did his job, patrolled, stood post. He was one of the guys involved in the Jaker drug bust, and about a month or two after he got kicked out, he shot himself in the head.

Gregory Postiglione came in with my generation of boots; he was from New Jersey and was absolutely wild, both on duty and off. But we all liked him, and his charismatic character. His wildness didn't help him very much administratively, where he was constantly getting in trouble for various things. One was for shooting a dog but the bullet somehow exited its skull and smacked into Toledo's leg, wounding him but not too severely. These Afghan dogs were really something, like wolves, and you didn't want to mess with them if you could avoid it. Post got NJP-ed because the company commander had given an explicit order not to shoot anymore dogs and Post did exactly that when one of them tried to attack him on a patrol. He got yoked up in the Jaker drug bust as well. The last time I remember seeing him was when I was in Snipers and he was talking to me about it in the Chicken Shack chow hall, and I was telling him about what a great deal it was and how he should try out for the next indoc. Of course, I didn't realize that he was getting kicked out, but he was enthusiastic about looking into the prospect of doing the indoc. Several months later, he was killed in an accidental shooting with a shotgun.

Ortiz, Schranz, Koppers, Post have joined the Twenty-Two.

The pain is real, and it hits home for everybody. I call up my roommate of boot day lore, Tom Smith. "Hey Smith, you alone man? You got a second?"

"Hey Vining, what's up? Is everything all right with Schranz?"

"Nah man … the story got out wrong … he killed himself earlier this morning."

"Fuck … Schranz …fucking hell …"

"Yeah man, I know. Now they haven't said anything about a funeral yet, but since you're in New York, want to coordinate on getting up to New Hampshire?"

"Yeah … yeah, of course, man … we really need to do that, keep me posted if you hear anything about it on Facebook."

"I will man, it fucking sucks, but I will, I'll be looking at flights shortly as well."

We got the Facebook details of the funeral. Schranz was actually buried in Ohio, but the family wanted to have a separate memorial gathering for all the Charlie guys, just for us. I flew out there, missing a couple days of school but I was not bothered in the least. Smith drove up from NYC, and I met him just outside of Boston. Together we headed to Nashua, New Hampshire, where we booked a hotel.

Unlike Taylor's funeral, which brought me to tears seeing the amount of support from his small all-American town of Marietta, Ohio, Schranz's death was completely different. Marietta had flags galore, with billboards packed with words about "We Honor Joshua Taylor." The entire population came out and lined the streets to the cemetery, half the roads were blocked for it. The Patriot Guard motorcycles came out and escorted the body. Not a single Marine paid for their hotel stay because the town got funds together to cover the hotel bills, absolutely amazing.

But for Schranz, for suicide, there was nothing. Just the grieving Charlie Company guys and his family, in addition to assorted friends from his Catholic church where the service was held. In fact, there were more Charlie guys than there were townspeople, quite the opposite with Taylor and Fenn. It was hard to bear the difference between the two: both were much more than deserving of the word "hero." These guys had done things most Americans of their own generation will never be capable of. Selfless service, unconditional love, sacrifice. Yet one was barely a news blip in the local atmosphere when it happened.

Throughout the memorial proceedings, Schranz brought us together like never before: seniors, our generation, the Charlie boots that Schranz trained, everyone turned up. We were more than fifty strong at times, and it was undoubtedly the most extensive collection of Charlie Company Marines since Charlie Company became an established line company. What he couldn't do in life, he achieved in death, by bringing us all together to mourn for him. And although I wish to God it had happened under the auspices of some battalion reunion, it happened at his memorial service.

The overwhelming emotion of being around these guys, of remembering where we came from, and what brought us together, was amazing. I felt like I was back in, back at the bricks, or at Loy Kolay, just sitting around and talking about drunken Jacksonville nights with Paulie, or flying down dusty dirt roads in Mat-Vs. I felt secure again, I felt safe as I had never felt since getting out. If the very earth below us had caved in and Armageddon was upon the world, I wouldn't have minded because to die in the company of these men would have been an honor in of itself. It was spiritual and mental healing similar to what I went through at the second round of Bridgeport.

I'm not advocating that maybe the cure for dealing with what we dealt with, is to revisit the place of death and to get everyone back together from the same unit and go drinking. But I will say, in my individual case, it certainly helped me cope. Sometimes I find myself inadvertently speeding through lines of traffic in my pathetic HHR. I have to catch myself and slow down. But sometimes I like it, I love the rush, the feeling that I'm a hand motion or a car length away from complete death and dismemberment. It reminds me of being on patrol, of being a dirt mound or a muddy hole away from certain death.

I do the same thing on a bicycle, raving through the campus and roads of Bloomington because it gives me a similar rush. My last class ends late at night, in almost complete darkness, and on the bike ride home, I go through a long patch of woods where the only light available is from the flashlight on my bicycle. It is dark, and the trees close in quickly, enveloping me in darkness. I'm not so scared of the black night as I am of some lowlife jumping out at me with a knife, demanding my bike, my money, or both. So often I tell myself, "What am I scared of? Death? I've already dealt with that, I need not be scared." But during the week that Schranz took his life, I can't help but think every time I go through those woods, that they might be dark, but they will never be as dark as the spot that Schranz was in, that Monday morning.

Shortly after Schranz, during the winter break of the school year, I decided to visit Todd. Previously I had connected with Dimauro, and he had told me about the state that Todd was in. Seeing Schranz go without actually seeing him in person made me sick, and I wanted to see Todd. The kid came from the poorest county in Pennsylvania, coal-mining, meth country. He had grown up in a broken household, with very little support. So instead, he got his help from crime and doing hard drugs. Heroin, cocaine, ecstasy, bath salts. Cannabis was morning refreshment to him. Rough around the edges, this kid was a little war machine, starting a fight just because someone looked at him funny, and hating people because they acted like "fucking faggots and bitches" as he would put it. But in the Fleet, his hard-charging bottom could outdo anyone in the platoon when it came down to it. He might not have been as savvy as the rest of us when it came to orders, 9-Lines, or Call for Fire, but the kid could hump. Whatever you put on his back, he picked up and moved with it. Especially the Thor in Loy Kolay, that kid would manhandle the thirty-pound piece of metal like he owned every square centimeter of it, and still come back for more. He never complained about this work, apart from the usual bitching and groaning. He stood his posts, conducted VCPs and was an overall BAMF.

Coming back to the States, he was a senior in the new generation of Charlie Company, now under that "Fat Sausage of a First Sergeant" as Schranz put it so brilliantly. I swear, that jerk ate rocks for breakfast, thus making his speech sound like gravel coming alive. In this new command, Todd did what was done to us: he hazed boots. He hazed boots because he knew what deployment was all about, knew it was going to be hard, knew it was going to suck, knew someone might die. So he hazed his guys because he wanted them to be tough, like we were hazed to be tough and obedient, to obey orders without question, and to carry heavy loads without complaint. But in Todd's case, one of his boots squealed, like a rat.

You just don't do that in the grunts, especially to higher officers. You don't do this because although the seniors might haze you, they'll also take care of you, like a little brother. But unfortunately for Todd, the chain of command was political and downright stupid. They put him up for court martial, even sending him off to Cax, time that he could have used to prepare his case with a lawyer. But no, instead he was guarding range roadblocks in Twentynine Palms. When he got back, all his wook-lawyer told him was, "You're basically fucked, there's nothing we can do." He got put up for an other-than-honorable discharge, and while waiting for that to come through, he blew all the $10,000 he had saved up to that point, on drugs, back to his comfort zone. When he was kicked out he had absolutely no money, and had to have his stepfather drive all the way down to go pick him up, and then drive him back to PA. He told me it was one of the most embarrassing times in his entire life, having his stepfather come down and take off work. By this point, most of our seniors had gotten out, I was back from the Leatherneck pump and starting the insane checkout process myself.

All of us were concerned for him. If anyone was going to extract themselves from this green earth via a GSW to the head, it would be Todd, hands down. Dimauro, whom I hooked up with in Pennsylvania on one of my rides back to college, even told me this after seeing him: "The poor guy was cracked out of his mind on drugs when we brought him down here with his cousin, in complete fairyland. Everything I was saying to him was bouncing off into outer space. But get this, whenever, I mean whenever I brought up something Marine Corps related, or third related, or our deployment-related, it was as if he shut off the fairytale, and clicked right back into it, getting into the stories with me, and telling me his side of things, how he and Haylock used to play around with the AUP, or how much he hated the Sir. However, as soon as it was over, he went right back to his drug-induced coma, snorting crack in bar bathrooms while we weren't watching."

Crazy right? The Marine Corps literally bends him over, and shoves the Green Weenie so far up Todd's ass, kicks him out, and he wants nothing to do with it. But yet, this thing, this experience that we shared together, is still a large part of his heart, and his soul, and it will be, for the rest of his life. He won't ever be able to get rid of it. The same thing happened when I came to visit him, also on a trip back to Indiana. His hot girlfriend had just broken up with him, he was working in the coalmines of Pennsylvania as that was the only work he could get with an other-than-honorable. I made it a point to go see him, spending the night at his place.

The text messages between us almost speak for themselves, about that bit of his heart:

Todd: Yea bro definitely I try to work 7 days a week but fuck it ... It would be really nice to see you man it would be awesome
Todd: Sweet dude so your for sure stopping by then
Todd: We'll crash at my parents when we're there just don't bring up the Marine Corps BC I'll probably start shit ... Please lol
Todd: I can't wait to see you bud it will be nice
Todd: I'm really poor so if your disgusted by my house I'd understand
Miles: Bro, we used to shit in fuel drums, and sleep in the dirt, I'll be fine haha!
Todd: Lol ok buddy can't wait

I drive out to the absolute middle of nowhere, U.S.A., and get to his place. I inch the car in his parent's driveway, and before I've even parked, he comes out to my car, and I get out, giving him a great big old hug. It was amazing to see him again. Although that time we had together, with all of third, was for a brief two years, that connection will last a lifetime. Every time I see one of the guys, seniors to me, guys I came in with, my boots ... it's like we're sharing that connection again, that small sliver of "I remember a time, in a moment in my life, when I would have died for you, and being in this group of guys, although horrible at times, although we hate each other at times, will probably be some of the greatest moments of my life."

I walk into his parents' house, and it's not bad at all, really. His mother greets me at the door, and I'm absolutely blown away: she's one of the sweetest women you'll ever meet. I'm thinking in my mind, "How the hell did a guy like Todd come from a sweet mother like that …" I get past the threshold of the door, and what do I see on the ground? The issued woodland ditty bag from boot camp. I move into the living room, and what else do I see? A perfectly clean, white dress blues barracks cover, still in the plastic wrap, on top of the TV set. In another corner I see his dress blues picture from boot camp. I move over to the other side of the room, and in a box there is a collage of pictures from our deployment, all depicting Todd. One of them is the picture of him about to kiss Yeah Right You, our cool AUP guy. Absolutely ridiculous, but it's great. Another is with him, Paul, and Naser.

His mother asks me in that angelic voice from the kitchen, "Miles? Do you need any more mac and cheese?"

Todd rocks back and forth on his legs, like he does, and shouts into the kitchen, "Hey Maa! Vining said FUCK You!" Typical Todd.

She replies, "Ahhh, I'm sure he didn't say that, Meyer …"

Todd gets his silly grin on, "I'm just kidding Maa … he didn't say that." Nothing's changed in his demeanor. I love it.

Contrary to his text messages, all we talk about is the Fleet. This guy went there, that guy did that, Paulie's a staff sergeant now, Kugler got married, Nwankwo is in school, Garner was out contracting, freakin' Stinson is still in! Todd tells me that one of the coal-miner bosses tried treating him like a boot, and Todd told him, "Look, you motherfucker, I was in the Marines and in Afghanistan; I'm not taking your shit." Hilarious, he still won't take crap from anyone one. We talk about Schranz, the tragedy of it, and the mini-reunion that transpired with all the Charlie guys.

The whole episode is so bizarre. The Marine Corps screwed him, hard, and yet, it is still part of him, his brothers are still part of him, he relives all our field ops, and all our patrols, and he relives our barracks lives, every day. He did his job of being a grunt to the T and was even kicked out for it. But yet, there is that shining dress blues cover on top of the TV set, there are those pictures on the wall, those memories are still hot with emotion. How do you explain that? How do you tell that this experience, of being an 0311, of doing what we do for a living, how is that still there? Still ever-present in his very soul, always central to his very existence, enough to make him tell a senior coalmining boss to go "Fuck yourself, I did my time in Afghanistan."

I don't think he misses the organization labeled "Department of the Navy, United States Marine Corps." I don't think he misses his Pog drill instructors who saw stepping out on the left foot to be more important than slamming bullets into bodies. I don't think he misses the chain of command that got him kicked out of the Marine Corps for trying to treat his boots the same way he was treated. I don't think he misses the trips back to Jaker and Geronimo and seeing those rear echelon higher-ups telling him how to win a war. He might miss the Afghan AUP he played grab-ass with. He might also miss the Afghan people whom he was partially risking his life for, the same ones he searched day in and day out, at VCPs all over Helmand. Maybe he misses sitting up on post alone with his thoughts or relaxing next to the burning shitter. But no, I don't think in his heart of hearts he really misses that either. I think he misses the same thing I miss, and the same thing that so many of us yearn for on this EAS side of the fence. I think he misses being a part of a group of fifteen men and in some cases loving them more than he loved himself. I think he misses the fact that at one point in his life he would have done anything and everything, even giving his own life, if it meant that one of those other men would come home instead of him.

You could be clichéd and call it a brotherhood, or as Junger would label it, a sense of tribal connection. But whatever it is, it was a sense of belonging, a feeling of love that will never, ever exist in this world we have now become a part of. The society we entered thereafter, the same community that we had supposedly fought and died for, lacked everything we had come to value so dearly.

A shrink from that society once asked me, "Did you go through anything traumatic over there?"

"Umm, sure, getting shot at, IEDs, friends dying."

She nods understandingly. She thinks she understands but she's missing the punchline. Everyone is missing the punchline. Violence through armed conflict can be an unimaginable tragedy, tearing apart families, maiming innocents, and causing severe trauma in the worst way possible. But it isn't the worst thing in the world. To not be loved, accepted, wanted, or needed can be a dark and lonely dungeon few can escape from. To not know who will be there for you in your time of need, especially when you've been ripped away from something so real and so visceral that you cannot escape it. That can be much worse. And is something our modern society sometimes cannot wrap its head around.

Epilogue: Saved Rounds

"When the child asks, 'What is it like to go to war?'
To remain silent keeps you from coming home."
　　　　　　　Karl Marlantes, *What Is It like to Go to War*

On a summer break, I went to Minnesota to be with one of the guys I was in Snipers with: Dragomir. We engaged in some pretty heavy drinking, and it felt great to cuss out the same idiots once again. But then we started talking about V, and I said to Drag, "I'd take all of it back, all the combat, all the helo missions, the whole deployment, my car, everything, if it meant that V could be here today." Up to this point, this is how I had rationalized his death.

Drag looked me in the eye and said, "Would you really? Would you absolutely really? No, don't say that."

Puzzled, I said to him, "What do you mean? I truly would."

He looked at me again, "No, no, you wouldn't."

What the heck was my buddy trying to tell me?

"No one put a gun to your head, or his head, and said, you will be going to Afghanistan as an infantryman. This wasn't the Russians in the Eighties, or 'Nam, or World War Two. No one did that to you. Both of you knew the risks going in. You both knew exactly what could have happened. And unfortunately for him, it did happen. You got lucky, and it didn't happen to you. But both of you knew this going in, and you wanted it. You wanted it so bad that you made sure your recruiter put you down as an 03 and not as anything else. You wanted to be in the shit, to get shot at, to be tested, to prove yourselves as men. So don't say that you would have traded everything away so he would have been here today because that's taking what he wanted away from him. Sure, it absolutely sucks, and it's horrible that his life was taken on a battlefield overseas, and his family is going to have to deal with this for the rest of their lives. But he knew the risks just as much as you did, and you know what? He accepted them, just like you did, and he went in guns blazing."

The healing process is different for us all. No one person can say this works, or that doesn't work. But healing from V's death began with that conversation. However, what we as a community of veterans are dealing with isn't a clear-cut case. What works for me will probably not work with other veterans who saw the same amount of combat as I did, or saw more combat, or saw no fighting at all. For some, maybe that one out of one hundred, as Heraclitus put it, there isn't much of an after-effect. We don't all have the same sort of PTSD that defines us and our experiences back home. Instead, we have a myriad of issues, problems and readjustment concerns that greet us in civilian life. Some of us don't have much of an issue at all. Some of us struggle with it every day, and some of us have demons in our closets from before enlisting in the Marine Corps. Schranz's widow, Abby, said it so well at his graveside. We were trying to define him by how we knew him in the Fleet; his family and friends were trying to define him by how they recognized him as a child, as a teenager. Yet Abby knew both of these definitions were wrong when it came to the man Schranz was after his EAS date and before his suicide. There is no clearcut, absolute pigeonhole you can fit us all into.

Just like Schranz said at the beginning of this book, we wrote these words because we strongly felt that this is a story that needs to be told, for the sake of every grunt who has spent a day in Helmand, but also for people out there who want to know what that day in Helmand was like, and every agonizing day after that. Too often, this war is portrayed through the lens of officers, staff NCOs, special ops guys or specialty infantrymen such as Snipers or Recon. Of course, these guys did their part, took their losses and, of course, they influenced the course of the war; no one is denying that. But there have been too few books that portray a narrative, a tale, a combat odyssey in the literary canon of Iraq and Afghanistan. There is little that shows what the overwhelming majority of 18- to 21-year-old active duty Marine infantrymen went through and are going through in this conflict. How we lived, why we lived, what we wanted, how we fought, and how we died.

One Nine didn't push Marjah or storm Fallujah. We patrolled our AO in Nawa, and we were the second to last victor battalion to leave Afghanistan before One Two completely pulled out from Leatherneck. Nothing we did was unusual or extraordinary compared to units before or after us. However, we endured loss, both accidental, combat, and suicidal. We got in gunfights, we stood our posts, and we patrolled. I went through a painfully serious relationship that typifies what many young Marines go through during service, and Schranz experienced a marriage that few grunts ever get to know. I don't think that my story or Schranz's, or Charlie Company's, Bravo's, or even One Nine's is something that uniquely stands out among the hundreds of platoons, companies, and battalions that have been to war during this period of time that is blankly labeled the "Global War on Terror."

But I do think we went through an experience that profoundly changed our lives, in more ways than one. And I think we have a curious, or at the very least oblivious, American society who wants to know what changed their sons so much that they miss this violent war and struggle in the very society that nurtured and raised them. That is a story that Schranz and I not only lived, but one we want to tell, and from our perspective, we need to tell. Hopefully, through these pages of the OEF chronicle of the Walking Dead, that story can once again come alive.

You would think being 8,000 miles away from home for eight months in a barren desert full of nothing but shit would be one of the most distraught experiences of your life. You would think not being able to take a shower for months would make you sick to your stomach. You would think not seeing loved ones, losing loved ones, and not being able to talk to them would make you depressed. To be frank, all of it is true. But there are things about fighting in a war like we fought in that makes you keep wanting more. I can never imagine having a bond with someone else like I have with my friends, my brothers. I don't think there will ever be another group of people or friends for that matter that I will be able to say to, "Hey bro, I got your back." To say I have your back means more than just me watching out for you. It means no matter what the odds, what happens, how bad the shit goes down, I will lay down my life to protect you. I will do everything in my power to make sure that they, my brothers, come back, even if I don't. It is a promise that I will never make with anyone else in my life. I will make sure that they get to go home to see their families, their wives, mothers, fathers, brothers, and sisters. To know that if putting my life in grave danger, to the point of sacrifice, will get my brother home, then that is what I will do. It is a bond that you cannot replicate. I have only known this group of men for a couple years of my life, yet it feels like I have known them for the entirety of my existence.

To know that I was fighting a war – a war now forgotten – with those men who felt the same way about the bond we shared, made me comfortable, happy that I belonged exactly where I was. That is something that will never be forgotten. That is also why, every single day since we have been back, I want to go back. Yeah, we had to deal with trying to be killed daily. We had to endure countless hours and miles of patrols, blistering hot days, and demented cold nights. We had to deal with idiotic higher-ups who didn't know their left from their right, IEDs, no showers, working parties, the smell of shit burning in a fire, no plumbing, and generators cutting out … I wouldn't trade it for the world. I WANT to go back to that. All of it. I miss it. We were in the suck, together. We fought in countless firefights, together.

We joked and laughed and played cards and got hurt together. It wasn't the most mesmerizing "vacation" you could have asked for, but it was one that if, given a chance, I would go back to in a heartbeat. Nobody but us will ever understand. We weren't fighting for America, our rights, or our freedom: we were fighting for each other. I would do anything to be with my family again. That family. And that war was my home. I miss that home. I miss that family. I will never be the same without them.

Appendix

Charlie Company Casualty Statistics, October 2013–May 2014

As compiled by Kevin Schranz

According to Lt. Shawn Consey USN, Assistant Battalion Surgeon 1st Battalion, 9th Marines, Charlie Company casualty statistics for this period were:

Purple Hearts: 13 (one US interpreter wounded in action)
FAS (First Aid Station) conducted 42 medical evacuations for trauma, illness, or non-combat related emergencies
101 total blast exposures
17 traumatic brain injuries (TBIs)
23 Marines received surgical procedures after return to the United States
35 point of injury traumas (zero killed in action), zero preventable diseases
65 total awards for the company
30 valor awards

The battalion averaged 1.5 engagements a day with the insurgency, one IED blast every 17.5 days, 16 local nationals treated for life-threatening conditions at the PB; over 1,000 patient medical encounters conducted by FAS team for accident, injury, blast exposure, or illness. Anyone the FAS, Corpsman, or CLS Marines got their hands on lived.

Acknowledgments & Sources

The quote at the beginning of the preface is something I wrote on a napkin at Schranz's memorial service in New Hampshire. The flow of the introduction is mostly based on a letter format posted by the Facebook page 'F'n boot' before it was deactivated. I have not seen it elsewhere since. Schranz's writings appear in the preface, and in the Burn Burn chapter (named after a song that V liked). The second half of 'Epilogue: Saved Rounds' is a part of Kevin's writings but was written by Austin Cox, one of Schranz's guys at Boldak. His widow, Abby, provided me with everything he had written to date, which amounted to twenty-one pages of text. The conversation between Hefner and V never took place; however, V's side of the discussion is taken verbatim from a combat camera–recorded interview done with him the day before he was killed, on December 23, 2013. Those are his actual words and expressions. The text conversation with Todd is also verbatim from the texts we exchanged as I drove out to visit him. All the memorial names of One Nine suicides are compiled from guys who served between 2010 and 2014 and are from word of mouth on the One Nine Facebook page. Sam Benson's writing is from a video that he produced trying to raise awareness about suicides among British vets in the U.K. The 'Welcome to the Infantry' lyrics were composed, recorded, and posted on YouTube by a former infantryman by the Youtube username of Fitzy Mess.

Sometime in 2016 the Islamic Emirate of Afghanistan announced on its website that among a number of patrol bases overrun in Helmand Province, Loy Kolay was one of them. This was one of the proverbial nails in the coffin of my service, seeing that all our efforts in that small part of Helmand appear to have been for nought. After leaving the service I went to school at Indiana University, trying to figure out what I just went through. I have returned to Afghanistan twice since that second deployment, the first time as a contractor to the embassy in Kabul, and the second time working with a media company called TechNation, also in Kabul. Someday, somehow, I want to return to Nawa. I would like to know what happened to Pritchna, Aakula, and Aratrura. There are perhaps no people in the world that have affected my life's trajectory as much as these amazing Afghans.

I want to thank Tom Hanney for continually encouraging me to keep up my writing, and always spot-checking me to keep me honest. But thank God I didn't go with "Four Year Comma" because that's just plain stupid, even for a knuckle-dragging machine-gunner. My professor Michelle Moyd, Catherine St. Pierre, Matthew Hoh, Kirby Vining and Ginny Maziarka for taking a brutally honest look at the draft and all did tremendous work with editing my scribble.

My editors, Claire Hopkins, Chris Cocks, and the entire team at Pen & Sword were absolutely fantastic to work with, and I couldn't have been more humbled when I got that first email from Claire stating that she was interested in publishing this project. Thank you so much for suggestions, deadlines, and being gracious in pushing things back.

I am blessed with my partner Mackenzie who has been the most perfect person that I have been able to share my life with and has shown me how to love again.

Maggie from Wilmington has been an excellent source of editing and friendship, someone whom I can count on to chase hood rats out my hotel room. Sergeants Michael, Early, Friend, and Vasselian, four giants of men who will forever be shining examples of leadership under fire and the epitome of the grunts I am trying to describe in these pages. I want to thank my seniors, Garner, Paul, Range, Dimauro, and many others from Charlie, for passing the grunt torch of hatred that I then bestowed on the best fireteam to ever grace the Fleet: Ayer, Hefner, Hoffman, Weaver, and Weider. The amazing friendships that I developed with Dragadouche, Prak, and Janka in Snipers that still last to this day. In addition to all the boys in first platoon, Bravo who had the pleasure of dealing with my horrible leadership and eventual demotion.

The time I spent at Patrol Base Loy Kolay still influences me today. I found God there one morning while standing post, I fell in love with Pashtu and the Afghan people, and was blessed with living in austere conditions with the likes of Hamaker, Martin, Nwankwo, Weitoish, Mauler, Paul, Haylock, Buck, Kugler, Miller, Todd, Randy, Volpe, Michael, Nasir, Faiz, "AK", and of course our non-working, bomb-sniffing dog Pete. You all have become a part of my life.

I cannot forget the brothers who came in with me to third platoon: Stinson, White, Smith, Mauler, Todd, and Weitoish. I'm so sorry for all the stupid Asian shenanigans I pulled that got us in so much trouble: please forgive me. With his wife's permission, I hope Smith gets to kiss Katy Perry again.

I want to thank my parents for being somewhat okay with their only son going into mortal combat at the age of nineteen. But your fascination with the unknown in both music and languages has propelled me to be as passionate about what you really find important in life.

Schranz, you made me do twice as much, in addition to your side of the work, but you'll never be forgotten, brother. I hope you were smiling from the heavens when we used your M1 in our *TFB TV* squad live-fire. And your amazing wife, Abby, who was determined to continue what you started; she is dedicated to your spirit coming alive, if only through these pages. I hope your story inspires generations of Marine infantry machine-gunners for decades to come.

I pray that I've described my relationship with Lynn accurately and fairly. The ending was one of the most painful things I've gone through and am still going through. I routinely find myself thinking what if you hadn't been a chapter in my life but instead formed its sturdy binding. I don't know what would have happened if things had worked out; it is hard for me to imagine leading the life I live now, knowing where you are today, but we never had to cross that intersection. I only know what my heart told me, regardless of anything logical, or any career move. I'll never feel that same strong love, for anyone, ever again.

Sean Gobin and Christine from Warrior Expeditions, an outstanding organization that helps American combat veterans reintegrate into the society they came back to. My new lifelong friend, Michael Maziarka, for working a lot out with me on the 1,200-mile Ice Age National Scenic Trail in Wisconsin. I'm sorry I couldn't ever get up on time.

My time volunteering with one of the most inspirational relief groups on the planet, the Free Burma Rangers, directly contributed to this project, with special mention to Miguel of 21st Century Asian Arms Race. I met David Eubank as a child in Thailand, and since then he has never stopped inspiring me to be a better person in every way. I highly recommend that any vet who wants to feel that sense of purpose, helping people in a tangible way somewhere overseas, to volunteer with the group. It does help.

But most importantly, I want to thank and remember Joshua Taylor. On March 18, 2013, a candle was extinguished from this world that I will never see lit again.

About the Authors

Miles Vining enlisted in the Marines in 2010 as an 0311 rifleman, assigned to 1st Battalion, 9th Marines at Camp Lejeune, NC. He rose to the rank of corporal while deploying with the battalion to Helmand Province in Afghanistan in 2011, to Nawa District, before a subsequent tour in 2013–14 to Camp Leatherneck. With a degree from Indiana University and as the editor of the online resource center, *Silah Report*, he volunteers in Syria and Burma with the Free Burma Rangers relief group. He met his partner Mackenzie and promptly sent her a draft of the manuscript. She didn't like the descriptions of Lynn too much. Despite that, they have been together for several wonderful years.

Kevin Schranz enlisted in the Marines in 2010 as an 0331 machine-gunner, before being assigned to Charlie Company, 1st Battalion, 9th Marines. He rose to the rank of corporal while deploying with the battalion to Helmand Province in 2011, to Nawa District, with a subsequent tour in 2013–14 at Patrol Base Boldak. Kevin married Abby, and, unlike many Jacksonville marriages, it truly worked out. Kevin left the Marines in 2014 and started school in Connecticut, then transferred to Ohio State University. On September 28, 2015, he took his own life.

Abby honors Kevin in her current work with suicide prevention and postvention. After volunteering at a local non-profit serving those bereaved by suicide, she accepted a position as a Suicide Prevention Initiatives Coordinator, where she teaches suicide prevention to community members, facilitates support groups for those bereaved by suicide, and provides immediate support to fellow suicide loss survivors. For any who need help while reading this, the national U.S. suicide hotline is 1-800-273-8255.